MICROCOMPUTERS / MICROPROCESSORS :

HARDWARE, SOFTWARE, AND APPLICATIONS

Prentice-Hall
Series in Automatic Computation

AHO, ed., *Currents in the Theory of Computing*
AHO AND ULLMAN, *The Theory of Parsing, Translation, and Compiling,*
   Volume I: *Parsing;* Volume II: *Compiling*
ANDREE, *Computer Programming: Techniques, Analysis, and Mathematics*
ANSELONE, *Collectively Compact Operator Approximation Theory and Applications
   to Integral Equations*
AVRIEL, *Nonlinear Programming: Analysis and Methods*
BENNETT, JR., *Scientific and Engineering Problem-Solving with the Computer*
BLAAUW, *Digital System Implementation*
BLUMENTHAL, *Management Information Systems*
BRENT, *Algorithms for Minimization without Derivatives*
BRINCH HANSEN, *Operating System Principles*
BRZOZOWSKI AND YOELI, *Digital Networks*
COFFMAN AND DENNING, *Operating Systems Theory*
CRESS, et al., *FORTRAN IV with WATFOR and WATFIV*
DAHLQUIST, BJÖRCK, AND ANDERSON, *Numerical Methods*
DANIEL, *The Approximate Minimization of Functionals*
DEO, *Graph Theory with Applications to Engineering and Computer Science*
DESMONDE, *Computers and Their Uses*, 2nd ed.
DIJKSTRA, *A Discipline of Programming*
DRUMMOND, *Evaluation and Measurement Techniques for Digital Computer Systems*
ECKHOUSE, *Minicomputer Systems: Organization and Programming (PDP-11)*
FIKE, *Computer Evaluation of Mathematical Functions*
FIKE, *PL/1 for Scientific Programmers*
FORSYTHE AND MOLER, *Computer Solution of Linear Algebraic Systems*
GEAR, *Numerical Initial Value Problems in Ordinary Differential Equations*
GILL, *Applied Algebra for the Computer Sciences*
GORDON, *System Simulation*
GRISWOLD, *String and List Processing SNOBOL4: Techniques and Applications*
HANSEN, *A Table of Series and Products*
HARTMANIS AND STEARNS, *Albebraic Structure Theory of Sequential Machines*
HILBURN AND JULICH, *Microcomputers/Microprocessors: Hardware, Software,
   and Applications*
JACOBY, et al., *Iterative Methods for Nonlinear Optimization Problems*
JOHNSON, *System Structure in Data, Programs, and Computers*
KIVIAT, et al., *The SIMSCRIPT II Programming Language*
LAWSON AND HANSON, *Solving Least Squares Problems*
LORIN, *Parallelism in Hardware and Software: Real and AApparent Concurrency*
LOUDEN AND LEDIN, *Programming the IBM 1130*, 2nd ed.
MARTIN, *Computer Data-Base Organization*
MARTIN, *Design of Man-Computer Dialogues*
MARTIN, *Design of Real-Time Computer Systems*
MARTIN, *Future Developments in Telecommunications*
MARTIN, *Principles of Data-Base Management*
MARTIN, *Programming Real-Time Computing Systems*

MARTIN, *Security, Accuracy, and Privacy in Computer Systems*
MARTIN, *Systems Analysis for Data Transmission*
MARTIN, *Telecommunications and the Computer*
MARTIN, *Teleprocessing Network Organization*
MARTIN AND NORMAN, *The Computerized Society*
MCKEEMAN, et al., *A Compiler Generator*
MEYERS, *Time-Sharing Computation in the Social Sciences*
MINSKY, *Computation: Finite and Infinite Machines*
NIEVERGELT, et al., *Computer Approaches to Mathematical Problems*
PLANE AND MCMILLAN, *Discrete Optimization: Integer Programming and Network Analysis for Management Decisions*
POLIVKA AND PAKIN, *APL: The Language and Its Usage*
PRITSKER AND KIVIAT, *Simulation with GASP II: A FORTRAN-based Simulation Language*
PYLYSHYN, ed., *Perspectives on the Computer Revolution*
RICH, *Internal Sorting Methods Illustrated with PL/1 Programs*
RUDD, *Assembly Language Programming and the IBM 360 and 370 Computers*
SACKMAN AND CITRENBAUM, ets., *On-Line Planning: Towards Creative Problem-Solving*
SALTON, ed., *The SMART Retrieval System: Experiments in Automatic Document Processing*
SAMMET, *Programming Languages: History and Fundamentals*
SCHAEFER, *A Mathematical Theory of Global Program Optimization*
SCHULTZ, *Spline Analysis*
SCHWARZ, et al., *Numerical Analysis of Symmetric Matrices*
SHAH, *Engineering Simulation Using Small Scientific Computers*
SHAW, *The Logical Design of Operating Systems*
SHERMAN, *Techniques in Computer Programming*
SIMON AND SIKLOSSY, eds., *Representation and Meaning: Experiments with Information Processing Systems*
STERBENZ, *Floating-Point Computation*
STOUTEMYER, *PL/1 Programming for Engineering and Science*
STRANG AND FIX, *An Analysis of the Finite Element Method*
STROUD, *Approximate Calculation of Multiple Integrals*
TANENBAUM, *Structured Computer Organization*
TAVISS, ed., *The Computer Impact*
UHR, *Pattern Recognition, Learning, and Thought: Computer-Programmed Models of Higher Mental Processes*
VAN TASSEL, *Computer Security Management*
VARGA, *Matrix Iterative Analysis*
WAITE, *Implementing Software for Non-Numeric Application*
WILKINSON, *Rounding Errors in Algebraic Processes*
WIRTH, *Algorithms + Data Structures = Programs*
WIRTH, *Systematic Programming: An Introduction*
YEH, ed., *Applied Computation Theory: Analysis, Design, Modeling*

MICROCOMPUTERS / MICROPROCESSORS: HARDWARE, SOFTWARE, AND APPLICATIONS

JOHN L. HILBURN

Electrical Engineering Department
Louisiana State University
Baton Rouge

PAUL M. JULICH

Electrical Engineering Department
Louisiana State University
Baton Rouge

PRENTICE-HALL, INC.

ENGLEWOOD CLIFFS, N.J.

Library of Congress Cataloging in Publication Data

HILBURN, JOHN L
  Microcomputers/microprocessors.

  (Prentice-Hall series in automatic computation)
  Includes bibliographical references and index.
  1. Miniature computers. 2. Microprocessors.
I. Julich, Paul M., II. Title.
TK7888.3.H48   001.6'4'04   76-5863
ISBN 0-13-580969-X

To our wives, Meme and Pat

10 9 8 7 6

Printed in the United States of America

PRENTICE-HALL INTERNATIONAL, INC., *London*
PRENTICE-HALL OF AUSTRALIA, PTY. LTD., *Sydney*
PRENTICE-HALL OF CANADA, LTD., *Toronto*
PRENTICE-HALL OF INDIA PRIVATE LIMITED, *New Delhi*
PRENTICE-HALL OF JAPAN, INC., *Tokyo*
PRENTICE-HALL OF SOUTHEAST ASIA (PTE.) LTD., *Singapore*

CONTENTS

PREFACE   **xi**

1 **INTRODUCTION**   **1**

References   6

2 **DIGITAL LOGIC**   **7**

2.1.   Basic Logic Gates   7
2.2.   Boolean Algebra   14
2.3.   Digital Integrated Circuits   22
2.4.   Flip-Flops   30
2.5.   Shift Registers   37
2.6.   Output Buffers   40
       References   43
       Exercises   43

3 **NUMBER SYSTEMS AND CODES**   **45**

3.1.   Decimal Number System   45
3.2.   Binary Number System   46

3.3. Octal Number System 53
3.4. Hexadecimal Number System 56
3.5. Signed Numbers and Complement Arithmetic 59
3.6. Binary-Coded Number Systems 66
3.7. Signed 10's Complement Decimal Arithmetic 69
3.8. American Standard Code for Information Interchange (ASCII) 70
     References 72
     Exercises 72

4 **MICROCOMPUTER ARCHITECTURE**   **74**

4.1. Introduction 74
4.2. Read-Only Memory (ROM) 79
4.3. Read/Write Memory 86
4.4. Microprocessor 94
     References 112
     Exercises 114

5 **SOFTWARE**   **116**

5.1. Introduction 116
5.2. Planning a Program 118
5.3. Flow Charts 119
5.4. Machine Language 121
5.5. Symbolic Language 124
5.6. Fundamentals of Programming in Assembly Language 128
5.7. Editors 141
5.8. High-Level Languages 145
     References 147
     Exercises 148

6 **INTERFACING AND PERIPHERAL DEVICES**   **150**

6.1. Introduction 150
6.2. Programmed-Data Transfers 153
6.3. DMA Transfer 168
6.4. Synchronization 170
6.5. IC Interface Elements 173
6.6. Programmable Interfaces 180
6.7. Peripherals 183
     References 193
     Exercises 194

7 **MICROPROCESSORS AND MICROCOMPUTER SYSTEMS**   **196**

7.1.   Microprocessor Selection   196
7.2.   Intel 4004   197
7.3.   Intel 4040   209
7.4.   National IMP-4   215
7.5.   Rockwell PPS-4   223
7.6.   Intel 8008/8008-1   234
7.7.   Intel 8080   243
7.8.   Motorola 6800   252
7.9.   RCA COSMAC   259
7.10. Rockwell PPS-8   266
7.11. National PACE   275
7.12. Microprocessor Summary   284
       References   284
       Exercises   286

8 **DESIGN METHODOLOGY AND APPLICATIONS**   **287**

8.1.   Design Methodology   287
8.2.   Examples of Microcomputer Applications   304
       References   321
       Exercises   321

APPENDIX A   INSTRUCTION SET FOR INTEL 4004 AND 4040   **323**

APPENDIX B   INSTRUCTION SET FOR THE NATIONAL IMP-4   **326**

APPENDIX C   INSTRUCTION SET FOR THE ROCKWELL PPS-4   **332**

APPENDIX D   INSTRUCTION SET FOR INTEL 8008   **338**

APPENDIX E   INSTRUCTION SET FOR INTEL 8080   **341**

APPENDIX F   INSTRUCTION SET FOR THE MOTOROLA 6800   **345**

APPENDIX G   INSTRUCTION SET FOR THE RCA COSMAC   **350**

APPENDIX H   INSTRUCTION SET FOR THE ROCKWELL PPS-8   **353**

APPENDIX I   INSTRUCTION SET FOR THE NATIONAL PACE   **362**

INDEX   **364**

PREFACE

A recent and fascinating innovation in the digital electronics field is the development of the microprocessor using large-scale integrated circuit technology. It is predicted that these devices will have a tremendous impact, much like the transistor on the vacuum tube, upon the design of conventional digital systems presently employed in instrumentation and computer networks. The microprocessor, combined with memory and input/output devices, forms a microcomputer whose cost is competitive with conventional random logic in an ever-increasing number of applications. The microcomputer is not only finding use in small systems, where it may replace a minicomputer, but it is also opening vast new areas of applications where larger machines are not economically feasible.

At the present time, or in the near future, microcomputers will be found in such new applications as automobiles, home appliances, point-of-sale terminals, educational and medical equipment, and many others. As the use of these devices increases, many individuals previously unfamiliar with digital devices will find it essential to understand their operation. In addition to new hardware, the application of these devices requires an understanding of computer programming (software).

The book is intended for all persons involved in the design, use, or maintenance of digital systems using microcomputers. Although a knowledge of either hardware or software is helpful, the book is written at a level that can be understood by individuals with little previous experience. The first chapter presents an introduction to the microcomputer and describes its significance to the field of digital electronics. Chapter 2 is devoted to conventional digital logic because a knowledge of this subject is necessary for proper use of these devices (e.g., interfacing networks). The chapter will be of particular interest to individuals with a knowledge primarily of computer software. This discussion is followed by a presentation of number systems, arithmetic operations, and codes employed in microcomputers (Chapter 3). Chapter 3 provides an adequate background for individuals having a knowledge primarily of hardware.

Chapter 4 presents a general description of microcomputer architecture covering the memory and microprocessor portions of a typical machine. This is followed by a general discussion of the software used in programming microcomputers (Chapter 5). Included in the chapter are explanations of machine, symbolic (assembly), and higher-level languages (PL/M) that are available for most machines. In Chapter 6, input and output methods are presented with descriptions of typical interfacing techniques. Several important peripheral devices commonly used in microcomputer systems are then discussed.

Chapter 7 is devoted to the description of several commercially available micro-processors and microcomputer systems. Included in these surveys are products of Intel, Motorola, National Semiconductor, RCA, and Rockwell International cor-porations. Finally, Chapter 8 presents a discussion of the design methodology employed for microcomputers. A number of applications, illustrating the use of microcomputers in selected systems, are presented to demonstrate the power and flexibility of these machines in solving everyday engineering problems.

Exercises are included at the end of the chapters so that the book may be used as either a reference book or as a textbook. It is hoped that the book will be a valuable reference for all persons interested in digital systems and will fill any void existing between hardware and software concepts, especially as applied to microcomputers.

JOHN L. HILBURN

PAUL M. JULICH

1 INTRODUCTION

The microprocessor is one of the most exciting technological developments since the transistor appeared in 1948. It is predicted that this device will not only revolutionize the digital electronics field, but will also have a great influence on the way of life of present and future generations. The first microprocessor, the Intel 4004, was introduced in 1971 by Intel Corporation. This device, developed primarily for calculator-oriented applications, is a monolithic integrated circuit (IC) employing large-scale integration (LSI) in metal-oxide semiconductor (MOS) technology. The 4004 was soon followed by a variety of microprocessors, with most of the major semiconductor manufacturers producing one or more types. Most microprocessors use LSI technology employing either p-channel MOS, n-channel MOS, silicon-on-sapphire MOS, complementary MOS, or bipolar processes.

A microprocessor is a central processing unit (CPU) which is usually implemented in one or several IC packages. When the microprocessor is combined with memory and input/output (I/O) devices, a microcomputer is formed, as shown in the block diagram of Fig. 1.1.

The microprocessor consists of an arithmetic/logic unit (ALU) and a control unit. The ALU performs arithmetical and logical operations on data received from memory or input devices. The control unit, as the name indicates, controls the flow of data and instructions within the computer. It fetches instructions from memory, decodes the instructions, and executes them by enabling the appropriate circuitry and by controlling the proper sequence of events performed by the ALU and I/O devices. The memory is used to store data and instructions. The I/O devices provide a mechanism for transferring data to and from the outside world.

A microprocessor generally requires some additional circuitry to function as a complete CPU. The amount of hardware necessary varies from processor to processor. It can be expected, however, that as newer devices are developed, less and less support circuitry will be required. A CPU module in the Intel MCS-80 microcomputer series is

1

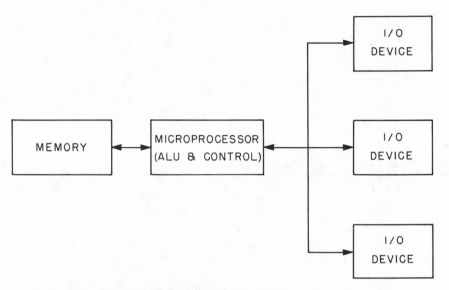

Fig. 1.1. Block diagram of a basic microcomputer.

Fig. 1.2. Intel MCS-80 CPU Module. (Courtesy of Intel Corporation).

shown in Fig. 1.2. The module includes an 8080 microprocessor, a crystal clock, and memory and I/O interface logic. The 8080 microprocessor is a second-generation 8-bit processor. Its predecessor, the Intel 8008, was the first 8-bit microprocessor to be produced.

Microcomputers, like all computers, manipulate binary information. The binary information is represented by *binary digits,* called *bits.* Microcomputers operate on groups of bits which are referred to as *words.* The number of bits making up a word varies among the different microprocessors. Common word sizes are 4, 8, 12, and 16 bits. Another commonly used binary quantity is the *byte,* which consists of 8 bits.

Microprocessors are having an impact on the design of virtually all digital systems. They are finding application in many systems which formerly used random logic [1]. In complex systems, a microcomputer is often cheaper than random logic. One can expect, as time and technology progress, that the processor cost will continue to diminish in a manner reminiscent of that of operational amplifier ICs.

Microcomputers are being employed in jobs which in the past have been performed by minicomputers. Many new applications are also being found for which the minicomputer could not be economically justified. Performance limitations (e.g., speed, shorter word length, limited addressing modes, fewer internal registers) limit the competitiveness of first- and second-generation microcomputers in areas where minicomputers are now used. These limitations, however, should diminish as more sophisticated technologies are developed.

The characteristics of the different microprocessors vary greatly, and some microprocessors are more suitable than others in particular applications. Typical applications for different machines, categorized by the machine size, include the following [2, 3]:

4-Bit Systems:

Accounting systems
Appliances
Calculators
Game machines
Intelligent instrumentation
Terminals (simple)

8-Bit Systems:

Control systems
Intelligent terminals and instruments
Point-of-sale terminals
Traffic controllers
Communications preprocessors (data concentrators)
Process control systems

16-Bit Systems:

Data acquisition systems
Numerical control
Process control
Intelligent terminals
Supervisory control (gas, power, water distributions)
Automatic testing systems

Most microprocessor manufacturers have *development systems*, sometimes called prototyping systems, available for the designer. These systems usually consist of a microcomputer with extensive memory and I/O capabilities. They are particularly useful in designing microcomputer systems which are tailored to specific applications. Two such systems are the Rockwell PPS-4 Assemulator (a 4-bit machine) and the Intellec 8 (an 8-bit machine) of Intel Corporation, as shown in Figs. 1.3 and 1.4.

The presentation of the material in the following chapters begins with a discussion of digital logic in Chapter 2. Basic logic gates, Boolean algebra, digital integrated circuits, flip-flops, and shift registers are presented. A knowledge of these topics is important for understanding and designing microcomputer systems. Individuals who have previously been involved only in computer programming, commonly referred to as *software*, will find this chapter very informative.

In Chapter 3, popular number systems and codes employed in microcomputers are discussed. Topics include binary, octal, and hexadecimal number systems, 1's and 2's complement arithmetic, binary-coded-decimal (BCD) number systems, 10's complement arithmetic, and the American Standard Code for Information Interchange (ASCII).

Chapter 4 deals with microcomputer architecture. Included in the chapter are descriptions of memory types, read-only memory (ROM) and random-access memory (RAM), and microprocessor structure. CPU registers, instructions, addressing modes, and instruction execution are described for a typical microprocessor.

Software is presented in Chapter 5. Machine language, symbolic language (assem-

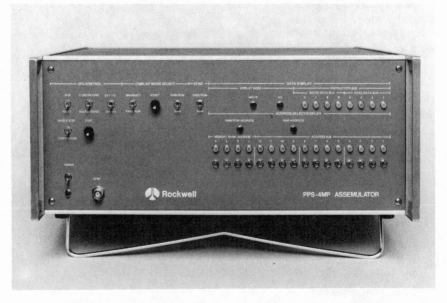

Fig. 1.3. Rockwell PPS-4 Assemulator (Courtesy of Rockwell International Corporation).

Fig. 1.4. Intel Intellec 8/MOD 80 (Courtesy of Intel Corporation).

bly language), and a higher-level language (PL/M) are described. Program planning, flow charting, and software aids (monitors, editors, assemblers, etc.) are also presented. In the chapter, as well as in Chapter 6, a number of programming examples are given. All examples use the mnemonics of either the Intel MCS-4/40 or the MCS-8/80 microcomputer systems. Only these instruction sets are used because they contain a representative repertoire of instructions, and confusion for the reader is avoided by not introducing numerous other instruction sets. The instructions are straightforward and are easily understood, even by the novice. In addition, these instruction sets are well known to most people familiar with microprocessors. Chapters 4 and 5 are of particular importance to designers with primarily a hardware background in conventional digital logic. The microprocessor introduces entirely new design methods in which both hardware and software take on equally important roles.

In Chapter 6, interfacing methods and peripheral devices are investigated. Program-control transfers employing synchronous, asynchronous, and interrupt transfers are described. Cycle-stealing transfers and direct memory access (DMA) are also presented. Typical interface networks are described for each type of transfer. Popular interface ICs and a number of microcomputer peripherals are discussed. Peripherals described include analog-to-digital and digital-to-analog converters, teletypewriters, tape cassettes, and floppy disks.

A number of popular microprocessors and microcomputer systems are described in Chapter 7. Microprocessors considered are the Intel 4004, 4040, 8008, and 8080, the Motorola 6800, the National IMP-4 and PACE, the RCA COSMAC, and the Rockwell PPS-4 and PPS-8. The selection considerations for a microprocessor in a specific application are also examined.

Chapter 8 concludes the book by presenting a design example which considers interfacing an IBM Selectric typewriter to a large-scale computer or a calculator. The design methodology for this system is analyzed, and a portion of an interface employing a microprocessor is designed. Several applications are then described which illustrate the utility and flexibility of the microcomputer.

REFERENCES

1. LEWIS, DONALD R. and W. RALPH SIENA, "Microprocessors or Random Logic" (three-part series). *Electronic Design*, Vol. 21, No. 18 (Sept. 1, 1973).

2. "Primer on Microprocessors" (two-part series). *Electronic Products*, Vol. 17, No. 9 (Feb. 17, 1975).

3. WEISSBERGER, ALAN J., "MOS/LSI Microprocessor Selection." *Electronic Design*, Vol. 22, No. 12 (June 7, 1974).

2 DIGITAL LOGIC

2.1. BASIC LOGIC GATES

A *logic gate* is an electronic device which performs logical manipulations on one or more *logic variables*. A logic variable is an electrical signal which has two distinct values known as *states*. These two states are commonly referred to as TRUE and FALSE. For example, a logic variable S could represent the condition of a SPST switch. The switch is either open or closed; therefore S has two values. If S is TRUE for a closed condition, then S is FALSE for an open condition, as shown in Fig. 2.1. Other assignments often used include HI and LO, YES and NO, ON and OFF, and logic "1" and "0," respectively.

In Fig. 2.1, the assignment HI and LO might be considered an obvious selection. When the switch is closed the battery voltage (HI) appears across the light bulb, whereas an open switch results in a zero voltage (LO) at the bulb. In this case, a lighted bulb represents a TRUE state and an extinguished bulb a FALSE state. Alternatively, using the 1 and 0 assignment for the switch, we could consider $S = 1$ for the TRUE state (closed) and $S = 0$ for the FALSE state (open).

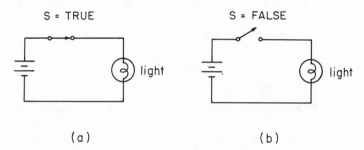

(a)   (b)

Fig. 2.1. A SPST switch representing (a) a TRUE state (b) a FALSE state.

7

The use of the 1 and 0 assignment to describe the state of a variable is of particular significance. Two-state electronic circuits are inherently *binary* devices. In a binary number system, 0 and 1 are the two required numerical digits. The mathematics for variables having only two values has been systematized by Claude E. Shannon [1] using the concepts developed by the mathematician George Boole [2]. As a result, this branch of mathematics is given the name *Boolean algebra*. This algebra manipulates *Boolean variables* which are variables having only two values such as the previously described logic variables. Boolean variables are normally assigned the logic values of 0 and 1.

The types of logic operations performed by digital computers are really few in number, but each may be performed a fantastically large number of times. The basic operations include those of gating and counting. The logic gates necessary to perform the gating functions will now be described.

The AND Gate

An AND gate is a digital device which performs the *logical product* or *conjunction* for two or more logic (Boolean) variables. This logical product is commonly called AND. Well-known expressions for the AND operation for two variables A and B are

$$X = A \cdot B = AB = A.B = A \cap B = A \wedge B \tag{2.1}$$

In this text, the symbol $\wedge$ will be used in order to avoid confusing the logical and arithmetical products.

Using a word definition, the AND operation of two or more logic variables is TRUE if and only if all the logic variables are TRUE. In the case of two variables in (2.1), X is TRUE when A *and* B are both TRUE. Otherwise, X is FALSE. The various combinations of A and B and the resulting values of X are readily displayed by the use of a *truth table*. A truth table for (2.1) is shown in Table 2.1; the 1 and 0 assignment has been used for TRUE and FALSE, respectively.

Table 2.1   TRUTH TABLE FOR
$X = A \wedge B.$

A	B	$X = A \wedge B$
0	0	0
0	1	0
1	0	0
1	1	1

An electrical network employing a series connection of SPST switches which performs the AND operation of (2.1) is shown in Fig. 2.2. The voltage of the battery is applied to the light bulb only when both switches A *and* B are closed. If X is represented by the lighting of the bulb (on-TRUE, off-FALSE), then this circuit performs the AND operation for A and B.

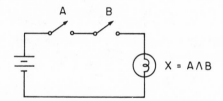

Fig. 2.2. Circuit for $X = A \wedge B$

Numerous logic symbols have been used to represent the various logic gates. A widely accepted standard is that specified by IEEE Standard No. 91 (ANSI-Y 32.14-1973) for distinctive-shape and rectangular-shape symbols [3]. The rectagular-shape symbol is substantially compatible with IEC (International Electrotechnical Commission) Publication 117–15, Recommended Graphical Symbols: Binary Logic Elements. The distinctive-shape and rectangular-shape symbols for a two-input AND gate are shown in Fig. 2.3.

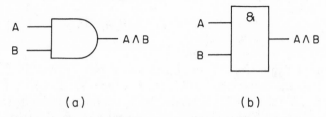

(a)   (b)

Fig. 2.3. Logic symbols for two-input AND gate (a) distinctive shape (b) rectangular shape.

Any number of variables can be ANDed. In the case of three variables

$$X = A \wedge B \wedge C \tag{2.2}$$

The truth table describing (2.2) is given in Table 2.2. The corresponding logic symbols are shown in Fig. 2.4.

Table 2.2 TRUTH TABLE FOR
$X = A \wedge B \wedge C.$

A	B	C	$X = A \wedge B \wedge C$
0	0	0	0
0	0	1	0
0	1	0	0
0	1	1	0
1	0	0	0
1	0	1	0
1	1	0	0
1	1	1	1

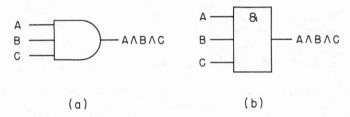

Fig. 2.4. Logic symbols for a three-input AND gate (a) distinctive shape (b) rectangular shape.

The OR Gate

An OR gate is a device which performs the *logical sum* or *disjunction* for two or more logic (Boolean) variables. This logical sum is commonly called OR. Well-known expressions for the OR operation for two variables A and B are

$$Y = A + B = A \lor B = A \cup B \tag{2.3}$$

The $\lor$ notation will be used hereafter.

Using a word definition, the OR operation of two or more logic variables is TRUE if any of the logic variables is TRUE. For the case of (2.3), Y is TRUE if A *or* B *or* both are TRUE. The truth table for this operation is shown in Table 2.3. This table demonstrates the difference between the logical sum and the arithmetic sum. In the last line we see that $1 \lor 1 = 1$ for the logical sum.

Table 2.3   TRUTH TABLE FOR
$Y = A \lor B.$

A	B	$Y = A \lor B$
0	0	0
0	1	1
1	0	1
1	1	1

An electrical network using a parallel connection of SPST switches which performs the OR operation of (2.3) is shown in Fig. 2.5. The voltage source will light the

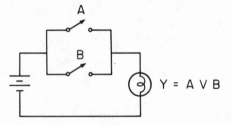

$Y = A \lor B$

Fig. 2.5. Circuit for $Y = A \lor B$.

bulb if either or both of the switches A and B are closed; therefore the light obviously represents $A \lor B$. The logic symbols for a two-input OR gate are shown in Fig. 2.6.

As in the case of the AND gate, the number of variables that can be ORed is unlimited. In the case of three variables

$$Y = A \lor B \lor C \tag{2.4}$$

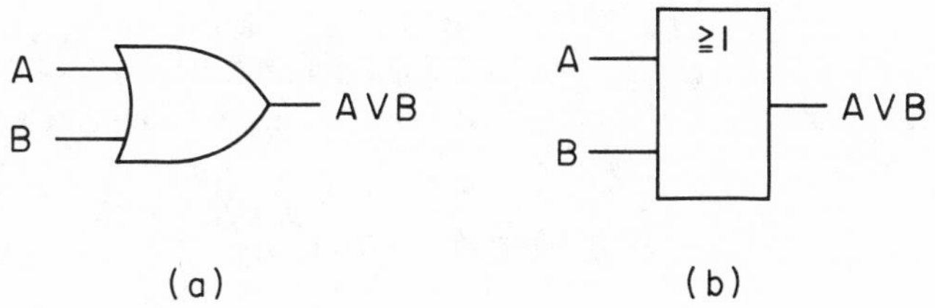

A ‒⟫‒ A∨B

A ‒|≥1|‒ A∨B
B

(a)   (b)

Fig. 2.6. Logic symbols for two-input OR gate (a) distinctive shape (b) rectangular shape.

The truth table which describes (2.4) is given in Table 2.4. The corresponding logic symbols are shown in Fig. 2.7.

Table 2.4 TRUTH TABLE FOR
$Y = A \lor B \lor C.$

A	B	C	$Y = A \lor B \lor C$
0	0	0	0
0	0	1	1
0	1	0	1
0	1	1	1
1	0	0	1
1	0	1	1
1	1	0	1
1	1	1	1

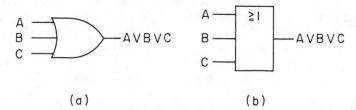

(a)   (b)

Fig. 2.7. Logic symbols for three-input OR gate (a) distinctive shape (b) rectangular shape.

The Inverter (NOT Gate)

The *inverter* is an electronic device which performs the NOT operation on a logic variable. This negation produces the *complement* of the variable. For example, if A is

TRUE, then the complement of A (not A) is FALSE. Conversely, if A is FALSE, then the complement of A is TRUE. Widely used expressions for the NOT operation for a variable A are

$$N = \bar{A} = A' \tag{2.5}$$

We shall use the $\bar{A}$ notation, which is read "not A" or the "complement of A."

When the 1 and 0 assignment is employed, if $A = 1$, then $\bar{A} = 0$, and vice versa. The truth table for an inverter is given in Table 2.5 and the corresponding logic symbols are shown in Fig. 2.8. Unlike the AND and OR gates, the inverter has only one input.

Table 2.5   TRUTH TABLE FOR
AN INVERTER

A	$\bar{A}$
0	1
1	0

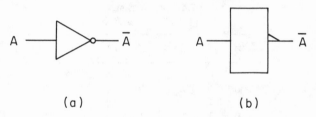

(a)   (b)

Fig. 2.8. Logic symbols for an Inverter (a) distinctive shape (b) rectangular shape.

The NAND Gate

A NAND gate is a device which performs a Not AND operation. The gate is formed by simply complementing the output of an AND gate by means of an inverter, as shown in Fig. 2.9. The expressions which are sometimes used for the NAND operation of variables A and B are

$$X = \overline{A \cdot B} = \overline{AB} = \overline{A.B} = \overline{A \wedge B} = \overline{A \cap B} = A \uparrow B \tag{2.6}$$

We shall use the $\overline{A \wedge B}$ notation, read "A nand B."

Since the NAND gate is composed of an AND gate and an inverter, it might

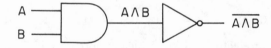

Fig. 2.9. NAND gate using an AND gate and Inverter.

appear that it is unnecessary to define another gate. However, as will be shown in Sec. 2.3, the basic gate in several IC logic types is a NAND gate. Therefore, the definition is fundamental and quite commonly used.

The truth table for a three-input NAND gate is given in Table 2.6 and the corresponding logic symbols are shown in Fig. 2.10. It is interesting to note from Figs. 2.9 and 2.10 that the inverter is replaced by a small circle at the output of the AND symbol. In general, a circle of this type at the input or output of a device represents complementation.

Table 2.6 TRUTH TABLE FOR $X = \overline{A \wedge B \wedge C}$.

A	B	C	$X = \overline{A \wedge B \wedge C}$
0	0	0	1
0	0	1	1
0	1	0	1
0	1	1	1
1	0	0	1
1	0	1	1
1	1	0	1
1	1	1	0

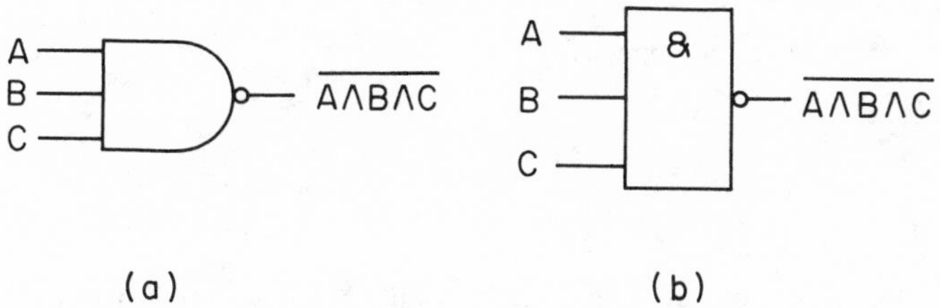

(a)   (b)

Fig. 2.10. Logic symbols for a three-input NAND gate (a) distinctive shape (b) rectangular shape.

The NOR Gate

A NOR gate is a device which performs a *Not OR* operation. The gate is formed by the series connection of an inverter at the output of an OR gate, as shown in Fig. 2.11. Expressions which are often used for the NOR operation of variables A and B are

$$Y = \overline{A + B} = \overline{A \vee B} = \overline{A \cup B} = A \downarrow B \qquad (2.7)$$

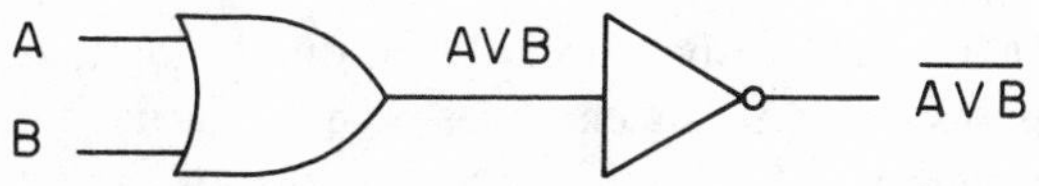

Fig. 2.11. NOR gate using an OR gate and Inverter.

We shall use the $\overline{A \vee B}$ notation, read "*A* nor *B*."

As in the case of the NAND gate, the NOR gate can be constructed from other gates. Again, however, the NOR gate is the basic building block of several IC logic types, which results in its definition being very useful and commonly used. The truth table for a three-input NOR gate is given in Table 2.7 and the corresponding logic symbols are shown in Fig. 2.12.

Table 2.7   TRUTH TABLE FOR
$$Y = \overline{A \vee B \vee C}.$$

A	B	C	$Y = \overline{A \vee B \vee C}$
0	0	0	1
0	0	1	0
0	1	0	0
0	1	1	0
1	0	0	0
1	0	1	0
1	1	0	0
1	1	1	0

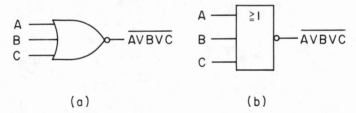

(a)   (b)

Fig. 2.12. Logic symbols for a three-input NOR gate (a) distinctive shape (b) rectangular shape.

2.2. BOOLEAN ALGEBRA

In this section, the mathematical fundamentals of Boolean algebra are presented. The use of this mathematical technique in describing the function and design of *combinational* logic networks is introduced. A combinational logic network is a digital circuit whose outputs at any time are determined solely by its inputs at this time. Obviously, all the gates previously described are combinational (sometimes called *combinatorial*) networks.

This text is not intended to be a treatise on digital logic design. No effort has been made to present minimization techniques such as Karnaugh mapping or Quine–McCluskey tabular methods. For excellent discussions of these topics, the reader is referred to References [4–10].

Basic Theorems

As in other branches of mathematics, Boolean algebra is based on a set of postulates such as those set forth by E. V. Huntington in 1904 [11]. As a result of these postulates, the following relations are valid for logic 0 and logic 1 values.

$$0 \wedge 0 = 0 \qquad (2.8a) \qquad\qquad 1 \vee 1 = 1 \qquad (2.8b)$$

$$1 \wedge 0 = 0 \qquad (2.9a) \qquad\qquad 0 \vee 1 = 1 \qquad (2.9b)$$

$$1 \wedge 1 = 1 \qquad (2.10a) \qquad\qquad 0 \vee 0 = 0 \qquad (2.10b)$$

$$\bar{1} = 0 \qquad (2.11a) \qquad\qquad \bar{0} = 1 \qquad (2.11b)$$

Equations (2.8a)–(2.10a) represent the AND operation for 0 and 1 as seen by the truth table of Table 2.1. Similarly, (2.8b)–(2.10b) satisfy the OR operation of Table 2.3, and (2.11) satisfies the inverter of Table 2.5. Examination of (2.8a)–(2.11a) and (2.8b)–(2.11b) reveals that a *duality* exists between Boolean operations. Note that replacing 0 by 1, 1 by 0, and $\wedge$ by $\vee$ in (2.8a)–(2.11a) yields (2.8b)–(2.11b). In order to illustrate this duality, these equations have been paired.

The above equations can be extended to include the algebraic properties for Boolean variables A, B, and C. Several important properties are given by the following equations which are paired:

$$A \wedge 1 \quad= A \qquad (2.12a) \qquad A \vee 0 \quad= A \qquad (2.12b)$$

$$A \wedge 0 \quad= 0 \qquad (2.13a) \qquad A \vee 1 \quad= 1 \qquad (2.13b)$$

$$A \wedge A \quad= A \qquad (2.14a) \qquad A \vee A \quad= A \qquad (2.14b)$$

$$A \wedge \bar{A} \quad= 0 \qquad (2.15a) \qquad A \vee \bar{A} \quad= 1 \qquad (2.15b)$$

$$\bar{\bar{A}} \quad= A \qquad (2.16)$$

$$A \wedge B \quad= B \wedge A \qquad (2.17a) \qquad A \vee B \quad= B \vee A \qquad (2.17b)$$

$$A \wedge (B \wedge C) = (A \wedge B) \wedge C \qquad\qquad A \vee (B \vee C) = (A \vee B) \vee C$$

$$= A \wedge B \wedge C \quad (2.18a) \qquad\qquad = A \vee B \vee C \quad (2.18b)$$

$$A \wedge (B \vee C) = (A \wedge B) \qquad\qquad A \vee (B \wedge C) = (A \vee B)$$

$$\vee (A \wedge C) \quad (2.19a) \qquad\qquad \wedge (A \vee C) \quad (2.19b)$$

$$A \wedge (A \vee B) = A \qquad (2.20a) \qquad A \vee (A \wedge B) = A \qquad (2.20b)$$

Equations (2.12)–(2.16) define the AND, OR, and complementation properties for the variable A, whereas (2.17)–(2.20) define the commutative, associative, distributive, and absorptive properties, respectively. Each of (2.12)–(2.20) can be implemented by the AND and OR gates and the inverter of the previous section. Consider, for example, the double complement of Eq. (2.16). An implementation is given in Fig. 2.13 utilizing two inverters.

Next, consider the relation of (2.19b) for the distributive law. Figure 2.14 shows

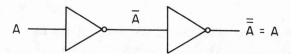

Fig. 2.13. Logic implementation of the double complement.

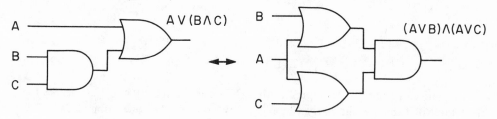

Fig. 2.14. Logic implementation of $A \lor (B \land C) = (A \lor B) \land (A \lor C)$.

the two circuit implementations for this property. Although both circuits are equivalent, one arrangement requires two gates while the other requires three.

Another very important relation in Boolean algebra is DeMorgan's theorem. This theorem relates the AND and OR properties of variables A, B, and C by the equations

$$\overline{A \land B \land C} = \bar{A} \lor \bar{B} \lor \bar{C} \qquad (2.21a) \qquad \overline{A \lor B \lor C} = \bar{A} \land \bar{B} \land \bar{C} \qquad (2.21b)$$

The application of DeMorgan's theorem is particularly useful in obtaining dual Boolean expressions. Note that $\lor$ and $\land$ are interchanged and all variables are replaced by their complements. Consider, for example, a three-input AND gate. From (2.16) and (2.21a)

$$A \land B \land C = \overline{\overline{A \land B \land C}} = \overline{\bar{A} \lor \bar{B} \lor \bar{C}} \qquad (2.22)$$

which gives two representations for the AND gate, as shown in Fig. 2.15.

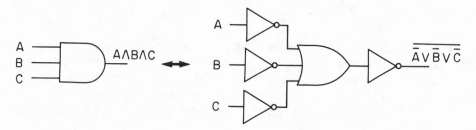

Fig. 2.15. Logic implementation of $A \land B \land C = \overline{\bar{A} \lor \bar{B} \lor \bar{C}}$.

Combinational Logic Networks

The outputs of a combinational logic network are functions only of its inputs at any given time. Because of this characteristic, the design of a combinational circuit is relatively straightforward. The first step in a design process is the specification of a truth table which defines the desired outputs for all combinations of the inputs.

For illustrative purposes, consider the design of an important anticoincidence gate which is known as an EXCLUSIVE-OR (XOR) gate. This gate is particularly useful in constructing arithmetic adders to be discussed in Chapter 3. The truth table for this gate is given in Table 2.8. Note that the output of this gate is TRUE only when the inputs are not equal (anticoincidence).

Table 2.8   TRUTH TABLE FOR AN
EXCLUSIVE-OR GATE.

Input		Output
A	B	X
0	0	0
0	1	1
1	0	1
1	1	0

The values in a truth table represent the variables in terms of their TRUE states. Therefore, a 1 in the table for variable A represents A, whereas a 0 represents $\bar{A}$. In Table 2.8, notice that the output X is TRUE only when "$\bar{A}$ *and B*" or "A *and* $\bar{B}$" conditions exist. As a Boolean equation, this is written

$$X = (A \wedge \bar{B}) \vee (\bar{A} \wedge B) \tag{2.23}$$

This form of a Boolean expression is known as a *sum-of-products* (SOP) form [10]. The product terms in this sum are called *minterms*.

A logic implementation of the EXCLUSIVE-OR gate of (2.23) is shown in Fig. 2.16. This implementation requires the use of AND and OR gates and inverters and

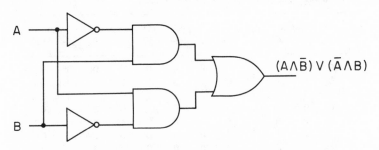

Fig. 2.16. Logic implementation of the EXCLUSIVE-OR gate in A-O-N form.

is known as an AND-OR-NOT (A-O-N) realization. Since any Boolean expression in SOP form can be implemented with these gates, the A-O-N combination is said to form a *complete set*. Several different gate combinations form such sets, two of which are NAND and NOR gates.

The commonly used notation for the EXCLUSIVE-OR gate is $A \oplus B$, read "A exclusive-or B." The corresponding logic symbols are shown in Fig. 2.17.

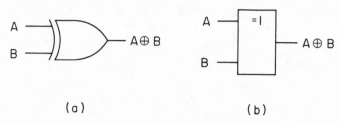

(a)   (b)

Fig. 2.17. Logic symbols for the EXCLUSIVE-OR gate (a) distinctive shape (b) rectangular shape.

Combinational logic is very useful in performing code-to-code conversions. As a second example, consider the design of a 1-of-8 decoder. Before proceeding, let us review the steps required for this procedure.

1. Construct a truth table for the desired logic function.

2. For *each* TRUE state in an output, form the logical product (AND) of the inputs.

3. For *each* output, form the logical sum (OR) of the logical products (minterms) found for this output in step 2.

A truth table for the 1-of-8 decoder is presented in Table 2.9. From this table, it is seen that there are three input variables having eight possible combinations. Of the eight outputs, only "one of eight" is TRUE for any given input. Performing step 2 for X_1, we see that only one TRUE state exists. The logical product of the inputs for this

Table 2.9 TRUTH TABLE FOR A 1-OF-8 DECODER.

Input			Output							
A	B	C	X_1	X_2	X_3	X_4	X_5	X_6	X_7	X_8
0	0	0	1	0	0	0	0	0	0	0
0	0	1	0	1	0	0	0	0	0	0
0	1	0	0	0	1	0	0	0	0	0
0	1	1	0	0	0	1	0	0	0	0
1	0	0	0	0	0	0	1	0	0	0
1	0	1	0	0	0	0	0	1	0	0
1	1	0	0	0	0	0	0	0	1	0
1	1	1	0	0	0	0	0	0	0	1

state is $\bar{A} \wedge \bar{B} \wedge \bar{C}$ since all other outputs are 0's. We now perform step 3; since only one product exists, then $X_1 = \bar{A} \wedge \bar{B} \wedge \bar{C}$. This can easily be transformed into the dual form $X_1 = \overline{A \vee B \vee C}$ by the direct application of (2.21a) (DeMorgan's theorem). Repeating this procedure for X_2 through X_8, we find

$$X_1 = \bar{A} \wedge \bar{B} \wedge \bar{C} = \overline{A \vee B \vee C}$$
$$X_2 = \bar{A} \wedge \bar{B} \wedge C = \overline{A \vee B \vee \bar{C}}$$
$$X_3 = \bar{A} \wedge B \wedge \bar{C} = \overline{A \vee \bar{B} \vee C}$$
$$X_4 = \bar{A} \wedge B \wedge C = \overline{A \vee \bar{B} \vee \bar{C}}$$
$$X_5 = A \wedge \bar{B} \wedge \bar{C} = \overline{\bar{A} \vee B \vee C}$$
$$X_6 = A \wedge \bar{B} \wedge C = \overline{\bar{A} \vee B \vee \bar{C}}$$
$$X_7 = A \wedge B \wedge \bar{C} = \overline{\bar{A} \vee \bar{B} \vee C}$$
$$X_8 = A \wedge B \wedge C = \overline{\bar{A} \vee \bar{B} \vee \bar{C}}$$

If the inputs and their complements are available, this decoder can be constructed from eight three-input AND gates described by the first expressions in the above equations, or by eight three-input NOR gates described by the second expressions. An implementation employing the AND gates is shown in Fig. 2.18.

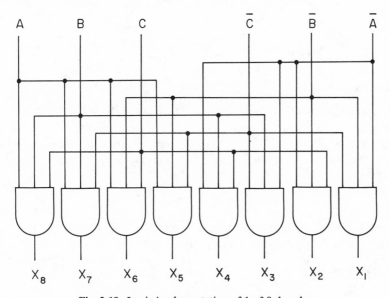

Fig. 2.18. Logic implementation of 1-of-8 decoder.

Positive and Negative Logic

In relating logical variables to electric signals, it is necessary to identify logics 0 and 1 with distinct voltage levels. Two methods are possible, *positive logic* and *negative logic*, defined by the following statements:

A "positive logic" convention means that the 1 state (TRUE) is the more positive voltage level and the 0 state (FALSE) is the less positive voltage level of a digital circuit.

A "negative logic" convention means that the 1 state (TRUE) is the less positive voltage level and the 0 state (FALSE) is the more positive voltage level of a digital circuit.

The use of these conventions is best illustrated by an example. For clarity, let a variable, say A, be denoted by A_+ and A_- for positive logic and negative logic, respectively. From the definitions above, it is obvious that

$$A_+ = \bar{A}_- \tag{2.24a}$$

$$A_- = \bar{A}_+ \tag{2.24b}$$

These relations are signified by the inverter symbols of Fig. 2.19. As shown in this figure, inverters can be used to convert from positive to negative logic, and vice versa.

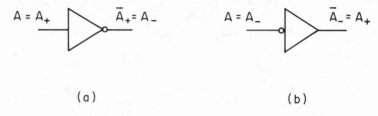

$$(a) \qquad\qquad\qquad\qquad\qquad (b)$$

Fig. 2.19. Inverter (a) positive logic (b) negative logic.

Next, consider the OR gate of Sec. 2.1. The truth table of Table 2.3 describes the OR operation in a positive logic convention. Suppose we now wish to use a negative logic convention. From (2.24), we need only complement the 0's and 1's on both inputs and the output, as shown in Table 2.10. Employing (2.21b) and (2.24b), we see that

$$\overline{A_+ \lor B_+} = \bar{A}_+ \land \bar{B}_+ = A_- \land B_-$$

Inspection of this relation or Table 2.10 shows that an OR gate in positive logic (positive-true OR) is an AND gate in negative logic (negative-true AND).

Table 2.10 TRUTH TABLE OF OR GATE FOR POSITIVE AND NEGATIVE LOGIC.

A_+	B_+	$A_+ \lor B_+$	$A_- = \bar{A}_+$	$B_- = \bar{B}_+$	$A_- \land B_- = \overline{A_+ \lor B_+}$
0	0	0	1	1	1
0	1	1	1	0	0
1	0	1	0	1	0
1	1	1	0	0	0

Positive Logic   Negative Logic

The negative AND circuit symbol is constructed in the following manner. Begin with an AND gate and label the inputs and outputs in positive logic. We are in negative logic, however; therefore the inverters of Fig. 2.19 are required at all inputs and the output. This circuit and the resulting logic symbol are shown in Fig. 2.20.

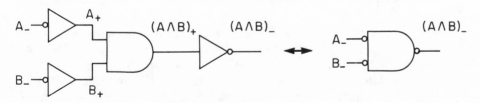

Fig. 2.20. Negative AND gate.

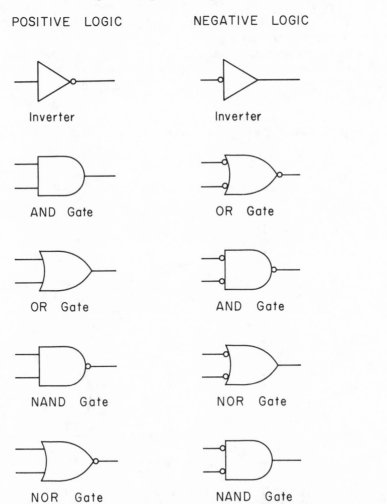

Fig. 2.21. Summary of positive and negative logic symbols.

A similar procedure can be used to develop the negative logic equivalent of the other gates. A summary of these gates is given in Fig. 2.21.

2.3. DIGITAL INTEGRATED CIRCUITS

The logic gates of the previous section are available as integrated circuits (ICs) [12]. ICs offer significant advantages over discrete circuits in size, power, and cost. Numerous complete gate circuits can be deposited on a single chip with greatly reduced overall power requirements. The fabrication techniques for ICs are similar to those for discrete transistors, and the cost of the ICs is often comparable to that of single transistors. ICs are classified according to their complexity. *Small-scale integration* (SSI) refers to circuits containing less than 12 gates, *medium-scale integration* (MSI) to circuits having more than 12 but less than 100 gates, and *large-scale integration* (LSI) to those having 100 or more gates.

All digital ICs have two voltage regions for the inputs and outputs which represent the 0 and 1 states. Figure 2.22 illustrates a typical input-versus-output voltage curve depicting the allowable operating regions and several important voltages for typical IC NOR and NAND gates. At the input to the device, an allowable 0 state is from $V_{\min}$ to V_{IL}, whereas an allowable 1 state is from V_{IH} to $V_{\max}$. Similarly, at the output a 0 state exists from $V_{\min}$ to V_{OL}, whereas a 1 state exists from V_{OH} to $V_{\max}$. Specifically,

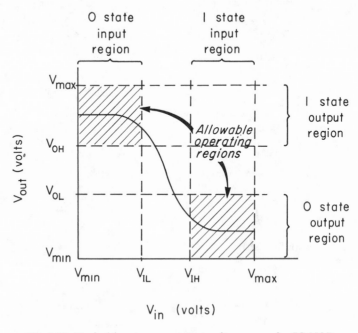

Fig. 2.22. Typical input versus output voltage curve for IC NOR and NAND gates.

V_{IL} and V_{OL} are the maximum input and output voltages, respectively, which will assure a 0 state. V_{IH} and V_{OH} are the minimum input and output voltages, respectively, which will assure a 1 state.

ICs are marketed under a variety of different names, but the majority fall into one of the categories to be described in this section. Since the IC logic families to be discussed employ bipolar or field-effect transistors, a discussion of these elements is presented first, followed by a description of each logic family.

Transistors as Digital Elements

Transistors are the basic elements in most of the IC logic families. They are also used as discrete elements in interfacing applications involving the interconnection of two or more logic networks. The two types which are used in IC fabrication are the bipolar junction transistor [13] and the metal-oxide semiconductor field-effect transistor (MOSFET) [14].

The bipolar junction transistor exists in two forms, the PNP and NPN types. The symbols for these are shown in Fig. 2.23. As a logic element, the transistor is normally

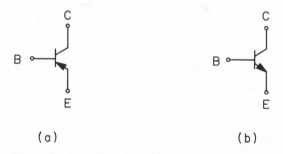

(a)   (b)

Fig. 2.23. Bipolar junction transistors. (a) PNP (b) NPN.

either "on" (conducting) or "off" (nonconducting). The PNP transistor is off if the base, B, is more positive than the emitter, E, and on if the base is more negative than the emitter. The collector, C, is biased negatively with respect to the emitter. Conventional current (flow of positive charges) is from emitter to collector. The base-to-emitter voltage necessary to cause the transistor to switch from an off condition to full on (saturation) is from -0.1 to -0.7 volts. The NPN transistor is off if the base is more negative than the emitter and on if the base is more positive. The collector is biased positively with respect to the emitter, and conventional current flows from collector to emitter. The base-to-emitter voltage necessary to cause the transistor to switch from off to on is from 0.1 to 0.7 volts.

A standard circuit using the bipolar junction transistor is the *common-emitter* configuration of Fig. 2.24(a). In this figure, the transistor is either PNP or NPN, and V_{CC} is less than or greater than zero, respectively. For this configuration, a logic variable, say A, at the input yields $\bar{A}$ at the output, which is the function of an inverter. For a PNP transistor in this circuit, the transistor is turned on for a negative voltage at the

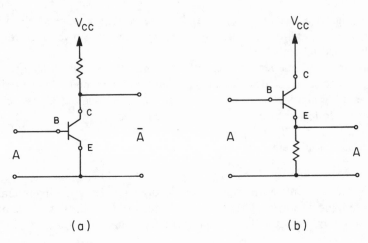

(a)   (b)

Fig. 2.24. Bipolar junction transistor circuits (a) common emitter
(b) emitter follower.

input, whereas for an NPN transistor, a positive voltage is required. Therefore, a
positive logic convention for the NPN transistor has as a dual the PNP transistor
employing a negative logic convention.

Another standard circuit is the *emitter-follower* (common-collector) configuration
of Fig. 2.24(b) which employs either a PNP or NPN transistor. In this configuration,
a logic variable A at the input results in A at the output; therefore this circuit functions
as a buffer amplifier. Once again, the NPN and PNP transistors are duals as described
above.

Another important transistor class, the MOSFET, also exists in two forms, the
p-channel and *n-channel* types. The symbols of these devices for the *enhancement mode*
are shown in Fig. 2.25. When used as a switch, the p-channel MOSFET is off if the
gate, G, is more positive than the source, S, and on if more negative. The drain, D, is

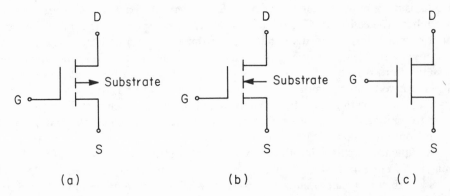

(a)   (b)   (c)

Fig. 2.25. MOSFET transistors (enhancement mode) (a) p-channel
(b) n-channel (c) a common manufacturer's symbol for (a) and (b).

biased negatively with respect to the source, and conventional current flow is from source to drain. The n-channel MOSFET is off if the gate is more negative than the source and on if the gate is more positive. The drain is biased positively with respect to the source, and current flows from drain to source. The substrate is normally connected to the source.

A circuit which is analogous to the bipolar circuit of Fig. 2.24(a) is the *common-source* circuit of Fig. 2.26 for either p-channel or n-channel devices. This circuit performs an inverter function for a logic variable A. As in the case of the bipolar transistors, the p-channel and n-channel MOSFETs exhibit a similar duality property.

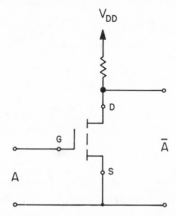

Fig. 2.26. MOSFET inverter.

Diode-Transistor Logic

A well-known family of logic is the *diode-transistor logic* (DTL). This logic, as the name indicates, is constructed of diodes and bipolar junction transistors. The basic gate in DTL is the NAND gate, as shown in Fig. 2.27 for two inputs. A qualitative description of the circuit function is as follows. If A and B are in a 1 state, then current from V_{cc} flowing via R_1 and R_2 turn Q_1 on. Current flowing through Q_1 via R_1 turns Q_2 on and the output is low. Next, if A or B or both are in a 0 state, the current flowing through R_2 is "sinked" to ground and Q_1 is off. Therefore, Q_2 is off and the output is high. These are the characteristics of a NAND gate in a positive logic convention. Since the device driving input A or B in the 0 state must sink the current through R_2, this logic family is a *current-sinking* type.

The possible number of inputs to any gate is called the *fan-in* factor of the gate. Similarly, the *fan-out* factor is the number of inputs of the same family that the output of the gate can drive. The DTL logic family typically has a fan-in of up to 10 and a fan-out of 8. Nominally, the power supply voltage, V_{cc}, is 5 V, the power dissipation is 10 mW/gate, and the propagation delay is approximately 30 ns/gate. At the input of the gate, nominal values of V_{IL} and V_{IH} (Fig. 2.22) are 1.2 and 2.0 V, respectively. At the output, V_{OL} and V_{OH} are 0.45 and 2.6 V, respectively.

Another important property to consider for any logic family is that of noise. Two

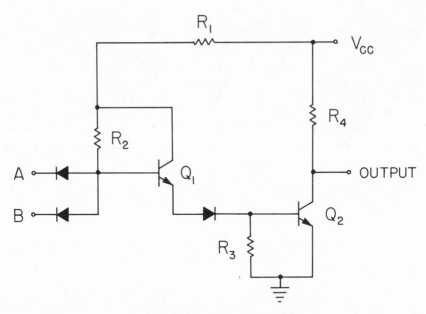

Fig. 2.27. Standard DTL NAND gate.

important factors associated with noise are known as *noise immunity* and *noise genera-tion*. Noise immunity is a measure of how much noise must be superimposed on a logic signal to cause the gate to change its output erroneously. Noise generation is primarily noise induced on power lines due to switching action of the gates. The noise immunity for DTL is good, and the noise generation is medium.

DTL devices employ SSI technology, and the variety of gating functions is mod-est. New designs normally employ one of the remaining families to be described.

Transistor-Transistor Logic

A very popular logic family is the *transistor-transistor logic* (TTL or T²L). In this logic, the inputs consist of a multiple-emitter transistor, as shown in Fig. 2.28 for a standard gate. This basic gate is a NAND gate in positive logic. Qualitatively, the circuit functions as follows. If A and B are in a 1 state, then current flowing from V_{cc} through R_1 enters the base of Q_2 via the forward-biased base-collector junction of Q_1. This current turns Q_2 on, which redirects the current in R_2 from the base of Q_3 to the base of Q_4. Hence, Q_3 is turned off, Q_4 is saturated, and the output is low (0 state). Next, if A or B or both are in a 0 state, then the current through R_1 is "sinked" to ground via the base-emitter junction or junctions of Q_1. Therefore, Q_2 is off, Q_3 is on, Q_4 is off, and the output is high (1 state). This logic family, like DTL, is a *current-sinking* type.

Standard TTL logic, e.g., the 54/74 series, typically has a fan-out capability of 10 and a fan-in up to 8. Nominal values of other quantities include a power supply, V_{cc},

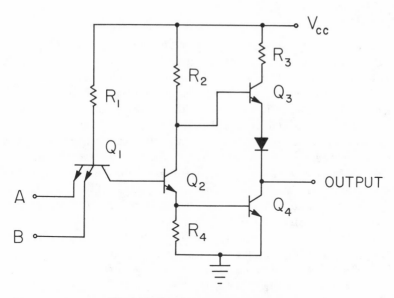

Fig. 2.28. Standard TTL NAND gate.

of 5 V, a power dissipation of 12 mW/gate, and propagation delay of 10 ns/gate. At the input of the gate, V_{IL} and V_{IH} (Fig. 2.22) are 0.8 and 2.0 V, respectively. Corresponding values at the output for V_{OL} and V_{OH} are 0.4 and 2.4 V, respectively. The device driving a TTL gate must have the capability of sinking 1.6 mA in the 0 state and $-40\ \mu A$ in the 1 state. This is defined as a *unit TTL load*.

Another important quantity related to noise immunity is *dc noise margin* [15]. This noise margin is the difference between the worst-case output voltage and the worst-case input voltage. When the output of a gate is connected to the input of another in the same family, a voltage margin, $V_{NL} = V_{IL} - V_{OL}$, exists to "hold" the driven gate in the 0 state. V_{NL} is called the *low-state noise margin*. Clearly, a gate being held in the 0 state would require a noise spike of at least V_{NL} at the input to cause the gate to erroneously leave this state. Similarly, a *high-state noise margin* is defined as $V_{NH} = V_{OH} - V_{IH}$. For a standard TTL gate, a typical value of V_{NL} and V_{NH} is 0.4 V. The noise immunity is considered very good for this family, but the noise generation is medium to high.

Standard TTL logic offers a great variety of different gating functions using SSI technology. In addition to standard TTL, several other forms of this logic are available. These include *low-power TTL, high-speed TTL, Schottky-clamped TTL* (STTL), and *low-power STTL*. Low-power TTL features a power dissipation of 1 mW/gate with a gate delay of 33 ns/gate. High-speed TTL has a gate delay of 6 ns but a power dissipation of 22 mW/gate. STTL and low-power STTL have propagation delays of 3 and 10 ns/gate, respectively, with corresponding power dissipations of 22 and 2 mW/gate. Other characteristics of these types are similar to standard TTL. The TTL family is compatible with the DTL family [8].

Emitter-Coupled Logic

In standard TTL logic, the changing from one state to another requires switching the output common-emitter transistor into and out of saturation. When a transistor is driven into this condition, the base region is saturated with minority carriers. To turn the transistor off, these minority carriers must be removed, which limits the speed of the device. A logic family which operates in the *active* region between saturation and cutoff is the *emitter-coupled logic* (ECL).

A basic circuit for an ECL gate is shown in Fig. 2.29. This network is made up of a differential amplifier, a bias network, and an emitter follower for the output. The bias network is designed such that Q_3 is on if A and B are in a 0 state (Q_1 and Q_2 off). In this condition, Q_4 is off and the output is low (0 state). If A or B is high (1 state), Q_1 or Q_2 is on and the current flowing through Q_3 is reduced, causing the collector to rise in potential. This causes Q_4 to conduct, resulting in a high (1 state) at the output. These combinations of inputs result in an OR operation. If an additional emitter follower is included at the output, with the base of the transistor connected to the collector of Q_2, a NOR output will result. For this reason, the basic gate in ECL is generally referred to as an OR/NOR gate.

In a standard ECL logic (e.g., the 1,000/10,000 series) fan-in and fan-out of 5 and 50 are typical. Power supply voltages are $V_{CC} = 0$ and $V_{EE} = -5.2$ V. The nominal values for the other quantities are a power dissipation of 25 mW/gate, a propagation

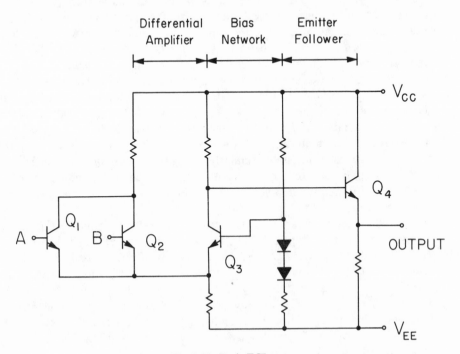

Fig. 2.29. Basic ECL gate.

delay of 2 ns/gate, $V_{IL} = -1.85$ V, $V_{IH} = -0.810$ V, $V_{OL} = -1.65$ V, and $V_{OH} = -0.96$ V (Fig. 2.22). Noise immunity is fair with $V_{NL} = 0.2$ V and $V_{NH} = 0.15$ V. Noise generation is low to medium.

ECL logic offers a fairly versatile set of different circuit functions. The two primary advantages of ECL are faster switching times (propagation delay is at least an order of magnitude smaller than that of TTL) and reduced switching transients on power supply lines. ICs are also available to interface ECL to TTL, and vice versa.

Complementary MOS Logic

An MOS circuit which features a low power dissipation and high noise immunity is *complementary MOS* (CMOS) logic. This logic family is fabricated from n-channel and p-channel MOS transistors, as shown in Fig. 2.30 for a basic CMOS gate. In operation, if A and B are high (1 state), then Q_1 and Q_2 are turned off, Q_3 and Q_4 are turned on, and the output is low (0 state). Next, if A or B (or both) are in a 0 state, then Q_1 and Q_2 are turned on, Q_3 and Q_4 are turned off, and the output is high (1 state). This is the function of a NAND gate. If the p-channel and n-channel transistors of Fig. 2.30 are interchanged, the gate becomes a NOR gate. Therefore, the basic gate in CMOS is either a NAND or a NOR gate.

In Fig. 2.30, both A and B are inputs to gates of MOS transistors. Since the input

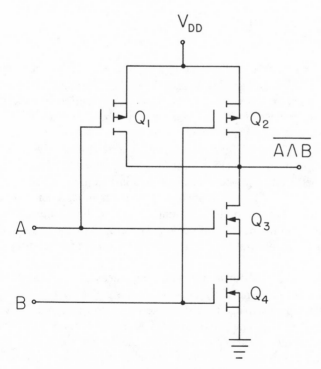

Fig. 2.30. Basic CMOS NAND gate.

resistance is of the order of 10^{12} ohms, virtually no current is drawn by the inputs. At the output, since one of the two transistors connected to each input (i.e., Q_1, Q_3 and Q_2, Q_4) is always in saturation, the output resistance is low and the fan-out is high. In addition, under static conditions, one transistor in each path from V_{DD} to ground (i.e., Q_1, Q_3 and Q_2, Q_4) is always cut off, and there are no resistive paths. Hence, the only quiescent power dissipation is that resulting from leakage in the MOSFETs, which in some circuits is nanowatts per gate. In dynamic operation, however, parasitic capacitances within the gate circuit cause increased power dissipation. At switching rates of 1 MHz, the power dissipation can increase to 1 mW/gate.

In a standard CMOS logic IC (e.g., the CD 4000 series by RCA and the MM 54C/74C series by National Semiconductor), the power supply voltage, V_{DD}, has a range from 3 to 15 V. These devices are voltage-level compatible with TTL and DTL if V_{DD} is 5 V. When $V_{DD} = 5$, nominal values for other quantities are a quiescent power dissipation of 10 nW/gate, a fan-out of 50 or higher, and a propagation delay of 70 ns. The noise generation is low to medium and the noise immunity is excellent (to 45% of V_{DD} in some cases).

A number of different circuit functions are currently available in CMOS. Most are voltage-level compatible with TTL and DTL; however, care must be exercised in interfacing these families [16]. A major disadvantage of CMOS is its lower operating speed, especially when there is a capacitive load at the output.

2.4. FLIP-FLOPS

The *flip-flop* (bistable multivibrator) is a 1-bit memory device for storage of a logic variable [7–10]. This device differs from the combinational networks of the previous section in that it is a *sequential network*. A sequential network is one in which the present value of the outputs is dependent not only on the present value of the inputs, but also on the past history of the circuit.

A good example of a sequential system is a telephone. In order to reach a desired party, the proper sequence must be dialed. When the last number is dialed, the party reached (output) is dependent on this last number (present value of input) and the past history of the system (previously dialed numbers). Another example is an electronic counter that is monitoring events. Suppose the counter has already monitored 377 events and the next event occurs. The output of the counter (378) depends not only on the present input (next event), but also on the past history of the counter (377).

Sequential systems perform systematic sequences of operations which are synchronized by a control signal. This control signal is called a *clock*. A clock is a device which generates a precise pattern of alternately occurring 0's and 1's (pulse train), as shown in Fig. 2.31. The time for one complete cycle of the clock is called a *period*. The frequency of the clock is the reciprocal of the period. Astable multivibrators operating at several megahertz are commonly used for generating clocking signals.

The flip-flop is the basic building block for larger sequential networks including

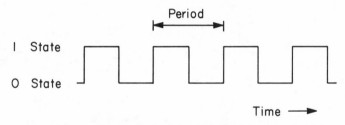

Fig 2.31. Clock voltage waveform.

counters, shift registers, and memory registers, all of which are fundamental in the operation of microcomputers. Although there is a variety of flip-flops, all are derived from a few simple types. In this section, we shall examine four important types in universal use. Other types of flip-flops are generally variations of these having different input gating circuitry.

Gated R-S Flip-Flop

The *gated R-S* (*reset-set*) *flip-flop* is a basic memory element sometimes referred to as an *RST flip-flop* or an *R-S latch*. Two logic symbols for this device are shown in Fig. 2.32. The first symbol is that commonly used by manufacturers and the second is

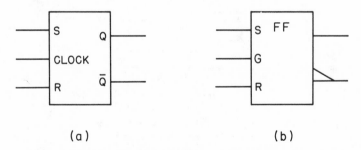

(a)   (b)

Fig. 2.32. Logic symbols for an *R-S* flip-flop (a) commonly used symbol (b) IEEE rectangular standard.

the rectangular shape defined by IEEE standard No. 91–1973 [3]. The first symbol consists of inputs S (set) and R (reset), a synchronizing CLOCK input (other notations used include C, CK, CL, CP, and T), and output Q and its complement $\bar{Q}$. On the IEEE rectangular standard, G represents the CLOCK input and the small triangle the $\bar{Q}$ output.

A circuit which functions as an *R-S* flip-flop is shown in Fig. 2.33. This circuit consists of AND and NOR gates with feedback from the output of the NOR gates returned to their inputs. The operation of this circuit is given by the truth table of Table 2.11. In this table, t_n is the time at which a pulse (clock or gating) is applied to the CLOCK input and t_{n+1} is the time the pulse ends. Q_n is the value of Q at time t_n. In the first set of conditions shown in the table, $S = 0$ and $R = 0$ at t_n. Under these

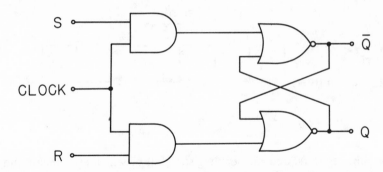

Fig. 2.33. Gated R-S flip-flop using AND and NOR gates.

conditions, $Q = Q_n$ and $\bar{Q} = \bar{Q}_n$ at t_{n+1}. For example, if $Q_n = 0$, then at t_{n+1}, $Q = 0$ and $\bar{Q} = 1$. Next, consider the conditions $S = 0$ and $R = 1$ at t_n. At t_{n+1} $Q = 0$ and $\bar{Q} = 1$. Now, consider inputs conditions of $S = 1$ and $R = 0$. At t_{n+1}, $Q = 1$ and $\bar{Q} = 0$. Obviously, for these latter two sets of conditions, Q at t_{n+1} is not dependent on Q_n. Finally, if $S = 1$ and $R = 1$, then the output is undefined. This condition is not permitted for this flip-flop.

Table 2.11 TRUTH TABLE FOR A
GATED R-S FLIP-FLOP.

t_n		t_{n+1}	
S	R	Q	$\bar{Q}$
0	0	Q_n	$\bar{Q}_n$
0	1	0	1
1	0	1	0
1	1	undefined	

Clearly, the R-S flip-flop functions as a 1-bit memory device. As long as $S = 0$ and $R = 0$, the flip-flop *remembers* the bit value. If $S = 1$ and $R = 0$, the output is set to 1, whereas if $S = 0$ and $R = 1$, the output is reset to 0. The reset-set operation of many R-S flip-flops occurs on either the leading or trailing edge of a clock pulse. The input gating circuitry is designed such that the inputs are enabled on either a low-to-high transition (positive edge-triggered) or a high-to-low transition (negative edge-triggered). These are known as *edge-triggered R-S flip-flops*. A timing digram for a negative edge-triggered device is shown in Fig. 2.34. In the figure, the S and R inputs cause Q transitions only on the negative edges of the clock pulses. Changes in S and R have no effect on Q until these transitions occur.

Another method used to activate the flip-flop inputs is a voltage-level enable. In this case, the S and R inputs are enabled by the HI (LO) voltage level of the CLOCK. During the time that this level is present at the CLOCK input, the output will follow the inputs. This flip-flop is generally referred to as an *R-S latch*. A typical timing

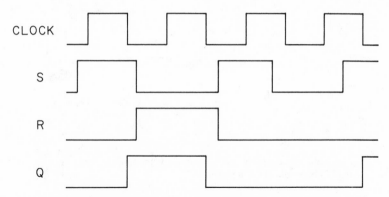

Fig. 2.34. Timing diagram for negative edge-triggered *R-S* flip-flop.

diagram for a HI-level enable is shown in **Fig. 2.35.** Note that *S* and *R* are enabled at all times when CLOCK is HI.

Another important type of *R-S* flip-flop is known as a *master-slave R-S flip-flop*. The master-slave operation is described for the *J-K* flip-flop.

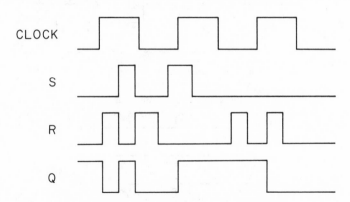

Fig. 2.35. Timing diagram for an *R-S* latch.

J-K Flip-Flop

The most versatile and commonly used flip-flop is the *J-K flip-flop*. Two important characteristics of this flip-flop are that it has no invalid input condition as does the *R-S* flip-flop and it can complement. Two logic symbols for this device are shown in Fig. 2.36. The *J-K* flip-flop, like the *R-S* flip-flop, has two data inputs (*J* and *K*), a CLOCK input, and outputs *Q* and $\bar{Q}$.

The truth table of Table 2.12 describes the operation of a *J-K* flip-flop. As in the case of the *R-S* flip-flop, t_n is the time immediately prior to the input enable time, and t_{n+1} is the time immediately after this input information is transferred to the output. A circuit which functions as a *J-K* flip-flop is shown in Fig. 2.37.

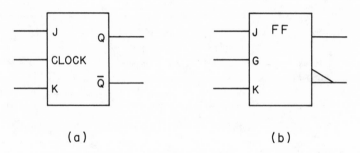

(a)   (b)

Fig. 2.36. Logic symbols for *J-K* flip-flop (a) commonly used symbol (b) IEEE rectangular standard.

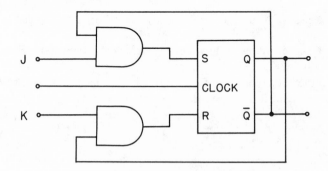

Fig. 2.37. Circuit for a *J-K* flip-flop.

Table 2.12   TRUTH TABLE FOR A
              J-K FLIP-FLOP.

t_n		t_{n+1}	
J	K	Q	$\bar{Q}$
0	0	Q_n	$\bar{Q}_n$
0	1	0	1
1	0	1	0
1	1	$\bar{Q}_n$	Q_n

Comparing Tables 2.11 and 2.12, we see that the *J-K* flip-flop performs identically to the *R-S* flip-flop for the first three conditions, with *J* and *K* replacing *S* and *R*, respectively. Because of this, the *R-S* flip-flop is rarely found in practice, having been supplanted by the *J-K* flip-flop. For the last condition in Table 2.12, if *J* and *K* are 1 at t_n, then at t_{n+1}, $Q = \bar{Q}_n$. Therefore, for this condition, the output complements (toggles) with each clock pulse. When operating in the toggle mode, the *J-K* flip-flop performs the function of a *T* (*toggle*) *flip-flop*. This flip-flop, frequently used in counters, is represented by the logic symbols of Fig. 2.38.

J-K flip-flops are generally one of two types, *edge-triggered J-K flip-flops* or

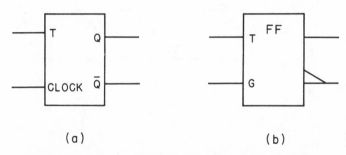

(a)   (b)

Fig. 2.38. Logic symbols for *T* flip-flop (a) commonly used symbol
(b) IEEE rectangular standard.

master-slave J-K flip-flops. The edge-triggered *J-K* flip-flops are those in which the
inputs are enabled and the outputs set either on the leading edge or the trailing edge
of the CLOCK pulse, as described for the *R-S* flip-flop. In most cases, the negative
edge-trigger (high-to-low transition) is used. In many applications (e.g., counters and
shift registers), a change in the input conditions at the time the state of the flip-flop is
to change can cause undesired or unpredictable results. This condition is known as
race. This problem is avoided by use of a master-slave type of flip-flop.

The *J-K* master-slave flip-flop is composed of two flip-flops. One is called the
master and the other the slave. In operation, the flip-flop is enabled by the CLOCK
pulse, as shown in Fig. 2.39. In this figure, at 1 the slave flip-flop is isolated from the

1. Isolate Slave FF from
   Master FF.
2. Enable J and K inputs
   to set Master FF.
3. Disable the J and K
   inputs.
4. Transfer data from
   Master FF to Slave
   FF.

Fig. 2.39. Timing pulse for CLOCK input of master-slave *J-K*
flip-flop.

master. At 2, the *J* and *K* inputs are enabled and the master flip-flop is set. At 3, the
J and *K* inputs to the master flip-flop are disabled. Finally, at 4, the output of the
master flip-flop sets the slave flip-flop, resulting in an output for the device at this time.
A typical timing diagram for a flip-flop of this type is shown in Fig. 2.40.

J-K flip-flops are available in all IC logic families. One such device is the TTL
type 7476, a dual *J-K* master-slave flip-flop with PRESET and CLEAR. A diagram of
the IC package is shown in Fig. 2.41. In this figure, V_{cc} is a 5-volt power supply terminal. The PRESET and CLEAR are used to set the state of the output. These inputs are
independent of the CLOCK input. A low (0 state) to PRESET sets Q to 1, whereas a

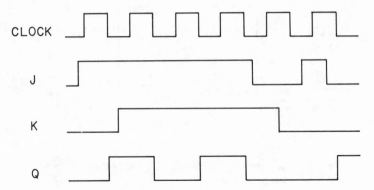

Fig. 2.40. Timing diagram for a master-slave *J-K* flip-flop.

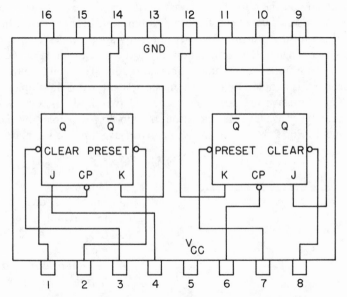

Fig. 2.41. TTL Type 7476 dual *J-K* flip-flop with PRESET and CLEAR.

low to CLEAR sets Q to 0. The small circle on the inputs of PRESET and CLEAR indicate that these inputs are enabled by logical 0's. It should also be noted that the small circle on CLOCK means that the outputs are set on a high-to-low transition (negative edge) of the CLOCK pulse. This device has a typical operating frequency of 20 MHz.

D Flip-Flop

A variation of the gated *R-S* flip-flop is the *D (data) flip-flop*. Logic symbols for this device are shown in Fig. 2.42, and the truth table is shown in Table 2.13. In this

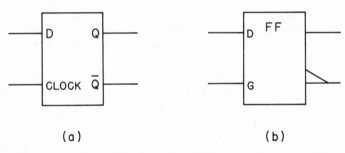

(a)　　　　　　　　　　　　　　(b)

Fig. 2.42. Logic symbols for D flip-flop (a) commonly used symbol (b) IEEE rectangular standard.

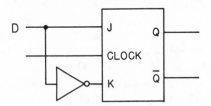

Fig. 2.43. Circuit for D flip-flop.

Table 2.13 TRUTH TABLE
FOR D FLIP-
FLOP.

t_n	t_{n+1}	
D	Q	$\bar{Q}$
0	0	1
1	1	0

table, if $D = 0$ (1), then $Q = 0$ (1) at t_{n+1}. Clearly, the data at D is transferred to Q when the input is enabled. A circuit which performs this function is shown in Fig. 2.43.

The D flip-flop, like the R-S and J-K flip-flops, is generally an edge-triggered or master-slave type. The edge-triggered type is normally positive edge-triggered. Another popular device is a D *latch*, sometimes called a *bistable latch*. This device is a D flip-flop which is enabled by a voltage level, as is the R-S latch. For a D latch which is enabled by a high CLOCK pulse, the output follows the input during the time the CLOCK is 1. Most D flip-flops and latches have PRESET and CLEAR inputs.

2.5. SHIFT REGISTERS

Shift registers are used extensively in microcomputers for data storage and manipulation. A shift register consists of a series of flip-flops (one per data bit) connected so that the output of each flip-flop becomes the input to the next flip-flop [7–10]. As the register is clocked, the data is shifted one position to the right or left for each clock pulse. This device is ideally suited to handling *serial data* (one bit at a time), converting *parallel data* (all bits simultaneously) to serial data, and converting serial data to parallel data.

IC shift registers are generally MSI devices constructed employing *R-S*, *J-K*, or *D*-type flip-flops, and differences among them are primarily related to the method used in managing the incoming and outgoing data. In this section, we shall describe the important types of these registers.

Serial-Entry Shift Register

A *serial-entry shift register* is a device in which the input data is entered serially to the input, as shown in Fig. 2.44 for a 4-bit shift register. In this figure, *D* flip-flops have been employed. In operation, the register can be loaded in the following manner. Initially, a clear pulse (logical 0) is applied to RESET, which sets Q_0–Q_3 to 0. Next, the first data bit, D_1, is applied to the SERIAL INPUT. On the leading edge of the first clock pulse, $Q_0 = D_1$. Next, D_2 is applied to the SERIAL INPUT. On the leading edge of the second clock pulse, $Q_0 = D_2$ and $Q_1 = D_1$. Continuing this process, after four clock pulses, $Q_0 = D_4$, $Q_1 = D_3$, $Q_2 = D_2$, and $Q_3 = D_1$. A timing diagram for a typical loading sequence is shown in Fig. 2.45.

In Fig. 2.44, the output data can be taken in either a serial or a parallel format. In the latter case, the shift register is functioning as a *serial-to-parallel converter*. Obviously, for shift registers having a large number of bits (greater than eight), parallel

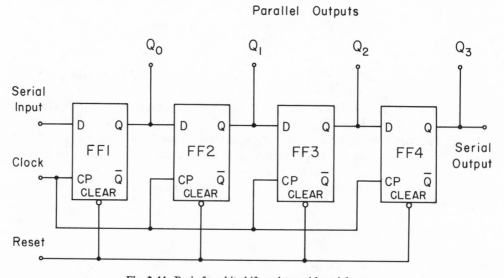

Fig. 2.44. Basic four-bit shift register with serial entry.

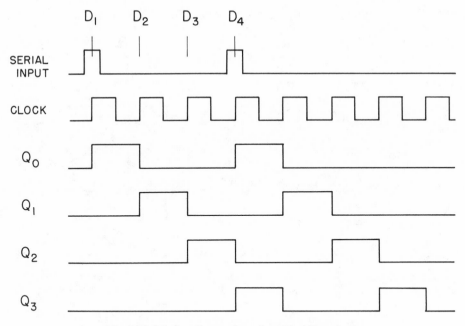

Fig. 2.45. Timing diagram for a four-bit shift register.

outputs are not practical because of the large number of pins required on the IC package. Shift registers are available having over 1000 bits.

Parallel-Entry Shift Register

A *parallel-entry shift register* is a device in which the input data is loaded simultaneously by use of parallel data lines, as shown in Fig. 2.46 for a 4-bit register using *J-K* flip-flops. In operation, this type of shift register can be loaded by the following sequence of events. First, the register is cleared by application of a pulse (logical 0) to the RESET. Next, D_1–D_4 are applied to the inputs and a pulse (logical 1) is applied to the LOAD terminal. This loads all flip-flops via the PRESET inputs. Following this loading operation, the data shifts one position to the right for each clock pulse. The data can be read out in either a serial or parallel format. Many IC shift registers have parallel input and serial output. These devices are known as *parallel-to-serial converters*.

The shift registers described so far have shifted in the same direction for each successive clock pulse. In many applications, however, it is desirable to be able to shift data either right or left. Registers which have this capability are known as *left-shift right-shift registers*. This is accomplished by gating the outputs of the flip-flops to the appropriate inputs for performing either a left or right shift. The shift direction is controlled by a MODE input. Flip-flops which have left-shift right-shift and serial and parallel input and output are known as *universal shift registers*.

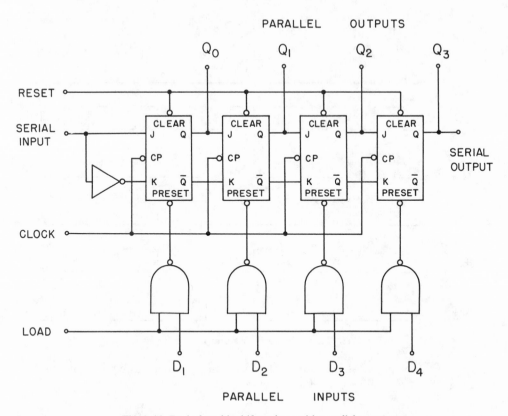

Fig. 2.46. Basic four-bit shift register with parallel entry.

2.6. OUTPUT BUFFERS

Two types of devices that are commonly used for buffers in microcomputer systems are open-collector gates and tri-state gates. These gates differ from the conventional ones in the design of their output circuitry.

Open-Collector Gates

Gates which have open-collector outputs are very useful in microcomputers. A circuit for a two-input open-collector TTL NAND gate is shown in Fig. 2.47. Referring to Fig. 2.28, we see that the components in the collector of the standard TTL NAND gate are omitted to form the open-collector gate. For standard TTL gates, if two outputs are connected together with one output in a low state and the other in a high state, a low-impedance path from V_{cc} to ground occurs through the low-state output transistor. The result is an excess current (30 to 40 mA) flowing in this transistor, which exceeds the power rating of the device [17]. Therefore, connecting the outputs of two or more standard gates is not permitted.

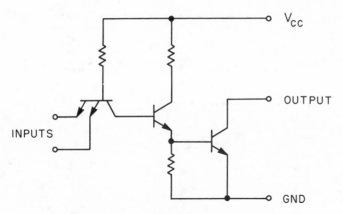

Fig. 2.47. Open-collector TTL NAND gate.

Open-collector TTL gates are usually operated by providing a *pull-up* resistor (2 kΩ) from the collector of the output transistor to V_{CC}. The gate functions as a standard NAND gate. If two or more outputs are connected in parallel, it is common practice to use only one of the 2-kΩ pull-up resistors. As a result, the collectors of all gates tied together return to V_{CC} via the 2-kΩ resistor. Therefore, no harm results to any gate. When a pair of two-input NAND gates are tied together, the output, F, of the combination is

$$F = \overline{(A \wedge B) \vee (C \wedge D)} \tag{2.25}$$

where A, B and C, D are the respective inputs to each NAND gate. The conventional circuit symbol for this connection is shown in Fig. 2.48. This capability is commonly referred to as a *wire-OR* or *dot-OR* connection.

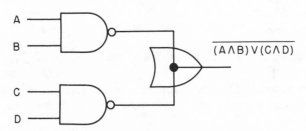

Fig. 2.48. Circuit symbolism for wire-ORing.

Tri-State Gates

Tri-state gates are designed so that the output exhibits three distinct states. In the case of a TTL device, it may act as a normal gate with low-impedance logical 1 and logical 0 states as long as the CONTROL input is enabled. A third state, having a very high output impedance, occurs if the CONTROL input is disabled. A basic circuit that performs a tri-state function is shown in Fig. 2.49 for TTL logic. When the gate

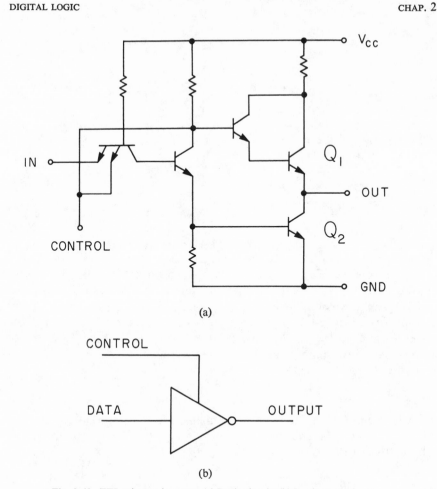

(a)

(b)

Fig. 2.49. TTL tri-state inverter. (a) Basic circuit. (b) Logic symbol.

is disabled (grounded), the drive current is removed from Q_1 and Q_2, which generates the third state. When the CONTROL input is activated (high), the gate acts as a conventional inverter. The truth table for the device is given in Table 2.14.

Tri-state gates are also produced in the other logic families such as those employing MOS technologies.

Table 2.14   TRUTH TABLE FOR A TRI-STATE
                  INVERTER.

Data	Control	Output
0	0	High Z
1	0	High Z
0	1	1
1	1	0

REFERENCES

1. SHANNON, C. E., "Symbolic Analysis of Relay and Switching Circuits." *Trans. of AIEE*, Vol. 57 (1938), pp. 713–723.

2. BOOLE, G., *An Investigation of the Laws of Thought*. New York: Dover Publications, Inc., 1954.

3. "IEEE Standard Graphic Symbols for Logic Diagrams (Two-State Devices)." IEEE Std. 91–1973 (ANSI Y32. 14–1973), August, 1973.

4. KARNAUGH, M., "The Map Method for Synthesis of Combinational Logic Circuits." *Trans. of AIEE*, Vol. 72, Pt. I (1953), pp. 593–598.

5. QUINE, W. V., "A Way To Simplify Truth Functions." *American Math. Monthly*, Vol. 62, No. 9 (1955), pp. 627–631.

6. McCLUSKEY, E. J., JR., "Minimization of Boolean Functions." *Bell System Tech. Journal*, Vol. 35, No. 6 (1956), pp. 1417–1444.

7. DIETMEYER, D. L., *Logic Design of Digital Systems*. Boston, Mass.: Allyn & Bacon, Inc., 1971.

8. HILL, F. J. and G. R. PETERSON, *Introduction to Switching Theory and Logical Design*, 2nd ed. New York: John Wiley & Sons, Inc., 1974.

9. McCLUSKEY, E. J., *Introduction to the Theory of Switching Circuits*. New York: McGraw-Hill Book Co., 1965.

10. RHYNE, V. THOMAS, *Fundamentals of Digital Systems Design*. Englewood Cliffs, N.J.: Prentice-Hall, Inc., 1973.

11. HUNTINGTON, E. V., "Sets of Independent Postulates for the Algebra of Logic," *Trans. American Math. Soc.*, Vol. 5 (1904), pp. 288–309.

12. *Digital Integrated Circuit D.A.T.A. Book*. Orange, N.J.: Derivation and Tabulation Assoc., Inc. (published semiannually).

13. ANGELO, E. J., JR., *Electronics: BJTs, FETs and Microcircuits*. New York: McGraw-Hill Book Co., 1969.

14. SEVIN, L.J., JR., *Field Effect Transistors*. New York: McGraw-Hill Book Co., 1963.

15. DEEM, W., K. MUCHOW, and ANTHONY ZEPPA, *Digital Computer Circuits and Concepts*. Reston, Va.: Reston Publishing Co., Inc., 1974.

16. *COS/MOS Digital Integrated Circuits*. Somerville, N.J.: RCA Solid State DATABOOK Series, 1973.

17. PEATMAN, JOHN B., *The Design of Digital Systems*. New York: McGraw-Hill Book Co., 1972.

EXERCISES

2.1. Reduce the following Boolean functions using Eqs. (2.12)–(2.20). Give a logic implementation for the reduced form.

(a) $F = (\bar{A} \wedge \bar{B}) \vee (\bar{A} \wedge B)$

(b) $F = (\bar{A} \vee \bar{B}) \wedge (\bar{A} \vee B)$

(c) $F = (\bar{A} \wedge B \wedge C \wedge D) \vee (A \wedge B \wedge C \wedge D) \vee (B \wedge \bar{C} \wedge D)$

(d) $F = (A \vee \bar{B} \vee \bar{C} \vee \bar{D}) \wedge (\bar{A} \vee \bar{B} \vee \bar{C} \vee \bar{D}) \wedge (\bar{B} \vee C \vee \bar{D})$

(e) $F = (\bar{A} \wedge \bar{B} \wedge \bar{C} \wedge \bar{D}) \vee (\bar{A} \wedge \bar{B} \wedge C \wedge \bar{D}) \vee (\bar{A} \wedge B \wedge \bar{C} \wedge D) \vee$
$\quad\ (\bar{A} \wedge B \wedge C \wedge D) \vee (A \wedge B \wedge \bar{C} \wedge D) \vee (A \wedge B \wedge C \wedge D) \vee$
$\quad\ (A \wedge \bar{B} \wedge \bar{C} \wedge \bar{D}) \vee (A \wedge \bar{B} \wedge C \wedge D)$

2.2. Use De Morgan's theorem to obtain an alternate expression for the following Boolean functions. Give the logic implementation.

(a) $F = (A \wedge \bar{B}) \vee (\bar{A} \wedge B)$

(b) $F = (A \wedge B) \vee (\bar{A} \wedge \bar{B})$

(c) $F = (A \wedge B \wedge C) \vee (A \wedge \bar{B} \wedge C)$

(d) $F = (A \wedge B) \vee (C \wedge \bar{A} \wedge B) \vee \bar{C}$

2.3. Write a Boolean expression and give a logic implementation for the following truth table.

A	B	F
0	0	1
0	1	0
1	0	1
1	1	1

2.4. Design a 1-of-16 decoder using the technique employed for the network of Fig. 2.18.

2.5. Verify the following:

(a) A positive AND gate is equivalent to a negative OR gate.

(b) A positive NAND gate is equivalent to a negative NOR gate.

(c) A positive NOR gate is equivalent to a negative NAND gate.

2.6. (a) Design a *J-K* flip-flop using a *T* flip-flop and appropriate logic gates.

(b) Repeat part (a) using a *D* flip-flop.

2.7. (a) Design a *D* flip-flop using a *T* flip-flop and appropriate logic gates.

(b) Design a *T* flip-flop using a *D* flip-flop and appropriate logic gates.

2.8. Construct a timing diagram for the circuit of Fig. 2.44 which is required for loading the binary number 1100 into the register using four successive clock periods.

2.9. Repeat Exercise 2.8 for the circuit of Fig. 2.46 to load the register using the parallel inputs.

2.10. Determine the output for three two-input open-collector NAND gates connected in parallel.

3 NUMBER SYSTEMS AND CODES

A knowledge of number systems is fundamental in using microcomputers. Number systems which we use today are based on a method devised by Hindu mathematicians in India about 400 A.D. The Arabs began to use this system, known as the *Arabic number system*, about 800 A.D. Around 1200 A.D., this system was introduced to the Europeans, and it is now commonly referred to as the *decimal number system*.

Other number systems, based on the same principles as the decimal number system, include the *binary*, *octal*, and *hexadecimal* number systems. Digital computers, being composed of binary circuits, make frequent use of one or more of these number systems. In this chapter, we will describe these systems and present methods for converting from one system to another. Addition and subtraction will be discussed and the appropriate hardware for performing these functions will be described for binary 2's complement arithmetic. Finally, *binary-coded-decimal* (BCD) number systems and an important alphanumeric code (ASCII) are presented.

3.1. DECIMAL NUMBER SYSTEM

The most commonly used number system is the decimal number system. It is composed of the *digits* 0 through 9. The word digit is derived from the Latin *digitus*, meaning finger or toe. The fact that this system has ten digits is commonly attributed to the ten fingers of man. The decimal system is an example of a system which employs *positional notation*. In such a system, the position of each digit in a number determines its value or weight. For example,

$$374.29$$

is a shorthand notation for

$$(3 \times 10^2) + (7 \times 10^1) + (4 \times 10^0) + (2 \times 10^{-1}) + (9 \times 10^{-2})$$

Obviously, the position of any digit determines the power of 10 by which the digit is multiplied. In this example, 3 is in the *hundreds* (10^2) position, 7 is in the *tens* (10^1) position, 4 is in the *ones* (10^0) position, 2 is in the *tenths* (10^{-1}) position, and 9 is in the *hundredths* (10^{-2}) position.

The *radix* or *base* of the decimal number system is 10. Three important characteristics of number systems having positional notation (place value) are:

1. The number of digits is equal to the base.
2. The largest digit is one less than the base.
3. Each digit is multiplied by the base raised to the appropriate power for the digit position.

In the above example, a *radix point* (called a decimal point for base 10) is used to separate the integer part of the number (terms having positive exponents of the base 10) from the fractional part of the number (terms having negative exponents of the base 10). Therefore, we may write

$$N = N_I + N_F \tag{3.1}$$

where N_I and N_F are the integer and fractional parts of the number, respectively. For the previous example, $N_I = 374$ and $N_F = 0.29$. Representing a number in this manner is very useful in conversions between bases, which is described in the following sections.

3.2. BINARY NUMBER SYSTEM

The simplest number system employing positional notation is the binary system. As the name implies, the system has a base of 2. The two binary digits (bits) employed are 0 and 1. For example, the number

$$1011.1101_2$$

is equivalent in decimal terms to

$$(1 \times 2^3) + (0 \times 2^2) + (1 \times 2^1) + (1 \times 2^0) + (1 \times 2^{-1})$$
$$+ (1 \times 2^{-2}) + (0 \times 2^{-3}) + (1 \times 2^{-4}) = 11.8125_{10}$$

The subscripts on the above numbers indicate the base of the number. These are often omitted when the base of the number is understood.

It should be noted in the above example that the radix (binary) point separates the integer and fractional parts of the number in a manner identical to that for the decimal point of the previous section. Also, the conversion from binary to decimal is straightforward and easily performed using the positional notation concept.

Decimal-to-Binary Conversion

Suppose we wish to convert a decimal number to a binary number. One method of accomplishing this is known as the *dibble-dabble* method [1]. Using this method, integer numbers are converted to the desired base with successive divisions by the base. In the previous example, the integer part of the number, N_I, is 11_{10}. This is converted to the base 2 by the following process:

$$11 \div 2 = 5 \quad \text{with remainder} \quad 1 \quad \text{(LSB)}$$
$$5 \div 2 = 2 \qquad\qquad\qquad\qquad 1$$
$$2 \div 2 = 1 \qquad\qquad\qquad\qquad 0$$
$$1 \div 2 = 0 \qquad\qquad\qquad\qquad 1 \quad \text{(MSB)}$$

The division process is continued until 0 results. The remainders are then collected beginning with the last or *most significant bit* (MSB) and proceeding to the first or *least significant bit* (LSB). In this case

$$N_I = 11_{10} = 1011_2$$

To change a fractional number to the desired base, successive multiplications by the base are performed. Referring to the same example, the fractional part of the number, N_F, is 0.8125_{10}. This is converted to base 2 as follows:

$$0.8125 \times 2 = 1.6250 = 0.6250 \quad \text{with overflow of} \quad 1 \quad \text{(MSB)}$$
$$0.6250 \times 2 = 1.2500 = 0.2500 \qquad\qquad\qquad\qquad 1$$
$$0.2500 \times 2 = 0.5000 = 0.5000 \qquad\qquad\qquad\qquad 0$$
$$0.5000 \times 2 = 1.0000 = 0.0000 \qquad\qquad\qquad\qquad 1 \quad \text{(LSB)}$$

The multiplication process is continued until either 0 (not always possible) or the desired number of binary places is obtained. The overflows are then collected beginning with the MSB and proceeding to the LSB. In this example

$$N_F = 0.8125_{10} = 0.1101_2$$

Therefore, from Eq. (3.1), we have

$$N = 11.8125_{10} = 1011.1101_2$$

Binary Counting

Counting in binary is less complex than in any other system since the only allowable digits are 0 and 1. In counting, when the first event occurs, the count is 1. When the second event occurs, however, the digit 2 does not exist. In this case, a *carry* into the next position results yielding a binary count of 10_2. Converting this to decimal we see that

$$10_2 = (1 \times 2^1) + (0 \times 2^0) = 2_{10}$$

which is the desired count. Table 3.1 shows a binary counting sequence from 0 to 9.

Table 3.1 BINARY COUNTING.

2^3	2^2	2^1	2^0	Decimal
			0	0
			1	1
		1	0	2
		1	1	3
	1	0	0	4
	1	0	1	5
	1	1	0	6
	1	1	1	7
1	0	0	0	8
1	0	0	1	9

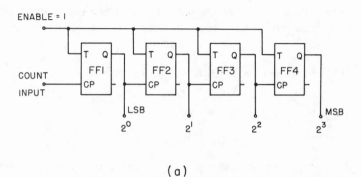

(a)

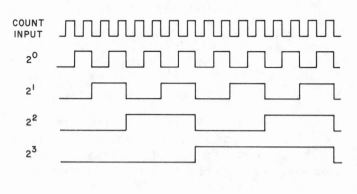

(b)

Fig. 3.1. (a) Circuit diagram; and, (b) timing diagram for a 4-bit binary counter.

Note that a carry results on all even counts. At the occurrence of the fourth and eighth counts, a carry propagates from the *units* bit (2^0) to the *fours* (2^2) and *eights* (2^3) bits, respectively.

A basic binary counter can be constructed using any of the flip-flops of the previous chapter. One flip-flop is required for each bit desired. A 4-bit binary counter employing negative edge-triggered T flip-flops is shown in Fig. 3.1. This counter is known as an *asynchronous* (ripple) counter since all flip-flops are not clocked simultaneously [2]. If all flip-flops are initially cleared, when the first clock pulse occurs, the 2^0 bit is set to 1 and all other bits remain in the 0 state. The next clock pulse resets FF1 to 0. Since this is the input to FF2, the 2^1 bit is set to the 1 state and the remaining bits are unchanged (0 state). A timing diagram for the successive chain of events is shown in Fig. 3.1, where the binary count of the clock input is given by the 2^3 through 2^0 bits. Note that the counter is also a frequency divider. The 2^0 bit divides the clock frequency by 2. Similarly, the 2^1, 2^2, and 2^3 bits divide the clock frequency by 4, 8, and 16, respectively.

Binary counters, both synchronous and asynchronous, are available in all IC logic families. Four-bit counters (e.g., the TTL 7493) and counters exceeding ten bits (e.g., the CMOS CD4020) are readily available in single packages.

Binary Addition

In binary addition, the sum of the digits 0 and 1 obeys the following rules:

(a) $0 + 0 = 0$

(b) $0 + 1 = 1$

(c) $1 + 1 = 0 + \text{carry}$

(d) $1 + 1 + 1 = 1 + \text{carry}$

To illustrate the use of these rules, consider the sum of 1110 and 1100 as shown in Fig. 3.2. In column 1, $0 + 0 = 0$ [rule (a)]. In column 2, $1 + 0 = 1$ [rule (b)]. In the third column, $1 + 1 = 0 + \text{carry}$ [rule (c)]. This carry is shown at the top of column 4.

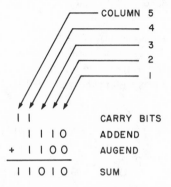

Fig. 3.2. Binary addition of 1110 and 1100.

Summing this column, $1 + 1 + 1 = 1 +$ carry [rule (d)]. This carry is placed at the top of column 5. Since this is the only 1 in this column, the sum is 1.

Suppose we consider the sum of binary bits A and B. The truth table for all possibilities of the sum of A and B is shown in Table 3.2. From this table, using the technique discussed in Chapter 2, we see that

$$\text{SUM} = (A \wedge \bar{B}) \vee (\bar{A} \wedge B) = A \oplus B$$
$$\text{CARRY} = A \wedge B$$

Table 3.2   TRUTH TABLE FOR THE SUM
OF A AND B.

A	B	SUM	CARRY
0	0	0	0
0	1	1	0
1	0	1	0
1	1	0	1

A circuit which performs these functions is shown in Fig. 3.3. This network is known as a *half-adder*, and it performs the arithmetic sum of two binary digits.

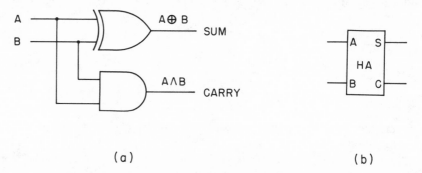

(a)   (b)

Fig. 3.3. (a) Half-adder circuit. (b) Half-adder symbol.

In the addition example of Fig. 3.2, we see that the half-adder would be sufficient for summing any column not having a carry. The fourth column, however, does have a carry bit. Therefore, a device is needed to form the arithmetic sum of two bits A and B and a carry bit C_i. A truth table for this sum is shown in Table 3.3. From this table we see that

$$\text{SUM} = (\bar{C}_i \wedge \bar{A} \wedge B) \vee (\bar{C}_i \wedge A \wedge \bar{B}) \vee (C_i \wedge \bar{A} \wedge \bar{B}) \vee (C_i \wedge A \wedge B)$$
$$\text{CARRY} = (\bar{C}_i \wedge A \wedge B) \vee (C_i \wedge \bar{A} \wedge B) \vee (C_i \wedge A \wedge \bar{B}) \vee (C_i \wedge A \wedge B)$$

Table 3.3 TRUTH TABLE FOR THE SUM OF
A, B, AND C_i.

C_i	A	B	SUM	CARRY
0	0	0	0	0
0	0	1	1	0
0	1	0	1	0
0	1	1	0	1
1	0	0	1	0
1	0	1	0	1
1	1	0	0	1
1	1	1	1	1

These expressions can be reduced using the theorems from Boolean algebra (an interesting exercise for the reader). Performing these reductions, we find

$$\text{SUM} = C_i \oplus (A \oplus B)$$

$$\text{CARRY} = [A \wedge B] \vee [C_i \wedge (A \oplus B)]$$

A circuit which performs these functions is shown in Fig. 3.4. This circuit is called a *full-adder* and performs the arithmetic sum of three bits.

In the previous addition example (Fig. 3.2), we added 1110 and 1100. Since these numbers have four bits, a 4-bit full-adder is needed to perform this sum. The schematic of a network made up of full-adders is shown in Fig. 3.5. To illustrate the operation of this network, the numbers 1110 and 1100 are shown at inputs A and B, respectively, of the full-adders. Notice that the carry input on the first (right-hand) full-adder is 0. The values of the carry bits generated in each full-adder are shown in parentheses at the C_0 outputs. It should be noted that these carries are identical to those of Fig. 3.2. The sum of the numbers is given by the highest-order carry (MSB) and the sum bits. The result is read from left to right (MSB to LSB), yielding 11010.

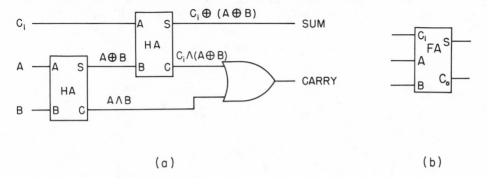

(a)   (b)

Fig. 3.4. (a) Full-adder circuit. (b) Full-adder symbol.

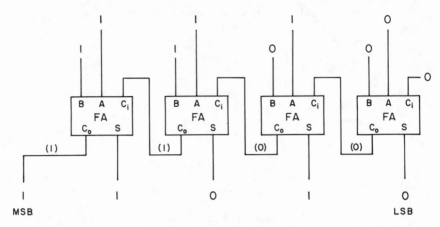

Fig. 3.5. 4-bit full-adder.

Full-adders are available in all IC logic families and they form the basic building block for the arithmetic/logic unit (ALU) in microprocessors.

Binary Subtraction

In binary subtraction, the difference of the digits 0 and 1 obeys the following rules:

(e) $0 - 0 = 0$

(f) $1 - 0 = 1$

(g) $1 - 1 = 0$

(h) $0 - 1 = 1 -$ borrow

The use of these rules is illustrated by subtracting 1100 from 10110, as shown in Fig. 3.6. In column 1, $0 - 0 = 0$ [rule (e)] and in column 2, $1 - 0 = 1$ [rule (f)]. In the third column $1 - 1 = 0$ [rule (g)]. Continuing to column 4, we have $0 - 1 = 1 -$

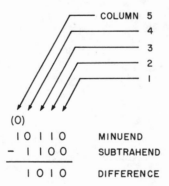

Fig. 3.6. Binary subtraction of 10110 and 1100.

borrow [rule (h)]. This borrow results in the 1 in column 5 being replaced by 0 (shown in parentheses). The resulting difference is 1010.

A subtraction procedure such as that in Fig. 3.6 can be implemented with circuits similar to those of the half-adder and the full-adder [3]. These circuits are often referred to as half-subtracters and full-subtracters. In most microcomputers, however, the subtraction process is performed using complement arithmetic with signed numbers in order to reduce the complexity of the arithmetic section of the computer. This method is discussed in Sec. 3.5, and the appropriate circuits required for its implementation are described.

3.3. OCTAL NUMBER SYSTEM

The octal number system is an important system which is often used in microcomputers. It has a base of 8 and employs the digits 0 through 7. To illustrate the positional value for this system, consider the octal number

$$673.12_8$$

The equivalent decimal number is given by

$$(6 \times 8^2) + (7 \times 8^1) + (3 \times 8^0) + (1 \times 8^{-1}) + (2 \times 8^{-2}) = 443.15625_{10}$$

As in the binary and decimal number systems, the radix (octal) point separates the integer and fractional parts of the number.

Decimal-to-Octal Conversion

Decimal-to-octal conversion can be accomplished using the dibble-dabble method presented in Sec. 3.2. The integer part of a number is converted with repeated divisions by the base 8. In the above example, the integer part of the number, N_I, is 443_{10}. This is easily converted by the following procedure:

$$
\begin{aligned}
443 \div 8 &= 55 \quad \text{with remainder} \quad 3 \quad \text{(LSD)} \\
55 \div 8 &= 6 \qquad\qquad\qquad\qquad 7 \\
6 \div 8 &= 0 \qquad\qquad\qquad\qquad 6 \quad \text{(MSD)}
\end{aligned}
$$

Collecting the remainders proceeding from the *most significant digit* (MSD) to the *least significant digit* (LSD), we find

$$N_I = 443_{10} = 673_8$$

For conversion of the fractional part of the number, repeated multiplications are required. In the above example, the fractional part of the number, N_F, is 0.15625_{10}. The conversion proceeds as follows:

$$0.15625 \times 8 = 1.25000 = 0.25000 \quad \text{with overflow of} \quad 1 \quad (\text{MSD})$$

$$0.25000 \times 8 = 2.00000 = 0.00000 \qquad\qquad\qquad\qquad 2 \quad (\text{LSD})$$

Collecting the overflows from the MSD to the LSD, we find

$$N_F = 0.15625_{10} = 0.12_8$$

Therefore, from Eq. (3.1), we have

$$N = 443.15625_{10} = 673.12_8$$

Binary-to-Octal Conversion

Numerical operations in microcomputers are performed in binary. Binary numbers, when used to represent large quantities, require many 0's and 1's. This is cumbersome and time-consuming; therefore, other systems are often used as a shorthand notation for binary numbers. One popular system is the octal system. As a result, frequent binary-to-octal conversions are necessary.

In binary, three bit positions represent exactly eight combinations (000 through 111). Therefore, octal numbers can be directly substituted for 3-bit binary numbers. For this reason, the conversion is simple and straightforward. The integer part of the binary number is separated into groups of three bits beginning at the binary point and proceeding to the left. The fractional part of the number is separated into 3-bit groups beginning at the binary point and proceeding to the right. Each group of three bits is then replaced by an octal equivalent. The process is demonstrated for the binary number 11101110100.00111101 by the following:

$$
\begin{array}{ccccccc}
11 & 101 & 110 & 100 & . & 001 & 111 & 01 \\
(011) & & & & & & & (010) \\
\\
3 & 5 & 6 & 4 & . & 1 & 7 & 2 \\
(\text{MSD}) & & & & & & & (\text{LSD})
\end{array}
$$

Therefore, $11101110100.00111101_2 = 3564.172_8$.

In forming the 3-bit groupings, 0's may be needed to complete the first (MSD) and last (LSD) groups, as shown above. In the last group, for example, 01 is not octal 1. In this case, 01 represents 010 or octal 2.

Octal-to-binary conversion is the reverse of the above procedure. This is easily accomplished by replacing each octal digit by its 3-bit binary equivalent.

Octal Addition

In an octal number system, when addition is performed, a carry is generated in each digit position for which a sum exceeds 7. This is illustrated by the counting sequence of Table 3.4. In this table, a carry occurs on the eighth and sixteenth decimal counts.

Table 3.4 OCTAL COUNTING.

Octal	Decimal	Octal	Decimal
0	0	12	10
1	1	13	11
2	2	14	12
3	3	15	13
4	4	16	14
5	5	17	15
6	6	20	16
7	7	21	17
10	8	22	18
11	9	23	19

To demonstrate octal addition, consider the sum of 5273_8 and 6432_8, as shown in Fig. 3.7. In column 1, $3 + 2 = 5$. Adding column 2, we have $7 + 3 = 8_{10} + 2 = 10_8 + 2 = 2 + \text{carry}$. This carry is shown at the top of column 3. In column 3, $1 + 2 + 4 = 7$. Next, summing column 4, we find $5 + 6 = 8_{10} + 3 = 10_8 + 3 = 3 + \text{carry}$. This carry is placed at the top of column 5. Finally, summing column 5 yields a 1. Therefore,

$$5273_8 + 6432_8 = 13725_8$$

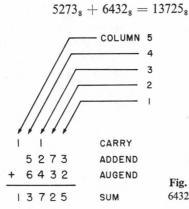

Fig. 3.7. Octal addition of 5273 and 6432.

Octal Subtraction

In octal subtraction, a borrow is required for each digit position in which the minuend digit is less than the subtrahend digit. In the octal system, a borrow requires that eight units (10_8 or 8_{10}) be added to the minuend digit and one unit be subtracted from the adjacent (left) minuend digit. An example of octal subtraction is shown in Fig. 3.8 for the difference of octal numbers 46534 and 6714. In column 1, $4 - 4 = 0$. Proceeding to column 2, $3 - 1 = 2$. Subtracting in column 3, we have $5 - 7 = 5 + \text{borrow} - 7 = 5 + 10_8 - 7 = 5 + 8_{10} - 7 = 6$. The borrow which is added to this position is obtained from column 4. Therefore, the 6 in the minuend of column 4 is

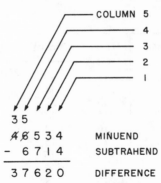

```
                          COLUMN 5
                                 4
                                 3
                                 2
                                 1
    3 5
    4̶ 5̶ 5 3 4      MINUEND
  -   6 7 1 4      SUBTRAHEND
  ─────────────
    3 7 6 2 0      DIFFERENCE
```

Fig. 3.8. Octal subtraction of 46534 and 6714.

replaced by $6 - 1 = 5$, shown at the top of this column. Continuing to column 4, $5 - 6 = 5 + \text{borrow} - 6 = 5 + 10_8 - 6 = 5 + 8_{10} - 6 = 7$. As before, the borrow added to this column was obtained from column 5. This results in the 4 of column 5 being replaced by 3. In column 5, $3 - 0 = 3$. Therefore,

$$46534_8 - 6714_8 = 37620_8$$

3.4. HEXADECIMAL NUMBER SYSTEM

The hexadecimal number system is another system often used in microcomputers. It has a base of 16 which requires sixteen digits. The digits used are 0 through 9 and A through F. The symbols A through F represent the equivalent decimal numbers of 10 through 15, respectively. This system is called an *alphanumeric* number system since numbers and letters are used to represent its digits. A counting sequence for this system is shown in Table 3.5.

Table 3.5   HEXADECIMAL COUNTING.

Hexadecimal	Decimal	Hexadecimal	Decimal	Hexadecimal	Decimal
0	0	A	10	14	20
1	1	B	11	15	21
2	2	C	12	16	22
3	3	D	13	17	23
4	4	E	14	18	24
5	5	F	15	19	25
6	6	10	16	1A	26
7	7	11	17	1B	27
8	8	12	18	1C	28
9	9	13	19	1D	29

The positional value of the hexadecimal system can be demonstrated using the hexadecimal number

$$F3D.C8_{16}$$

The decimal equivalent for this number is given by

$$(15 \times 16^2) + (3 \times 16^1) + (13 \times 16^0) + (12 \times 16^{-1}) + (8 \times 16^{-2}) = 3901.78125_{10}$$

The radix (hexadecimal) point, as in the previously described number systems, separates the integer and fractional parts of the number.

Decimal-to-Hexadecimal Conversion

Decimal-to-hexadecimal conversion can be performed using the previously described dibble-dabble method. The integer part of a decimal number is converted by repeated divisions by the base 16. In the previous example, the integer part of the number, N_I, is 3901_{10}. This is converted by the following procedure:

$$3901 \div 16 = 243 \quad \text{with remainder} \quad 13_{10} = D \quad (\text{LSD})$$
$$243 \div 16 = 15 \qquad\qquad\qquad 3$$
$$15 \div 16 = 0 \qquad\qquad\qquad 15_{10} = F \quad (\text{MSD})$$

The remainders are collected proceeding from the MSD to the LSD. Therefore,

$$N_I = 3901_{10} = F3D_{16}$$

The fractional part of the number is converted by repeated multiplications by the base. In our example, $N_F = 0.78125_{10}$. The conversion is performed by the following:

$$0.78125 \times 16 = 12.5 = 0.5 \quad \text{with overflow} \quad 12_{10} = C \quad (\text{MSD})$$
$$0.5 \quad\times 16 = 8.0 = 0 \qquad\qquad\qquad 8 \quad (\text{LSD})$$

Collecting the overflows from the MSD to the LSD, we find

$$N_F = 0.78125_{10} = 0.C8_{16}$$

Therefore, from Eq. (3.1), we find

$$N = 3901.78125_{10} = F3D.C8_{16}$$

Binary-to-Hexadecimal Conversion

The hexadecimal number system is another system often used as a shorthand notation for binary numbers. In binary, 4-bit positions are necessary to obtain sixteen combinations (0000 to 1111). As a result of this, hexadecimal numbers can be directly substituted for 4-bit binary numbers. The integer part of the binary number is separated into groups of four bits beginning at the binary point and proceeding to the left. The fractional part of the number is separated into 4-bit groups beginning at the binary point and moving to the right. Each group of four bits is then replaced by a hexadecimal equivalent. For the binary number 11010101000.1111010111, the conversion is performed as follows:

$$110 \quad 1010 \quad 1000 \quad . \quad 1111 \quad 0101 \quad 11$$
$$(0110) \qquad\qquad\qquad\qquad\qquad (1100)$$
$$6 \quad\; A \quad\;\; 8 \quad . \quad F \quad\;\; 5 \quad\; C$$
$$(MSD) \qquad\qquad\qquad\qquad\qquad (LSD)$$

Therefore, $11010101000.1111010111_2 = 6A8.F5C_{16}$.

In forming the 4-bit groupings, 0's may be required to complete the first (MSD) and last (LSD) groups, as shown above. Of particular interest is the last group where 11 is not 3, but 1100 or hexadecimal C.

Hexadecimal-to-binary conversion is the inverse of the above procedure. This is easily performed by replacing each hexadecimal digit by its 4-bit binary equivalent.

Hexadecimal Addition

In hexadecimal addition, a carry is generated in each digit position for which a sum exceeds 15_{10} or F. This is illustrated in Table 3.5 for the sixteenth decimal count, which is hexadecimal 10. To demonstrate addition in hexadecimal, consider the sum of $8A36_{16}$ and $C271_{16}$ as shown in Fig. 3.9. In column 1, $6 + 1 = 7$. Summing column

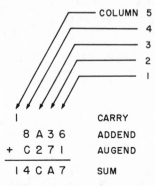

Fig. 3.9. Hexadecimal addition of 8A36 and C271.

2, we find $3 + 7 = A$. Similarly, in column 3, $A + 2 = C$. Adding column 4, we have $8 + C = 16_{10} + 4 = 10_{16} + 4 = 4 + \text{carry}$. This carry is shown at the top of column 5. Finally, summing column 5 yields 1. Therefore,

$$8A36_{16} + C271_{16} = 14CA7_{16}$$

Hexadecimal Subtraction

For hexadecimal subtraction, a borrow is required for each digit position in which the minuend digit is less than the subtrahend digit. In this system, a borrow requires that sixteen units (10_{16} or 16_{10}) be added to the minuend digit and one unit be subtracted from the adjacent (left) minuend digit. The subtraction process for numbers $3A76F_{16}$ and $1CB39_{16}$ is shown in Fig. 3.10. In column 1, $F - 9 = 6$. In column 2, $6 - 3 = 3$. Subtracting in column 3, we find $7 - B = 7 + \text{borrow} - B = 7 + 10_{16} - B = 7 + 16_{10} - 11_{10} = C$. This borrow is obtained from the minuend digit, A, of column 4. Therefore, this digit must be replaced by $A - 1 = 9$, shown at the top of column 4. Continuing to column 4, $9 - C = 9 + \text{borrow} - C = 9 + 10_{16} - C = 9 + 16_{10} - 12_{10} = D$. The borrow in this digit results in $3 - 1 = 2$ replacing the 3 of column 5. Therefore, we have

$$3A76F_{16} - 1CB39_{16} = 1DC36_{16}.$$

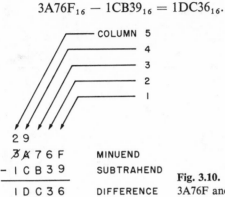

Fig. 3.10. Hexadecimal subtraction of 3A76F and 1CB39.

3.5. SIGNED NUMBERS AND COMPLEMENT ARITHMETIC

In all number systems, both positive and negative values are possible. A conventional method of denoting these values is to use a plus (+) or a minus (−) sign preceding the number. This representation is called a *signed number*. Computers are constructed of binary circuits and use the symbols 0 and 1 to represent the binary states. We must therefore use the same symbols to indicate whether numbers are positive or negative. Generally an additional bit, known as a *sign bit*, is placed at the most significant end to represent the sign. 0 and 1 are normally used to indicate positive and negative values, respectively.

In this section, we will describe three important signed number systems known as *sign-and-magnitude*, *1's complement*, and *2's complement* representations [3–5].

Sign-and-Magnitude Representation

The simplest signed number system is the sign-and-magnitude notation often referred to as *signed binary*. An *n*-bit number employs the MSB to represent the sign of the number and the remaining $n - 1$ bits to express the magnitude in binary. As an example, consider -13_{10} expressed using five bits. We have

$$-13_{10} = 1,1101$$
$$\phantom{-13_{10} = 1,}\text{sign bit } (-)$$

In this representation, a comma has been used to separate the sign bit from the magnitude bits for clarity; it is omitted by many authors. Another example is

$$+27_{10} = 0,11011$$

$\hookleftarrow$ sign bit $(+)$

Table 3.6 shows the decimal equivalents for 4-bit signed binary numbers. In this table, there are two representations for 0: 0,000 and 1,000. Therefore, the four bits used in this notation can represent only fifteen values, resulting in a loss of one value.

Table 3.6   DECIMAL EQUIVALENTS OF 4-BIT SIGNED BINARY NUMBERS.

Binary	Decimal	Binary	Decimal
0,000	+0	1,000	−0
0,001	+1	1,001	−1
0,010	+2	1,010	−2
0,011	+3	1,011	−3
0,100	+4	1,100	−4
0,101	+5	1,101	−5
0,110	+6	1,110	−6
0,111	+7	1,111	−7

It is a simple matter to visualize whether to add or subtract a number by inspection of the sign bit. The required addition or subtraction is performed for the magnitude bits, as described in Sec. 3.2. However, different arithmetic circuits are required, one for subtraction and one for addition. The complement representation for a negative number, to be described next, avoids this difficulty.

1's Complement Representation

In a 1's complement representation for a number, a negative weight of $-[2^{n-1} - 1]$ is assigned to the sign bit. For positive numbers, the 1's complement representation is identical to that of signed binary. For negative numbers, however, the negative weight alters the magnitude portion of the operand. An n-bit (including the sign bit) 1's complement representation for an integer number, x, is

$$N(x) = 0, x, \qquad\qquad\qquad x \geq 0 \qquad\qquad (3.2a)$$

$$= 1, \{[2^{n-1} - 1] - |x|\}, \qquad x \leq 0 \qquad\qquad (3.2b)$$

As an example of Eq. (3.2a), consider the decimal number 6. In binary, $6_{10} = 110_2$. Therefore, in order to include the sign bit, a 4-bit number is required.

$$N(6) = 0,110$$

This result is identical to the signed binary representation.

Next consider the number -6_{10}. In this case, $|x| = 6_{10} = 110_2$. Since $|x|$ requires three bits, inclusion of a sign bit will require four bits. Therefore, in Eq. (3.2b), $n = 4$, $2^{n-1} = 2^3 = 8_{10} = 1000_2$, and $2^{n-1} - 1 = 7_{10} = 111_2$. This yields

$$N(-6) = 1, [111 - 110] = 1,001$$

Comparing the results for these two examples, we see that $N(6) + N(-6) = 1,111$, which demonstrates the property that a number plus its 1's complement yields all 1's. Also, it should be noted that if each bit is complemented for $N(6)$, we obtain $N(-6)$. This is an extremely important property. For example, consider

$$N(17) = 0,10001$$

Replacing 0's by 1's and 1's by 0's (complementing all bits) yields

$$N(-17) = 1,01110$$

The conversion of a negative value from 1's complement to decimal can be performed in two ways. The first method is the reverse of the complementing procedure. For example, consider the 4-bit number 1,011. Complementing each bit we have 0,100. This is 1's complement for $+4$. Therefore, $1,011 = -4$.

The second method uses the fact that the sign bit has a negative weight of $2^{n-1} - 1$ for an n-bit number. In our case $n = 4$, $2^{n-1} - 1 = 7$, and the weight of the sign bit is -7. Therefore,

$$1,011 = -7 + 3 = -4$$

This method is easy to apply since we simply convert the magnitude bits to decimal and add the result to the negative weight of the sign bit.

Table 3.7 shows the decimal equivalents for 4-bit 1's complement numbers. From this table, the bit-by-bit complement property is readily verified between positive and negative numbers. Also, as in the case of signed binary, there exist two representations for 0. These are 0,000 and 1,111.

Table 3.7   DECIMAL EQUIVALENTS OF 4-BIT 1's COMPLEMENT
            NUMBERS.

1's Complement	Decimal	1's Complement	Decimal
0,000	$+0$	1,111	-0
0,001	$+1$	1,110	-1
0,010	$+2$	1,101	-2
0,011	$+3$	1,100	-3
0,100	$+4$	1,011	-4
0,101	$+5$	1,010	-5
0,110	$+6$	1,001	-6
0,111	$+7$	1,000	-7

The primary advantage of complement numbers is that the subtraction process is performed by *adding* the complement of the number. Suppose, for example, we wish to perform the operation $17_{10} - 12_{10} = 17_{10} + (-12_{10})$. In 1's complement, $N(17) = 0,10001$ and $N(12) = 0,01100$. Therefore, $N(-12) = 1,10011$. $N(17) + N(-12)$ is shown in Fig. 3.11. In this figure, the numbers are added using addition as described in Sec. 3.2. This sum, neglecting the carry generated in the sign bit, is $0,00100$ or $+4_{10}$. The correct answer is $+5_{10}$. This requires adding $+1$ to the original sum, which is called *end-around carry*. The result is then $0,00101$ or 5_{10}.

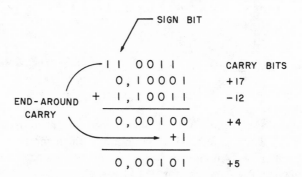

Fig. 3.11. 1's complement arithmetic for $17 - 12 = 5$.

Because of the necessity of the end-around carry, 1's complement arithmetic is not generally used to perform subtraction in microprocessors. This operation is usually performed using the 2's complement arithmetic of the next section. A knowledge of the 1's complement numbers, however, is very useful in generating 2's complement numbers.

2's Complement Representation

The 2's complement representation for positive numbers is identical to that for 1's complement or signed binary. For negative numbers, the 2's complement is equal to the 1's complement plus 1. Therefore, an n-bit 2's complement representation for an integer number x is

$$M(x) \doteq N(x), \qquad x \geq 0 \tag{3.3a}$$

$$= N(x) + 1, \qquad x < 0 \tag{3.3b}$$

where $N(x)$ is defined in (3.2). The weight of the sign bit in 2's complement is -2^{n-1} for $x < 0$.

As an example, consider the steps in finding the 2's complement for -13_{10}:

1. Express 13_{10} as a 1's complement number.

$$N(13) = 0{,}1101$$

2. Complement each bit of $N(13)$.

$$N(-13) = 1{,}0010$$

3. Add 1 to $N(-13)$.

$$M(-13) = N(-13) + 1 = 1{,}0011$$

This method is generally used in computers since it is easily implemented with hardware. An alternate method, performed by inspection, is executed by starting from the right (LSB) and duplicating each bit until the first 1 is encountered; thereafter, complement all bits.

The decimal equivalents for 4-bit 2's complement numbers are shown in Table 3.8. In this table, we see that there is only one representation for 0. Also, -8 exists

Table 3.8   DECIMAL EQUIVALENTS OF 4-BIT 2'S COMPLEMENT NUMBERS.

2's complement	Decimal	2's complement	Decimal
0,000	+0		
0,001	+1	1,111	−1
0,010	+2	1,110	−2
0,011	+3	1,101	−3
0,100	+4	1,100	−4
0,101	+5	1,011	−5
0,110	+6	1,010	−6
0,111	+7	1,001	−7
		1,000	−8

as a 4-bit number in 2's complement, but not as a 4-bit number in signed binary or 1's complement. This presents an apparent problem in using (3.3). Since -8 does not exist as a 4-bit 1's complement number, how does one obtain a 2's complement representation? Recall that the negative weight of the sign bit of a 4-bit number is $-2^3 = -8$. Since we add the magnitude bits to this negative weight to get the number, we see that $1{,}000 = -2^3 + 0 = -8$.

Next, consider the 5-bit representation of -8. $N(8) = 0{,}1000$ and $N(-8) = 1{,}0111$. Therefore, $M(-8) = N(-8) + 1 = 1{,}1000$. Comparing this result to 4-bit representation, we see that the number of bits employed determines the value of the magnitude portion of the operand.

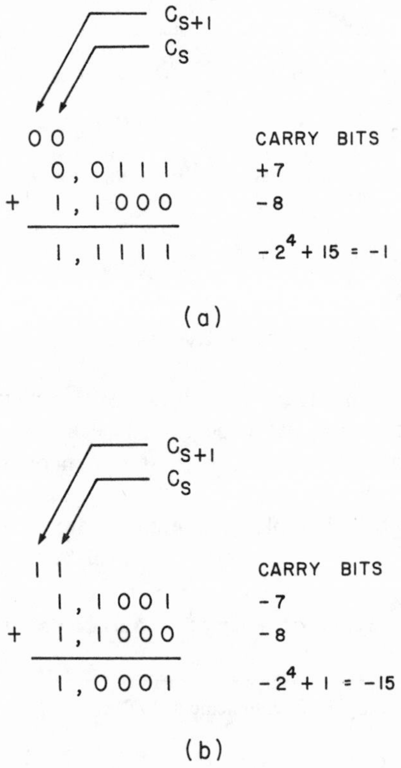

```
        Cs+1
        Cs

  0 0                    CARRY  BITS
    0 , 0 1 1 1          + 7
 +  1 , 1 0 0 0          - 8
    ──────────
    1 , 1 1 1 1          - 2⁴ + 15 = - 1
```

$$-2^4 + 15 = -1$$

(a)

```
        Cs+1
        Cs

  1 1                    CARRY  BITS
    1 , 1 0 0 1          - 7
 +  1 , 1 0 0 0          - 8
    ──────────
    1 , 0 0 0 1          - 2⁴ + 1 = -15
```

$$-2^4 + 1 = -15$$

(b)

Fig. 3.12. 2's complement arithmetic for (a) $7 - 8$ (b) $-7 - 8$.

Let us now examine the properties of 2's complement arithmetic. Consider, for example, the difference $7 - 8 = M(7) + M(-8)$, as shown in Fig. 3.12(a) for 5-bit numbers. In this example, the sign-bit carry, C_S, and the carry out of the sign bit, C_{S+1}, are both equal to 0. The sum yields -1 in 2's complement form. Next, consider the sum of -7 and -8, as shown in Fig. 3.12(b). In performing the sum, we see that C_S and C_{S+1} are both 1. However, the correct result is given by $1,0001 = -15$, which requires that we neglect C_{S+1}. In the examples of Fig. 3.12, no numeric overflow occurs because both results are between 15 and -16. (This range includes all 5-bit numbers.) Therefore, C_{S+1} is neglected. It should be noted that when no overflow occurs, $C_S = C_{S+1}$.

Now let us inspect the cases of numeric overflow. Overflow can occur only when both numbers have the same sign. Consider the sum of 5-bit numbers 12 and 14, as shown in Fig. 3.13(a). This sum gives $+26$ which cannot be expressed as a 5-bit 2's complement number. As a result, overflow occurs, and the comma we have used (for convenience) to separate the magnitude and sign bits must be moved one place to the left, as shown. The C_{S+1} carry is now included in the sum. Note that C_S and C_{S+1} are not equal.

Next, consider the sum of -12 and -14, shown in Fig. 3.13(b). As before, the C_{S+1} carry must be included in the result and the comma moved one place to the left.

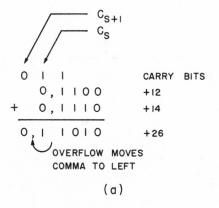

(a)

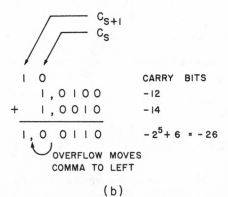

(b)

Fig. 3.13. 2's complement arithmetic illustrating overflow for (a) $12 + 14$ (b) $-12 - 14$.

Again, C_S and C_{S+1} are not equal. Therefore, overflow occurs only when C_S and C_{S+1} are not equal. This is expressed logically by

$$\text{OVERFLOW} = C_S \oplus C_{S+1}$$

A circuit which performs 2's complement addition and subtraction is shown in Fig. 3.14. In the case of addition, the ADD/SUBTRACT terminal and the input carry into the full-adder, C_{in}, are 0. B_0 through B_{n-1} pass through the exclusive-OR gates unchanged since 0 is on one input of each gate. Therefore, the sum $A + B$ results with any overflow being generated by the exclusive-OR gate having inputs of C_S and C_{S+1}.

In the case of $A - B$, the ADD/SUBTRACT terminal and the input carry, C_{in}, are 1. B_0 through B_{n-1} are complemented as a result of the 1 at one input of each EXCLUSIVE-OR gate. This complementation yields the 1's complement for $-B$. Since $C_{in} = 1$ is added to this 1's complement, the 2's complement for $-B$ results, which is added to A. As in the case of addition, C_S and C_{S+1} generate any overflow.

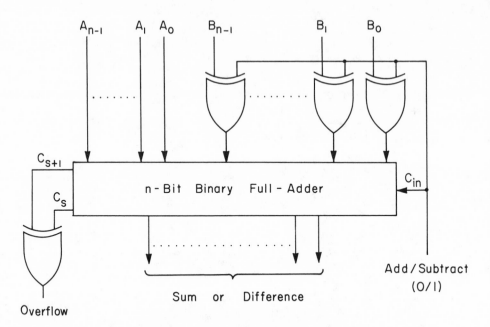

Fig. 3.14. 2's complement adder/subtractor.

3.6. BINARY-CODED NUMBER SYSTEMS

The binary number system is the most convenient system for computers; however, people are more accustomed to decimal numbers. An ideal method is to perform all computer functions on binary data and convert the results to decimal for display to the operator. The conversion from binary to decimal and vice versa, although straightforward, requires implementation of a complex algorithm. In many small computer systems the time spent in executing the conversion algorithm may greatly exceed the time spent in data manipulations. Figure 3.15 illustrates the steps necessary for a conversion between decimal and 2's complement representations. If a lengthy computation is to be made, it may be most efficient to make these conversions and calculate in 2's complement.

For less extensive calculations, however, a compromise is to encode each decimal digit with a binary number. Such a system is called *binary-coded decimal* which is commonly abbreviated *BCD* [2–6]. The decimal weighting is maintained, but the digit is represented by a combination of the binary digits 0 and 1. A large number of methods exist for encoding each decimal digit by a binary number. Since ten digits must be represented, a minimum of four bits must be used to encode each digit. The most common method is to represent each digit by its binary equivalent using four bits. For example, the digit 5 is equivalent to binary 0101, and the digit 9 is equivalent to

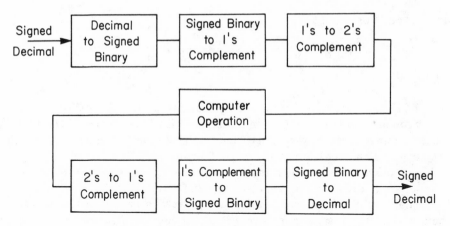

Fig. 3.15. Number conversion in a computer.

binary 1001. By this method, the decimal number 59 is represented as

$$
\begin{array}{ccc}
5 & 9 & \text{decimal} \\
0101 & 1001 & \text{BCD}
\end{array}
$$

Note that for each decimal digit the binary representation may be interpreted by a binary-to-decimal conversion. For example,

$$0111 = (0 \times 2^3) + (1 \times 2^2) + (1 \times 2^1) + (1 \times 2^0) = 7$$

Since each bit carries a particular weighting (2^0, 2^1, 2^2, etc.), the code is referred to as a *weighted code*. The weighting in this case is 8, 4, 2, 1; thus, this particular code is called 8421 BCD [3]. Table 3.9 illustrates 8421 BCD along with several other popular BCD codes. Note the ease with which conversions from BCD to decimal, and vice versa,

Table 3.9 BCD Codes.

Decimal	8421 BCD	2′421 BCD	Excess-3	Gray Code
0	0000	0000	0011	0000
1	0001	0001	0100	0001
2	0010	0010	0101	0011
3	0011	0011	0110	0010
4	0100	0100	0111	0110
5	0101	1011	1000	0111
6	0110	1100	1001	0101
7	0111	1101	1010	0100
8	1000	1110	1011	1100
9	1001	1111	1100	1000

may be made. For example,

0101	0000	1000	0011	BCD
5	0	8	3	Decimal

In BCD, there are sixteen possible combinations of four bits (0000–1111); therefore, six combinations are not used. In the case of 8421 BCD, the last six (1010–1111) are not permitted. Since the weight of each bit is the same as that in binary numbering, this system is often referred to as *natural BCD* or simply BCD.

Next, consider the sum of 5 and 8 in this code, as shown in Fig. 3.16. In this figure, we see that the conventional sum for BCD 5 and 8 yields 1101 (binary 13), which is not permitted in this code. In decimal, a carry is generated on the tenth count; therefore, in BCD this same carry must be created. Since a higher-order carry occurs on the sixteenth count for a 4-bit binary number, we see that adding six (0110) to numbers 1010 through 1111 in BCD addition will generate the decimal carry, as illustrated in Fig. 3.16. As a result of correction factors such as this, BCD arithmetic circuits are more complex than those of binary circuits and require more time in executing numeric computations.

```
        0 1 0 1      BCD 5
    +   1 0 0 0      BCD 8
    ─────────────
        1 1 0 1      BINARY 13
    +   0 1 1 0      ADD 6
    ─────────────                   Fig. 3.16. Addition of 5 and 8 in 8421
  0 0 0 1   0 0 1 1  BCD 13         BCD.
```

Suppose we wish to subtract two BCD digits. If no borrows are generated, the subtraction is straightforward and corrections factors are not necessary. If a borrow occurs, however, then a correction is required as illustrated in Fig. 3.17. The correction is required because a borrow from the fifth binary digit has a weight of 16 instead of 10, as required for BCD. Thus, an additional six must be subtracted. Arithmetic units, counters, and various encoders and decoders for 8421 BCD are available in most IC logic families.

```
     0 0 1 0   1 0 0 0    BCD 28
  -  0 0 0 1   1 0 0 1    BCD 19
  ──────────────────
     0 0 0 0   1 1 1 1    BINARY 15
  -          0 1 1 0    SUBTRACT 6
  ──────────────────                 Fig. 3.17. Subtraction of 19 from 28 in
     0 0 0 0   1 0 0 1    BCD 9       8421 BCD.
```

Another weighted code is the 2′421 BCD of Table 3.9 [4]. In this code, the weight of the MSB position is 2 instead of 8, and the remaining bits are 4, 2, and 1 as in the previous code. This leads to the anomaly of having two representations for digits

2 through 7. In the table, we have selected the weights such that digits 0–4 begin with 0 and digits 5–9 begin with 1.

The excess-3 code of Table 3.9 is another BCD code [5]. This is an *unweighted* code since the bit positions cannot be assigned a fixed weight for representing each digit. The excess-3 code is used when it is desirable to obtain the *9's complement* of the decimal digit represented by the code. The 9's complement for a decimal digit, x, is given by

$$P(x) = x, \qquad x \geq 0 \qquad\qquad\qquad (3.4a)$$

$$ = 9 - |x|, \qquad x < 0 \qquad\qquad (3.4b)$$

As an example of the utility of the excess-3 code, consider finding the 9's complement for -4. From (3.4b), we see $P(-4) = 9 - 4 = 5$. Another method of obtaining this result uses a self-complementing property. In excess-3, $0111 = 4$. Complementing each bit, we find $1000 = 5$, which is the 9's complement for -4. Thus, the 9's complement is generated by complementing each bit of the excess-3 number. The 9's complement of a decimal number is analogous to the 1's complement in binary, and it is therefore useful in performing decimal subtraction. A similar self-complementing property exists for $2'421$ BCD, which may be easily demonstrated by the reader.

Another important unweighted code is the Gray code (reflected code) [3, 6]. In Table 3.9, we see that only one bit changes in going from one number to the next. This code is very useful for certain analog-to-digital converters (especially shaft encoders) because it results in errors of not more than one count.

3.7. SIGNED 10's COMPLEMENT DECIMAL ARITHMETIC

In ordinary decimal arithmetic, numbers are represented in a sign-and-magnitude notation (e.g., $+47$ or -81). As in the case of binary numbers a decimal number may also be represented in a complement notation. If the sign is represented by a binary bit ($1 = -$, $0 = +$) having a weighting of -10^n for a negative n-digit decimal number, the result is a signed 10's complement representation [3, 7, 8] given by

$$Q(x) = 0, x, \qquad x \geq 0 \qquad\qquad\qquad (3.5a)$$

$$ = 1, 10^n - |x|, \qquad x < 0 \qquad\qquad (3.5b)$$

This representation is sometimes referred to as 100's complement for $n = 2$, 1000's complement for $n = 3$, etc.

Arithmetic operations using 10's complement arithmetic are very similar to those of 2's complement in Sec. 3.5. For example, consider subtracting 147 from 124. In obtaining this difference, we add 124 to the 10's complement of -147. From (3.5b), $n = 3$ since 147 has three digits and

$$Q(-147) = 1,10^3 - 147 = 1,853$$

The subtraction process is demonstrated in Fig. 3.18.

As in the case of 2's complement arithmetic, overflow in 10's complement is given by

$$\text{OVERFLOW} = C_S \oplus C_{S+1}$$

In our example, $C_S = C_{S+1} = 0$ and no overflow occurs. Since the sign bit equals 1, the decimal number is obtained by adding the magnitude digits (977) to the weight of the sign bit (-10^3). If an overflow occurs, appropriate steps must be performed to properly interpret the result.

In performing decimal arithmetic, computers must use a BCD code for the digits. If a self-complementing code is employed (e.g., excess-3), the 9's complement is easily obtained by complementing the bits of each digit. When all digits of the number have been complemented, adding 1 to the number yields the 10's complement for the magnitude bits in excess-3 code. The sign bit (1) is then included, and arithmetic operations can be performed in a manner similar to that in Fig. 3.18 using excess-3 arithmetic.

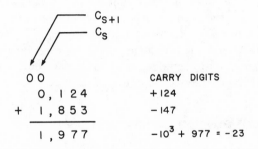

Fig. 3.18. 10's complement arithmetic for $124 - 147$.

3.8. AMERICAN STANDARD CODE FOR INFORMATION INTERCHANGE (ASCII)

The most common alphanumeric code used to represent characters is the American Standard Code for Information Interchange (ASCII) [9]. This code uses either six or seven bits for data representation. 6-bit ASCII excludes lowercase characters. The 7-bit code is called full ASCII, extended ASCII, or USASCII. In the ASCII code, 64 characters are available, including uppercase alphabetics with numerics and control characters. With full ASCII, both uppercase and lowercase characters are possible. Table 3.10 shows the most commonly used 6-bit and 7-bit ASCII characters. The 7-bit code is generally used for input and output devices such as the teletypewriter or teleprinter.

In the 7-bit code, an eighth bit is often used as a *parity* or *check bit* to determine if the data has been transmitted correctly. The value of this bit is specified by the type of parity. *Even parity* means that the sum of all 1 bits, including the parity bit, is an even number. For example, if 3 is the data in question, the ASCII code in binary is 0110011. Since four 1's are in the code and 4 is an even number, the parity bit would be 0.

Odd parity means that the sum of all bits, including the parity bit, is an odd number. In the example, the parity bit for odd parity would be 1. Another parity often

Table 3.10   OCTAL VALUES FOR 7-BIT AND 6-BIT ASCII CODES.

Printing Character	7-Bit ASCII	6-Bit ASCII	Printing Character	7-Bit ASCII	6-Bit ASCII
@	100	00	(Space)	040	40
A	101	01	!	041	41
B	102	02	"	042	42
C	103	03	#	043	43
D	104	04	$	044	44
E	105	05	%	045	45
F	106	06	&	046	46
G	107	07	'	047	47
H	110	10	(	050	50
I	111	11	)	051	51
J	112	12	*	052	52
K	113	13	+	053	53
L	114	14	,	054	54
M	115	15	−	055	55
N	116	16	.	056	56
O	117	17	/	057	57
P	120	20	0	060	60
Q	121	21	1	061	61
R	122	22	2	062	62
S	123	23	3	063	63
T	124	24	4	064	64
U	125	25	5	065	65
V	126	26	6	066	66
W	127	27	7	067	67
X	130	30	8	070	70
Y	131	31	9	071	71
Z	132	32	:	072	72
[	133	33	;	073	73
\	134	34	<	074	74
]	135	35	=	075	75
↑	136	36	>	076	76
←	137	37	?	077	77
Null	000				
Horizontal Tab	011				
Line Feed	012				
Vertical Tab	013				
Form Feed	014				
Carriage Return	015				
Rubout	177				

encountered is called *mark parity*. In this case, the parity bit is always 1. Finally, *space parity* means the parity bit is always 0.

The ASCII code is used almost exclusively in most microcomputer systems.

REFERENCES

1. HURLEY, R. B., *Transistor Logic Circuits*. New York: John Wiley & Sons, Inc., 1961.

2. MALMSTADT, H. V. and C. G. ENKE, *Digital Electronics for Scientists*. New York: W. A. Benjamin, Inc., 1969.

3. RHYNE, V. T., *Fundamentals of Digital Systems Design*. Englewood Cliffs, N. J.: Prentice-Hall, Inc., 1973.

4. KOHONEN, T., *Digital Circuits and Devices*. Englewood Cliffs, N. J.: Prentice-Hall, Inc., 1972.

5. DEEM, W., K. MUCHOW, and A. ZEPPA, *Digital Computer Circuits and Concepts*. Reston Va.: Reston Publishing Co., Inc., 1974.

6. HUSKEY, H. D. and G. A. KORN, *Computer Handbook*. New York: McGraw-Hill Book Co., 1962.

7. CHU, Y., *Digital Computer Design Fundamentals*. New York: McGraw-Hill Book Co., 1962.

8. RICHARDS, R. K., *Arithmetic Operations in Digital Computers*. New York: Van Nostrand Reinhold Co., 1955.

9. KORN, G. A., *Minicomputers for Engineers and Scientists*. New York: McGraw-Hill Book Co., 1973.

EXERCISES

3.1. Perform the following conversions:
(a) 101101.101_2 to decimal
(b) 47_{10} to binary
(c) 0.74_{10} to binary
(d) 24.31_{10} to binary

3.2. Perform the following binary arithmetic operations:
(a) $1011 + 1101$
(b) $1101 - 0110$
(c) $101.1101 + 1101.101$
(d) $1110.1001 - 1010.011$

3.3. Perform the following conversions:
(a) 87.1_{10} to octal
(b) 1011.101_2 to octal
(c) 724.6_8 to decimal
(d) 62.42_8 to binary

3.4. Perform the following octal arithmetic operations:
(a) 674.276 + 561.43
(b) 1074.26 − 741.356

3.5. Perform the following conversions:
(a) $BAD.DAD_{16}$ to decimal
(b) 374.971_{10} to hexadecimal
(c) 11011.101101_2 to hexadecimal
(d) $8AF.CB4_{16}$ to octal

3.6. Perform the following hexadecimal arithmetic operations:
(a) ABCD.EF + 138F.014C
(b) 9A4DF.C1 − 47F.A27

3.7. Give the sign-and-magnitude, 1's complement, and 2's complement representations for the following decimal numbers:
(a) −24
(b) −7462

3.8. Using 1's and 2's complement arithmetic, find
(a) 974 − 356
(b) 721 − 846

3.9. Give the 8421 BCD representations for the following decimal numbers:
(a) 974
(b) 1092

3.10. Perform the following arithmetic operations using 8421 BCD numbers:
(a) 257 + 896
(b) 4719 − 825

3.11. Determine the 9's and 10's complement representations for the following decimal numbers:
(a) −31
(b) −7469

3.12. Repeat Exercise 3.8 for 9's and 10's complement arithmetic.

3.13. Give the 8-bit binary, octal, and hexadecimal codes using even, odd, mark, and space parities for the following 7-bit ASCII characters:
(a) A
(b) 6
(c) LINE FEED
(d) =

4 MICROCOMPUTER ARCHITECTURE

4.1. INTRODUCTION

A microcomputer is a machine which manipulates binary numbers (*data*) following an organized sequence of steps (*program*). Each step in the sequence is called an *instruction*. Microcomputers, like all computers, are machines which have the following features [1]:

1. An *input* medium, by which data and instructions may be entered.

2. A *memory*, from which data and instructions may be obtained and where results may be stored in any desired order.

3. A *calculating* section, which is capable of performing arithmetical and logical operations on any data taken from memory.

4. A *decision* capability, by which it may select alternate courses of action on the basis of computed results.

5. An *output* medium, by which results may be delivered to the user.

Machines which satisfy these five properties are known as *Harvard* class computers. If, in addition to these properties, instructions are stored in the same form as data in the same memory, each equally accessible to the calculating section of the computer, then instructions may be treated as data, and the machine can modify its instructions. Such a machine is called a *von Neumann* or *Princeton* class computer. Microcomputers are available in Harvard and von Neumann classes.

The design of all microcomputers is based on four basic building blocks. These are input devices (feature 1), memory (feature 2), a microprocessor (features 3 and 4), and output devices (feature 5). The input devices convert input signals into the proper binary form for the microprocessor. Some typical devices are analog-to-digital (A/D)

74

converters, teletypewriters, cassette tape decks, etc. An interface is usually necessary to transform the input data into the proper digital form.

Memory has the capability to store binary numbers which describe, in detail, the instructions the computer is to implement. It also stores data (in binary form) upon which the computer is to operate and finally output to the outside world.

The microprocessor contains a *central processing unit* (CPU) which consists of the circuitry required to access the appropriate locations in memory and interpret resulting instructions. The execution of these instructions also takes place in this unit. The CPU contains the *arithmetic/logic unit* (ALU), a combinational network that performs arithmetical and logical operations on the data, a *control* section which controls the operations of the computer, and various data registers for temporary storage and manipulation of data and instructions. Microprocessors are implemented in one to ten IC packages using LSI technology [2]. They are available in various word sizes, ranging from four to sixteen bits [3].

Output devices convert the binary output data into a useful form. Examples of these devices include printers, tape punches, cathode ray tube displays, digital-to-analog (D/A) converters, etc.

The microcomputer building blocks are interconnected by a group of lines (one for each bit to be transferred) called a *bus*. Figure 4.1 illustrates a simplified microcomputer block diagram. Note that the input and output (I/O) devices share the same bus. Frequently in microcomputers the memory and I/O devices share the same bus.

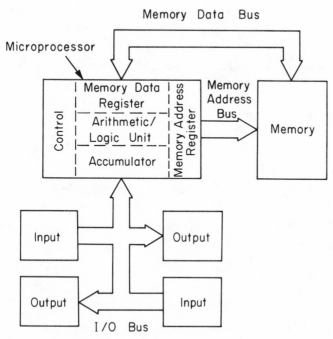

Fig. 4.1. Basic block diagram of a microcomputer.

In this case, the microprocessor may treat an I/O device as a memory element [4]. Figure 4.2 illustrates a system in which the memory and I/O devices share the same bus.

The computer operates in synchronism with a clock. A number of clock cycles are required to accomplish the tasks specified by one instruction. The execution of one instruction is called an *instruction cycle*. An instruction cycle typically consists of

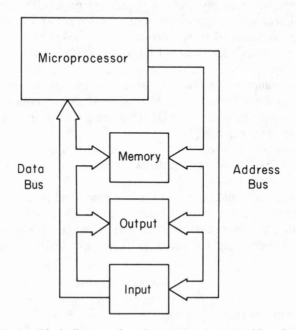

Fig. 4.2. Block diagram of a microcomputer system with a single data bus.

one or more *machine cycles*. During a machine cycle, the following subcycles are performed:

1. Fetch cycle.

    (a) The CPU provides the address of an instruction in a memory location via the memory address register.

    (b) The address is decoded and the instruction is read from memory into the memory data register of the CPU.

2. Execute cycle.

    The instruction is decoded and the requested operation is performed.

Figure. 4.3 illustrates a typical timing sequence for these cycles.

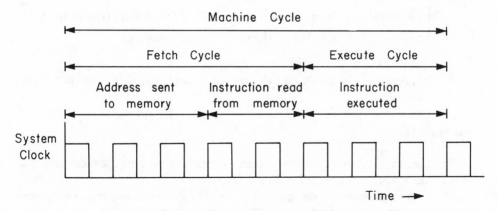

Fig. 4.3. Typical machine cycle.

Instruction Word Flow

During an instruction cycle, two types of words are processed. These are *instruction words* and *data words* [5]. Consider first the operations which take place on instruction words. The flow of an instruction word is shown in Fig. 4.4.

During a machine cycle the following operations take place with respect to an instruction word.

1. At the beginning of a cycle, the content of the program counter is placed in the memory address register (MAR).

2. The content of the MAR is transferred to the memory and decoded to determine the appropriate word.

3. The instruction is read from memory via the memory data bus to the memory data register (MDR).

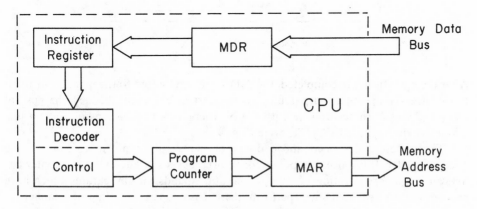

Fig. 4.4. Flow of an instruction word.

4. The instruction is then placed into the instruction register (IR) in the CPU.

5. The instruction is decoded by the instruction decoder.

6. The instruction is executed.

7. The program counter (PC) is incremented or reset according to the instruction being executed.

Data Word Flow

The execution of an instruction frequently requires an operation on data. The flow of a data word is illustrated in Fig. 4.5.

Data is input from either the memory or an I/O device. In many microcomputers, the data input must enter the CPU by way of a register called the *accumulator* (AC). The accumulator also functions as the destination of all data operated on by the ALU.

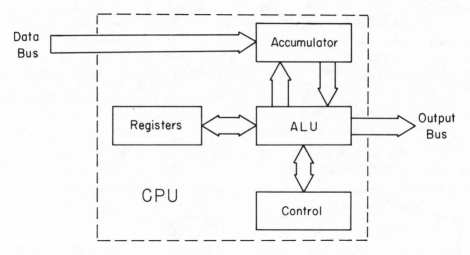

Fig. 4.5. Flow of a data word.

After the operations are completed, the data words are output to the memory or to an I/O device via the input/output bus. All operations are controlled by the control section (Sec. 4.4) in accordance with the instruction. All operations on data words take place during an EXECUTE cycle (Fig. 4.3).

The structure described above does not necessarily conform to any specific microcomputer. It has been simplified for tutorial purposes. Each microcomputer has its own unique organization which combines or expands certain features which have been described. All machines perform these basic operations in one manner or another. In Chapter 7 specific machines will be discussed and their individual characteristics examined.

Memory

Program steps and data must be stored and recalled at the appropriate time in order for the computer to perform its function. This is the task of the memory elements. Memory may be broadly divided into two classes, read-only memory (ROM) and read/write memory (RWM). ROM is used to store program steps and constant data values. It is difficult and time-consuming to write into ROM; therefore, it is used in situations where the memory values do not change, e.g., in dedicated systems. Since this is a primary application of microcomputers, most of these machines use ROM for program storage. Some microcomputers use only ROM for storing program steps.

Read/write memory is used to store data which changes during the operation of the system, e.g., results of calculations, or programs which are changed frequently. For either type, the function of memory is to store and provide on command a word of data or a program step.

In the following sections, detailed discussions of read-only memory, read/write memory, and the microprocessor unit are presented.

4.2. READ-ONLY MEMORY (ROM)

Read-only memory forms an important part of the memory requirement in most microcomputer systems [6]. This memory is generally referred to as ROM, an acronym for read-only memory. Other names for this type of memory are dead memory, fixed memory, permanent memory, and read-only store (ROS). *The ROM functions as a memory array whose contents, once programmed, are permanently fixed and cannot be altered by the microprocessor using the memory.*

The ROM, being a fixed memory, is nonvolatile; i.e., loss of power or system malfunction does not change the contents of the memory. Also, most ROMs have the feature of *random access*, which means that the access time for a given memory location is the same as that for all other locations. Stated concisely, random access means memory access time is independent of the memory location being accessed.

As a result of the recent advances in IC technology, ROMs exist in many forms. The technique employed for storing information in the ROM (called programming) provides a convenient method for classifying all ROMs into one of three categories [7]. The first category consists of ROMs that are *custom programmed* or *masked programmed* when manufactured. These ROMs are programmed as specified by the user during fabrication and cannot be changed after packaging.

A second category includes ROMs which are programmable by the user. This type includes those often referred to as *programmable ROMs*, *field-programmable ROMs* (pROMs), or *read-only memory, programmable* (ROMP) [8]. A common form of this type of ROM uses fusible links which can be modified by the user. These ROMs, once programmed, have the contents of the memory permanently fixed as those of the first category.

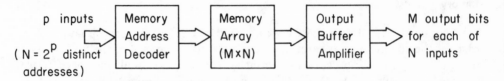

Fig. 4.6. Block diagram of a ROM.

The third category of ROMs consists of those which are programmable again and again [9]. These are *reprogrammable* and are often referred to as pROMs and *read-mostly memory* (RMM). This type of ROM is reprogrammable in an off-line procedure using electrical, optical, etc., techniques.

A block diagram of a typical read-only memory is shown in Fig. 4.6. In this figure, the memory address decoder is a combinational network which directs the desired one of N possible addresses to the appropriate M bits (word) in the $M \times N$ memory array. The contents of these M bits are then transferred to the output buffer amplifier for use by the system. In order to generate the N possible input combinations (addresses), p input terminals ($N = 2^p$) are necessary at the memory address decoder. This results in p input bits. The $M \times N$ memory array contains the permanently stored bit pattern. The output buffer amplifier provides drive for the M output bits.

The basic structure of Fig. 4.6 can be realized by two distinct addressing schemes known as *linear selection* and *coincident selection* [10]. Linear selection, while somewhat simpler than coincident selection, is generally used in smaller-capacity ROMs such as code converters, whereas larger-capacity ROMs normally use coincident selection.

Linear-Selection Addressing

ROMs can be characterized by the method in which the memory array is addressed by the memory address decoder. In ROMs employing linear selection, the memory address decoder of Fig. 4.6 is generally a 1-of-N decoder similar to that described in Sec. 2.2. The decoder output enables one of N word lines as shown in Fig. 4.7. Each word line is composed of M bits. This arrangement of the $M \times N$ memory array is a two-dimensional memory known as a *crossbar (rectangular) matrix*.

When the memory is addressed, the memory address decoder applies a voltage (1 state) to the appropriate one of the N word lines. Each bit line which is connected to this word line by a coupling element receives an excitation voltage. This voltage represents a 1 state being stored in these bit positions. At junctions where no coupling element joins the selected word line to the bit line, a 0 state is stored.

The various types of ROMs using linear selection differ primarily in the kind of coupling element employed. The use of passive circuit elements such as resistors or capacitors for coupling forms the simplest ROM structures. In the case of resistors, severe attenuation problems result for large arrays. Consider, for example, the 4×4 resistive array shown in Fig. 4.8. The state of the decoder is shown for an input of 10.

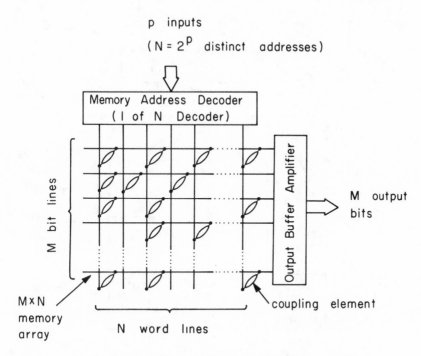

p inputs

$(N = 2^P$ distinct addresses)

Memory Address Decoder
(1 of N Decoder)

M bit lines

Output Buffer Amplifier

M output
bits

M×N
memory
array

coupling element

N word lines

Fig. 4.7. Basic structure of a ROM employing linear selection.

This activates the W_2 word line with a resulting output word of 1011. The input voltage to the output buffer amplifier for the B_0 bit line is equal to the voltage division of V between resistors R_1 and R_2. Since all resistors are equal, this voltage is $V/2$.

Next, consider bit line 1. In this case, the input voltage to the buffer amplifier is the voltage division of V between R_3 and the parallel combination of R_4 and R_5 and is equal to $V/3$. In general, the maximum voltage that can occur as a 1-state input to the buffer amplifier is easily shown to be

$$V_{\max} = \frac{V}{n} \tag{4.1}$$

where n is the total number of resistors connected to the bit line under consideration. From Eq. (4.1), it is obvious that as n becomes large, $V_{\max}$ becomes small and causes great difficulty in distinguishing between the 0 and 1 states.

The problems associated with passive coupling elements can be greatly reduced by the use of nonlinear or active devices. The use of diodes in place of each resistor in Fig. 4.8, with cathodes connected to the bit lines and anodes to the word lines, eliminates the loading effect present in resistive ROMs. With the recent advances in MSI and LSI IC technologies, bipolar and MOS transistors have come into common use. A bipolar transistor-coupled version of the resistor-coupled memory matrix of Fig. 4.8 is shown in Fig. 4.9.

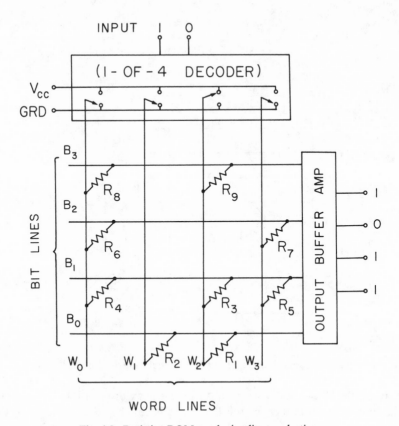

Fig. 4.8. Resistive ROM employing linear selection.

Coincident-Selection Addressing

Large ROMs are now available having capacities of hundreds of words [11]. If linear selection is used, it is seen from Fig. 4.7 that the memory address decoder becomes a very complex network for large N. A method of overcoming this difficulty is to replace each bit line with an X-Y array of N bits. Since there are M bit lines, this will require M of the X-Y arrays. The memory is addressed by supplying an X address and a Y address simultaneously. In Fig. 4.6, the memory address decoder will now consist of a 1-of-X and a 1-of-Y decoder, and the memory array will consist of M of the X-Y arrays.

A single X-Y array for a ROM using coincident selection is shown in Fig. 4.10. There are q input terminals into the 1-of-X decoder, which requires that $X = 2^q$. Similarly, r input terminals for the 1-of-Y decoder requires that $Y = 2^r$. Since $X \times Y = N$, then $2^q \cdot 2^r = 2^{q+r} = N$. Recalling that $N = 2^p$ for the linear-selection case, we see that $p = q + r$. Therefore, the same number of input terminals is necessary for the ROM network irrespective of the selection method chosen.

When a memory word in the ROM is accessed, q inputs are applied to the X

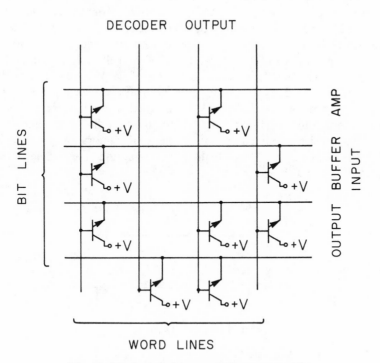

Fig. 4.9. Bipolar transistor coupled memory matrix.

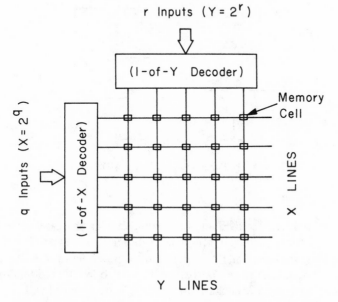

Fig. 4.10. Single X–Y array in a ROM using coincident selection.

decoder which activates the appropriate X line. Other names for the X input are *row select* and *word select*. Similarly, r inputs applied to the Y decoder activate the appropriate Y line. The Y inputs are known as *column select* or *bit select*. The activated X and Y lines intersect a single memory cell in the array. Incorporated into this memory cell is steering logic which outputs the stored bit of this cell to the output buffer amplifier by way of a *sense line*. This output is one bit of an M-bit word. The remaining $M - 1$ bits are generated in the same manner. M arrays, known as *planes* or *segments*, are connected in parallel such that the planes are excited simultaneously. One bit from each plane is then transferred by a sense line to an output buffer amplifier.

An MOS transistor-coupled version of the X-Y memory array of a coincident-select ROM is shown in Fig. 4.11. Transistors having the gates connected to the X lines represent 0's, and those having the gates open represent 1's.

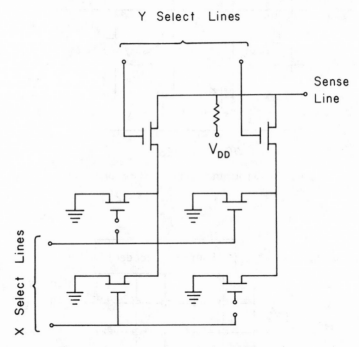

Fig. 4.11. X-Y memory array using MOS transistors.

Semiconductor ROMs

ROMs are well suited to MSI and LSI manufacturing processes using both bipolar and MOS transistor technologies. In general, bipolar devices are faster with higher drive capability (fan-out), while MOS circuits consume less power and occupy less space. Access times range from approximately 1 μs to less than 50 ns for MOS and bipolar, respectively. Both MOS and bipolar ROMs are designed with capacities up to 8K bits.

In the fabrication of bipolar ROMs, both TTL and ECL devices are popular. A block diagram of a type 7488 TTL 256-bit read-only memory is shown in Fig. 4.12. This device, produced by numerous manufacturers, is a custom-programmed ROM which employs linear selection in addressing 32 words having 8 bits per word. The device is available in 16-pin dual in-line and 16-pin flat packages. The Chip Select (CS) terminal is used to enable the outputs B_0 through B_7. This terminal is necessary for expanding the memory size by employing multiple ROM circuits. An additional combinational network is necessary in this case to activate the proper Chip Select input.

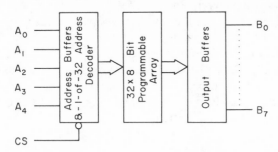

Fig. 4.12. Block diagram of a type 7488 TTL 256-bit Read-Only Memory.

Many semiconductor memories have the important feature of tri-state outputs (see Sec. 2.6) [12]. In a memory of this type, the circuitry of the output lines is designed such that the outputs are essentially open-circuited when the memory is not enabled. This allows the parallel operation of numerous memories on a data bus since the loading effects of nonenabled outputs are eliminated. When these memories are enabled, the conventional 0 or 1 states are present.

Field-programmable bipolar ROMs are now available from a number of manufacturers. These pROMs often employ a fusible metal for the connections to the individual emitters of the memory cells which can be open-circuited in a controllable fashion for programming after packaging [8]. Another method utilizes a cell structure which involves avalanching the base-emitter junctions of the individual transistors within the memory cells [9]. This results in a metal migration which sets a permanent base-emitter short for programming the memory cell bit. Numerous manufacturers now produce equipment for programming pROMs. Some of these include Pro-Log, Spectrum Dynamics, and Data I/O Programmers.

MOS ROMs are constructed using p-channel (pMOS), n-channel (nMOS), and complementary-symmetry MOS (CMOS) technologies. These ROMs are available featuring custom-programming, field-programming, and reprogramming capabilities. In general, pMOS is slower but less expensive, whereas nMOS is faster, approaching the speed exhibited by bipolar in some cases. CMOS construction leads to extremely low-power and relatively high-speed operation. Operating frequencies of 20 MHz are readily obtained with CMOS [7]. Unfortunately, the fabrication process for CMOS is more complex and hence more costly.

At least two types of reprogrammable MOS pROMs are now available. The type better known and most readily available is an arrangement utilizing an array of floating gate pMOS transistors [13]. A high voltage applied between the source and drain results in negative charges on the gate due to avalanche injection of electrons from the source. These isolated negative charges create a conducting channel with a lifetime, under normal operating conditions, of up to 100 years having been quoted. The stored information in this device can be cleared by exposing the circuit to ultra-violet light. The IC package is provided with a quartz cover to permit this erasure. A popular pROM of this type is the Intel 1702A.

Semiconductor memory is either *static* or *dynamic*. Information stored in static memory, in general, requires no additional circuitry to retain this information. Dynamic memory, however, requires circuitry for a refresh cycle which must be performed periodically. Each of the ROMs discussed in this section has been static. Although dynamic ROMs are available, the static type is much more common. Since dynamic read/write memory is of much greater importance, the discussion of dynamic memory is presented in the next section.

4.3. READ/WRITE MEMORY

Read/write memory elements for microcomputers are generally semiconductor devices. An array of flip-flops or similar storage devices is produced as a single integrated circuit. For example, as many as 4096 bits are common on one IC chip. Even though ROMs are technically random-access memory (RAM) elements, the read/write memory, which is an array of active, volatile elements, is frequently referred to as simply a RAM [10]. Hence, RAM will be used to refer to read/write memory.

The two classes of RAMs are static and dynamic. A static RAM stores each bit of information in a flip-flop, and this information is retained as long as power is supplied to the circuit. Dynamic RAMs are devices in which the information is stored in the form of electric charge on the gate-to-substrate capacitance of an MOS transistor. This charge dissipates in a few milliseconds, and the element must be *refreshed* (capacitance recharged) periodically. Dynamic RAMs are important because fewer elements are required to store a bit (typically three or four transistors as opposed to six or eight), so that more bits can be packed into an IC of a given physical area [14]. They are also faster than the static RAM and consume less power in the quiescent state. The refreshing cycle requires additional circuitry, however, which is often external. Therefore, there are a certain number of memory elements required before dynamic memory becomes profitable. Smaller memories are generally static elements, whereas larger memories are typically dynamic. The break point is gradually moving lower as more of the refresh circuitry is included in the integrated circuit.

Static RAM

The static RAM is the main memory element for many microcomputers. Consider an $N \times 1$ static RAM. This RAM has the following input and output lines, as shown in Fig. 4.13 [15].

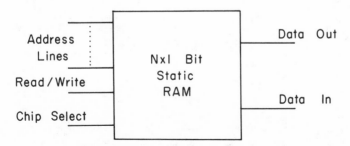

Fig. 4.13. $N \times 1$ bit static RAM.

(a) *Address Lines.* The number of Address Lines, r, depends on the size of the RAM (N bits, $N = 2^r$). For example, a 1024-bit RAM has ten address lines.

(b) *Data Out.* The Data Out is a single line to output the particular bit which is addressed.

(c) *Data In.* The Data In is a single line to input the particular bit to be stored in memory.

(d) *Read/Write.* The Read/Write is a single line on which the command to READ (output) or WRITE (input) is supplied to the circuit. This line is held in a READ state except during the precise time that a WRITE is desired.

(e) *Chip Select (Chip Enable).* The Chip Select is a single line employed to disconnect the memory from the output data bus (using a tri-state device) and to inhibit the WRITE circuitry of the chip. It is used to control the accessing of the chip if more than N words of memory are required.

From a terminal standpoint, operation of the memory element can be described in terms of two cycles, a READ and a WRITE cycle. To read a bit of information stored in the memory requires the following steps.

1. The Read/Write line is placed in a READ state.

2. The address of the memory cell to be read is loaded onto the Address Lines.

3. The memory is enabled by applying the proper level to the Chip Select line.

4. After a length of time required to propagate the information to the output, the bit is read from the Data Out line.

A READ cycle for a typical 1024-bit static RAM requires approximately 1 μs (Fig. 4.14).

The WRITE cycle is similar to the READ cycle with the exception that the Read/Write line must reach the WRITE state only after the address has been applied

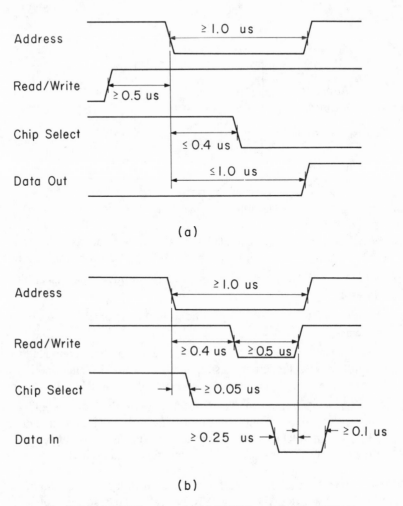

Fig. 4.14. (a) READ cycle; and (b) WRITE cycle for the 1024 bit static RAM (Type 2602).

for a time sufficient for the address to propagate through the memory. Steps in the WRITE cycle are as follows.

1. The address at which the bit is to be stored is applied to the Address Lines.
2. The memory is enabled by applying the proper level to the Chip Select line.
3. A pulse is applied to the Read/Write line.
4. The bit to be written is applied to the Data In line.

A WRITE cycle for a typical static RAM requires 1.0 μs (Fig. 4.14).

An $N \times M$ RAM contains N words which are M bits long. The procedure for accessing a location is the same for an M-bit word as for a 1-bit word. Instead of one Data Out and one Data In line, there are M Data Out and M Data In lines.

Static RAM Cell

RAMs are composed of a number of single memory cells. They may be arranged in such a manner that linear- or coincident-selection addressing is employed. Large RAMs generally make use of coincident selection. The RAM may be organized as a bit storage or a word storage element. In a RAM organized for word storage, several cells are addressed simultaneously. Semiconductor RAMs are fabricated using various technologies, such as TTL, ECL, and MOS [7, 10].

A typical MOS memory cell is shown in Fig. 4.15. Q_1 and Q_2 form the flip-flop which is the basis of the storage cell. A single bit is stored in each flip-flop. Q_3 and Q_4 serve as pull-up resistors for Q_1 and Q_2. If coincident selection is used, a part of the address is decoded to choose a particular row (X address). The X-address line controls Q_5 and Q_6 of all cells in the appropriate row. The remainder of the address is decoded to determine the particular column (Y address) that is to be read. This output from

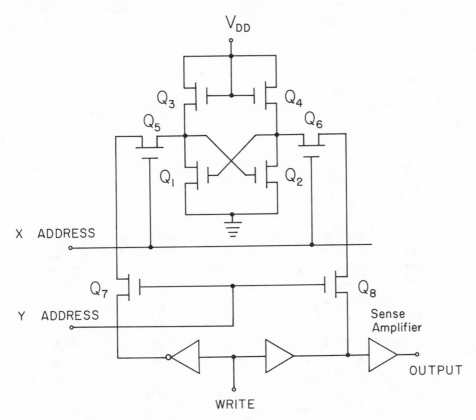

Fig. 4.15. A typical MOS static memory cell.

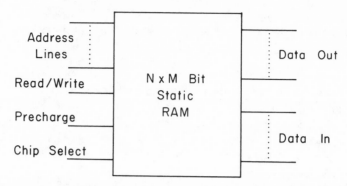

Fig. 4.16. Typical $N \times M$ dynamic RAM.

the decoder is applied to the Y-address line and controls Q_7 and Q_8 of the appropriate column of cells. If Q_5 through Q_8 are turned on, a current will flow in one and only one of the two bit lines.

A sense amplifier is provided to convert the current signal into a voltage level. The state of the flip-flop (Q_1 and Q_2) is not altered by the READ operation. In order to perform the WRITE operation, the proper cell must be addressed (Q_5 through Q_8 turned on) and the appropriate voltage levels must be applied to the bit lines by the WRITE amplifiers. This sets the desired state of the flip-flop.

Dynamic RAM

The operation of a dynamic RAM is complicated by the temporary nature of the data storage. A typical dynamic RAM has the following input and output lines, as illustrated in Fig. 4.16.

(a) *Address Lines.* As in static RAM, the number of Address Lines depends on the number of words which may be stored in the RAM. For example, a 1024-word RAM would have ten address lines because $2^{10} = 1024$. Most dynamic RAMs use coincident selection.

(b) *Data Out.* The number of Data Out lines is a function of the size of the word which is stored in the RAM. For example, a 256×4 RAM has 256 addresses, and each address corresponds to four bits (i.e., four data lines would be output from the RAM).

(c) *Data In.* The number of Data In lines is dependent on the word size of the RAM. Input bits are placed on the Data In lines.

(d) *Precharge.* The Precharge line must be pulsed before the output lines are read in order to charge the output capacitors. The timing of this pulse in relation to the Chip Select pulse is critical.

(e) *Read/Write.* The Read/Write line is a single line on which the command to READ (output) or WRITE (input) is given. The line is normally in the READ state.

(f) *Chip Select* (*Chip Enable*). This line is employed to control the input and output from the memory. A pulse on this line is required for each READ or WRITE cycle, and its timing in relation to the Precharge pulse is critical.

To READ a word from the RAM requires the following steps.

1. The address of the word to be read is placed on the address lines and allowed to stabilize.

2. The chip is precharged via the Precharge line.

3. The Read/Write line is placed in the READ state. After a WRITE operation, the Read/Write line must return to the READ state for a sufficient time period before the address lines are altered.

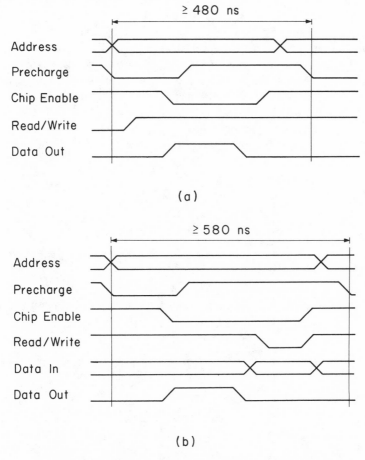

(a)

(b)

Fig. 4.17. Timing diagram for a Type 1103 dynamic RAM for (a) a READ cycle; and, (b) a WRITE cycle.

4. While the Precharge line is enabled, the Chip Enable line is activated. The time in which Precharge and Chip Enable lines are both on must be carefully controlled.

A typical READ cycle timing diagram is shown in Fig. 4.17(a) [16].

A WRITE cycle or READ/WRITE cycle is identical to the READ cycle with the addition of the following step.

5. While the Chip Enable is enabled, a WRITE pulse is applied to the Read/Write line and data applied to the Data In lines.

The timing diagram for a typical WRITE or READ/WRITE cycle is given in Fig. 4.17(b).

MOS Dynamic RAM Cell

A typical three-transistor dynamic RAM cell [6, 10] is illustrated in Fig. 4.18. In addition to the three transistors required to implement the basic cell, a fourth transistor needed to gate the precharging of the output capacitor is shown. A bit is stored as a charge on the gate-to-substrate capacitance, C_g. To interrogate the cell, a pulse is applied to Precharge which turns Q_4 on. The output capacitor, C_R, is then charged to V_{DD}. The Read Select line is then enabled. This action results in Q_3 being on, which supplies a voltage to Q_2. If the bit is 0 (C_g is discharged), Q_2 is off and the charge will

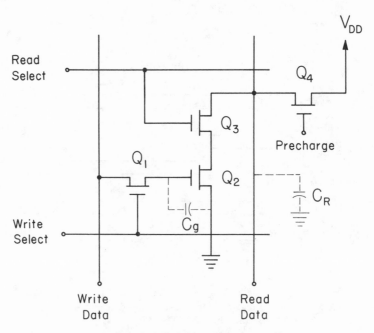

Fig. 4.18. A typical dynamic memory cell.

remain on C_R. If the bit is 1 (C_g is charged), Q_2 is on, and C_R will discharge. The output bit is the inverse of the bit stored in this case.

A WRITE operation is accomplished by applying the appropriate voltage level to the Write Data line and then pulsing the Write Select line. Q_1 is turned on and C_g charges to the value of the Write Data line.

There are numerous circuits designed to implement a dynamic RAM. All of these circuits employ MOS technology because of the high input impedance required to prevent the rapid discharging of C_g. Even with MOS devices, it is necessary to refresh (recharge C_g) the cell periodically. The length of time between refresh operations is a function of temperature and is generally 1 to 3 ms for state-of-the-art devices at 0 to 55°C.

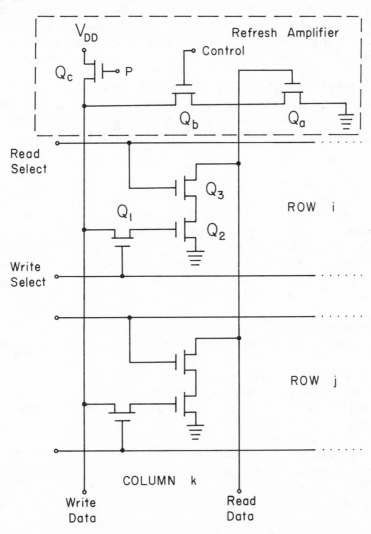

Fig. 4.19. Refresh circuitry for a Type 1103 dynamic RAM.

Refreshing the Dynamic RAM

Refreshing of a dynamic RAM cell is accomplished by reading the stored bit, and then transmitting this bit to the Write Data line and writing it back into the cell by applying a Write Select pulse [7, 17]. The type 1103 RAM cell uses the circuitry shown in Fig. 4.19. When a 1 is read from a cell in column k, the Read Data line will contain a 0. Thus, Q_a is off. If P and Control are made negative, then the Write Data line will be at potential V_{DD} (1 state). If the Write Select line is pulsed, the capacitance, C_g, will be recharged. The reader can verify that if C_g is initially discharged, it remains discharged.

One refresh amplifier is provided for each column of cells. Therefore, all the elements in a row may be refreshed in one cycle. During a refresh operation the row address must be applied to the decoders. Since all elements in a row are refreshed simultaneously, it is not necessary to supply the column address. All the rows in the memory must be refreshed every 2 ms. This refreshing may be accomplished for all rows in one burst of 32 cycles, or the refresh cycles may be interspersed with the normal READ and WRITE cycles. External logic must be provided to supply the address from the memory address register during a normal memory cycle and to supply the address of the row to be refreshed during a refresh cycle. The sequencing of the addresses to be refreshed requires a counter to increment the bits associated with the row address.

4.4. MICROPROCESSOR

The execution of a program takes place in the microprocessor. It contains the central processing unit (CPU) which consists of an arithmetic/logic unit (ALU), appropriate registers, and control circuitry. Using LSI technology, the microprocessor is usually implemented in one or several ICs. The steps involved in executing a program consist of transferring binary quantities from one register to another and performing arithmetical and logical operations (AND, OR, INVERT, ADD, etc.) on these quantities.

A number of registers are normally included in the CPU. These are used for temporary storage of data and instructions to the machine. The most common registers included are:

(1)   Memory Address Register (MAR)

The MAR holds the address of the word to be accessed in memory. The size of the MAR determines the number of words in memory which can be directly addressed. For example, a 16-bit register will allow $2^{16} = 65,536$ words to be directly addressed.

(2)   Memory Data Register (MDR)

The MDR receives and holds the word from memory. The size of the MDR is determined by the number of bits in the data word (e.g., a 2-byte word size requires a 16-bit MDR). A word which is being written into memory is also held in this register until the write operation is complete. It may be thought of as a buffer in the microprocessor.

(3)   Accumulator (AC)

The results of arithmetical and logical operations in the ALU are typically stored in the accumulator. The accumulator also serves as one input to the ALU. As illustrated in Fig. 4.20, it accumulates the results of operations performed by the ALU. Suppose the accumulator is initially cleared (contains all 0's). If the register contains 0101 initially, then an ADD operation in the ALU will result in 0101 being stored in the accumulator (0000 + 0101 = 0101). If 0110 is then placed in the register, an ADD operation will result in 1011 being stored in the accumulator (0110 + 0101 = 1011). The sum of the numbers appearing in the register is therefore accumulated in the accumulator.

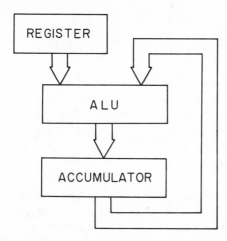

Fig. 4.20. Function of the accumulator (2 input functions).

Frequently in microprocessors all input/output data must pass through the accumulator. Thus, it is a key register. The size of the register is equal to the size of a data word. Some microprocessors have two or more accumulators [18]. This makes the processor more flexible and allows certain tasks to be performed more efficiently.

(4)   Program Counter (PC)

The program counter contains the address in memory of the instruction which is being processed. The set of instructions (or program steps) is normally stored sequentially in memory. For example, the following steps might be desired:

(a) Read a data word from the I/O device into the accumulator (call this instruction I_1).

(b) Add a number to the accumulator (I_2).

(c) Write the result into a certain memory location (I_3), etc.

The location of these instructions in memory is illustrated in Fig. 4.21. In the normal step-by-step set of instructions, the computer accesses sequential locations in memory. For this reason the program counter is normally incremented during execution of an instruction.

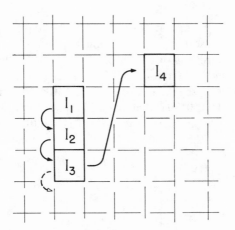

Fig. 4.21. Location of instructions in memory.

It may be desirable, however, to change the order of the instructions, depending on the data received and the result of operations on this data. This may be accomplished by branching to a nonsequential location in memory (e.g., the instruction I_4 in Fig. 4.21). Such a step requires that the program counter be directly set with the location of I_4 rather than being incremented. Much of the power of the computer is derived from this branching capability.

(5) Stack

The stack is an array of registers which allows words or addresses to be accessed from the top of this array on a *last-in, first-out* basis. This is often abbreviated as an *LIFO* array or it may be referred to as a *pushdown* (or *push-pop*) array [19]. When a word is placed in the stack, all words previously in the stack are moved down one location. This is referred to as a *push* operation. When a word is retrieved from the stack, all words are moved up one location. This is referred to as a *pop* operation. The

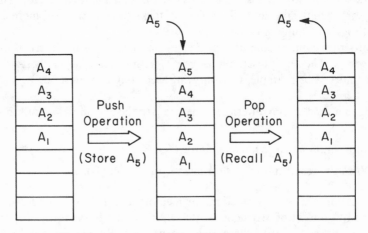

Fig. 4.22. Operation of a stack illustrating the storage and recall of a word.

procedure is illustrated in Fig. 4.22. In this example, the stack consists of seven registers. As a word, say A_5, is pushed onto the stack, it is placed in the top register, and A_1 through A_4 are moved down one register. A pop operation will then recall A_5 and shift A_1 through A_4 up one register in the stack.

Note that it is not possible to recall A_4 before A_5. The elements are automatically accessed on a last-in, first-out basis. The stack is typically used in microprocessors to store return addresses for subroutines and to store the condition of internal registers during the processing of interrupts. Some microprocessors allow only return addresses to be stored in the stack [20]. The stack may be implemented in memory [21], but this requires a memory cycle in order to access the stack. The operation is made much faster by providing a special set of registers within the CPU for this purpose. An important parameter in this case is the number of registers included in the stack. If one attempts to place more words in the stack than there are registers, the first word will be lost (Fig. 4.23). If this goes undetected, unusual and difficult-to-diagnose errors may occur [18]. Some microprocessors eliminate this problem by placing the overflow from the stack into a stack in memory.

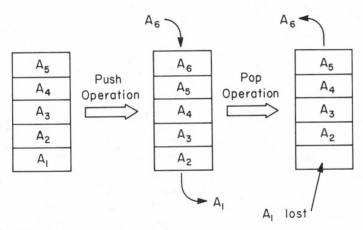

Fig. 4.23. Illustration of the result of the overflow of a finite stack.

Many push-pop arrays are implemented in a manner reminiscent of a stack of papers. Each input is placed on top of the pile. This requires a register, called the *stack pointer* (SP), to hold the address of the top element of the stack. Figure 4.24 illustrates this type of operation. The stack pointer is represented as a 3-bit register with the binary representation shown. The stack pointer initially holds 011 (binary 3). This means that the top of the stack is at register 3. A push operation loads A_5 into register 4 and changes the stack pointer to indicate that the top of the stack is now located at register 4. A pop operation reverses the procedure.

(6) Scratch-Pad Memory (General-Purpose Registers)

In most microprocessors, a number of registers are provided in the CPU for temporary storage of data and addresses. The number of these registers and the

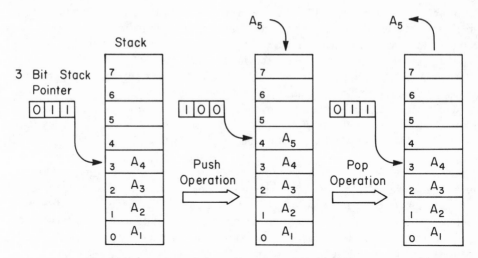

Fig. 4.24. Operation of the stack pointer (SP) for addressing a stack element.

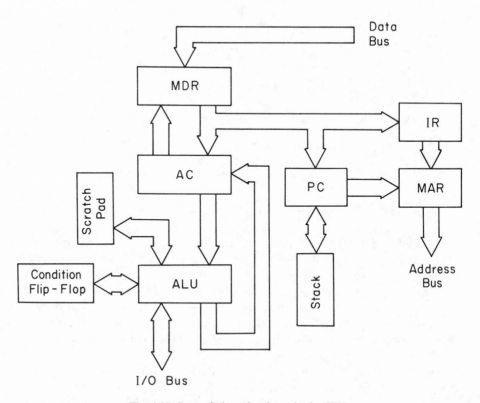

Fig. 4.25. Interrelation of registers in the CPU.

flexibility of accessing them varies greatly from computer to computer (Chapter 7). Manufacturer's literature sometimes provides suggestions on their usage which are valuable for the novice.

(7)   Instruction Register (IR)

The IR contains the instruction which is being decoded and executed. Input to the IR is typically from memory as the program steps are read sequentially. Usually provision is also made for an input to this register via a set of switches or push buttons on the front panel of a computer system. This input is typically used to direct the computer to the location of the first program step.

(8)   Status Register

A status register consisting of one or more flip-flops, often called *flags*, is used to provide indication of overflow from operations, presence of zeros in the accumulator, sign of a number in the accumulator, and carry (or link) from the accumulator. This information is vital in many arithmetic operations and is often used as a basis for deciding which program step is to be executed. A typical interrelation between these registers is illustrated in Fig. 4.25.

In single-chip microprocessors the number of terminals available is limited. This often requires that the three buses shown in Fig. 4.25 be combined into one or two buses. This is accomplished by time-sharing the bus or buses. If the I/O bus and the memory data bus are combined, then an I/O device is handled in the same manner as a memory element [22].

Instructions

All operations to be performed by the computer must be broken down into a series of individual tasks. The power of the computer does not result from the complexity of the individual steps, but from the rapidity with which it performs these steps. These individual steps are called *instructions*. The details and number of these instructions vary greatly from computer to computer. The instructions must be encoded into binary because they are stored in memory. Theoretically, any program may be written using the instruction set of any computer. The length of the program and the time of execution, however, may differ greatly with different instruction sets.

Computer instructions may be divided into five functional categories [23]. The categories are: (1) Transfer of Data, (2) Control, (3) Subroutine Linking, (4) Operation, and (5) Input/Output. The instructions may reference data from memory, CPU registers, or simply control the operation of the machine. Those which reference memory require an extra memory cycle to obtain the data and, therefore, require more time to execute. The functions of these categories are as follows.

(1)   Transfer of Data

This category includes the moving of data from one memory location to another or from register to memory, or vice versa. The simple transfer of information is often referred to as MOVE, LOAD, STORE, or EXCHANGE. As the data is transferred, it may be operated on by the ALU. Operations such as ADD, SUBTRACT, AND, OR, EXCLUSIVE-OR, and COMPARE are common capabilities. Figure 4.26 illustrates

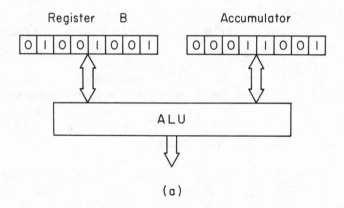

(a)

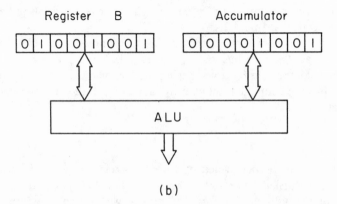

(b)

Fig. 4.26. AND operation illustrating the condition of register B and the accumulator (a) prior to the AND operation; and, (b) after the AND operation.

the results of an AND operation on the contents of register *B*. Some machines provide the capability to include the link or carry flag in the addition or subtraction, which facilitates multiple precision arithmetic.

The capability to move data to and from the stack may be provided. This instruction (PUSH or POP) makes it possible to restore the status of the computer after processing an interrupt.

(2)   Control

Control instructions can be classified as *conditional* or *unconditional*. The condition of a status flip-flop (CARRY, ZERO, SIGN, etc.) determines whether or not a conditional instruction will be executed. Some common instructions in this category are:

(a)   *HALT*. This instruction directs the control section to suspend execution of the program. External action is required for program execution to resume.

(b) *JUMP.* This instruction causes the program counter to be set directly to a nonsequential location in memory for the next instruction.

(c) *SKIP.* This instruction is generally conditional. If the condition is met, the program counter is incremented a sufficient number of times to skip the next instruction. If the condition is not met, the program counter is incremented and the next instruction is executed. A conditional skip is shown in Fig. 4.27 which is dependent on the state of the carry status flip-flop. If the carry flag is reset, the program counter is incremented to $2A36_{16}$. If, however, the carry flag is set, the counter is advanced to $2A37_{16}$, which skips the instruction at location $2A36_{16}$.

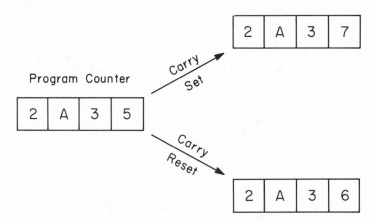

Fig. 4.27. Result of a SKIP IF CARRY SET on program counter.

(3) Subroutine Linking

These instructions may also be conditional or unconditional. Some typical members of this category are:

(a) *CALL Subroutine.* This instruction causes the program counter to be incremented and the new address to be stored in the stack. This address is the return address for the subroutine when execution is completed. The program counter is then loaded with the address of the subroutine and execution proceeds. In Fig. 4.28, the program is executing an instruction at location 2600_{16}. The stack contains a return address of $1AAC_{16}$. The instruction calls a subroutine beginning at location $00BE_{16}$. When the call is executed, the program counter is incremented to 2601_{16} and pushed onto the return address stack. Execution of a conditional CALL is dependent on the status of the appropriate conditional flag.

(b) *RETURN.* RETURN causes the return address in the stack to pop. This address is loaded into the program counter and program execution proceeds. In Fig. 4.29 a RETURN is executed. Before the execution of the RETURN,

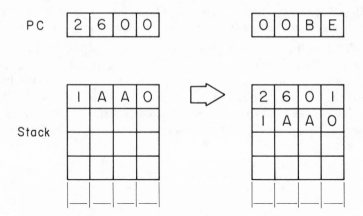

Fig. 4.28. Result of a CALL SUBROUTINE AT ADDRESS 00BE (Hexadecimal) on Program Counter and the Stack. Note: The stack contains the return address.

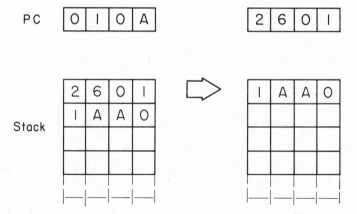

Fig. 4.29. Result of a RETURN instruction. The top address in the stack is transferred to the program counter.

the stack holds the return addresses illustrated in Fig. 4.28. The execution of RETURN pops the first register in the stack 2601_{16} into the program counter. The computer will then execute the instruction at 2601_{16}.

(c) *RESTART.* The RESTART instruction is a special-purpose CALL which allows the computer to jump to one of several fixed locations and continue the execution. It is used instead of a CALL in some cases because it does not require the complete specification of a memory location. Thus, it executes more rapidly.

(4) Operation

This category of instructions includes those that perform operations on a particular register or status flip-flop. No data transfer takes place. Typical members of this class are:

(a) *CLEAR.* Zeros are stored in the appropriate register (e.g., the accumulator).

(b) *INCREMENT.* The value stored in the register is increased by 1.

(c) *DECREMENT.* The value stored in the register is decreased by 1.

(d) *COMPLEMENT.* This instruction results in each bit in the appropriate register being complemented (1's complementation).

(e) *ROTATE.* The contents of the accumulator are rotated one bit to the right or left.

For a right rotation, the least significant bit is rotated into the position of the most significant bit, and every other bit is moved one place to the right. Figure 4.30 illustrates the result of a right rotation of the accumulator.

The ROTATE instruction may include the CARRY (or LINK) flip-flop in the rotation. Figure 4.31 illustrates this for a left rotation.

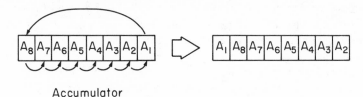

Accumulator

Fig. 4.30. Right rotation of contents of the accumulator.

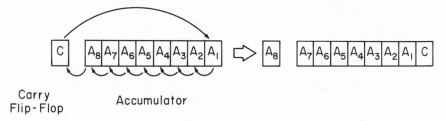

Carry
Flip-Flop   Accumulator

Fig. 4.31. Left rotation through the carry flip-flop.

Since the conditional instructions depend on the status of the flags, the ROTATE instruction enables a sequence of instructions to be dependent on an individual bit in a data word. For example, before a data word may be read from an I/O device, the computer must determine if a word is ready to be read. This is done by reading a *status word* from the I/O device. The status word will contain a certain pattern if the data word is ready. Suppose a 1 in the LSB is used to indicate this status. A right rotation may now be performed to shift this bit to the carry flip-flop, and then a conditional branch to an input instruction may be performed.

(f) *RESET CONDITION FLIP-FLOP.* This instruction clears the appropriate flag.

(g) *DECIMAL ADJUST ACCUMULATOR.* The addition and subtraction instructions are frequently implemented using 2's complement arithmetic. If the data being processed is in BCD, then the resulting addition will be erroneous if the sum of two digits is greater than 9. The instruction logically examines the result for this condition (>9) and performs a correction by adding 6 (see Sec. 3.6). Inclusion of this instruction in the repertoire of a computer is valuable when the input/output data is in BCD.

(5)   Input/Output

This category contains two fundamental instructions:

(a) *INPUT.* This instruction causes the contents of the I/O bus to be loaded into the accumulator.

(b) *OUTPUT.* This instruction causes the contents of the accumulator to be placed on the I/O bus.

Machines with large instruction sets frequently combine two or more of these operations into one instruction. The utility of these instructions and their effectiveness is strongly dependent on the particular application.

Encoding of Instructions

Instructions are stored in memory in the same manner as data. In Harvard class computers, separate memory is provided for instruction words and data words. In von Neumann class computers, the machine does not recognize a data word as being different from an instruction word. The distinction is made strictly on the basis of location in memory. All instructions are encoded by a binary word. Instructions in this form are in *machine language* or *machine code*. Memorization of these codes is tedious and often results in errors. For this reason, all manufacturers provide a set of mnemonics (alphanumeric representations) for the instructions. These are often the actual operation or an abbreviation of the operation to be performed, as shown in Table 4.1.

Table 4.1   TYPICAL INSTRUCTIONS AND MNEMONICS.

Instruction	Mnemonic
Add	AD
Subtract	SUB or SU
Move	MOV
Load	LD or L
Or	OR
And	AN
Exclusive OR	XOR or XO

For ease of reference to the machine code and addresses, the binary numbers are frequently written in octal or hexadecimal. For example, the instruction "Move the contents of register *B* to register *A*" (Intel 8008) is represented in the following fashion:

Mnemonic	Representation		
	Binary	Octal	Hexadecimal
MOV *A*, *B*	11001000	310	C8

Addressing Modes

An instruction word must convey the operation to be performed (*operations code*) and the address of the memory location or registers containing the data on which the operation is to be performed (*operand*). An *n*-bit instruction may be divided into three basic parts: (1) an operations code, (2) an address mode, and (3) an operand address, as shown in Fig. 4.32. The number of bits in each of these parts varies from microprocessor to microprocessor.

OP CODE (m bits)	ADDR MODE (n bits)	ADDRESS (p bits)

Fig. 4.32. Instruction format.

The instruction length depends on the machine and the operation being performed. An 8-bit instruction format would allow only $2^8 = 256$ possible combinations of operations and addresses. This is obviously inadequate if a reasonable-size memory is to be accessed. For this reason 2- and 3-byte instructions are frequently used for memory access [20]. Such an instruction is 16 or 24 bits long. In most cases, one byte is used to represent the operations code and address mode portions of an instruction. The number of bits used for each of these and their relative locations within the byte vary from processor to processor.

The address mode and operand part of the instruction combine to indicate the location in which the operand is stored. There are numerous modes of addressing the operand [24]. The most important for microprocessors include direct, indirect, relative, indexed, and immediate addressing. The address mode portion of the instruction specifies how the address is to be interpreted. These addressing modes are defined as follows:

(a) *Direct Addressing*. With direct addressing, the address of the operand is specified directly in the instruction. For example, consider the instruction "add the contents of memory at address 032 to the accumulator." Such an instruction could be symbolized by

AD   032

The operand address (032) is directly specified in this instruction (Fig. 4.33). This is a common form of addressing used in microcomputers. Direct addressing usually requires multiword instructions in 4- or 8-bit microprocessors.

(b) *Indirect Addressing.* In this mode, the instruction provides the address at which the address of the operand is to be found. Figure 4.34 illustrates this type of addressing. The data to be operated on is 301, located in memory location 543. Indirect addressing allows a large block of memory to be addressed by a single-word instruction. In microprocessors, a form of address-

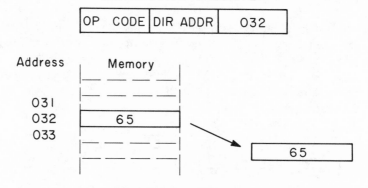

Fig. 4.33. Direct Addressing.

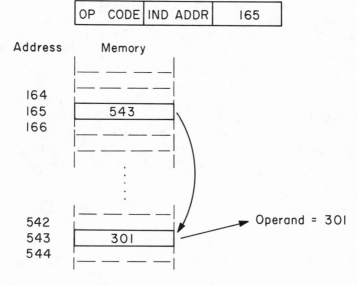

Fig. 4.34. Indirect Addressing.

ing called *register indirect addressing* is commonly used. The address is stored in one or more registers within the CPU. In most cases, this architecture allows any location in memory to be addressed with a single-word instruction.

(c) *Relative Addressing.* In relative addressing, the address is specified by its relation to the program counter. In this mode the address specified in the instruction is added to the number in the program counter to obtain the address of the operand. For example, if the address in the instruction is 11 and the program counter contains 124, then the address of the operand will be $11 + 124 = 135$ (Fig. 4.35). The use of relative addressing simplifies the transfer of programs to different areas of memory.

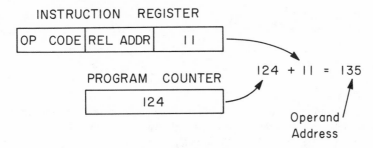

Fig. 4.35. Relative Addressing.

Microcomputer memory is frequently structured into *pages*. A page may consist of 256 words of memory and is frequently located on a single IC. A page structure divides the memory into small blocks. The use of paging reduces the necessity for multiword memory reference instructions. In conjunction with a memory page structure, a form of relative addressing called *page relative addressing* is frequently used. In page relative addressing, an operand address given in the instruction is interpreted as a location on the same page of memory addressed by the program counter. In *page-0 relative addressing*, the operand address refers to a location on page 0 of the memory, regardless of the program counter contents.

(d) *Indexed Addressing.* This mode is similar to relative addressing. The address specified in the instruction, however, is relative to a prespecified register other than the program counter. This register is called the *index*. The address given in the instruction is added to the contents of the index register to determine the address of the operand. In Fig. 4.36, register *B* is the index register. Since the address mode is indexed, the number stored in register *B* (341) is added to the operand address (32) to obtain the location of the operand (373).

Indexed addressing is valuable in programs involving tables or arrays of numbers. The address of the first element of the table may be stored in the index register, and all other elements in the table may be addressed in relation to the first element.

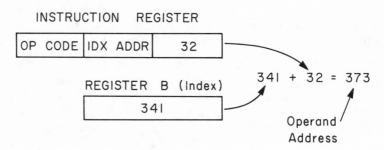

Fig. 4.36. Indexed Addressing.

(e) *Immediate Addressing.* In this mode the data is given directly in the instruction. For example, consider the instruction "load the accumulator immediately with the number 7." Such an instruction could be symbolized by

$$LAI \quad 7$$

The operand (7) is specified directly in the instruction. The operand (7) in this instruction is located in the memory byte directly following the memory location containing the LAI instruction.

Execution of Instructions

In the preceding paragraphs, we have described the execution of a program in terms of its basic steps or instructions. These instructions are implemented in the CPU under the direction of the control section. The control section provides the appropriate timing pulses at the proper time to implement the instruction. For example, Fig. 4.37 illustrates the connection of registers within the CPU. These registers are linked by a bus to reduce the number of interconnections.

In order to transfer information from register B to register $C(B \longrightarrow C)$, the control section must provide a logic level to enable the AND gates on register B. This makes the output of the OR gates (the bus) equal to the contents of the B register. After the contents of register B have reached the bus, the control section supplies a pulse to the clock input of register C and the information on the bus is loaded into register C. Each bus can carry information from only one register at a time. The execution of all instructions is controlled in this manner by the control section. All pulses are produced in synchronism with the clock pulses. Figure 4.38 illustrates a typical timing sequence for the signals which are generated by the control section to produce the data transfer of Fig. 4.37.

The output of the control section is a function of the instruction code. Most microprocessors have fixed instruction sets [25] and software must be written around these instructions. A few microprocessors have *microprogrammable* control units which allow one to partially or totally change the instruction set to fit the application. A microprogrammable controller contains a ROM which is programmed with the

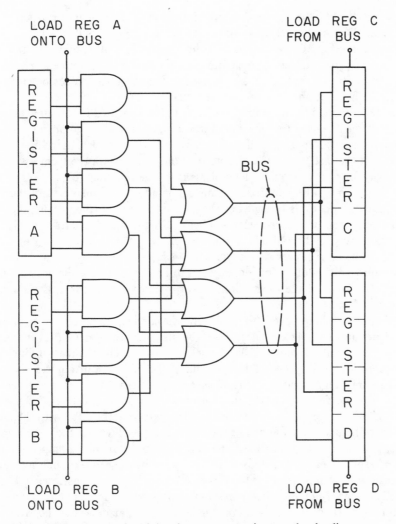

Fig. 4.37. Transfer of data between two registers under the direction of the control section.

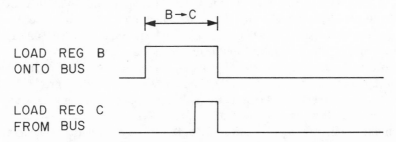

Fig. 4.38. Typical timing signals generated by the control section for the B ⟶ C transfer of Fig. 4.37.

microinstruction [26]. This gives the capability of customizing the instructions to a particular application [2, 27]. Few users take advantage of this flexibility because of difficulties in developing instruction sets and supporting software. Often the ROMs used are masked programmed and cannot be altered once programmed. In some processors, the microprogrammed ROM is located on the microprocessor chip, and a change in the instructions requires manufacturing a new CPU chip.

Transfers external to the microprocessor are implemented in the same manner as transfers between registers in the microprocessor. Consider a complete instruction cycle as shown in Fig. 4.3. The fetch cycle consists of two subcycles. In the first subcycle, the address of the instruction is transferred to the memory via the memory data bus. If this bus is four bits wide and the address is twelve bits long (e.g., the Intel 4040), three clock cycles will be required to transfer the address to memory. In the second subcycle, the instruction is returned to the microprocessor. If the instruction word is eight bits wide, then two clock cycles will ber equired to make this transfer. The fetch cycle in this case would require a total of five clock cycles.

Some of the more powerful microprocessors have both a data bus and an address bus. This allows the address for a data word to be output to the memory simultaneously with the input of the instruction. This capability reduces the instruction cycle time.

During the execution cycle, the instruction is carried out as a number of distinct microinstructions, i.e., place register B on the bus, load register C from the bus, etc. Each microinstruction requires at least one clock cycle. The number of clock cycles required depends on the type of instruction. If the instruction requires access to a data word in memory (*memory reference instruction*), then five additional clock cycles would be required for referencing an 8-bit data word on a 4-bit bus with a 4096-bit memory (12 address bits). The width of the bus connecting the CPU with the memory and the peripherals is an important factor in the speed with which the computer operates, as one can easily see from the above example. In single-chip (monolithic) microprocessors, the size of the bus is limited by the number of terminals available on the package. A typical IC package has the inputs and outputs as illustrated in Fig. 4.39. In this figure, the *Data Bus Status line* indicates whether data is being input by the microprocessor. It is used as a status signal to external devices. The *Synchronize* terminal provides a pulse at the beginning of each instruction cycle which is used to synchronize memory and I/O devices. The *Wait, Ready*, and *Write* terminals provide external information on the status of the CPU. This status information varies with different systems. Refer to Chapter 7 for manufacturer's data and descriptions of several popular processors. The *Interrupt* (1 or more terminals) provides a capability of interrupting the processor in the middle of a program. Whether or not the processor may be restarted to continue the overall program after processing the interrupt depends on the structure of the computer. Finally, the *Reset* simply clears the program counter and the instruction register. Manufacturer's data supplies information on other actions that may result when a reset occurs.

Monolithic microprocessors have 16 to 48 pins. Those with 40 or more pins generally have separate data, address, and/or instruction buses, whereas the 18-pin

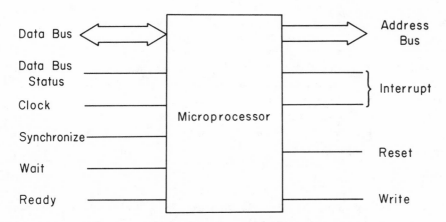

Fig. 4.39. A typical monolithic IC microprocessor package.

packages frequently have only a single I/O bus which must be *multiplexed*. In a multiplexed system, the interpretation of the information on the bus depends on the time in the instruction cycle. A timing diagram (Fig. 4.40) for the fetch cycle of an Intel 4040 microprocessor shows that the data bus carries five different words during the fetch cycle.

Every microprocessor has its own idiosyncrasies, and therefore one should refer to the appropriate manufacturer's literature. The information in this chapter gives a description of certain functions which are common to most systems.

Microprocessors are fabricated using PMOS, NMOS, CMOS, and bipolar

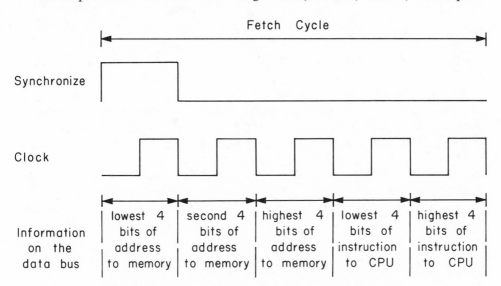

Fig. 4.40. Example of fetch cycle showing the multiplexing of data and addresses of the data bus.

technologies. The first systems to appear used PMOS technology. Machines in this class typically have minimum instruction cycles of 4–13 μs. NMOS chips allow greater gate density and improved speed. Typical minimum instruction cycle times are 2–5 μs. For lower power density, CMOS is used. Typical cycle times for CMOS are 6 μs. The fastest microcomputers are designed using bipolar technology. Cycle times in the range of 0.3 to 1 μs are obtained from these machines. It must be pointed out that the time required to execute a given program does not necessarily relate to the instruction cycle time. Frequently, the structure of the machine and the instruction set provided are of much greater importance.

Direct Memory Access

In Sec. 4.1 we stated that all input data usually pass to the accumulator, from which they may be stored in memory. If it is necessary to input large arrays of data, this can be a time-consuming task because several instructions are required to make a transfer from input to memory or memory to output. To solve this problem, some microcomputers provide the capability of directly accessing memory without passing through the CPU. A computer with this capability is said to have *direct memory access* (DMA).

In order to provide DMA, it is necessary to remove the CPU from the memory address bus and the data bus. This is accomplished by temporarily suspending the operation of the computer (a HOLD condition) and isolating the CPU from the buses by the use of tri-state gates. External circuitry must be provided to supply the address to the memory address bus and to place the data on the memory data bus during a DMA transfer.

Paralleling of Microprocessors

Some microprocessors are designed with the capability of paralleling several processors to increase the word size. One such device is the Intel 3002, a 2-bit central processing element which allows paralleling of two or more units. For example, if eight central processing elements are interconnected, a 16-bit microprocessor is obtained. Microprocessors in this class are called *bit-slice processors*. Each slice of the processor contains sections of the registers, ALU, status bits, and a pushdown stack [28]. Parallel arrangement of the processors produces a word size processor which must be microprogrammed by the user to generate the macroinstructions. This has the disadvantage that software aids (from the manufacturer) are not available since the instruction set is generated by the user. Bit-slice processors of two and four bits are available.

REFERENCES

1. HILL, FREDERICK, JR., and GERALD R. PETERSON, *Digital Systems: Hardware Organization and Design.* New York: John Wiley & Sons, Inc. 1973.

2. SCHULTZ, G. W., R. W. HOLT, and H. L. MCFARLAND, JR., "A Guide To Using LSI Microprocessors." *Computer*, Vol. 6, No. 6 (June, 1973), pp. 13–19.

3. HOLT, RAYMOND W. and MANUEL R. LEMOS, "Current Microcomputer Architecture." *Computer Design*, Vol. 13, No. 2 (February, 1974), pp. 65–73.

4. SCHMID, HERMAN, "Monolithic Processors." *Computer Design*, Vol. 13, No. 10 (October, 1974), pp. 87–95.

5. MALEY, GEORGE A. and MELVIN F. HEILWELL, *Introduction to Digital Computers*. Englewood Cliffs, N. J.: Prentice-Hall, Inc., 1968.

6. DAVIS, SIDNEY, "Selection and Application of Semiconductor Memories." *Computer Design*, Vol. 13, No. 1 (January, 1974), pp. 65–77.

7. LUECKE, G., J. P. MIZE, and W. N. CARR, *Semiconductor Memory Design and Application*. New York: McGraw-Hill Book Co., 1973.

8. ROSTKY, GEORGE, "Focus on Semiconductor Memories." *Electronic Design*, Vol. 19, No. 19 (September, 1971), pp. 50–63.

9. FROHMAN-BENTCHKOWSKY, DOV, "A Fully Decoded 2048-Bit Electrically Programmable FAMOS Read-Only Memory." *IEEE Journal of Solid State Circuits*, Vol. SC-6, No. 5 (October, 1971), pp. 301–306.

10. MILLMAN, JACOB and CHRISTOS C. HALKIAS, *Integrated Electronics: Analog and Digital Circuits and Systems*. New York: McGraw-Hill Book Co., 1972.

11. RILEY, WALLACE B., "Semiconductor Memories Are Taking over Data-Storage Applications." *Electronics*, Vol. 46, No. 16 (August, 1973), pp. 75–90.

12. CALEBOTTA, STEPHEN, "Use Three-State Logic with Confidence." *Electronic Design*, Vol 20, No. 14 (July, 1972), pp. 70–72.

13. *The Intel Memory Design Handbook*. Santa Clara, Calif.: Intel Corp., August, 1973.

14. KOEHLER, H. FREDERICK, "Advances in Memory Technology." *Computer Design*, Vol. 13, No. 6 (June, 1974), pp. 71–77.

15. KROEGER, JOSEPH H., "Free Your Memory System from the Pause that Refreshes." *Electronic Products*, Vol. 15, No. 10 (March, 1973), pp. 73–75.

16. HOFF, MARCIAN E., JR., "The 1103–1024 Memory Bits on a Chip," (three-part series). *Electronic Design*, Vol. 20, No. 2, pp. 40–45; No. 4, pp. 76–81; No. 5, pp. 50–53 (January–March, 1972).

17. WALTHER, T. R., "Dynamic N-MOS RAM with Simplified Refresh." *Computer Design*, Vol. 12. No. 2 (February, 1973), pp. 53–58.

18. OGDIN, JERRY L., "Microcomputers: Promises and Practices." 1974 IEEE INTERCON, March 26–29, 1974, New York, N. Y.

19. KORN, G. A., *Minicomputers for Engineers and Scientists*. New York: McGraw-Hill Book Co., 1973.

20. *MCS-8 Assembly Language Programming Manual*. Intel Corp., November, 1973.

21. SHIMA, MASATOSHI and FREDERICO FAGGIN, "In Switch to N-MOS Microprocessor Gets a 2-μs Cycle Time." *Electronics* (April, 1974), pp. 95–100.

22. WEITZMAN, CAY, *Minicomputer Systems Structure, Implementation and Application.* Englewood Cliffs, N. J.: Prentice-Hall, Inc., 1974.

23. SOUCEK, B., *Minicomputers in Data Processing and Simulation.* New York: Wiley Interscience, 1972.

24. DEITMEYER, DONALD L., *Logic Design of Digital Systems.* Boston: Allyn & Bacon, Inc., 1971.

25. LEWIS, D. R. and W. RALPH SIENA, "Microprocessors or Random Logic?" *Electronic Design*, Vol. 21, No. 18 (September, 1973), pp. 106–110.

26. KOHNEN, TUEVO, *Digital Circuits and Devices.* Englewood Cliffs, N. J.: Prentice-Hall, Inc., 1972.

27. McDERMOTT, JIM, "Suddenly Everybody Is Building Microprogrammed Computers." *Electronic Design*, Vol. 19, No. 24 (November, 1971), pp. 23–28.

28. SNYDER, F. G., "The Microprocessor Shake-Out." *Digital Design*, Vol. 4, No. 9 (September, 1974), pp. 20–22.

EXERCISES

4.1. Explain the difference between the von Neumann and Harvard class computers.

4.2. In many Harvard class computers, the program memory is composed of ROM. What problems does this cause in program development?

4.3. The resistive ROM in Fig. 4.8 stores four 4-bit words. What word is stored in location
(a) 00
(b) 01
(c) 11

4.4. Any combinational network can be realized using ROM. Consider a 16×4 ROM. What pattern of 1's and 0's should be stored in the ROM in order to implement
(a) $F = (A \wedge B) \vee (\bar{C} \wedge D) \vee C$
(b) $F = A \vee (C \wedge \bar{B}) \vee D$
(c) $F = A \oplus (B \oplus C)$

4.5. How many Boolean functions of four variables can the following ROMs store?
(a) 16×4 ROM   (c) 32×8 ROM
(b) 32×4 ROM   (d) 256×8 ROM

4.6. What is the minimum number of input and output terminals required for the following ROMs?
(a) 256×4 ROM   (c) 512×8 ROM
(b) 256×8 ROM   (d) 1024×4 ROM

4.7. (a) Explain the difference between static and dynamic RAM.
(b) What is meant by *volatile*?

4.8. The accumulator of an 8-bit microprocessor contains $C5_{16}$. The carry is set. What will the accumulator contain following:
(a) Two ROTATE LEFT instructions.
(b) Three ROTATE RIGHT THROUGH CARRY instructions.

(c) A COMPLEMENT ACCUMULATOR instruction.

(d) A DECIMAL ADJUST ACCUMULATOR instruction.

(e) EXCLUSIVE-OR of the accumulator with itself.

4.9. The program counter of a microprocessor contains 554_{16} and the stack contains $7D7_{16}$. What is the content of the program counter and the stack immediately following a CALL to subroutine at location $3AF_{16}$. Two RETURN instructions are now executed. What is the content of the program counter.

4.10. Explain:

(a) Direct addressing.

(b) Register-indirect addressing.

(c) Page-relative addressing.

(d) Indexed addressing.

5 SOFTWARE

5.1. INTRODUCTION

In Chapter 4 the hardware aspects of microcomputers were discussed. This chapter will present programming, which by way of contrast is called *software*. A program consists of a sequence of detailed instructions to the computer. Instructions are stored in memory and are recalled as they are needed. Since the memory can store only 1's and 0's, the instructions must be encoded in binary. A program in this form is in *machine language*. In this chapter the development of a typical machine language program will be illustrated. This example will demonstrate the disadvantages of programming in machine language. *Symbolic language* provides the ability to represent instructions and storage locations by alphanumeric symbols. These symbols are chosen to make memorization easy and are therefore called *mnemonics*. If a program is written in symbolic language, it must be translated to machine language before it can be stored and executed. The translation is performed by a computer program called an *assembler*. In symbolic (or assembly) language, most statements translate to one instruction in machine language.

To make programming easier, additional languages have been developed in which statements more clearly resemble English and mathematics. A great many of these languages are used on large-scale computers. Each is developed with a particular class of problems in mind. Some of the more popular languages are FORTRAN, ALGOL, APL, COBOL, and PL/I. In these higher-level languages, one statement may correspond to many machine language instructions. The conversion from a higher-level language to machine code is performed by a program called a *compiler*.

In the preparation of a program, it is frequently necessary to make numerous corrections and changes. It may be necessary, for example, to correct a symbol or to insert one or more instructions into the program. This task is facilitated by the use of a special program called an *editor*. The editor allows the program to be stored into RAM (RWM) and accessed on an instruction-by-instruction basis for the purpose of making alterations easy. Each instruction is numbered to aid in identification and correction, and the editor automatically corrects line numbers as instructions are added or deleted. Finally, the corrected program may be listed and/or punched on paper tape for later entry into the computer memory.

Once written, a program is stored in one of the two types of memory. If the program is stored in ROM, then it is always present in the machine and may be executed by branching to the address of the first instruction. This is accomplished by jamming a JUMP command via the console switches or by a RESTART button which performs the same function. This is the normal operating procedure in dedicated microcomputers. If the program is to be stored in RAM, which is volatile, then the program is usually loaded from a keyboard or tape reader. To facilitate this loading, a special program called a *loader* is necessary. This program is often resident in the computer in ROM. It is frequently combined with the capability to READ or WRITE directly into locations in memory and performs various housekeeping and debugging chores. In this case it is called a *monitor*. Once a program is loaded, it is started by jumping

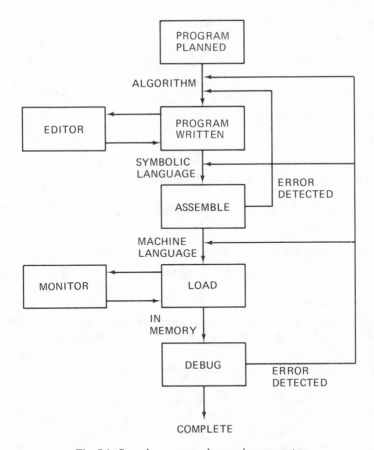

Fig. 5.1. Steps in programming a microcomputer.

to the first address in the program. Since most microprocessors are in dedicated systems, the program is usually stored in ROM. During the development process, however, it is very advantageous to store the program in RAM. The procedure for programming a microcomputer is depicted in Fig. 5.1.

5.2. PLANNING A PROGRAM

The first step in writing a program is to derive an overall plan of attack. This should be envisioned as a step-by-step procedure. Such a functional description of the task is called an *algorithm* [1]. It is similar to a cookbook recipe but more precisely defined. In particular, an algorithm has five properties.

1. *Finiteness.* An algorithm must terminate after a finite number of steps.

2. *Definiteness.* Each step of the algorithm must be precisely defined and un-ambiguous.

3. *Inputs.* An algorithm may or may not require some initial quantities to be specified.

4. *Outputs.* An algorithm has one or more outputs which are related to the inputs or characteristic of the algorithm.

5. *Effectiveness.* The outcome of an algorithm has a predictable result which has an application.

Example 5.1.

Suppose we wish to add two 16-digit BCD numbers, *NA* and *NB*, and store the result in *NA*. A simple outline of the steps involved is:

1. Specify memory addresses of *NA* and *NB*.

2. Load *NA* into the accumulator.

3. Decimally add *NB* to the contents of the accumulator.

4. Write the result into the memory location specified for *NA* in step 1.

Even simple statements like these usually cannot be executed directly in the particular microprocessor to be used. In order to implement directly the steps outlined above, the accumulator would have to be capable of handling sixteen BCD digits at once. In other words, a 64-bit machine would be required. If an 8-bit (two BCD digits) microprocessor is to be used, it is clear that the addition of a 16-digit number will require eight separate addition steps. As a first consideration, the steps above could be repeated eight times, once for each two digits. It is more efficient, however, to employ a loop arrangement which uses the same steps eight times. This is illustrated by the following algorithm. A symbol such as (SYMB) is used to represent the contents of symbolic address SYMB.

Algorithm for Adding Two 16-digit Numbers

1. Identify the addresses of the least two significant digits of NA and NB: $(LOCA) = NA_1$ and $(LOCB) = NB_1$. The remaining digits of each number are stored in sequential locations.

2. Initialize a counter to indicate when eight 2-digit words have been added (e.g., set IC = 8).

3. Load the contents of LOCA into the accumulator: ACC ← (LOCA).

4. Decimally add the contents of LOCB to the contents of the accumulator: ACC ← ACC + (LOCB).

5. Store the accumulator in LOCA: (LOCA) ← ACC.

6. Increment LOCA and LOCB: LOCA ← LOCA + 1; LOCB ← LOCB + 1.

7. Decrement the counter: IC ← IC − 1.

8. If IC is zero, all sixteen digits have been added; if not, then return to step 3 and continue.

In step 1, the statement $(LOCA) = NA_1$ means that the contents of the address symbolized by LOCA is NA_1. Thus the two LSD of NA and NB are stored in LOCA and LOCB, respectively. In step 6, LOCA and LOCB are incremented so that on the second pass through the loop, LOCA and LOCB will be the addresses of the third and fourth digits of NA and NB, respectively. At the termination of the algorithm, the sum will be stored in the location formerly occupied by NA. NA, of course, will be lost.

The next task is to write these steps in terms of the instruction set of the microprocessor selected. The selection of a microprocessor should not be passed over lightly. There are significant differences in the capabilities of different microprocessors to implement a particular program. Particular microprocessors are discussed in Chapter 7.

5.3. FLOW CHARTS

A *flow chart* is a schematic representation of the flow of information through the components of a processing system [2]. At some point in the program development, it is desirable to construct a flow chart of the program. There are differences of opinion among authors on the stage at which a flow chart should be drawn. Some say (with unquestionable logic) that the flow chart should be drawn before any of the program is written. This principle is often ignored in practice because of the difficulty of drawing a good flow chart a priori. There is no question, however, that a flow chart is an essential means of documenting an operational program. For this reason we will introduce flow charting and suggest further study in References [2–4]. Symbols are used which distinguish among the various classes of operations from input to output. Figure 5.2

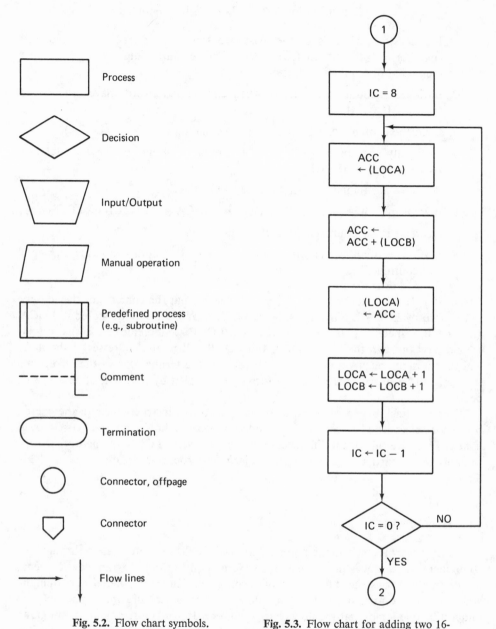

Fig. 5.2. Flow chart symbols.

Fig. 5.3. Flow chart for adding two 16-digit numbers in an 8-bit processor.

lists the common symbols. These are used in Fig. 5.3 to draw a flow chart for the program of Example 5.1. Note that each block does not necessarily correspond to only one step.

The location of the two numbers to be added is assumed to be known prior to entry into the program at connector (1). When connector (2) is reached, the sum of NA and NB is stored in the memory locations originally assigned to NA.

5.4. MACHINE LANGUAGE

Since machine language is unique with each microprocessor, it is necessary to choose a specific one for our example. Suppose we wish to write the program flow charted in Fig. 5.3 for an Intel 8080 microprocessor.

The first step is to allocate the storage locations for the variables encountered in the problem. The 8080 has sixteen address bits and can address 65K bytes of memory directly. Suppose the example program is to use locations $100\text{--}10F_{16}$. Then we may make the following allocations of memory.

$$
\begin{array}{lll}
\text{MEMORY} & 100\text{--}107_{16} & NA \\
 & 108\text{--}10F_{16} & NB \\
\end{array}
$$

$$
\begin{array}{lll}
\text{8-BIT} & & \\
\text{REGISTERS} & D \text{ and } E & \text{LOCA} \\
\text{WITHIN} & H \text{ and } L & \text{LOCB} \\
\text{MICROPROCESSOR} & C & \text{IC} \\
\end{array}
$$

Once the locations of the variables have been specified, the program may be written. Appendix E contains a complete listing of the instruction set for the 8080. In Table 5.1

Table 5.1 SELECTED 8080 INSTRUCTIONS (Intel MCS-80).

Mnemonic	Machine Code	Instruction
LXI D	0001 0001	$E \leftarrow \langle B_2 \rangle$; $D \leftarrow \langle B_3 \rangle$
LXI H	0010 0001	$L \leftarrow \langle B_2 \rangle$; $H \leftarrow \langle B_3 \rangle$
MVI C	0000 1110	$C \leftarrow \langle B_2 \rangle$
XRA A	1010 1111	$A \leftarrow A \oplus A$
LDAX D	0001 1010	$A \leftarrow [(D)(E)]$
ADC M	1000 1110	$A \leftarrow A + [(H)(L)] + \text{Carry}$
DAA	0010 0111	Decimal Adjust Accumulator*
STAX D	0001 0010	$[(D)(E)] \leftarrow A$
INX H	0010 0011	$H, L \leftarrow H, L + 1$
INX D	0001 0011	$D, E \leftarrow D, E + 1$
DCR C	0000 1101	$C \leftarrow C - 1$
JNZ	1100 0010	IF $(\overline{\text{ZERO}})$; $PC \leftarrow \langle B_3 \rangle \langle B_2 \rangle$

*Addition is performed in binary. A carry is provided from the third bit (LSB + 3) and the seventh bit (MSB) which are used in testing and correcting the result in BCD during the DAA instruction (Sec. 3.6).

Note: $\langle B_2 \rangle$ and $\langle B_3 \rangle$ refer to bytes 2 and 3 of the instruction in multibyte instructions and $[(D)(E)]$ symbolizes the contents of memory location whose address is contained in registers D and E.

we have listed the instructions necessary for this example. Although the machine code for the instruction set of a microprocessor is unique, the mnemonic representations are not. The representations are deciphered by the assembler. Therefore different microcomputers using the 8080 microprocessor may have different mnemonic representations for the instructions. The mnemonics listed for the 8080 microprocessor in this text will be those of the MCS-80 microcomputer system [5].

Suppose the numbers being added are

$$NA = 0001003890010173$$
$$NB = 0000963210340002$$

When the program begins execution, the RAM memory will contain the followin data:

Location	Contents (Decimal)	
100	73	(i.e., 0111 0011)
101	01	
102	01	
103	90	
104	38	NA
105	00	
106	01	
107	00	
108	02	
109	00	
10A	34	
10B	10	NB
10C	32	
10D	96	
10E	00	
10F	00	

A program to perform the addition may be written in terms of the 8080 instructions as follows:

1. Load D and E immediately with 100_{16}, the address of NA_1.
2. Load H and L immediately with 108_{16}, the address of NB_1.
3. Load C with 8.
4. Clear the carry flag by the exclusive-OR of A with A.
5. Load A with contents of the address specified by D and E.
6. Add A and carry to contents of the address specified by H and L.

7. Decimal Adjust Accumulator.

8. Store A in the location addressed by D and E.

9. Increment the address stored in H and L.

10. Increment the address stored in D and E.

11. Decrement C.

12. Jump to step 5 if zero flag is not set by step 11.

Suppose the program is to be stored in ROM beginning in location 500_{16}. Then the ROM will contain the binary information shown in Table 5.2. Nineteen memory locations are required for the program. It is necessary for the programmer to specify each instruction in binary code. In addition, the location of each instruction must be cataloged in order to implement the JUMP instruction. The second and third bytes of the JUMP instruction at location 510, for example, must refer to the address of a previous instruction. Suppose it were necessary to insert an instruction prior to location 500 which required moving all of the instructions in the program down one location. This would require that the second byte of the JUMP instruction be corrected to reflect the new location of the LOAD ACCUMULATOR instruction.

In summary, the writing of programs in machine language requires that the programmer keep up with the location of all instructions and data in the program. This is a tedious task which easily results in errors. Since microprocessors are inexpensive

Table 5.2 MACHINE LANGUAGE PROGRAM FOR EXAMPLE 5.1.

Location (Hexadecimal)	Contents (Binary)		Operation
500	0001 0001		
501	0000 0000	$(\langle B_2 \rangle)$	$E \leftarrow 0$
502	0000 0001	$(\langle B_3 \rangle)$	$D \leftarrow 1$
503	0010 0001		
504	0000 1000		$L \leftarrow 08$
505	0000 0001		$H \leftarrow 01$
506	0000 1110		$C \leftarrow 08$
507	0000 1000		
508	1010 1111		Carry Flag $\leftarrow 0$
509	0001 1010		$A \leftarrow [(D)(E)]$
50A	1000 1110		$A \leftarrow A + [(H)(L)] + \text{Carry}$
50B	0010 0111		Decimal Adjust Accumulator
50C	0001 0010		$[(D)(E)] \leftarrow A$
50D	0010 0011		$H, L \leftarrow H, L + 1$
50E	0001 0011		$D, E \leftarrow D, E + 1$
50F	0000 1101		$C \leftarrow C - 1$
510	1100 0010		IF $(\overline{\text{ZERO}})$
511	0000 1001		PC $\leftarrow 0509$
512	0000 0101		

and are often used with very short programs, it is feasible to program in machine language for some applications. The programmer should be aware, however, of the stumbling blocks awaiting him. In all but the simplest applications, symbolic language is recommended.

5.5. SYMBOLIC LANGUAGE

In symbolic language, all operations and addresses may be identified by symbols. This frees the programmer from memorizing or looking up the machine code for instructions and from keeping track of the absolute addresses of all data and instructions. A symbol may contain any combination of four to six characters (depending on the assembler) with the usual limitation that the first character be alphabetic. Table 5.1 gives a sample of the mnemonics used in the Intel 8080. The instruction symbols relate closely to the actual operation performed.

The representation of addresses by symbols is an important characteristic of symbolic programming. We may refer to the address of data or instructions by a symbol.

A typical assembly language statement is divided into four fields as follows.

$$\text{label : code operand ; comment}$$

The fields are separated by *delimiters* such as a space, comma, : , ; , /, -. The label is the symbolic address for the instruction. As the program is assembled, the label will be given the value of the address in which the instruction is stored. This facilitates referencing the instruction at any point in the program. Of course, not all instructions will have labels. It is not necessary to define a symbol for the address of an instruction unless that address is needed by a branch statement elsewhere in the program. For instance, in Example 5.1, only one instruction is referred to by a branch statement. Suppose one wishes to identify the address of this instruction by the mnemonic LOOP. In symbolic language, for the 8080, this instruction would appear as

$$\text{LOOP : LDAX   D ; Start of loop}$$

| Label field | Code field | Operand field | Comment field |

Therefore, in Table 5.2, LOOP would take on the value of 509.

The code field contains a symbolic representation of the instruction. The operand field contains the symbolic address of the operand. Everything in the comment field is ignored by the computer. It is supplied for documentation only. In a similar manner, the numbers NA and NB from the example could be referred to symbolically as NA and NB without specifying their addresses. In this case, NA would have a numerical value of 100_{16} (the address of the first byte of NA) and NB would have a value of 108_{16}. Using symbolic language, the program of Table 5.2 could be written as in Table 5.3.

Table 5.3 PROGRAM FOR EXAMPLE 5.1 IN SYMBOLIC LANGUAGE [5].

	LXI	D,NA	;	Load address of NA in D and E.
	LXI	H,NB	;	Load address of NB in H and L.
	MVI	C,8		
	XRA		;	Clear carry.
LOOP :	LDAX	D	;	Load byte of NA into accumulator.
	ADC	M	;	Add byte of NB to accumulator.
	DAA			
	STAX	D		
	INX	H		
	INX	D		
	DCR	C		
	JNZ	LOOP		

Pseudo-Instructions

Since the assembler is required to assign addresses to data and instructions, it is necessary to supply the starting address to be used by the assembler. This information and other information, which allow the assembler to perform more sophisticated functions, are provided through *pseudo-instructions*. Pseudo-instructions are written in the same fashion as machine instructions; however, they serve merely as instructions to the assembler to be used during the assembly process. The more significant of these instructions are in one of four classes:

1. *ORIGIN (ADDRESS)*. This statement always appears or is assumed at the beginning of each assembly language program. It specifies the address at which the following instructions are to be stored. Consecutive locations are used by the assembler until another ORIGIN statement is encountered. Some commonly used mnemonics include ORG, BEG, ∗, etc.

2. *EQUATE*. Assigns a numerical value to a symbol. A statement, $X = 40$ or X EQ 40 simply stores 40 in the address which is symbolically identified by X. Two symbols may be assigned the same storage location by this statement. For example, $X = RO$ would cause X and RO to be interchangeable. This operation is useful in condensing programs during the development process.

3. *BLOCK*. Defines a sequence of numbers such as an array or table. For example LIST: BLK 26, 3, 76, 44 would cause the four numbers listed to be stored in consecutive locations in memory beginning at location LIST. Reference to LIST would imply the first data word in the block. Most assemblers allow relative addressing to access other members of the block. For example LIST + 2 would refer to 76, the third word in the block. Among the symbols used to represent this operation are BLK and DB.

4. *END*. A termination (or end) command is a symbol to indicate the end of a source program. When the assembler encounters this pseudo-instruction, the assembly process stops.

Table 5.4   PSEUDO-INSTRUCTIONS FOR
EXAMPLE PROGRAM (Intel 8080).

```
        ORG   100H†
NA:     DB    73,01,01,90,38,00,01,00
NB:     DB    02,00,34,10,32,96,00,00
        ORG   500H
        ..........
        ..........          Symbolic
        ..........          Program
        ..........             of
        ..........          Table 5.3
        END
```

†H signifies a hexadecimal number.

Suppose an assembly language program is to be written for the Intel 8080 micro-computer system (MCS-80). The instructions for Example 5.1 are given in Table 5.3. If we desire *NA* and *NB* to be stored beginning at location 100_{16}, then the statements shown in Table 5.4 would be required.

Literals

Suppose the number 3 is to be added to the contents of the accumulator at some point in a program. Then

THREE EQ 3

would define THREE as having the value 3 and assign an address to the symbol THREE. Suppose the instruction,

AD THREE

would cause the contents of THREE to be added to the accumulator. This approach requires the programmer to keep track of the symbols assigned to each constant.

Another method of achieving the same result is to employ an add-immediate instruction, e.g., ADI 3. In this case the 3 will be stored in memory immediately following the instruction. If in the course of programming it is necessary to use this constant again, it must be placed in memory unless the programmer retains the absolute address of the number 3.

A *literal* is a pseudo-instruction that is a direct specification of a quantity to be operated on. If an assembler allows the use of literals, then the addition may be accomplished by one instruction, namely,

AD =3

The equals sign is normally used to signal the assembler that a literal will follow. In this case the computer assigns a storage location to the symbol 3 and stores the number 3 in it. If the same literal is used later in the program, the assembler will recognize the symbol and use the address in which 3 is stored. The use of literals reduces the number of symbol definitions required at the beginning of the program and is more efficient in terms of storage than immediate instructions.

Macros

The translating of symbolic language statements to machine language is normally performed on a one-to-one basis. In some cases, however, it is convenient to be able to use one symbol to stand for a group of instructions. This is accomplished by using a pseudo-instruction called a *macro*. In those assemblers which permit macro programming, the programmer may choose the macro name and the instructions it is to represent.

Consider the steps required to load the memory address register in the course of a program. This is a very common operation; in some microcomputers, it may be accomplished by a single instruction. In the Intel 8008, however, the MAR is composed of two registers H and L, as shown in Fig. 5.4.

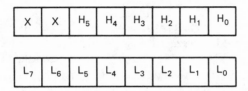

Fig. 5.4. H and L registers which compose the MAR for the 8008.

The MAR is fourteen bits long. The X's in the first two bits indicate that these two bits are not used in the address (*don't cares*). In the 8008 each of these registers must be loaded separately. Suppose that an address, Y, is defined by two bytes. Then the MAR may be loaded with Y by the following MOVE IMMEDIATE (MVI) instructions [11]

$$\text{MVI H,Y SHR 8}$$
$$\text{MVI L,Y AND 0FFH}$$

In the first instruction, H is loaded with the number symbolized by Y which has been shifted eight bits to the right (SHR 8). Then L is loaded with the number Y ANDed with 00000000 11111111(0FF$_{16}$). The steps in this operation are shown in Fig. 5.5.

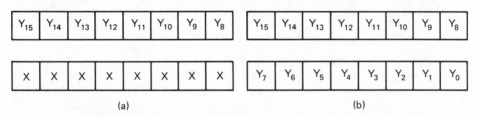

Fig. 5.5. Loading the H and L registers for the 8008 (a) after first MVI instruction (b) after second MVI instruction.

Of course Y_{14} and Y_{15} will not be used in determining the address. This sequence of two instructions is repeated many times during the course of a program. For this reason it is convenient to write a macro to refer to these instructions by a single symbol.

There are three steps in the application of a macro: (1) definition, (2) reference, and (3) expansion. Every macro must be defined once in a program. The definition generally contains an indication that a macro is being defined, a symbol which will stand for the macro, a dummy parameter list which will allow the operation to be changed slightly each time the macro is referenced, and an indication of the end of the macro definition. For example, in the Intel MCS-8 software, the definition of a macro LOAD to load the MAR would be as follows.

Macro Definition

```
LOAD   MACRO   ADDR
       MVI     H,ADDR SHR 8
       MVI     L,ADDR AND 0FFH
       ENDM
```

ADDR is a dummy parameter which stands for the address which is to be specified at the time the macro is referenced. ENDM signals the end of the macro definition.

A macro is referenced by simply stating the macro and the parameters to be used with the macro. Suppose that the address to be placed in the MAR is Y. Then the macro reference would be as follows.

Macro Reference

```
LOAD Y
```

When the program is assembled, the assemblers will insert the appropriate instructions for every macro reference. In this example, the assembled program would contain the following.

Macro Expansion

```
MVI  H,Y SHR 8
MVI  L,Y AND 0FFH
```

An assembler with macro capabilities can be very powerful. The use of macros also enables one to emulate other computers by using macros to implement the instructions of the emulated computer.

5.6. FUNDAMENTALS OF PROGRAMMING
IN ASSEMBLY LANGUAGE

Symbolic language programs are a step-by-step logical implementation of an algorithm as defined in Sec. 5.2. The most important characteristic of writing a program is preciseness. Writing efficient assembly language programs, however, is an art requiring experience, cleverness, and insight. The more complicated the program, the more important efficient (requiring less time and/or memory) programming becomes. In this chapter we will introduce some basic concepts which will lead to more efficient programming [7].

Loops

Frequently in programs it is necessary to repeat a sequence of instructions many times, as illustrated in the following example.

Example 5.2.

Suppose one wishes to obtain $8 * X$ ($*$ represents multiplication) and store it in Y. In the 8008 (MCS-8) instruction set (Appendix D), this could be accomplished by clearing the accumulator and then adding X eight times. The program could be written using the following instructions:

```
XRA  A    ; Clear accumulator.
LOAD X    ; Macro to load MAR.
ADD  M    ; Add X to accumulator.
ADD  M
ADD  M
ADD  M
ADD  M
ADD  M
ADD  M
ADD  M
LOAD Y    ; Load MAR with Y address.
MOV  M,A  ; Store accumulator in Y.
```

The exclusive-OR instruction is used to clear the accumulator. The LOAD macro, defined in Sec. 5.5, is used to load the H and L registers with the address corresponding to X. Once these registers have been set, the ADD M instruction adds the contents of X to the accumulator. The LOAD Y macro is then used to place the address, Y, into H and L, and the MOV M,A instruction places the result of the multiple addition $8 * X$ into location Y in memory.

Since the instruction ADD M occurs repeatedly, the program may branch back and repeat the same instruction eight times. Such a procedure is called *looping*. Example 5.1 made use of such a loop. Of course looping requires some additional logic to determine when to exit the loop. If we are using a loop, it is no more difficult to program the general problem of computing

$$Y = r * X$$

The summation is simply performed sequentially with each pass through the loop accomplishing

$$A \leftarrow A + (X)$$

If this operation is repeated r times, the A register will contain $r * X$. Figure 5.6 is a flow chart of this simple loop. A program for this loop is:

```
          XRA    A      ;  Clear accumulator.
          LOAD   R      ;  Set MAR to address R.
          CMP    M      ;  Compare R with 0.
          JZ     FIN    ;  Branch if R = 0.
          MOV    B,M    ;  Store R in B.
          LOAD   X
REPT  :   ADD    M
          DCR    B
          JNZ    REPT
FIN   :   LOAD   Y
          MOV    M,A
```

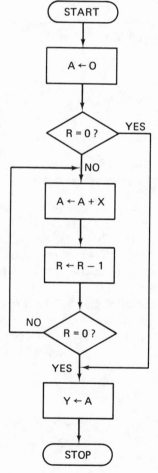

Fig. 5.6. Flow chart of a simple loop.

Note that the program requires one less instruction than the program without a loop. Of course this program is more general because it uses the same program to obtain $3 * X$, $5 * X$, etc. The comparison will be much more dramatic in many situations. The program is a straightforward implementation of the flow chart in Fig. 5.6. The variable R was assigned to the B register to reduce the number of memory references. If a microprocessor has general-purpose registers in the CPU, then these should be used for implementing a counter which is illustrated by the variable R. This reduces the time required to execute the program.

The equivalent of a rather extensive AND/OR network of discrete logic can be implemented using a loop [8].

Example 5.3.

Suppose one desires to compare an input word with a number of words stored in memory and, if a match is found, execute a particular routine MATWD. If no match occurs, proceed to a routine labeled NOMAT. The 8080 will be used in this example.

First the number of words against which the input word is to be tested is stored in register C. This register serves as an index to allow exit from the loop when the test is completed. In general, one may wish to examine only a portion of each incoming data word. For this reason, provision is made to mask the data word to eliminate "don't cares." Test words are stored in memory with the mask to be used immediately preceding it, as shown in Fig. 5.7. A program to implement this search is the following:

```
             MVI   C,N          ; Set C with number, N, of test
                                ; words to be searched.
             LXI   H,TWORD      ; Set MAR to location of test
                                ; word list.
INWORD :     IN    0            ; Input data word from device #0.
             ANA   M            ; Apply mask.
             INX   H            ; Increment MAR.
```

MASK 1
TEST WORD 1
MASK 2
TEST WORD 2
MASK 3
TEST WORD 3
. . . .

Fig. 5.7. Storage of test words and corresponding mask for Example 5.3.

```
CONT    :  CMP   M          ;  Compare with test word.
           JZ    MATWD      ;  If a match, perform routine
                            ;  MATWD.
           DCR   C
           JZ    NOMAT      ;  Jump, no match occurred.
           INX   H          ;  Increment MAR.
           JMP   INWORD     ;  Read another word.
```

After C is loaded with the number of test words to be used and the location of the test word list is placed in the MAR, then a word is input from the device designated 0. The mask for test word 1 is applied with an AND instruction. Only those bits of the input word which are in the same locations as 1's in the mask word will be tested. The instruction INX H is required to increment the MAR. The test word is then compared with the masked input word, and appropriate status flags are set. If the two words agree, the zero flag will be set and in the next instruction a jump to MATWD will occur. If a match does not occur on this word, then C is decremented and tested to determine if all the test words have been used. If they have, then no match has occurred and NOMAT should be executed. If all the test words have not been used, then the program branches back to the mask instruction and another test word is tried.

Another application of looping is to generate time delays [8]. If we place the computer in a loop, we can control the length of *time* that it stays in the loop by controlling the number of times the loop is executed.

Example 5.4.

Consider the following time-delay implementation using the MCS-40 (4040). The instruction set for the MCS-40 is given in Appendix A. *Note*: In the MCS-40 the ; delimiter indicates that a comment field follows.

```
         FIM  0 , 0BH   ;  Loads an 8-bit hexadecimal number into
                        ;  register pair 0 consisting of registers
                        ;  0 and 1.  The instruction loads
                        ;  R₀ ← 0 and R₁ ← B.
LOOP : ISZ  0 , LOOP   ;  Increments register 0, and if the result
                        ;  is zero, the program continues to the
                        ;  next sequential location.  Otherwise it
                        ;  branches to LOOP (and repeats itself).
       ISZ  1 , LOOP   ;  Increments register 1 and branches to
                        ;  LOOP unless register 1 is zero.  If
                        ;  register 1 is zero, the loop is terminated
                        ;  and the program continues with the next
                        ;  instruction.
```

The amount of time delayed in the loop may be determined from the number of cycles completed. A single-word instruction for the 4040 requires 10.8 μs to execute, and a two-word instruction requires 21.6 μs. The statement labeled LOOP will execute sixteen times before it reaches zero and moves to the next instruction. Since the ISZ instruction is a two-word instruction, the sixteen loops will require approximately 0.35 ms. Since register 1 was set to 11 initially, it must be incremented five times before the routine will be completed. Thus, the entire routine will require approximately 1.7 ms to execute. The delay may be varied from 0.35 to 5.5 ms in increments of 0.35 ms by selection of the number initially loaded into register 1. The delay could be further altered by inserting additional one- or two-word instructions in the loop.

Branch Statements

An important characteristic of a digital computer is its ability to alter the sequence of instructions it performs as a result of the data it receives. This is accomplished using branch statements such as JUMP or SKIP. In a straightforward manner, the data may be tested for each of the numerous possible conditions and the program sequence determined accordingly. Figure 5.8 illustrates a flow diag am of a typical program for a set of possible conditions A_1, A_2, A_3, and A_4.

A more efficient method of performing this branching, if several conditions must be checked, uses a branch table. In this approach the addresses of the various routines are stored in tabular form in memory, and the routines are addressed indirectly.

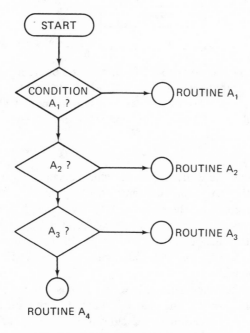

Fig. 5.8. A typical branching program.

Example 5.5.

Suppose we wish to execute one of eight routines R1 through R8 depending on which bit of the accumulator is set [6].

$$
\begin{array}{lllllll}
\text{Jump to R1 if accumulator holds} & 00000001 \\
\prime\prime \quad \prime\prime \ \ \text{R2} \ \prime\prime \quad \prime\prime \qquad \prime\prime \quad & 00000010 \\
\prime\prime \quad \prime\prime \ \ \text{R3} \ \prime\prime \quad \prime\prime \qquad \prime\prime \quad & 00000100 \\
\prime\prime \quad \prime\prime \ \ \text{R4} \ \prime\prime \quad \prime\prime \qquad \prime\prime \quad & 00001000 \\
\prime\prime \quad \prime\prime \ \ \text{R5} \ \prime\prime \quad \prime\prime \qquad \prime\prime \quad & 00010000 \\
\prime\prime \quad \prime\prime \ \ \text{R6} \ \prime\prime \quad \prime\prime \qquad \prime\prime \quad & 00100000 \\
\prime\prime \quad \prime\prime \ \ \text{R7} \ \prime\prime \quad \prime\prime \qquad \prime\prime \quad & 01000000 \\
\prime\prime \quad \prime\prime \ \ \text{R8} \ \prime\prime \quad \prime\prime \qquad \prime\prime \quad & 10000000 \\
\end{array}
$$

The branch table might be located in memory in the form shown in Fig. 5.9. Each address requires two bytes or words of memory storage in this case, $\langle R_i \rangle_1$ and $\langle R_i \rangle_2$.

$\langle R1 \rangle_1$
$\langle R1 \rangle_2$
$\langle R2 \rangle_1$
$\langle R2 \rangle_2$
$\langle R3 \rangle_1$
$\langle R3 \rangle_2$
. . . .

Fig. 5.9. Branch table stored in memory.

Consider programming the 8080 to perform the one-of-eight routines required by this example. The program shown in Fig. 5.10 would perform the indicated function.

Writing this program for one of the other microprocessors whose instruction set is given in the appendices is an interesting and informative exercise for the reader.

Subroutines

In many programs there are processes which occur several times but are not available as individual instructions. In assemblers so equipped, it may be advantageous to write a macro to accomplish the process. A disadvantage, however, is the fact that in the assembly process every macro reference is replaced by the set of instructions making up the macro. Thus, if a macro stands for 10 instructions and the macro is referenced 10 times in a program, then 100 memory locations will be dedicated to the task performed by the macro.

A *subroutine*, on the other hand, allows the same sequence of instructions to be repeated at different locations in the program. Each time the subroutine is referenced (a subroutine CALL) the location of the subroutine in memory is loaded into the program counter. Following execution of the subroutine, the address of the instruction immediately following the CALL is placed in the program counter and execution

```
START  :  LXI H,BRTAB  ;  POINTS H AND L TO BRANCH TABLE
GTBIT  :  RAR          ;  SHIFT LSB TO CARRY
          JC GETAD     ;  CHECK CARRY
          INX H        ;  (H,L) ← (H,L) + 1
          INX H
          JMP GTBIT
GETAD  :  MOV E,M      ;  LOAD ADDRESS FROM BRANCH TABLE INTO D,E
          INX H
          MOV D,M
          XCHG         ;  (H,L) ⇆ (D,E)
          PCHL         ;  LOAD PC WITH CONTENTS OF H,L


BRTAB     DW    R1     ;  DEFINE TWO BYTE WORD
          DW    R2
          DW    R3
          DW    R4
          DW    R5
          DW    R6
          DW    R7
          DW    R8
```

Fig. 5.10. Program for 8080 using branch table.

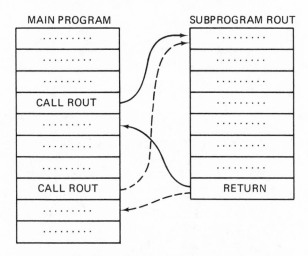

Fig. 5.11. Accessing a subroutine from the main program.

of the main program continues. This is illustrated in Fig. 5.11 for the CALL of a subroutine symbolized by ROUT. As the subroutine is assembled, it is assigned an address in memory. The symbol for the subroutine (ROUT) is assigned the address of the first instruction in ROUT. Since the processor must know where to find the next instruction in the main program after it completes execution of the subroutine, the address of the next instruction in the main program is pushed onto a pushdown stack (Sec. 4.4). When execution reaches the RETURN instruction in the subroutine, the return address is popped from the stack and execution continues. If later in the program ROUT is called again (Fig. 5.11), the same instructions are executed again, with a return to the next instruction following the CALL. Using our example of 10 instructions which must be executed 10 times during a program, the subroutine method would require only 21 memory locations (10 CALL, 1 RETURN, 10 instructions) as compared to 100 if a macro is used. Execution time for a macro may be shorter, however, so it is necessary to weigh the requirements of each application carefully. If the subroutine requires data from the main program, then this data or its address must be passed to the subroutine in one of the processor registers. There are numerous methods of doing this, depending on the processor architecture. One simple method, if enough registers are available, is to simply load the data to be passed into the scratch-pad memory before calling the subroutine.

Example 5.6.

Suppose one wishes a subroutine symbolized by ASUM that will add two numbers ALPHA and BETA and store the result (SUM) in a third location [6]. Using the general-purpose registers of the 8008, we may make the assignments

$$(C) = ALPHA$$
$$(D) = BETA$$
$$(B) = SUM$$

The subroutine might then contain the instructions:

```
ASUM :   MOV   A,C
         ADD   D
         MOV   B,A
         RET
```

Prior to calling the subroutine in the main program, the numbers to be added must be placed in the C and D registers. After the RETURN, the result is located in register B. In this case, the main program could employ the previously described LOAD MACRO and contain the following instructions:

```
LOAD   ALPHA
MOV    C,M
LOAD   BETA
MOV    D,M
CALL   ASUM
LOAD   SUM
MOV    M,B
```

Frequently scratch-pad registers are not available for data passing to the subroutine. In this case, an address parameter list (PARML) could be passed using the scratch-pad memory. PARML would contain the address of the data to be used. For example, suppose the H and L registers (MAR) of the 8008 are used to pass the memory address of PARML. If ALPHA is stored in PARML, BETA in PARML + 1, and SUM is placed in PARML + 2, then the following subroutine could be written:

```
ASUM2 :  MOV   A,M
         INR   L
         JNZ   CONT
         INR   H
CONT  :  ADD   M
         INR   L
         JNZ   CONT2
         INR   H
CONT2 :  MOV   M,A
         RET
```

In this subroutine, the MAR (H and L registers) must be incremented twice. Some economy may be realized by writing another subroutine to increment the MAR. Such a routine, MEMIN, could consist of the following instructions:

```
MEMIN :  INR   L
         RNZ        ;  Return if L is not zero.
         INR   H
         RET
```

Using this subroutine, ASUM2 would become:

```
ASUM2 :  MOV    A,M       ;  for 8008
         CALL   MEMIN
         ADD    M
         CALL   MEMIN
         MOV    M,A
         RET
```

Subroutine MEMIN is called by an instruction in subroutine ASUM2. This is called *nesting* of subroutines. Microprocessors differ in the level of nesting allowed. Some allow only two-level nesting, while others with the return address stack implemented in memory have essentially unlimited nesting capability. In general, microprocessors designed for calculator applications will allow only a few levels of nesting, while other machines will allow more levels. As an illustration of the difference in programming different microprocessors, the 8080 has a single instruction INX H to increment the MAR, which is equivalent to the SUBROUTINE MEMIN.

The CALL instruction described above is a multiword instruction on most machines. Some processors provide a RESTART instruction which is essentially a single-word subroutine call. The RESTART instruction has only a limited number of addresses, sometimes called *trap cells*, at which the subroutine may be located. It is useful in processing interrupts or subroutines in which speed is essential.

Input/Output

All input and output operations require one or more of the following steps [9].

1. Test to see if the peripheral device is available.

2. When the device is available, activate it.

3. Transfer data.

4. Deactivate the device.

Two classes of information may be exchanged: data information and status information.

Many microprocessors are designed to communicate with the data bus. In this case, the microprocessor must provide control information to the peripherals to assure that the proper device places data on the bus or receives it from the bus at the appropriate time. This generally requires software for implementation.

The simplest type of transfer assumes that the external device is always available. A particular device is selected and the CPU requests an input from the device via the data bus. The CPU then waits (via a time-delay loop, e.g., Example 5.4) until the peripheral device or corresponding interface has had enough time to load a word on the bus. An input instruction is then executed to read the word from the data bus. This method assumes that the peripheral device is able to respond within the allotted time. It is open-loop in nature; i.e., there is no feedback from the peripheral to inform the processor that the data is available on the bus. We will define such a transfer of data as a *synchronous data transfer* (Chap. 6). A flow diagram of the program required to execute this type of input is shown in Fig. 5.12.

The program steps required to implement the time-delay routine have been discussed in 5.6, and the input instruction (block 3, Fig. 5.12) has been discussed in Sec. 4.4. The program steps required to address the peripheral (block 1) depend upon the architecture of the microprocessor. In some of these devices (e.g., Motorola 6800), an I/O device is addressed as a memory element. Communication with an I/O device is carried out in the same manner as communication with a memory element. In other systems (e.g., Intel 8008), a device enable must be sent to the peripheral. This may be accomplished by using an output instruction to direct the peripheral to place its data or status on the bus.

This approach might be used to read an analog-to-digital converter. If the analog signal is varying slowly, one may simply supply a convert pulse to the converter and gate the converter output onto the data bus via one or more OUTPUT instructions. After a sufficient length of time, the conversion is assumed to be complete and the data bus is read by execution of an INPUT instruction.

Another common method of communicating with external devices is the "handshake" method (asynchronous data transfer) [10]. In this approach status information

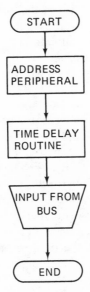

Fig. 5.12. Flow chart of input routine using an open-loop operation.

is provided by the peripheral interface. This generally consists of one or more flag bits which may be read by the microprocessor. Such flags generally indicate whether the peripheral is ready to accept input from the processor or whether the peripheral has a data word ready to be transmitted to the CPU. If the microprocessor desires to transmit a word to the peripheral, it first reads the status of the peripheral. If the status bits indicate that the device is ready, the transfer takes place. If, however, the device is "busy," the microprocessor is programmed to loop and continue reading the status word. During this operation, the microprocessor will wait until the external device is ready for a transfer to take place.

Example 5.7.

Suppose one wishes to read a character from a teletypewriter (TTY) using this procedure. Also suppose that the status word, derived from the interface (Sec. 6.2), has been wired as device 2, and the TTY is wired as device 0. The status of the TTY will be indicated by the LSB of the status word. If a 1 is in the LSB, the TTY interface is ready to transmit the character. If a 0 is present, it is not ready. Using the 8008 instruction set, the character is read by the following instructions:

```
IN      2 ;   Input status word.
RAR       ;   Rotate LSB into carry.
JNC .— 2 ;   Jump if device not ready.
IN      0 ;   Input character from the teletype.
```

The appropriate status bit is tested by rotating the accumulator through the carry bit until the appropriate bit is in the carry flip-flop. In this case, only a single rotation is required. Then, a branch is made conditional upon the value of the carry bit. Relative addressing is used in this case to cause the program to branch back to the

IN instruction. ("." indicates the address of the instruction which is currently being processed.) Such relative addressing, however, should be used with caution because the relative address is based on word count and not on instruction count. In this case both IN and RAR are single-word instructions. If, however, a multiword instruction had occurred in the loop, it must be accounted for in the relative address.

In the preceding example, the microprocessor simply loops, waiting for the TTY to indicate that it is ready. This approach is frequently used in microprocessors; but if a lengthy wait is anticipated, say 100–1000 microseconds [8], it may be desirable to allow the microprocessor to perform some useful task while it waits for the external device to be available. If this approach is to be taken, some means must be provided for the external device to signal the microprocessor that it is ready. The signal must be capable of altering the course of action which the microprocessor takes. Such a capability is called an *interrupt* and is available on many microprocessors.

Handling an interrupt requires a number of actions and is somewhat complicated. The microprocessor must recognize the interrupt and then ignore other interrupts until the first one is acted upon. If the microprocessor is to return to the task it was performing prior to the interrupt, the contents of the status flags and perhaps other registers must be stored before action on the interrupt takes place. This information will allow the microcomputer to pick up where it left off. The capability (instruction set) to rapidly store this information varies from microprocessor to microprocessor and greatly affects its ability to handle interrupts.

In many microprocessors, an interrupt causes an instruction to be jammed into the instruction register. This instruction is generally a branch or subroutine CALL instruction. In some processors it is supplied by the hardware [11]. In others, the program counter is automatically pushed onto the stack so that return to the original program can be made after the interrupt is processed. The interrupt may also automatically mask (or disable) other interrupts. If so, then software must provide an INTERRUPT ENABLE before processing of the current interrupt is completed.

The condition bits must be stored before the interrupt routine is processed and then restored prior to the return to the main program. This is an essential operation. Suppose, for example, that the program had just completed processing the instruction

RAR

when an interrupt occurred. If the next step in the main program is

JNC   .-2

then returning to this instruction after the processing of the interrupt will produce an error unless the status of the carry flag is restored before returning.

As an example of the processing of an interrupt, suppose that the task of reading a character from the TTY is to be implemented using an interrupt approach with an 8080 microprocessor. The main program would request a character from the TTY via an output command. Suppose

OUT   1

notifies the TTY interface that an input is requested. After the processing of this instruction, the microcomputer would continue to execute its program while waiting for an interrupt to occur. Suppose that the TTY interface is designed to place an RST 0 instruction on the data bus when the interrupt, indicating that a character is ready to be transmitted, occurs. The RST instruction is a single-word subroutine call which directs the program counter to octal memory locations 0, 10, 20, 30, 40, 50, 60, 70. Thus RST 0 directs the microprocessor to location 0. The following instructions would then serve to process the interrupt by reading the character from the TTY.

```
PUSH   PSW ;   Stores the status bits and accumulator.
PUSH   H   ;   Stores MAR (usually necessary).
IN     0   ;   Input character from TTY.
  .        ;   Instructions for processing and storing the
  .        ;   character.
  .
POP    H_;     Restores H and L registers.
POP    PSW ;   Restores condition flag and accumulator.
EI         ;   Enables interrupt.
RET        ;   Returns to point of interrupt occurrence.
```

The status word (PSW) and the MAR (H and L registers) are stored in the stack. The return address is stored automatically with the execution of the RST instruction. Other registers could also be stored in the stack. After these registers are stored, the program steps required by the interrupt are executed. In this case, a character is read from the TTY and then the character is processed and stored in memory. If this processing requires the use of the other general-purpose registers, B, C, D, E, then the value of these registers at the time of the interrupt should be stored by the programmer in the stack prior to executing the interrupt routine. After the processing is complete, the registers are restored to their original values by popping the stack. Remember that the stack is an LIFO list. Since H and L were the last values pushed on the stack, they are the first to be popped. Finally, the EI instruction enables the interrupt allowing the system to be interrupted again. Then a RET instruction causes the original value of the program counter to be popped from the stack, and execution continues on the main program.

5.7. EDITORS

After a program has been written in symbolic language, it must be translated by the assembler into machine language. (In small systems this may be performed by the programmer.) In order to translate a program, a copy must be available in some form (e.g., paper tape) for input into the assembler. Of course a paper tape can be made with a TTY in an off-line mode, but any errors in keying the program will require the use of the RUBOUT key to eliminate incorrect characters. Such operations make correcting a tape very tedious. Considerable simplification arises when an editing program, supplied by many microcomputer manufacturers with their prototyping systems, is used to key-in the program. The editor accepts the symbolic language statements and stores them in a portion of the random-access memory called a *text buffer*. From there commands are provided to enable the operator, via a TTY or CRT, to call any instruction from memory, make corrections, and then replace the corrected form in RAM. After the program has been corrected in memory, the editor then outputs the result in a usable form such as paper tape. For the purpose of correcting a program in memory, various commands are recognized by the editor. Some of the typical ones are:

1. *DELETE*. Allows the operator to eliminate an entire line of text. The editor assigns line numbers for the purpose of identification and automatically corrects the line numbers as lines are added or deleted.

2. *APPEND*. Adds the statements which follow to the end of the program.

3. *INSERT*. Adds a line between two existing lines of the program.

4. *CORRECT*. Allows a line to be corrected by typing in the correct line.

5. *SEARCH*. Searches one or more lines for a specified character and stops when the character is located to allow for correction.

6. *READ*. Allows the operator to read in a program or a portion of a program from a tape.

7. *LIST*. Lists the line or lines specified to enable the operator to check for errors and to locate a particular instruction.

8. *PUNCH*. Causes the contents of the text buffer to be punched on paper tape for later input into the assembler.

In addition to these commands, some commands are provided to allow the operator to determine the number of lines in the program and the amount of space occupied by the text buffer. This feature is necessary on editors which use the microcomputer itself to insure the operator that he is not running out of memory in the text buffer.

Operation of Assemblers

The corrected copy of the symbolic language program is translated by the assembler. Most microcomputer manufacturers produce an assembler to aid in program writing using their machines. Most microcomputer assemblers are multipass assemblers. In these the symbolic program must be processed by the assembler more than one time. During the first pass, the assembler constructs a symbol table which is stored in memory. This is a listing of all the symbols used in the program and the address or value which has been assigned to it. The assembler assigns addresses to those symbols which have not been assigned by a psuedo-instruction.

Typically, during a second pass, the assembler translates each instruction into machine language, provides the addresses, and lists both the symbolic language and the machine language side by side on an output device (e.g., TTY). Figure 5.13 illustrates the results of a second pass through the MCS-80 assembler [11]. Certain types of errors may be detected by the assembler. Duplicate address labels, undefined labels, and unrecognized instruction mnemonics are commonly detected by assemblers.

```
0000                ORG     500H
0500   310004       LXI     SP,400H  ; SET SP AT 400H
                    SPACE   MACRO
                    MVI     C, ' '   ; LOAD ASCII CODE FOR SPACE
                    CALL    TO       ; OUTPUT TO TTY
                    ENDM
0503   0E41         MVI     C, 'A'   ; LOAD ASCII CODE FOR A
0505   CD9205       CALL    TO       ; PRINT A
                    SPACE            ; PRINT SPACE
0508   0E20         MVI     C, ' '   ; LOAD ASCII CODE FOR SPACE
050A   CD9205       CALL    TO       ; OUTPUT TO TTY

050D   0E3D         MVI     C, '='   ; LOAD ASCII CODE FOR =
050F   CD9205       CALL    TO       ; PRINT =
                    SPACE
0512   0E20         MVI     C, ' '   ; LOAD ASCII CODE FOR SPACE
0514   CD9205       CALL    TO       ; OUTPUT TO TTY

0517   CD8705       CALL    TI       ; INPUT FIRST CHARACTER
051A   47           MOV     B,A
051B   4F           MOV     C,A
051C   CD9205       CALL    TO       ; PRINT FIRST CHARACTER
051F   CD9E05       CALL    CRLF
0522   0E42         MVI     C, 'B'
0524   CD9205       CALL    TO       ; PRINT B
                    SPACE
0527   0E20         MVI     C, ' '   ; LOAD ASCII CODE FOR SPACE
0529   CD9205       CALL    TO       ; OUTPUT TO TTY

052C   0E3D         MVI     C, '='
052E   CD9205       CALL    TO
                    SPACE
0531   0E20         MVI     C, ' '   ; LOAD ASCII CODE FOR SPACE
0533   CD9205       CALL    TO       ; OUTPUT TO TTY
```

Fig. 5.13. The output of the second pass of an assembler for a typical system (Intel MCS-80).

A third pass may be required to produce an output tape of the machine language program. This is the form which may be loaded into memory for execution of the program. It may be possible to output the tape in different codes and formats (Sec. 6.7).

There are various types of assemblers. National Semiconductor supplies a conversational assembler for its PACE microprocessor which allows one to edit and assemble a program that is keyed into the microprocessor [12].

If the assembler operates within the microcomputer itself, it is called a *self-assembler* or a *resident assembler*. The most important limitation of self-assemblers is the time required to load the assembler and make the translation when using low-speed input/output devices (e.g., a TTY). Typical programs may require 20–30 minutes for translating using a self-assembler. The finalization of a properly functioning program usually requires several iterations of correcting and reassembling, which can be very time-consuming. A high-speed paper tape reader or a floppy disk system can dramatically reduce this time.

Most manufacturers provide an assembler which is written to run on a larger computer. Such assemblers are called *cross-assemblers*. These programs are usually available on the nationwide time-sharing networks (e.g., TYMSHARE) and are frequently available in FORTRAN for use on in-house computers.

Some manufacturers also have a simulation program available to simulate the microprocessor on a large computer. This program is frequently used in conjunction with the cross-assembler to enable the programmer to debug his program rapidly. I/O operation is difficult to simulate, however, and testing of the program on the actual microprocessor and I/O equipment is essential.

Loading and Debugging

The assembled program will ultimately be stored in pROM or ROM for application. In the prototyping stage, however, most microcomputer development systems allow the operator to store his program in RAM which provides easier debugging [13]. In order to place a program in memory, a loader program must be provided to read the program into the proper location in memory. If the loader is stored on ROM, it is always accessible because ROMs are nonvolatile.

If the loader program is not present in the machine on ROM, a *bootstrap loader* must be used. Such a program is usually on tape and requires a few instructions to be keyed in to initialize the reading of the loader. The bootstrap program loads itself and is then capable of loading a machine code program.

With the program loaded into memory, it may be executed by loading the starting address into the program counter. This may be done by jamming a JUMP instruction into the instruction register via the console. Microcomputer prototyping systems generally contain a program on pROM with debugging capabilities. Some of the more important features are the ability to read the contents of a memory location, to change the contents of a memory location, and to execute the program on a step-by-step basis. More advanced features include the ability to relocate a program in memory and to specify the conditions under which the operator desires to examine the contents of registers or memory.

5.8. HIGH-LEVEL LANGUAGES

With high-level languages, the programmer specifies a relatively small number of general commands (source code) which are translated into the specific instructions (machine code) necessary for the microcomputer to perform the task indicated. The program which performs the translation is called a *compiler*. The complexity of many compilers makes it necessary to execute them on a medium- or large-scale computer. Compilers make programming easier and faster because fewer statements are required to implement an algorithm. The need to write detailed code for loops and complex data structures is eliminated [14]. The reduction in programming cost must be balanced against slower speed and a decrease in efficiency of memory utilization. Also, a reduction in mechanical errors may be offset by new errors introduced by a lack of understanding of the conventions built into the compiler.

High-level languages have little application for small programs; however, as the complexity of the program increases, the applicability of a high-level language increases. One high-level language in use on microcomputers is PL/M, a version of PL/I, which has been developed by Intel for the MCS 8/80 microcomputers. PL/M language consists of a number of basic statement types in which complicated arithmetical, logical, and character operations on 8-bit and 16-bit quantities can be expressed in a form resembling algebraic notation. Relational tests can be naturally stated to control branching through the program.

Example 5.8.

Consider the PL/M statement [15]:

$$\text{IF } X > Y, \text{ THEN } Z = X, \text{ ELSE } Z = Y$$

If X is greater than Y, Z is made equal to X; otherwise, Z is made equal to Y. This single statement in PL/M requires twelve instructions in symbolic code to implement in the 8008 when expressed as follows:

```
          MVI    H,Y SHR 8
          MVI    L,Y AND 0FFH   ;  Load address of Y.
          MOV    A,M            ;  Move Y to accum.
          MVI    H,X SHR 8
          MVI    L,X AND 0FFH   ;  Load address of X.
          CMP                   ;  Compare Y with X.
          JNC    TWO            ;  Jump if Y > X.
          MOV    A,M            .  ;  Move X to accum.
   TWO :  MVI    H,Z SHR 8
          MVI    L,Z AND 0FFH   ;  Load address of Z.
          MOV    M,A            ;  Move accum. to Z.
          END
```

The structure of the PL/M language may be illustrated by an example program described by Kildall [15].

Example 5.9.

Suppose a TTY is connected to the LSB of the data bus of an 8008. Consider writing a program to print the short message "What hath God wrought" on the TTY. The program is to transmit a serial bit stream to the TTY in the proper time space. A 7-bit ASCII code (Sec. 3.8) using odd parity will be used. Each character must be preceded by a start bit and followed by two stop bits, as shown in Fig. 5.14 for the character W. The ASCII code for W is 127_8 (Table 3.10). A PL/M program to perform this operation is listed in Fig. 5.15.

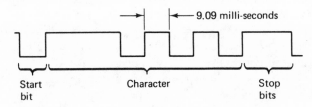

Fig. 5.14. Output pattern for a single character W.

```
DECLARE MESSAGE DATA ('WHAT HATH GOD WROUGHT'),
    (CHAR,I,J,SENDBIT) BYTE;
/* SEND EACH CHARACTER FROM MESSAGE TO TTY */
DO I = 0 TO LAST(MESSAGE);
CHAR= MESSAGE(I);
SENDBI T = 1;
/* SEND EACH BIT FROM CHAR TO TTY */
DO J = 1,11;
OUTPUT(0)= SENDBIT;
CALL TIME(91); /* WAIT 9.1 MSEC */
SENDBIT= CHAR AND 1;
/* ROTATE CHAR FOR NEXT ITERATION */
CHAR = ROR(CHAR 0R 1,1);
END;
END;
```

Fig. 5.15. PL/M program for Example 5.9.

The program begins with a data declaration that defines MESSAGE as a string of ASCII characters within the quotes. These 21 characters (spaces included) are numbered 0 to 20 for reference. The second line defines several variables CHAR, I, J, and SENDBIT which are used in the program. Any name may be selected for these variables as long as it is declared at the beginning of the program. CHAR holds each character of the message as it is transmitted. I identifies the particular character in the message and J specifies the bit in each character. The LSB of the variable SENDBIT is the bit which is to be transmitted next. The DO statement in line 4 causes instructions 4–15 to be repeated 21 times (once for each character in the message). As these statements are repeated, I is incremented, causing each character to be sent in succession. The DO statement on line 8 causes statements 9–14 to be implemented 11 times, once for each bit to be transmitted for a single character (one start bit, plus 8 bits for the ASCII character, plus two stop bits).

Setting SENDBIT to 1 allows the START bit to be transmitted the first time line 9 is carried out. After each bit is transmitted, a 9.1-ms space is required by the TTY before the next pulse is transmitted. Line 10 causes this to occur. Such a time delay is a standard feature in PL/M. The compiler implements it by inserting a wait loop for the prescribed amount of time. After this delay, the next bit (always the rightmost bit) to be transmitted is placed in SENDBIT by line 11, and the next bit to be transmitted is specified by placing a 1 in the rightmost bit of CHAR and then rotating CHAR one bit to the right in line 13. As each successive bit is transmitted, the bits in the word are shifted to the right and a 1 is added in the leftmost bit. Thus, as the character is transmitted, CHAR fills up with 1's from the left and after all eight bits have been transmitted CHAR contains all 1's. The next two repetitions of the loop will produce the stop bits for the character.

PL/M requires two passes of the program for translation. The first pass produces a listing of the source program, symbol listing, error diagnostics, program structure analysis, and an intermediate file containing a linearized version of the original program. The second pass uses the intermediate file as an input and produces machine code at the output.

REFERENCES

1. CLARE, CHRISTOPHER R., *Designing Logic Systems Using State Machines.* New York: McGraw-Hill Book Co., 1973.

2. WAYNE, MARK N., *Flowcharting Concepts & Data Processing.* San Francisco: Canfield Press, 1973.

3. FLORES, IVAN, *Computer Software.* Englewood Cliffs, N.J.: Prentice-Hall, Inc., 1965.

4. STARK, PETER A., *Digital Computer Programming.* Toronto: The Macmillan Co., 1967.

5. *8080 Single-Chip Eight-Bit Parallel Central Processor Unit.* Intel Corp., April, 1974.

6. *Programming Manual for the 8080 Microcomputer System.* Intel Corp., May, 1974.

7. SHERMAN, PHILLIP M., *Programming and Coding Digital Computers.* New York: John Wiley & Sons, Inc., 1963.

8. GLADSTONE, BRUCE, "Designing with Microprocessors Instead of Wired Logic Asks More of Designers." *Electronics* (Oct. 11, 1973), pp. 91–104.

9. HILL, FREDERICK, JR. and GERALD R. PETERSON, *Digital Systems: Hardware Organization and Design.* New York: John Wiley & Sons, Inc., 1973.

10. KORN, GRANINO A., *Minicomputers for Engineers and Scientists.* New York: McGraw-Hill Book Co., 1973.

11. *MCS-8 Assembly Language Programming Manual.* Intel Corp., November, 1973.

12. *Conversational Assembler Manual.* Publication No. 4200076X, National Semiconductor Corp., March, 1975.

13. FALK, HOWARD, "Microcomputer Software Makes Its Debut." *Spectrum* (October, 1974), pp. 78–84.

14. WEISS, C. DENNIS, "MOS/LSI Microcomputer Coding." *Electronic Design*, Vol. 8 (April 12, 1974), pp. 66–71.

15. KILDALL, GARY A., "High-Level Language Simplifies Microcomputer Programming." *Electronics* (June 27, 1974), pp. 103–109.

EXERCISES

5.1. Explain the relationship between symbolic language and machine language.

5.2. Write an algorithm for finding the roots of a quadratic equation

$$ax^2 + bx + c = 0$$

5.3. Draw a flow chart for the algorithm obtained in Exercise 5.2.

5.4. A binary number can be multiplied by 2 by simply shifting the number one bit to the left. Using this approach,
(a) Define an algorithm to multiply two 4-bit numbers.
(b) Draw a flow chart to implement the algorithm.

5.5. Write a program for the Intel 8008 (Appendix D) in symbolic language to implement the algorithm defined in Exercise 5.4. Assume the two 4-bit numbers are stored in locations AA and BB, respectfully, and that the resulting 8-bit number is to be stored in location CC.

5.6. Write the program for Exercise 5.5 in machine language.

5.7. Write the program of Exercise 5.5 for the Intel 8080 (Appendix E) microprocessor.

5.8. A frequent programming subtask is moving the data stored in one memory location to another. Using the Intel 8008, write a macro to transfer a data word from one location in memory to another.

5.9. Write a subroutine to perform an 8421 BCD to Gray code (Table 3.9) conversion for the following systems.
(a) Intel 4040
(b) Intel 8080

5.10. The accumulator of an 8008 microprocessor contains $C5_{16}$ and the carry is set (1). What will the accumulator and carry contain following each of the instructions?
(a) ANA A   (e) ACI 94_{16}
(b) ORA A   (f) SBI $0D6_{16}$
(c) XRA A   (g) RRC
(d) ADI 94_{16} (h) RAL

5.11. In an 8080 microcomputer system, the following conditions exist: A contains $4F_{16}$, B contains 27_{16}, H contains 00_{16}, L contains $0F_{16}$, and memory location $000F_{16}$ contains $2D_{16}$. The following program begins at memory location 0100_{16}.

```
ADD   B
ADC   M
DAA
MOV   M,A
```

Determine the new contents of all registers and memory locations that are altered. What is the content of the program counter following the MOV instruction?

5.12. Data sent to a computer is frequently formatted in blocks. The accuracy of the data is tested by summing the words in the block modulo n and comparing the result with the last word in the block (the checksum). Consider a system transmitting data to an 8080 system. A block of 24 8-bit words is transmitted. The first word in a block is always a RUBOUT (ASCII code FF_{16}, if space parity is used). The last word in the block is a checksum modulo 256. Write a program to read in the data words, test the checksum and output a 01_{16} on PORT 0 if an error occurs.

5.13. Consider a microcomputer system to aid in the preparation of income tax returns. The system automatically spaces to the next blank on the return, reads input data from the keyboard, performs the required arithmetical operations, and prints appropriately on the income tax form. Suppose that the system has read in the various components of income and has calculated the adjusted gross income. Write a program to space 30 spaces and then print the 7-digit number XXXXX.XX whose MSD is stored in INCOME. The teletypewriter (using 7-bit ASCII with space parity) is connected to PORT 0 through a parallel-to-serial converter (UART). The status of the interface may be read on bit 0 of PORT 1. Use the 8080 mnemonics.

6   INTERFACING AND PERIPHERAL DEVICES

6.1. INTRODUCTION

Microcomputers communicate with the outside world through the use of peripheral (I/O) devices. Peripherals that are commonly employed include teletypewriters, analog-to-digital (A/D) and digital-to-analog (D/A) converters, paper tape readers and punches, CRT displays, magnetic tape cassettes, and disk memories. When one or more I/O devices are connected to a microcomputer, an interface network for each device, called a *peripheral interface*, is required. This interface is necessary to convert information being transferred from the peripheral to the computer into a compatible format for the computer and, during a reverse transfer, to convert information from the computer to the peripheral into the required peripheral format. In addition, the interface usually must supply status information to the computer (e.g., READY· or BUSY) and reconcile any timing differences occurring between the computer and a peripheral [1].

Four functions which are common in peripheral interfaces are buffering, address decoding or device selection, command decoding, and timing and control [2]. Buffering is necessary to synchronize data exchanges between the processor and peripherals. Address decoding is required for selecting an I/O device in systems having more than one peripheral. Command decoding is provided in some systems for I/O devices that perform actions other than data transfers, such as rewinding a tape drive. Finally, each of these functions requires timing and control.

Data exchanges which occur between a microcomputer and peripheral devices fall into one of two categories, *programmed-data transfers* and *cycle-stealing transfers* [3–6]. In programmed-data transfers, the data exchange is controlled by the microcomputer program which transfers data, one word at a time, between the computer and an I/O device. On the other hand, cycle-stealing transfers, or direct memory access (DMA), are controlled by the peripheral device to allow mass transfer of a large block of data.

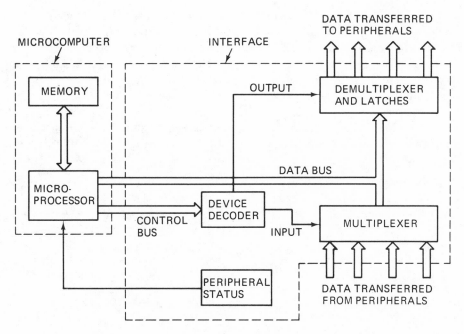

Fig. 6.1. Block diagram of a typical programmed-data transfer.

Programmed-data transfers are commonly used in all microcomputer systems. A block diagram for a typical transfer of this form is shown in Fig. 6.1. In this figure, a programmed I/O instruction to perform an input from one of the peripheral devices sends a command over the control bus to the device decoder. The decoder selects the appropriate channel in the multiplexer (Sec. 6.5). Each channel provides the necessary number of data paths required by the I/O device output. Next the status of the peripheral is received and tested by the microcomputer to determine if the device is ready (i.e., not busy processing another I/O command issued prior to the one in progress). The status of the peripheral is usually indicated in the interface by use of a flip-flop called a *flag*. When the device is ready, the appropriate multiplexer channel is enabled, and the data is transferred into the computer (e.g., into the accumulator) via the data bus. The multiplexer, in most systems, consists of a group of logic gates connected between the data bus and the output of each peripheral device. Gates having tri-state outputs (Sec. 2.6) are particularly useful in placing the multiplexed data onto the data bus. Since tri-state gates have very high impedances when not enabled, the outputs of all gates can be connected directly to the data bus. This virtually eliminates the calculation of impedance-loading effects necessary for conventional logic gates and substitutes, instead, the selection of the appropriate control lines for the tri-state gates.

For an output to a peripheral device, an I/O instruction issues a command to the device decoder to select the appropriate demultiplexer channel. The status of the peripheral is then tested and, when the device is ready, data from the computer is transferred to the peripheral through groups of latches (Sec. 2.4) in the demultiplexer channel. Since most peripherals are slower than microcomputers, the latches are used to hold the data from the bus until the transfer to the peripheral is completed. The latches, in this case, eliminate any errors which otherwise would occur due to timing differences between the processor and the peripheral. The logic gates making up the multiplexer and demultiplexer permit data exchanges for numerous peripherals via a single data bus. This method of operation is called *party line I/O*.

In the case of a DMA transfer, the data exchange is controlled entirely by hardware. As a result, the interface is more complex than that required for a programmed-data transfer. A block diagram for a typical DMA exchange is shown in Fig. 6.2.

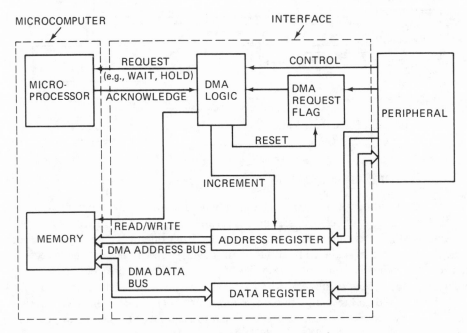

Fig. 6.2. Block diagram for a DMA transfer.

A DMA request is issued by the peripheral device which sets the request flag (flip-flop). This action causes the DMA logic to place the microprocessor in an idle condition via a processor terminal provided for this purpose (e.g., a HOLD or WAIT terminal). When the processor enters this state, it notifies the DMA logic by use of an ACKNOWLEDGE terminal on the processor. Most processors with DMA capability have tri-state gates on the data and address buses. When the processor acknowledges a HOLD or WAIT state, these gates are used to isolate the data and address buses from the processor. This allows external logic to take command of these buses and perform the DMA transfer.

Control information is supplied to the DMA logic to specify an input or output (WRITE or READ) operation in memory. The address register is loaded with the starting address, and a data exchange between the memory and a peripheral is executed. Following each transfer, the address register is incremented to select the next memory location. When the information exchange is completed, the peripheral issues a control command which resets the request flag and the request line to the processor. This action allows the microcomputer to continue with a normal programmed sequence.

Peripheral devices generate and accept data in either parallel or serial formats. Those that employ parallel formats, such as keyboards, A/D converters, and D/A converters, send or receive all bits in a data word simultaneously. In using these devices, the interface simply provides electrical compatibility and proper timing for transfers to and from the processor or DMA data bus. In devices that use serial formats, such as teletypewriters, tape cassettes, and modems, a data word is sent or received one bit at a time. The interface, in this case, must perform serial-to-parallel and parallel-to-serial transformations in exchanging data to and from the processor or DMA data bus. Special ICs for making these transformations, such as the universal asynchronous receiver-transmitter (UART), may be used for this purpose.

Extensive hardware is now available for designing custom interfaces. In this chapter, we will discuss interfacing methods for the different types of transfers. Since each microprocessor has a unique architecture, variations in I/O interface designs are quite extensive. The descriptions and circuits in the following sections, therefore, are structured to illustrate design concepts rather than the design of specific interfaces. Next, several IC interfacing components and programmable interfaces are described. Programmable interfaces are integrated circuits which can be programmed to perform many different interface functions. Finally, several popular, widely used peripherals are described.

6.2. PROGRAMMED-DATA TRANSFERS

Programmed-data transfers are employed in all microcomputers. These exchanges are executed under control of the program and are one of three types known as *synchronous transfers*, *asynchronous transfers*, and *program-interrupt transfers*.

Synchronous Transfers

A synchronous transfer is performed for peripherals whose timing is known. In this type of exchange, the I/O device must be ready for communication and accept or transmit data within the specified instruction time of the processor. The synchronous transfer is the most straightforward of all transfers and requires, in general, the least amount of hardware and software to implement.

As an example of a typical software routine, consider a system in which peripheral device 2 is an 8-bit A/D converter which is communicating with a microcomputer system having an 8-bit data bus. In addition, assume that this information is

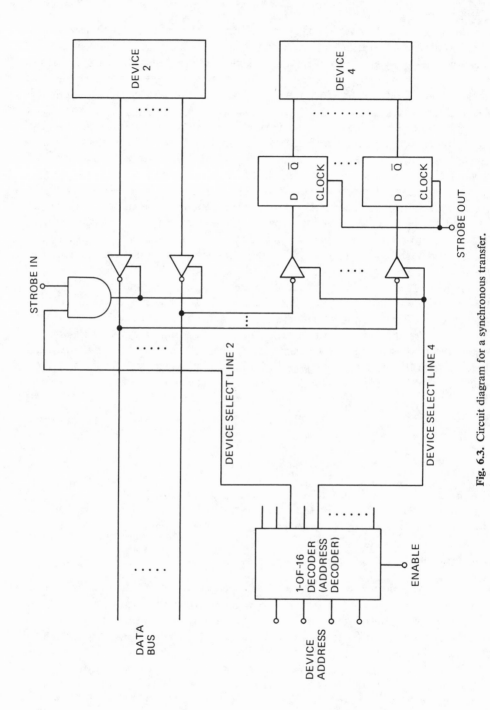

Fig. 6.3. Circuit diagram for a synchronous transfer.

154

processed by the microcomputer, and at some time later in the program sequence, the content of the accumulator is outputted to device 4, a D/A converter. A symbolic program, using the mnemonics of Appendix D (8008), is

.
.
.

IN   2

.
.
.

OUT 4

.
.
.

In this program, IN 2 issues a command to place the contents of device 2 (port 2) on the data bus irrespective of the status of the device. That is, the device is assumed to be ready and the contents of the data bus are transferred into the accumulator. Similarly, OUT 4 places the contents of the accumulator on the data bus and transfers this data to device 4 (port 4) without checking the status of the device.

A basic circuit which will perform the above-described exchange is shown in Fig. 6.3. When the input instruction is fetched from memory, a DEVICE ADDRESS (0010 in this case) is applied to the 1-of-16 decoder. The decoder allows a total of sixteen I/O devices to be accessed. An ENABLE pulse is applied to the decoder which activates DEVICE SELECT LINE 2. A STROBE IN pulse is then applied to the NAND gate which enables the tri-state inverters and transfers the data into the accumulator via the data bus. A timing diagram for this sequence is shown in Fig. 6.4.

In the case of an output to device 4, an output instruction is fetched and the content of the accumulator is placed on the data bus. A DEVICE ADDRESS (0100) pulse and ENABLE pulse are applied to the 1-of-16 decoder which activates DEVICE SELECT LINE 4. This line enables the tri-state inverters, placing the information on the data bus at the D inputs of the latches. A STROBE OUT pulse (Fig. 6.4) latches the data at the input to peripheral 4. The data remains latched until another output command is issued to this device.

In Fig. 6.3, the STROBE IN, STROBE OUT, ENABLE, and DEVICE ADDRESS are generated by the microprocessor with appropriate external logic. Since each processor has a unique architecture, the circuitry is dependent on the particular processor. All processors have status terminals which are used, in conjunction with status information issued on a data bus, to generate the timing and control signals. Normally, the DEVICE ADDRESS is issued on the address bus during the execute cycle of the I/O instruction. If the address is held on the bus for the duration of the transfer, it can be transferred to the decoder using AND gates or tri-state buffers which are activated by the ENABLE pulse. Some processors, however, use a single

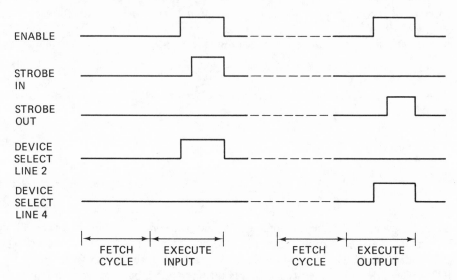

Fig. 6.4. Timing diagram for synchronous transfer of Fig. 6.3.

multiplexed bus for both addresses and data (e.g., the 8008). In this case, the address must be latched from the bus at the proper time in the cycle. The outputs of the latches then supply the DEVICE ADDRESS to the decoder.

In the above example, the A/D converter was assumed to be ready for the data transfer when the input command was issued. This requires that the device be activated and a time delay be allowed, sufficient for the A/D conversion to be completed, before the input instruction is executed. This could be accomplished, for instance, by performing an output instruction to another port (e.g., port 5) in a manner similar to that described above for port 4. The data at this port could then be used to activate the converter. This is a common method of activating devices in microcomputer systems prior to an I/O operation. A specific example of this method is presented in Sec. 8.2, Example 8.2.

In addition to the functions described in the above example, some processors (e.g., the Rockwell PPS-4) have I/O instructions which issue command information for peripheral control via a data bus. The COMMAND CODE from the bus is usually connected to all peripheral devices and is gated to the appropriate device with the device address line, as shown in Fig. 6.5. This information is decoded by the peripheral for use in controlling actions such as READ, WRITE, start a motor, etc. Processors having this capability are more efficient in many I/O operations since the command data does not pass through the accumulator to reach the peripheral. In processors not having this capability, these commands are generated using output instructions. Specific devices are dedicated to DEVICE SELECT LINES (ports), as described for the activation of the A/D converter.

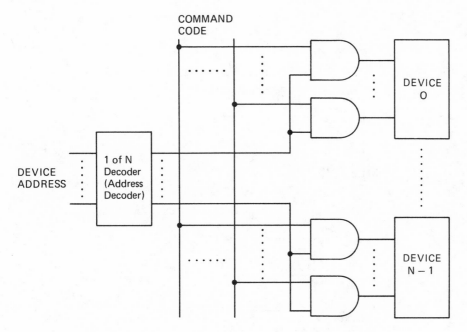

Fig. 6.5. Circuit for transfer of command code to peripheral devices.

Asynchronous Transfers

Asynchronous transfers, often called *handshaking I/O*, are commonly used in microcomputer systems [2–6]. In this type of transfer, the computer tests the peripheral before executing an I/O operation. A typical exchange consists of the following events (see Sec. 5.6):

1. Check the device status.

2. Activate the device when READY.

3. Transfer the data (input or output).

4. Deactivate the device.

In the first step, an instruction is executed to input the status of a selected peripheral. A conditional jump is then performed based on the condition of the status bit (step 2). If the device is busy, the program branches to repeat testing of the device status. If the device is ready, an I/O instruction is issued for either an input or output data exchange (step 3). At the termination of the transfer, the device is deactivated (step 4). A flow chart for this transfer is shown in Fig. 6.6.

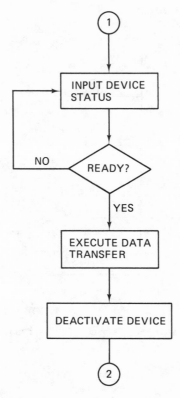

Fig. 6.6. Flow chart for an asynchronous transfer.

To illustrate an asynchronous transfer, consider a data input for an 8-bit A/D converter which is in the process of performing the analog-to-digital conversion. Suppose the converter is connected in a microcomputer system as device 1 (port 1) with a status flip-flop connected as device 2 (port 2) communicating with BIT LINE 4 of an 8-bit data bus. A symbolic program, using the mnemonics of Appendix E (8080), is

```
              .
              .
              .
TEST :  IN  2     ;  Contents of port 2 to accumulator (AC).
        ANI  10H  ;  Mask for bit 4.
        JZ  TEST  ;  If BUSY, jump to TEST.
        IN  1     ;  Transfer data to AC.
              .
              .
              .
              .
              .
```

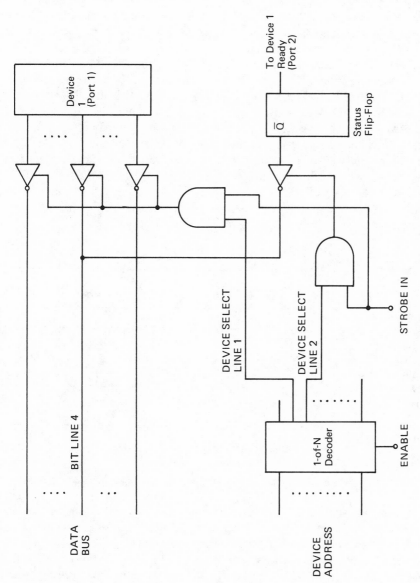

Fig. 6.7. Circuit for an asynchronous transfer.

159

In this program, IN 2 places the contents of port 2 (status of device 1) into the accumulator. If the device is ready, bit 4 is true. ANI 10H masks all bits except bit 4 and sets the ZERO flag if the device is not ready. JZ TEST loops the program until the device is ready. IN 1 then places the data from device 1 into the accumulator. It should be noted that the status of seven other devices could be tested using port 2 and appropriately masking the accumulator bits in the input program sequence.

A basic circuit to perform the transfers of the above program is shown in Fig. 6.7. When the input instruction (IN 2) to test the status of the device is issued, the DEVICE ADDRESS is applied to the 1-of-N decoder. This decoder allows N I/O ports to be addressed. An ENABLE pulse to this decoder activates DEVICE SELECT LINE 2 which places the status of device 1 into the status flip-flop ($\bar{Q} = 0$ for ready). A STROBE IN pulse then transfers this data into the accumulator via BIT LINE 4. If the device is busy ($\bar{Q} = 1$), the test sequence is repeated. When the device becomes ready, the instruction IN 1 is executed and the DEVICE ADDRESS activates DEVICE SELECT LINE 1. A STROBE IN pulse transfers the data of device 1 into the accumulator via the data bus. Port 1 is then deactivated at the termination of the ENABLE pulse. A typical timing diagram is shown in Fig. 6.8.

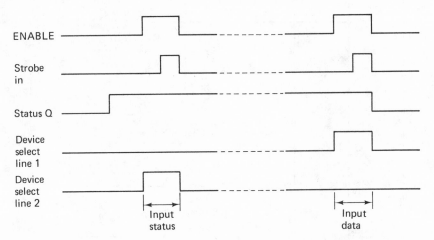

Fig. 6.8. Typical timing diagram for an asynchronous transfer.

In this example, the A/D converter is assumed to be performing the conversion when the input sequence is initiated. Prior to initiating the sequence, a start-conversion signal is required by the device. The signal may be generated either externally or by the computer. If the computer starts the conversion, an output instruction using a dedicated output port is necessary, as described in the synchronous-data transfer example.

An asynchronous transfer is ideal for reconciling timing differences between the peripheral and the processor. A disadvantage, however, is that the processor must delay (loop) until the peripheral is ready for the exchange. This is not only wasteful of computer time (if long delays are involved), but is impractical in many applications. In control processes, for instance, it may be necessary to maintain control signals while waiting for a transfer. A method of avoiding such difficulties is the use of program-interrupt transfers.

Program-Interrupt Transfers

Program-interrupt transfers are exchanges that alter the normal sequence of a computer program to permit an I/O operation [2–7]. They are particularly useful with slow peripherals or in applications where the occurrence of data to be transferred into the computer is unpredictable, e.g., in communications links. The main characteristic of this transfer is that data exchanges between the computer and peripheral devices are initiated by the devices. The implementation of such a system consists of replacing the wait loop of the asynchronous transfer with an equivalent loop in hardware to test for an external interrupt. During each machine operation, the microprocessor automatically checks for the presence of an interrupt signal.

In performing a simple interrupt transfer, the following steps usually occur:

1. An interrupt is requested by a peripheral device.
2. An acknowledgement of the interrupt is issued by the processor at the end of the current processor instruction.
3. The program counter is saved and the program branches to a memory address which contains a routine to process the interrupt.
4. The contents of internal (working and status) registers are saved and the data transfer is executed under software control.
5. Program execution is returned to the pre-interrupted program sequence.

Two methods of implementing the above sequence are commonly used in micro-computers. These are called *polled interrupts* and *vectored interrupts*. Polled interrupts are those in which each peripheral device is tested, using either hardware or software, until the requesting device is found. Program execution is then directed to the appropriate *interrupt-service routine* which executes the data exchange. In this method, the *priority* of the device is determined by the relative position of a device in the polling sequence. In contrast, vectored interrupts are those in which the requesting device causes program execution to proceed directly to the appropriate service routine. Therefore, in simple vectored systems, all devices have the same priority. Since polling is not required, vectored interrupts are generally faster than polled interrupts.

An interrupt request (step 1) is initiated by placing a signal on the microprocessor INTERRUPT terminal. In some processors, a software instruction is available for disabling this terminal. If disabled, the request is ignored and program execution continues in its normal sequence. When enabled, however, the interrupt is acknowledged at the termination of the current instruction cycle by a signal on an INTERRUPT ACKNOWLEDGE terminal or by simply beginning an interrupt cycle (step 2). Normally, the interrupt is disabled when step 2 is performed. This permits the processing of an interrupt to be completed before another interrupt is recognized. Next, the device requesting service is determined and the program counter is saved, or vice versa.

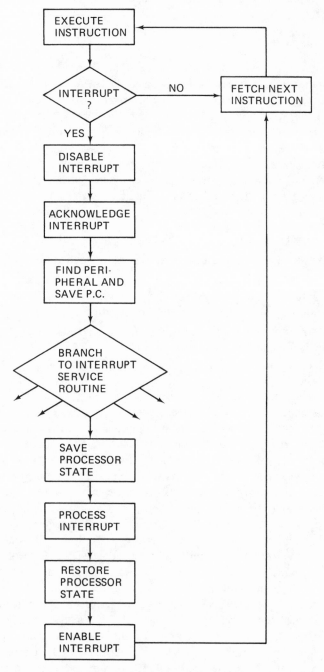

Fig. 6.9. Diagram for a program-interrupt transfer.

162

In a polling system, the polling sequence is performed in either hardware or software. In a vectored system, the device identifies itself following the interrupt acknowledgement. A branch to the appropriate interrupt-service routine is performed, completing step 3.

The initial instructions in a typical routine save the contents of the internal CPU registers. Instructions are then executed which perform the desired data exchange (step 4). Following the exchange, the CPU registers are restored to their pre-interrupted values. An interrupt enable instruction is performed (in processors having this capability) and program execution is returned to the original program, completing the transfer. A diagram for a typical transfer described above is shown in Fig. 6.9.

A simple method of implementing interrupt service is known as *software polling*. This technique requires that the interrupt status (flag) of each device be ORed on a single interrupt line. This line is connected to an INTERRUPT terminal on the processor. When an interrupt occurs, the flag of each device is tested according to a software polling routine. A flow chart for a simple testing sequence is shown in Fig. 6.10

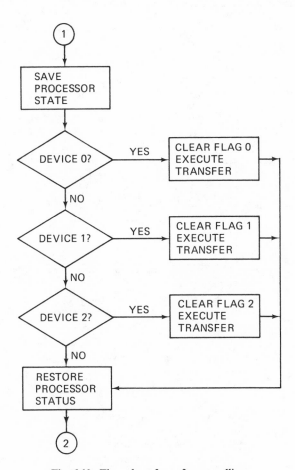

Fig. 6.10. Flow chart for software polling.

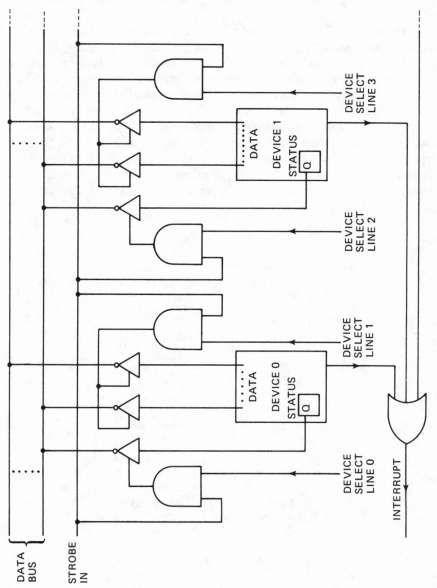

Fig. 6.11. Circuit for a software polled interrupt.

for three devices. Since the priority of each device is specified by its position in the polling sequence, device 0 obviously has the highest priority.

A circuit that performs software polling is shown in Fig. 6.11. In some processors (e.g., the Intel 4040), the interrupt request is acknowledged, the program counter is automatically saved (pushed on the stack), and program execution is directed to a specific position in memory ("trap cell"). Instructions in the trap cell result in saving the CPU status and testing the interrupt status of each device, as described for an asynchronous transfer. When the requesting device is found, program execution usually branches to an appropriate interrupt-service routine to perform the data exchange.

A common hardware-polling technique is known as *daisy-chaining*. In this method, the software polling previously described is replaced by random logic. A block diagram of a daisy-chain system is shown in Fig. 6.12. When an interrupt request is acknowledged, the INTERRUPT ACKNOWLEDGE is passed to device 0, the highest-priority device. If device 0 is requesting service, it will identify itself on the data bus and the ACKNOWLEDGE will not be passed to device 1. If device 0 has not generated an INTERRUPT REQUEST, it will pass the ACKNOWLEDGE to device 1. The procedure is continued until the requesting device is located.

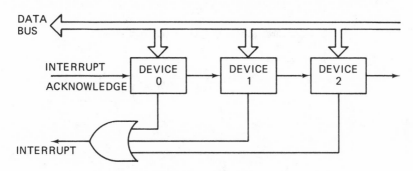

Fig. 6.12. Block diagram of a daisy-chain polling system.

The hardware necessary to convert the network of Fig. 6.11 into a daisy-chain system is shown in Fig. 6.13. In this figure, the DATA ENABLE lines replace the inputs from the DEVICE SELECT LINES of Fig. 6.11. When an interrupt occurs, the INTERRUPT ACKNOWLEDGE is activated, causing the device requesting service to supply the necessary information for addressing the correct interrupt-service routine. The data exchange is then executed.

A basic circuit for performing a vectored interrupt is shown in Fig. 6.14. For simplicity, the peripheral in this circuit is assumed to be device 2. In response to an interrupt request, the INTERRUPT ACKNOWLEDGE enables the tri-state buffers placing an interrupt address or a vector identity on the data bus. This immediately identifies the requesting device (device 2) and causes the program to branch to the appropriate interrupt-service routine. The DEVICE SELECT LINE 2 is activated and STROBE IN is pulsed, placing the data on the data bus. The content of the data bus

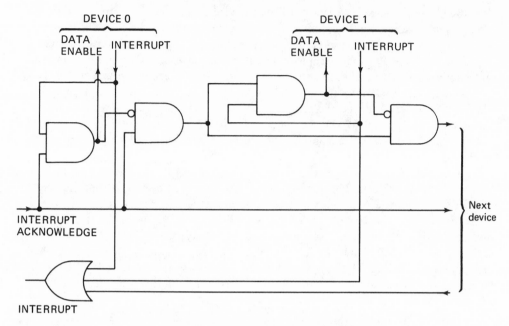

Fig. 6.13. Circuit for a daisy-chain interrupt transfer.

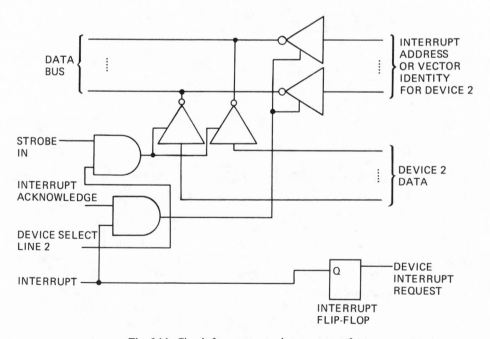

Fig. 6.14. Circuit for a program-interrupt transfer.

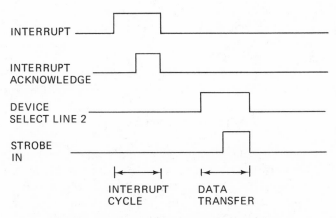

Fig. 6.15. Timing diagram for interrupt transfer of Fig. 6.14.

is loaded into the accumulator, which completes the transfer. A timing digram for the transfer of this circuit is shown in Fig. 6.15.

An assembly language program for the above transfer, using the mnemonics of the 8080, is

```
            JMP     INTR2 ;  Jump to interrupt-service
                  .         ;  routine for device 2.
                  .
                  .
                  .
   INTR2  : PUSH   B      ;  Save B and C registers.
            PUSH   D      ;  Save D and E registers.
            PUSH   H      ;  Save H and L registers.
            PUSH   PSW    ;  Save accumulator and status.
                  .
                  .         ;  Transfer instructions for
                  .         ;  device 2.
                  .
            POP    PSW    ;  Restore accumulator and status.
            POP    H      ;  Restore H and L registers.
            POP    D
            POP    B
            EI            ;  Enable interrupt.
            RET           ;  Return to pre-interrupt location.
                  .
                  .
```

In response to an interrupt request by device 2, the program counter is "vectored" to the JMP INTR2 instruction. In the Intel 8080, for example, a one-byte subroutine call (RST) is available for addressing one of eight locations in memory. The code for

RST 2, for instance, could be placed on the data bus in response to the interrupt. The JMP INTR2 instruction would then reside at this memory location. In addition, since RST is a subroutine call, the program counter is automatically pushed on the stack.

INTR2 is the interrupt-service routine for device 2. The PUSH instructions save the contents of the internal CPU registers. These are followed by instructions to perform the data transfer. At the termination of the transfer, the POP instructions restore the CPU registers, and EI enables the interrupt prior to returning to the regular program sequence.

In this example, all devices have the same priority when connected directly to the INTERRUPT ACKNOWLEDGE. A hardware priority system can be implemented by daisy-chaining the INTERRUPT ACKNOWLEDGE to each device. Some processors have two or more terminals for processing interrupts. For example, the National PACE has six INTERRUPT terminals which provide a priority vectored interrupt for six devices.

Multilevel or cascaded interrupts (interrupting an interrupt) are possible in many processors using interrupt enable flags to mask or unmask individual levels. This capability is particularly useful in systems having both slow and fast peripheral devices.

6.3. DMA TRANSFER

In a direct memory access (DMA) transfer, the peripheral device communicates directly with memory without disturbing the internal registers of the microprocessor. For a programmed-data transfer, such as an interrupt transfer, the task of processing an I/O exchange may require many hundreds of microseconds. If numerous external events occur, say once every 4 or 5 milliseconds on the average, then execution of the main program will be severely impeded [2]. In applications that require high-speed exchanges between a peripheral device and memory (e.g., loading memory from a floppy disk), the DMA transfer is the most efficient. It requires, however, a more complicated interface than that necessary for a programmed-data transfer.

Most processors with DMA capability have a terminal (e.g., a HOLD, WAIT, or PAUSE) which is activated by a peripheral device for a DMA transfer. When activated, it places the processor in an idle condition at the end of its current instruction and disables the address and data buses. Other terminals, such as HOLD ACKNOWLEDGE, acknowledge the request and permit external circuitry to execute the DMA transfer. Some processors, such as the RCA COSMAC, have a cycle-stealing capability [1]. There are normally two cycles for each program instruction, a fetch and an execute cycle. When the cycle-steal line is activated, the processor completes the execute cycle of the current instruction and then allows a one-cycle interval before beginning the next instruction. During this interval, data may be moved directly between memory and a peripheral.

The steps necessary for execution of a DMA transfer are:

1. A DMA request from a peripheral device.
2. Acknowledgement of the request by the processor.
3. Addressing of memory by external logic.
4. Data exchange between the peripheral device and memory (READ or WRITE).
5. Termination of the DMA.

In step 1, the peripheral requests a DMA transfer by enabling the appropriate processor terminal. The processor acknowledges this request after execution of its current instruction and disables the address and data buses (step 2). Most processors with DMA capability employ tri-state devices for output buffers to facilitate disabling the buses. During this state, the processor remains in an idle condition. External logic (a controller) takes command of the address and data buses and supplies an address to memory (step 3). The data exchange is then performed between memory and the selected device (step 4). In the case of transfers involving a block of data, the controller must supply the starting address, increment the memory address upon each data-

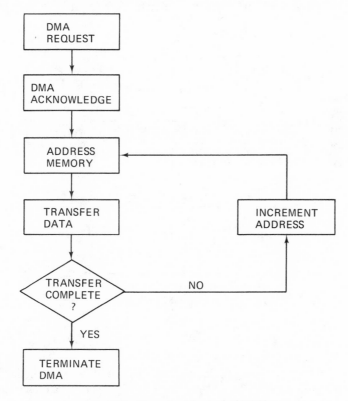

Fig. 6.16. Flow chart for typical DMA.

word exchange, and maintain a word count for the number of words to be transferred. Following the transfer, the controller terminates the DMA by disabling the appropriate processor terminal (HOLD, etc.), which completes step 5. In processors using this method (e.g., the Intel 8080), the enabling and disabling of this terminal usually must be synchronized with the microprocessor clock (Sec. 6.4). In others (e.g., the Motorola 6800), the DMA is terminated by use of an interrupt. A flow chart of a typical DMA is shown in Fig. 6.16.

A block diagram of a DMA system is shown in Fig. 6.2. In this figure, the DMA logic network to perform the above-described transfer includes the elements shown in the diagram of Fig. 6.17. The DEVICE ADDRESS activates the appropriate peripheral when the device decoder is enabled. The STARTING ADDRESS and the WORD COUNT are loaded into the memory counter and word counter, respectively. The WORD COUNT, in this case, represents the number of words in the block to be transferred. The first word of the block is then transferred, and the memory counter and word counter are incremented and decremented via the COUNT UP and COUNT DOWN inputs, respectively. The exchange continues and the word counter is decremented until it passes 0, generating a borrow signal. This signal is used to terminate the DMA. In transfers involving more than one data block, a block counter must also be included in the network to establish a reference for the number of blocks to be transferred.

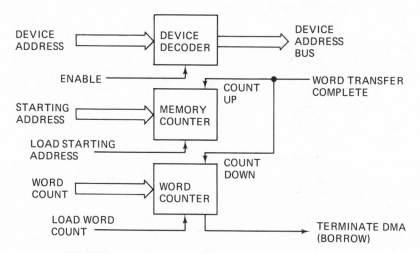

Fig. 6.17. Logic elements for DMA transfer of a data block.

6.4. SYNCHRONIZATION

Interfacing networks must provide timing compatibility between the microprocessor and peripheral devices. These networks generally operate in a *fundamental mode* to insure a stable and predictable response for the system [8]. Stated simply, the fundamental mode restriction requires that the inputs (both level and pulse) not be

allowed to change in logical value unless the system is in a stable state. Such a restriction requires that changes be synchronized with the system clock. In microcomputer systems, peripherals often operate from a separate clock, and synchronization of signals occurring between these units is required (e.g., during DMA and interrupt operations). Synchronization may also be required for time delays which result when a peripheral is remote from the processor. Interface circuits that are used to implement fundamental-mode operation are called *synchronizers*. They fall into two categories: synchronizers for pulse inputs and synchronizers for level inputs [3, 8].

A basic pulse synchronizer is a circuit that accepts a nonsynchronous pulse and delays it for a period of time necessary for synchronization with the system clock. A simple pulse synchronizer is shown in Fig. 6.18(a). This network consists of two

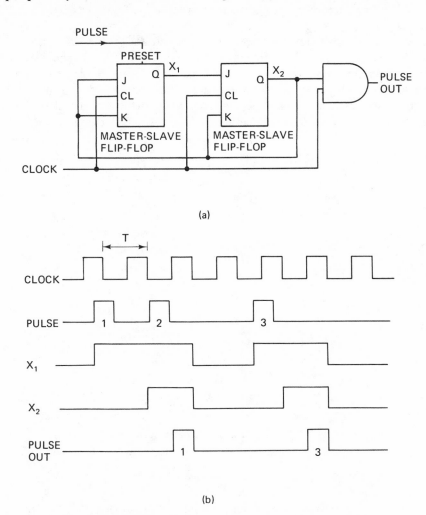

Fig. 6.18. Pulse synchronizer. (a) Circuit diagram. (b) Timing diagram.

master-slave J-K flip-flops and an AND gate. A nonsynchronous pulse occurring at the PRESET input of the first flip-flop sets the output (X_1) to 1. The first clock pulse following this event sets the second flip-flop (X_2) to 1. A second clock pulse generates an output pulse which is synchronized with CLOCK by the AND gate. Since the J and K inputs of both flip-flops are 1 at this time, they are reset at the termination of the clock pulse.

A timing diagram of the above sequence for three pulses is shown in Fig. 6.18(b). In this figure, we see that pulse synchronization is guaranteed only for pulses which are separated in time by at least two clock periods. This is illustrated by the loss of pulse 2 in the timing diagram. It should be noted that both flip-flops must be reset before the occurrence of another pulse for proper synchronization.

Level synchronizers are needed where unsynchronized data levels (e.g., data in peripheral registers) are present. Data levels which are being transferred, say to the processor data bus, must not be allowed to change until the exchange is completed. A simple circuit which performs this function is shown in Fig. 6.19(a). The circuit consists of a single D flip-flop. The timing diagram of Fig. 6.19(b) shows a typical data sequence for the device. Level synchronization is guaranteed only for a data input whose duration is at least one clock period. This is illustrated by the loss of data level 2 in the timing diagram. A level that occurs between two successive clock pulses will be lost.

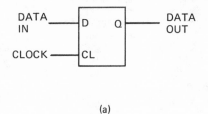

(a)

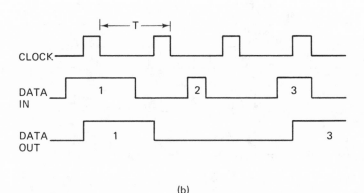

(b)

Fig. 6.19. Simple level synchronizer. (a) Circuit diagram. (b) Timing diagram.

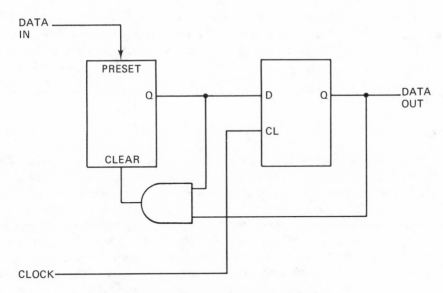

Fig. 6.20. Double-buffered level synchronizer.

An improved version of a level synchronizer which eliminates the data-loss problem is shown in Fig. 6.20. This network is a form of a *double-buffered* level synchronizer.

6.5. IC INTERFACE ELEMENTS

Numerous IC elements are available for use in constructing interfaces [9–12]. Included in these are multiplexers, line drivers and receivers, level translators and buffers, multivibrators, and special-purpose circuits. In this section, we shall discuss several typical devices that are often used in microcomputer interfaces to illustrate the variety of components available to the designer.

Multiplexers and Demultiplexers

A multiplexer is a device that selects data from one of two or more input data channels and transfers this data to its output. A mechanical equivalent of a solid state multiplexer is a multi-terminal rotary switch. Multiplexers are used extensively in microcomputer systems for permitting two or more devices to communicate with a single data bus. A simple circuit that functions as a multiplexer is the AND/OR gate combination of Fig. 4.37, which places data on the bus from either register A or B. This network represents a 2-input, 4-bit multiplexer.

Integrated circuit multiplexers are available in all logic families. These devices offer a wide variety of gating combinations. Typical circuits are the 8232 (8-input, 1-bit), 8233 (2-input, 4-bit), and 8263 (3-input, 4-bit) multiplexers.

A demultiplexer places data at its input into one of two or more output data channels. It performs the reverse function of a multiplexer. In Fig. 4.37, registers C and D represent a simple demultiplexer. Integrated circuit demultiplexers are available in a wide variety of gating combinations in most logic families. Typical devices are the 74154 (1-line to 16-line) and the 74155 (dual 1-line to 4-line or a 1-line to 8-line) demultiplexers.

Line Drivers and Receivers

Line drivers and receivers are used in microcomputer systems for communicating with peripheral devices. Data links constructed using these circuits fall into one of two classes known as *single-ended systems* and *differential systems* [9].

A single-ended system consists of a driver with a single output driving a line connected to a receiver with a single input and a common ground path, as shown in Fig. 6.21. A disadvantage of this method is that the current supplied by the driver must return through the common ground along with other system currents. These additional currents cause undesired signals to be generated at the receiver which may produce errors. The problem is reduced by providing a low-impedance ground system or by using several ground returns. Over short distances, standard or high-noise-immunity logic gates are generally suitable elements for implementing this type of system.

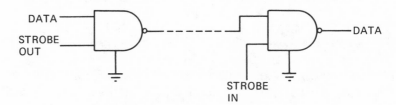

Fig. 6.21. Typical single-ended system.

Differential systems are used in communication links in which peripherals are far from or have different ground systems than the microcomputer. They are also used in high-noise environments. Differential systems are either *balanced* or *unbalanced*.

A balanced differential system consists of a driver with complementary outputs that drive a balanced two-wire transmission line into a receiver having differential inputs [Fig. 6.22(a)]. The inputs to the receiver must generally be matched to the transmission line using external components since most receivers have large input impedances. A balanced system largely ignores noise or voltages common to both lines (common-mode noise and common-mode voltage) [13]. A disadvantage, however, is that a balanced system is more complex than a single-ended system.

An unbalanced differential system consists of a driver having a single output and a differential input receiver, as shown in Fig. 6.22(b). This system gives protection from

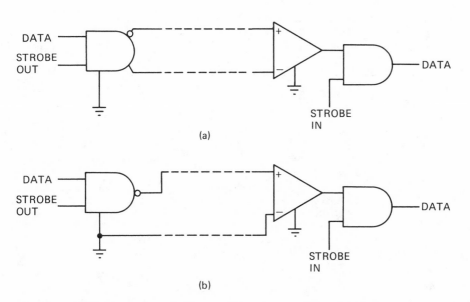

Fig. 6.22. Typical differential system. (a) Balanced. (b) Unbalanced.

noise common to the signal and ground lines, but inductive coupling between different signal lines is increased by a common ground return. This disadvantage must be weighed against the hardware and cost savings of an unbalanced system with common ground (including the single-ended system) over a completely balanced system.

Many different types of line drivers and receivers are available in the various IC logic families. Some are very important in bus-organized systems for transmitting and receiving information. A popular form of bus driver employed by designers is the open-collector TTL logic because of its wire-OR capability [14]. An example of one such device is a 7426 quad two-input high-voltage NAND gate (Sec. 2.6). This device features a high-voltage open-collector output for interfacing with high-level circuits (e.g., MOS circuits, lamps, and relays) or TTL inputs. Simple TTL receivers for single-ended systems include standard gates such as the 7400.

Another important type of line driver employs tri-state output circuitry. A typical device of this kind is the 8T09 quad bus driver shown in Fig. 6.23. Each inverter in this device can sink 40 mA and drive a 300-pF load with a guaranteed propagation delay of less than 22 ns. Tri-state devices eliminate the need for pull-up resistors which are required by open-collector devices. In addition, they improve system speed in many applications as compared to those employing open-collector circuits [15]. Systems which are designed using tri-state elements are usually single-ended. Many of the gates in the descriptions of the previous sections (e.g., Fig. 6.3) are tri-state devices.

A quad D-type bus flip-flop (8T10) is shown in Fig. 6.24. This device is particularly useful in applications where data to be transferred to a bus requires latching (see

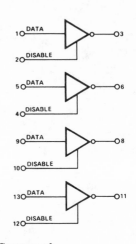

Data	Disable	Output
0	0	1
1	0	0
0	1	Hi- Z
1	1	Hi- Z

V_{CC} = (14)
GND = (7)
( ) = Denotes Pin Numbers for
14 Pin Dual-in-Line Package

Fig. 6.23. Logic diagram and truth table for the 8T09 (Courtesy of Signetics Corporation, Sunnyvale, California).

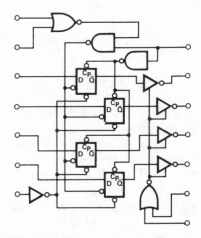

D_n	IN_{DIS}	OUT_{DIS}	0_{n+1}
0	0	0	0
1	0	0	1
X	1	0	0_n
X	X	1	High Z

0_n refers to the output state before a clock pulse.

0_n + 1 refers to the output state after a clock pulse.

Fig. 6.24. Logic diagram and truth table for the 8T10 (Courtesy of Signetics Corporation, Sunnyvale, California).

Fig. 6.7). Data held in each latch is outputted via a tri-state inverter. Each inverter permits up to twenty standard loads to be interconnected to a single data bus. The maximum clock frequency is typically 50 MHz.

Line drivers and receivers are also available for data transmission between data communication and terminal equipment. Devices such as the 8T15 and 8T16 are dual communications EIA/MIL line drivers and receivers, respectively. These circuits are designed for systems with equipment employing industry standards such as the EIA RS-232B and C [16], MIL STD 188B, and CCITT V 24. They are very useful for serial data transmission, and differential inputs are provided at the receiver for high common-mode noise immunity.

Level Translators and Buffers

Level translators and buffers are used for interfacing circuits of different logic families as well as for interconnecting logic families and I/O hardware, such as relays and lamps. Since many microprocessors employ MOS technology, translators from MOS-to-TTL and TTL-to-MOS are very useful. A circuit that can be used to perform TTL-to-MOS translation is the 8T90 hex-interface buffer of Fig. 6.25. Each buffer can couple low-level (typically 5 V and 25 mW) logic to a higher level (typically 28 V and 280 mW).

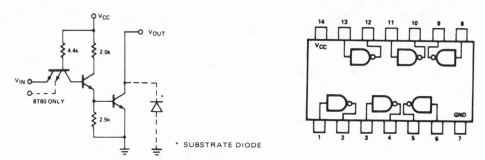

Fig. 6.25. Schematic and logic diagram for an 8T90 (Courtesy of Signetics Corporation, Sunnyvale, California).

An interface element that complements the 8T90 in performing the opposite translation from high to low level is the 8T18 (Fig. 6.26). This circuit has an extremely stable logic threshold and can entirely eliminate up to 6.5 volts of noise on an information signal. The 8T18 effectively couples a high signal, such as that occurring in a MOS circuit, to a lower level while providing digital threshold noise separation and buffer isolation.

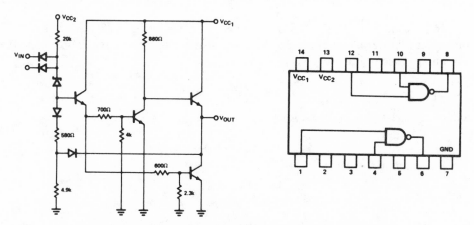

Fig. 6.26. Schematic and logic diagram for an 8T18 (Courtesy of Signetics Corporation, Sunnyvale, California).

Multivibrators

Two important classes of multivibrators for use in generating timing signals are *astable* and *monostable* multivibrators. Astable multivibrators are oscillators whose free-running frequency and duty cycle are controlled by one or more external resistors and capacitors. Monostables, often called *one-shots*, are circuits that produce a single output pulse as a result of a transition at the input. The duration of the output pulse is generally controlled by a single resistor and capacitor.

Astable multivibrators are useful in generating clock signals for microprocessors and microcomputer peripherals. A popular IC timing circuit is the type 555 of Fig. 6.27. This particular device is capable of operating in both the astable and monostable modes, giving timing from microseconds to hours.

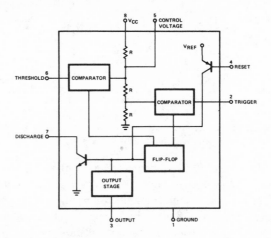

Fig. 6.27. Block diagram of the 555 timer (Courtesy of Signetics Corporation, Sunnyvale, California).

In the astable mode, the 555 is connected as shown in Fig. 6.28(a). The values of the necessary external resistors (R_A, R_B) and capacitor (C) are shown in Fig. 6.28(b). The charge time (output high) is given by

$$t_1 = 0.693(R_A + R_B)C$$

and the discharge time (output low) by

$$t_2 = 0.693R_B C$$

The free-running frequency is

$$f = \frac{1.44}{(R_A + 2R_B)C} = \frac{1}{T}$$

where T is the period of oscillation. The frequency, f, is easily found from Fig. 6.28(b).

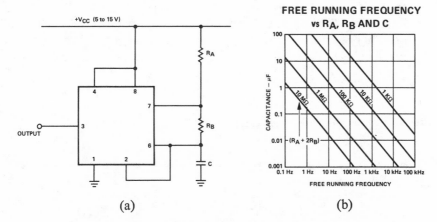

(a)   (b)

Fig. 6.28. Astable operation of the 555. (a) Circuit diagram. (b) Timing chart. (Courtesy of Signetics Corporation, Sunnyvale, California).

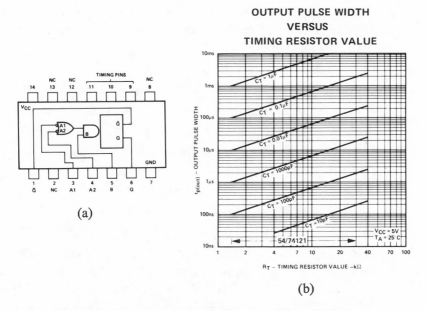

(a)   (b)

Fig. 6.29. 74121 Monostable Multivibrator. (a) Logic diagram. (b) Timing chart. (Courtesy of Signetics Corporation, Sunnyvale, California).

Monostables, or one-shots, are useful for generating precise time delays which are often necessary in interface networks. A popular TTL one-shot is the 74121 of Fig. 6.29(a). In this circuit, A1 and A2 are negative edge-triggered logic inputs that trigger the one-shot when either or both go to logical 0 with B at logical 1. B is a positive

Schmitt-trigger input for slow transitions that trigger the device when B goes to logical 1 with either A1 or A2 at logical 0. A desired pulse width is obtained by connecting a capacitor C_T (10 pF to 10 μF) between pin 10 (positive) and pin 11. An external variable resistor R_T (2–40 kΩ) is connected between pin 9 and pin 14 for variable pulse widths, given by

$$t_p = 0.693 C_T R_T$$

This relationship is shown by the timing chart of Fig. 6.29(b).

6.6. PROGRAMMABLE INTERFACES

A *programmable interface* is one whose function may be altered by an instruction from the microprocessor. Such an interface may provide bidirectional data flow between a peripheral and a processor, control the transmission of serial data, implement a DMA transfer, assist in the handling of interrupts, etc. Programmable interfaces usually require little or no external hardware in interconnecting a peripheral and a microprocessor.

A very important programmable element is the universal asynchronous receiver transmitter (UART). The UART converts asynchronous serial data to a parallel format, and vice versa, as shown in Fig. 6.30.

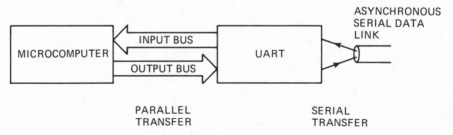

Fig. 6.30. Block diagram of a typical system employing a UART.

A typical UART is the Texas Instruments TMS 6011 shown in Fig. 6.31 [17]. The receiver section of the circuit accepts serial data from a transmission line and converts it to parallel data. The serial word can have a start bit, five to eight data bits, a parity bit, and one or two stop bits. The number of data bits desired is programmable from five to eight bits. The parity can be selected as either even or odd, or it can be completely disabled. One or two stop bits can also be selected. The transmitter section accepts parallel data and converts it to the above-described serial format. The receiver and transmitter sections are separate, and the device can operate in either a full-duplex (simultaneous transmission and reception) or in a half-duplex mode (alternate transmission and reception).

Operation of the 6011 is most easily understood by considering it as three separate sections: (1) transmitter, (2) receiver, and (3) common control. The transmitter and

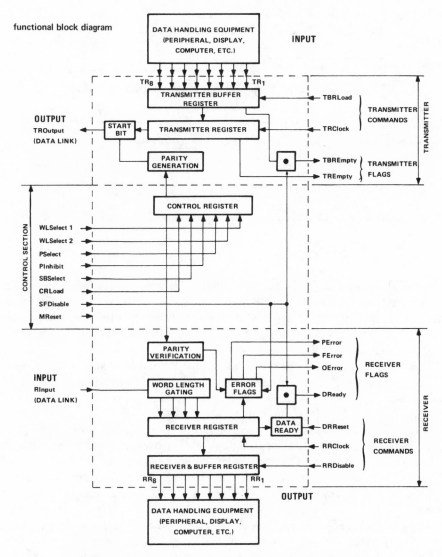

Fig. 6.31. Functional block diagram of the TMS 6011 UART.
(Courtesy of Texas Instruments).

receiver are independent, while the control section directs both receive and transmit functions.

The transmitter section receives parallel input data on input terminals TR_1 through TR_8. The data is loaded into the transmitter buffer register and transferred to the transmitter register using the TBRLoad terminal. Serial data is transmitted on the TROutput terminal as a result of a clock input to TRClock. The clock rate is 16 times the data rate.

operation timing diagram

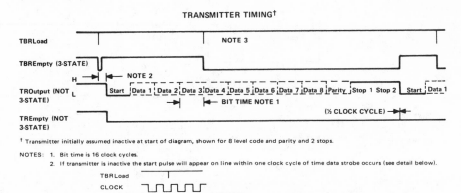

Fig. 6.32. Diagram of TMS 6011 transmitter timing. (Courtesy of Texas Instruments).

Flags TBEmpty and TREmpty are provided. TBEmpty flag indicates that a word has been transferred to the transmitter/receiver and that the transmitter buffer register is ready to accept a new word. The TREmpty flag indicates that the transmitter section has completed the transmission of a complete word. A diagram for the transmitter timing is shown in Fig. 6.32.

The receiver section accepts serial data on the RInput terminal. Data, clocked at 1/16 the rate of RRClock, is transferred from the receiver register to the receiver buffer register (RR_1 through RR_8). The RRDisable terminal is used to place the RR tri-state outputs into the high-impedance state.

Several flags are provided in the receiver section. The PError, FError, and OError flags indicate a parity error, framing error, or overrun error, respectively. An overrun error occurs when the previous word has not been read, i.e., when the DReady line has not been reset before the present data was transferred to the receiver register. DRReset is used to reset DReady. A diagram of the receiver timing is shown in Fig. 6.33.

The control section directs both the receiver and transmitter sections. MReset (master reset) is used to initialize the device. WLSelect 1, WLSelect 2, PSelect, PInhibit, and SBSelect are used to select the data, parity, and stop bits. The Baud rate (bits/s) is determined by the clock frequency which can vary from 0–200 kHz. The device is packaged in a 40-pin DIP and requires power supply voltages of $+5$ V and -12 V.

A useful programmable interface for the Rockwell PPS systems is the Telecommunications Data Interface (TDI) circuit [18]. The TDI is a combination modem (Sec. 6.7) and UART which allows asynchronous data transmission over telephone lines at a data rate up to 1200 bits/s. Other interfaces for these systems include a General Purpose I/O (GPI/O) circuit and a DMA Controller.

The Peripheral Interface Adapter (PIA) by Motorola is a programmable interface for use with the 6800 microprocessor [1]. It is used to control bidirectional data flow and interrupt requests from peripherals. Another interface developed for this system

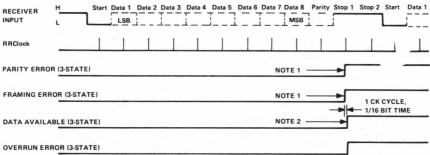

NOTES: 1. This is the point at which the error condition is detected, if error occurs.
2. Data available is set only when the received data has been transferred to the buffer register. Data available going High also transfers PE, FE, or the status word holding register (see block diagram).
3. All information is good in buffer register until data available tries to set for next character.
4. Above shown for 8-level code, parity and 2-stop. For no parity, stop bits follow data.
5. For all-level code, the data in the buffer register must be right-justified, i.e., RD_1 (pin 12).

Fig. 6.33. Diagram of the TMS 6011 receiver timing. (Courtesy of Texas Instruments).

is the Asynchronous Communications Interface Adapter (ACIA) which performs the functions of a UART.

6.7. PERIPHERALS

Peripherals are used in microcomputer systems to communicate with the outside world. Generally these devices are relatively small in size and can be placed on a table top or rack-mounted. In contrast to peripherals employed in large computer systems, microcomputer peripherals are usually at the lower end of the performance scale. Peripheral selection is important because in many instances, the cost of these devices exceeds that of the microcomputer system. In this section, we shall describe several peripherals which are in common use.

Analog-to-Digital and Digital-to-Analog Converters

Analog-to-digital (A/D) converters are devices that convert analog input data, which are usually voltages or currents, into digital form [19]. Three types of A/D converters are commonly available from manufacturers. One uses a counter-comparator technique and another uses a dual-slope integrator method. A third type, which uses successive-approximation, is the most popular because it offers the user an excellent compromise between speed and accuracy.

An ideal 3-bit binary A/D converter has a staircase transfer characteristic as shown in Fig. 6.34. An analog input voltage is quantized into 2^n levels for a converter with n bits. The true analog value corresponding to a given output code is centered between two decision levels. There are $2^n - 1$ non-zero analog decision levels, and the quantization size, Q, is equal to the full-scale range of the converter divided by 2^n. Q in this case is equal to the value of the LSB. The maximum conversion error is $\pm Q/2$.

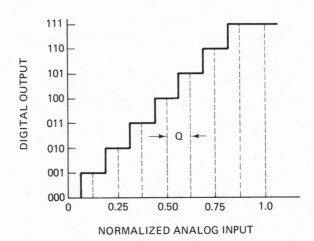

Fig. 6.34. Transfer characteristics for a 3-bit A/D converter.

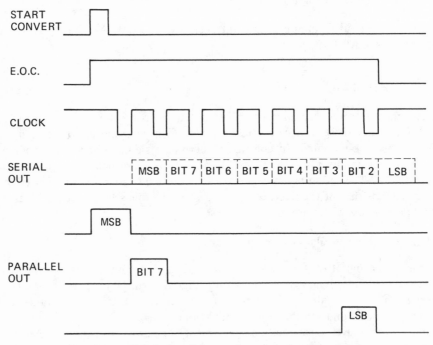

Fig. 6.35. Typical timing diagram of a successive-approximation A/D converter.

A typical timing diagram for a successive-approximation 8-bit A/D converter is shown in Fig. 6.35. A START CONVERT pulse is applied to the device which sets an END-OF-CONVERSION (E.O.C.) output terminal HI and initiates the A/D conversion process. The digital output bits are generated sequentially beginning with the

MSB and proceeding to the LSB. When the conversion is completed, the E.O.C. returns to a LO state. This signal is normally tested by the device requesting the conversion (e.g., a microcomputer) to determine when the converter is "ready" following a START CONVERT pulse. A/D converters are available with serial and/or parallel data outputs.

Digital-to-analog (D/A) converters perform the inverse A/D process of converting digital data into analog signals. These devices usually consist of a weighted-resistor network or a resistor-ladder network [19]. The resistor-ladder network is the best-known and most widely used.

An ideal 3-bit D/A converter transfer characteristic is shown in Fig. 6.36. There is a one-to-one correspondence between the input and output that does not exist for an A/D converter.

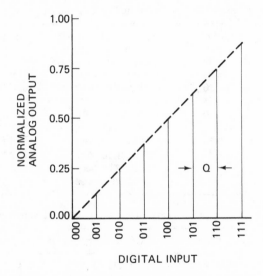

Fig. 6.36. Ideal 3-bit D/A converter transfer characteristic.

A/D and D/A converters are available with both unipolar and bipolar codes. Unipolar converters usually have positive inputs, whereas bipolar converters allow positive and negative inputs. Codes used with unipolar converters include straight binary, complementary binary, and BCD codes. Bipolar converter codes include 1's complement, 2's complement, offset binary, and sign-and-magnitude binary or BCD codes. There are also reflective and error-detecting codes such as the Gray and Hamming codes. Several popular codes are shown in Tables 6.1–6.3.

Paper Tape Readers/Punches

Paper tape is often used in microcomputer systems as an economical method of recording programs and data. Readers are available in low-speed to high-speed versions which read from 10 to 1000 characters/s. Punches, on the other hand, punch from

Table 6.1 UNIPOLAR CONVERTER BINARY CODES (12-bit converter)

Scale	+10 V FS	Straight Binary	Complementary Binary
+FS−1 LSB	+9.9976	1111 1111 1111	0000 0000 0000
+7/8 FS	+8.7500	1110 0000 0000	0001 1111 1111
+3/4 FS	+7.5000	1100 0000 0000	0011 1111 1111
+5/8 FS	+6.2500	1010 0000 0000	0101 1111 1111
+1/2 FS	+5.0000	1000 0000 0000	0111 1111 1111
+3/8 FS	+3.7500	0110 0000 0000	1001 1111 1111
+1/4 FS	+2.5000	0100 0000 0000	1011 1111 1111
+1/8 FS	+1.2500	0010 0000 0000	1101 1111 1111
0+1 LSB	+0.0024	0000 0000 0001	1111 1111 1110
0	0.0000	0000 0000 0000	1111 1111 1111

Table 6.2 UNIPOLAR CONVERTER BCD CODES (3-digit converter)

Scale	+10 V FS	Binary-Coded Decimal	Complementary BCD
+FS−1 LSB	+9.99	1001 1001 1001	0110 0110 0110
+7/8 FS	+8.75	1000 0111 0101	0111 1000 1010
+3/4 FS	+7.50	0111 0101 0000	1000 1010 1111
+5/8 FS	+6.25	0110 0010 0101	1001 1101 1010
+1/2 FS	+5.00	0101 0000 0000	1010 1111 1111
+3/8 FS	+3.75	0011 0111 0101	1100 1000 1010
+1/4 FS	+2.50	0010 0101 0000	1101 1010 1111
+1/8 FS	+1.25	0001 0010 0101	1110 1101 1010
0+1 LSB	+0.01	0000 0000 0001	1111 1111 1110
0	0.00	0000 0000 0000	1111 1111 1111

Table 6.3 BIPOLAR CONVERTER BINARY CODES (12-bit converter)

Scale	±5 V FS	Offset Binary	2's Complement
+FS−1 LSB	+4.9976	1111 1111 1111	0111 1111 1111
+3/4 FS	+3.7500	1110 0000 0000	0110 0000 0000
+1/2 FS	+2.5000	1100 0000 0000	0100 0000 0000
+1/4 FS	+1.2500	1010 0000 0000	0010 0000 0000
0	0.0000	1000 0000 0000	0000 0000 0000
−1/4 FS	−1.2500	0110 0000 0000	1110 0000 0000
−1/2 FS	−2.5000	0100 0000 0000	1100 0000 0000
−3/4 FS	−3.7500	0010 0000 0000	1010 0000 0000
−FS+1 LSB	−4.9976	0000 0000 0001	1000 0000 0001
−FS	−5.0000	0000 0000 0000	1000 0000 0000

10 to 150 characters/s. The tape is normally stored on a reel or is folded into a rectangular container (*fan-fold*) and is generally available in 1000-ft lengths.

Paper tape varies in width from $\frac{1}{2}$ to 1 inch, having 5- to 8-bit characters, respectively [20]. The bits are represented by perforations in the tape at each bit site. Usually a hole represents a 1, and the absence of a hole represents a 0. A commonly used paper tape is the 8-level tape shown in Fig. 6.37. It has eight lateral bit sites which are

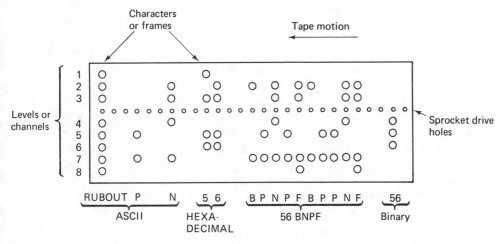

Fig. 6.37. 8-level paper tape.

called *characters* or *frames*. The bits within each character are called *levels* or *channels*. The row of holes positioned between levels 3 and 4 are necessary for the mechanical sprocket drive to advance the tape.

Many codes are available for representing data on the tape. In Fig. 6.37 the 7-level ASCII code (Sec. 3.7) is shown for the characters RUBOUT, P, N, 5, and 6. Note that these characters are represented by levels 1 through 7. The eight level can be used as a parity bit (lateral parity) for each character. In Fig. 6.37, the eight level represents an even parity.

Numerous formats are used for representing data on paper tapes. A common one is the *BNPF* format. In this representation, the ASCII character B is used to designate the beginning of a data word. ASCII characters P and N follow to represent 1's and 0's, respectively. An ASCII F denotes the end of the data word. With BNPF tapes, lateral parity can be employed. Error detection using this format is extremely good. Tapes can also be punched directly from a standard ASCII keyboard. The efficiency in terms of the number of characters required to represent a given amount of data is poor. In Fig. 6.37, it is shown that at least ten ASCII characters are required to represent the decimal number 56.

Other popular representations include the *binary* and *hexadecimal* formats. In the binary case, the data is represented by eight binary characters per frame. Since the eight level is used in this representation, lateral parity is not permitted. In the hexadecimal format, the ASCII codes for the hexadecimal numbers 0 through F are employed to represent each character. The use of the ASCII code permits a lateral parity check for error detection. It also allows tapes to be generated directly from a standard ASCII keyboard, a feature not possible for a binary tape. Binary and hexadecimal formats are shown in Fig. 6.37 for the decimal number 56. Notice that the hexadecimal representation requires twice as many characters as the binary case for a given number of data words.

Tapes for machine language programs (object tapes) are usually in binary or hexadecimal formats. They are read into the computer in discrete *records* or *blocks*. A typical block format includes a start character, record-length characters, load-address characters, data characters, and a checksum character. The start character indicates the beginning of a block. The record-length characters are used to notify the computer (via the loader program) of the actual number of data bytes in the record. Load-address characters provide the starting memory address into which the data is to be loaded. The data characters are loaded into memory and the checksum character is used as a longitudinal parity check. The checksum character contains the sum of all bytes in the record evaluated modulo 256 (i.e., the carry bit in the sum is neglected). The loader program performs this sum during the loading process and compares the result to the checksum. An error has occurred during the loading procedure if the two are not equal. Most object tapes consist of many blocks. A typical block contains 256 data bytes.

Teletypewriters

Teletypewriters are commonly used, general-purpose I/O devices. One very popular, economical type is the ASR-33 (automatic send-receive teletypewriter set) manufactured by the Teletype Corporation [21]. This device offers a keyboard which transmits 7-level ASCII characters, a typing unit for producing hard copy, a paper tape reader, and a paper tape punch. The device is a low-speed unit which transmits or receives data at a maximum rate of 10 characters/s.

The ASR-33 can be operated in a so-called LINE or LOCAL mode. In the LOCAL mode, the unit does not communicate with the microcomputer. Characters entered from the keyboard are typed. If the paper tape punch is turned on, keyboard characters are punched on an 8-level tape in the ASCII format described previously. Parity options available include even, mark, and space parities. The contents of a tape inserted into the reader are typed and also reproduced on tape if the punch unit is activated.

In the LINE mode, the ASR-33 communicates with the computer. Keyboard characters are transmitted as serial ASCII characters. Serial ASCII characters which are received from the computer are typed or perform special functions such as line feed and carriage return. In addition, all 256 binary combinations may be punched, read, and transmitted from paper tape.

Communication between the ASR-33 and a microcomputer is performed in a serial code. The code consists of eleven elements per character in which a 0 and 1 are called a *space* and *mark*, respectively. The first element is a start bit (always a space). This is followed by eight elements (bits) which comprise the character being transmitted. The final two elements are stop bits (always marks). The start and stop bits or pulses are used for synchronization purposes. Each element or bit within the code requires 9.09 ms, which results in a total of 10 characters/s or a 110 Baud rate. The TROutput of Fig. 6.32 represents the timing sequence for the serial information if the parity bit following bit 8 is eliminated.

The ASR-33 can be operated in either a half- or full-duplex mode. A current interface is standard for either a 20-mA or 60-mA current loop. This connection can be several hundred feet in length. An EIA RS 232C voltage interface is also available, but the hardwired connection is limited to approximately 100 ft.

Magnetic Tape Cassettes

Magnetic tape cassette units provide a substitute for paper tape readers and punches as a means of data manipulation and storage. Cassettes have the advantages of low cost, compact size, ease of loading, and superior editing capability [7]. A disadvantage, however, is the relatively high error rate for the device. This rate, depending on the recording technique, can approach one bit per 10^6 recorded, which represents five to ten errors per cassette.

A popular cassette is the Philips cassette which consists of two flangeless reels mounted in a plastic package having approximate dimensions of $2\frac{1}{2} \times 4 \times \frac{3}{8}$ inches. The cassette contains 300 ft of oxide-coated Mylar tape having a width of 0.15 in. Access to the tape is obtained through an aperture in the edge of the container. Numerous mechanisms have been designed for driving the tape. The simpler designs use friction drives in which the tape is driven between a roller and capstan. More sophisticated designs actually remove the portion of the tape being read from the cassette.

Cassette drives are available using either continuous recording or incremental recording techniques. Both methods usually record serially with one or two *tracks* on the tape, where a track is analogous to a channel or level of a paper tape. In continuous recorders, serial groups of eight to sixteen bits form *characters* or *words*. Groups of words (two to several thousand) form *blocks* or *records*, and groups of records (two to several hundred) constitute *files*. Records are separated by *interrecord gaps* which are typically 0.5 to 1 in. long. Continuous recorders can record up to 700,000 characters per cassette, depending on the number of interrecord gaps and the recording density (bits/inch).

Incremental recorders read and record on the tape by starting and stopping the tape for each bit or character. This eliminates the need for large interrecord gaps. A disadvantage, however, is a lower recording density due to the mechanical inertia of the tape drive mechanism in starting and stopping. The cassette storage capacity is typically 50,000 to 100,000 characters per cassette.

Important cassette tape characteristics include cassette capacity, record file length, recording technique, number of tracks, recording density, error rate and detection capability, interrecord gap length, and character transfer rates. Industrial standards for cassettes have been established by the European Computer Manufacturers Association (ECMA) and the American National Standards Institute (ANSI). Most manufacturers, however, prefer to design units for the broadest of user markets and do not necessarily adhere to the above standards.

A typical continuous recorder has a data format as shown in Fig. 6.38 for the Texas Instruments Silent 700 ASR twin cassette hard copy terminal [22]. The cassette

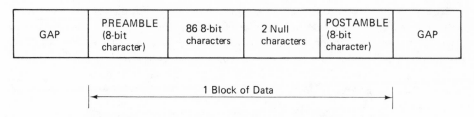

GAP	PREAMBLE (8-bit character)	86 8-bit characters	2 Null characters	POSTAMBLE (8-bit character)	GAP

1 Block of Data

Fig. 6.38. Tape data format for the Texas Instruments Silent 700 ASR twin cassette terminal.

unit has a recording density of 800 bits/in. with a recording speed of 8 in./s. The error rate is 1 in 10^6 maximum. The terminal consists of a standard ASCII keyboard which provides hardcopy at 10, 15, or 30 characters/s using a thermal printer and special heat-sensitive paper. The unit is a medium-speed replacement for the 10-characters/s teletypewriter.

Modems

The term *modem* is an acronym for *mo*dulator-*dem*odulator. The primary modem function is to convert digital data into an analog form which is suitable for transmission on common carrier circuits (e.g., telephone lines) [23, 24]. Modulation is the D/A conversion in which the digital data is placed on the transmission line by modulation of a tone or carrier. Demodulation is the reverse process.

In a data communication system (Fig. 6.39), transmitting and receiving modems are necessary at each end of the analog transmission line. The interfaces in the modulator and demodulator sections are usually EIA RS 232C or current loop interfaces providing connections for standard external devices. The output transmitting circuits and receiving circuits are networks required for transmitting and receiving analog information to and from the transmission line.

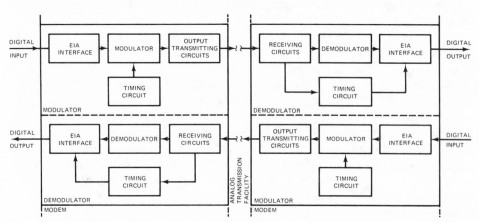

Fig. 6.39. Block diagram of a data communication system employing modems.

Three modulation techniques in common use are amplitude, frequency, and phase modulation. In a simple amplitude-modulation system, the amplitude of the modulated carrier frequency corresponds to the value of the data bits. The spectrum of the modulated waveform includes the carrier frequency plus the upper and lower sidebands. The sidebands are displaced from the carrier by the frequency of the modulating input. The resulting bandwidth is therefore twice that of the data rate.

In a frequency-modulation system, digital signals are converted to one of two frequencies corresponding to the 0 and 1 values of the data. Modulation of this form is known as *frequency-shift keying* (FSK). FSK is a commonly used technique for low-speed transmission (typically 0 to 600 bits/s) [25]. The modems operate with one functioning as an "originate" unit and the other as an "answer" unit. The originate modem transmits on a low-frequency channel using 1.270 kHz for a mark and 1.070 kHz for a space. It receives on a high-frequency channel using 2.225 and 2.025 kHz, respectively, for mark and space. The answer modem transmits on the high-frequency channel and receives on the lower. These frequencies are industry standards and assure compatibility with most commercially available low-speed data channels, including national time-sharing services. The carrier frequencies occupy discrete portions of the passband; however, the frequency modulation generates sidebands whose deviation from the carrier is directly dependent on the transmission bit rate. The total required bandwidth therefore depends on the transmission speed.

Phase modulation is widely utilized in high-speed systems. In its simplest form, two carriers are used which have identical frequencies but are 180 degrees out of phase with one another. Each phase is used to represent a mark or space condition. In such a system, both phase angles are referenced to a defined phase angle that is known by the transmitter and receiver. Another method transmits information contained in the relationship of two successive phase angles, known as differentially coherent *phase-shift keying* (PSK). PSK eliminates the need for a stable phase reference at the receiver.

The transmission timing for the digital data exchange rate can be either asynchronous or synchronous. Asynchronous timing is simpler and less expensive, but has the disadvantage of a lower data-exchange efficiency. Start and stop bits are used for each character, which can account for nearly 30% of the transmission time. In operation, the start bit is recognized by the receiver and the following bits are received at a specified data rate. The stop bit(s) permits the receiver to reset and prepare for the next start bit. Low-speed data systems employing devices such as teletypewriters often operate in this fashion.

Synchronous timing is used in higher-speed data systems. The transmitter and receiver are timed from synchronized clocks. A synchronized preamble code is transmitted first. The code is followed by the information to be transmitted without start or stop bits. The receiving modem maintains synchronism by sampling the received bits. Elimination of the start/stop bits substantially increases the throughput of the synchronous system.

Modems operate in both half- and full-duplex modes. Since full-duplex operation allows simultaneous transmission and reception, two transmission lines are required.

The public telephone network is the most commonly used transmission system. Dial-up lines having bandwidths of 3 kHz may be used for transmission rates up to 4800 bits/s, whereas lines used for high-speed transmission must be leased.

Floppy Disks

The floppy disk can be used as a replacement for paper tape and magnetic tape cassette units [7, 26]. It has the advantages of low cost, semirandom access capability, and high reliability. The floppy disk combines magnetic-tape and conventional-disk technologies. The recording medium, called a diskette, is oxide-coated Mylar, the material used for magnetic tape.

The IBM 3740-type diskette consists of a $7\frac{3}{4}$-inch disk housed in an 8-inch square plastic case. The recording head of the disk drive moves radially over the diskette to select one of 77 tracks which permit up to 243,000 bytes to be recorded. The diskette rotates within the plastic case at 360 rpm. The plastic case has three holes, one for the read/write head, one for the mechanical mechanism that spins the diskette, and one for index mark access. The read/write head actually comes into physical contact with the diskette, which is typical of most floppy disk systems produced by various manufacturers. The physical contact causes wear which limits the life of the diskette.

The data on a diskette is recorded in tracks. Each track is divided into sectors. The sector size depends on the application and usually contains one or more blocks of data. Manufacturers produce two types of sectored disks: hard-sectored disks and soft-sectored disks. In hard-sectored disk drives, a sector is identified using a photoelectric cell to detect a sector hole in the diskette. Most hard-sectored disks have 32 holes which allow 32, 16, 8, 4, 2, or 1 sector per track. The principle advantage of this type is that most sectoring work is performed by hardware.

Soft-sectored disks make use of software for sectoring. They can have any number of sectors per track. This technique allows the mixing of data and sectoring information on the diskette, but requires software or additional hardware for decoding the latter. A single photoelectrically detected hole indicates the start of a track. In a soft-sectored disk, the user must usually provide the software and interface for the disk drive supplied by the manufacturer. Since it is difficult to coordinate solutions to problems of user-supplied software and interface, most manufacturers offer hard-sectored disk drives.

Floppy disk units are designed with a moving read/write head for track selection which almost exclusively consists of a combination of a stepper motor and a rack-and-pinion drive. Floppy disk manufacturers generally quote a track-to-track access time of 10 ms for most units [27]. An average positioning time can be determined from the the track-to-track access time by multiplying it by one-third the total number of tracks and adding a head settling time (typically 10 ms) and a head loading time (typically 50 ms) to the result. For a floppy disk with 77 tracks, the average positioning time is 310 ms. For a rotation of 360 rpm, its average latency is approximately 83 ms, yielding a total average access time of about 393 ms. The data transfer rate equals the product of the disk's rotational speed and bit density. The transfer rate of an average floppy disk is 250,000 bits/s.

REFERENCES

1. FALK, HOWARD, "Linking Microprocessors to the Real World." *IEEE Spectrum*, Vol. 11, No. 9 (September, 1974).

2. GLADSTONE, BRUCE, "Designing with Microprocessors Instead of Wired Logic Asks More of Designers." *Electronics* (Oct. 11, 1973).

3. HILL, F. J. and G. R. PETERSON, *Digital Systems: Hardware Organization and Design*. New York: John Wiley & Sons, Inc., 1973.

4. KORN, GRANINO A., *Minicomputers for Engineers and Scientists*. New York: McGraw-Hill Book Co., 1973.

5. PEATMAN, JOHN B., *The Design of Digital Systems*. New York: McGraw-Hill Book Co., 1972.

6. SOUČEK, BRANKO, *Minicomputers in Data Processing and Simulation*. New York: John Wiley & Sons, Inc., 1972.

7. WEITZMAN, CAY, *Minicomputer Systems Structure, Implementation and Application*. Englewood Cliffs, N.J.: Prentice-Hall, Inc., 1974.

8. RHYNE, V. THOMAS, *Fundamentals of Digital Systems Design*. Englewood Cliffs, N.J.: Prentice-Hall, Inc., 1973.

9. *Advanced Micro Devices Data Book*. Advanced Micro Devices, Inc., Sunnyvale, Calif., 1974.

10. *Fairchild TTL Data Book*. Fairchild Semiconductor, Mountain View, Calif., 1972.

11. *Interface Integrated Circuits*. National Semiconductor Corp., Santa Clara, Calif., 1974.

12. *Signetics Digital, Linear, MOS*. Signetics, Sunnyvale, Calif., 1972.

13. MORRISON, RALPH, *Grounding and Shielding Techniques in Instrumentation*. New York: John Wiley & Sons, Inc., 1967.

14. "Unified Bus Maximizes Minicomputer Flexibility." *Electronics* (Dec. 21, 1970).

15. *Signetics Digital, Linear, MOS Applications*. Signetics, Sunnyvale, Calif., 1973.

16. *Interface Between Data Terminal Equipment and Data Communication Equipment Employing Serial Binary Data Interchange*. EIA RS 232C Standard, Electronic Industries Assoc., Washington, D.C., August, 1969.

17. *TMS 6011 JC, NC Asynchronous Data Interface*. Texas Instruments, Inc., Dallas, Texas, June, 1973.

18. *1200 BPS Telecommunications Data Interface*. Document No. 10371 N10, Microelectronic Device Division, Rockwell International, Anaheim, Calif., 1974.

19. SCHMID, HERMAN, *Electronic Analog/Digital Conversions*. New York: Van Nostrand Reinhold Co., 1970.

20. FLORES, IVAN, *Peripheral Devices*. Englewood Cliffs, N.J.: Prentice-Hall, Inc., 1973.

21. *Technical Manual 33 Teletypewriter Sets*. Bulletin 310B, Vol. 1, Teletype Corp., Skokie, Ill., April, 1973.

22. *Silent 700 Electronic Data Terminals*. Manual No. 959227–9701, Rev. A, Texas Instruments, Inc., February, 1974.

23. DAVIS, SIDNEY, "Modems: Their Operating Principles and Applications." *Computer Design*, Vol. 12, No. 9 (September, 1973).

24. "Shaping Up Your Data." *Digital Design*, Handbook Issue, Part 2, Vol. 5, No. 1 (January, 1975).

25. NASH, GARTH, "Build Compact Modems." *Electronic Design*, Vol. 23, No. 1 (Jan. 4, 1975).

26. SWITHENBANK, T. and L. SOLOMON, "Floppy Disks." *Digital Design*, Vol. 4, No. 11 (November, 1974).

27. BACKLER, JORDAN, "Disk Storage Devices." *Digital Design*, Handbook Issue, Part 1, Vol. 4, No. 12 (December 1974).

EXERCISES

6.1. Design an interface for a synchronous transfer in a microcomputer having an 8-bit data bus in which device 1 and device 3 are input and output devices, respectively. The ENABLE, STROBE IN, and STROBE OUT signals of Fig. 6.3 are available from the processor. The DEVICE ADDRESS is placed on the DATA BUS with bits 0 through 2 in synchronism with a SYNC DEVICE ADDRESS pulse available from the processor prior to execution of an input or output operation. Sketch a timing diagram for the transfer.

6.2. Write a program using the mnemonics of the Intel 8080 (Appendix E) to perform an asynchronous transfer in which device 1 and device 2 are input and output devices, respectively. Test the status of each device via bits 0 and 1 of port 0. Assume a data byte which is read from device 1 is outputted to device 2. Construct a flow chart for the transfer.

6.3. Design an interface for the transfer of Exercise 6.2. Assume that the DEVICE ADDRESS, STROBE IN, STROBE OUT, and ENABLE (Fig. 6.7) are available. Sketch a timing diagram for the transfer.

6.4. Devices 0 and 1 of Fig. 6.11 interrupt the processor at random times. Write a program using the 8080 mnemonics to perform software polling to locate the interrupting device. Read a data word from the interrupting device and store it sequentially beginning at location 100_{16}. After ten data words have been read, disable the interrupt to allow for processing the data.

6.5. Repeat Exercise 6.4 using the mnemonics of the Intel 4040 (Appendix A).

6.6. Repeat Exercise 6.4 employing a system using the daisy-chain interrupt structure of Fig. 6.13. Write a program to process the interrupt using the 8080 mnemonics.

6.7. Repeat Exercise 6.6 using a vectored interrupt transfer similar to that of Fig. 6.14.

6.8. Modify the logic diagram of Fig. 6.17 to include a BLOCK COUNTER for transferring one or more blocks of data.

6.9. Sketch the timing diagram for Fig. 6.20.

6.10. Determine resistor and capacitor values necessary for the 555 timer to oscillate at 0.1 MHz with $t_1 = 4t_2$. Sketch the circuit diagram.

6.11. Determine resistor and capacitor values necessary for a 74121 to have an output pulse of 250 ms. Sketch the various circuit diagrams which result in negative-edge and positive-edge triggering.

6.12. Design an interface for an asynchronous transfer for the A/D converter of Fig. 6.35. Assume an 8-bit converter with parallel output capability. Show all necessary latches. Write a program to perform the transfer using (a) 4004, (b) 4040, (c) 8008, and (d) 8080 mnemonics.

6.13. For the instruction MVI A,47H (Appendix E), sketch the paper tape formats for the following:
  (a) BNPF and ASCII formats in assembly language code for even, odd, mark, and space parities.
  (b) Binary and hexadecimal formats in machine language code with even, odd, mark, and space parities for the latter.

6.14. Design an asynchronous interface for a teletypewriter using a UART to transfer information to an 8-bit processor. Assume full-duplex operation.

6.15. Write a program to perform an asynchronous transfer between a UART and an 8-bit microcomputer to input a block of data from a tape cassette unit (Fig. E.6.15). The tape format is shown in Fig. 6.38. Assume the tape unit has been activated and the READ HEAD is at a GAP position. The PREAMBLE and POSTAMBLE are given by 01010101_2 and the NULL character by 00000000_2. Store the block of data (86 bytes) in memory beginning at location 500_{16}. Assume the time for serial input into the UART is much longer than the time required to read an 8-bit character from the UART into the computer (e.g., 300 bits/s). Use the 8080 mnemonics.

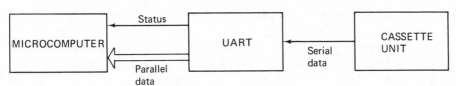

Fig. E6.15.

6.16. Design a modem to communicate with a telephone line using a UART. The modem is to operate as a low-speed FSK type.

7 MICROPROCESSORS AND MICROCOMPUTER SYSTEMS

Numerous microprocessors are available for the designer from various manufacturers. The operational characteristics of different processors vary greatly. In this chapter, we discuss several important factors governing the selection of a processor. Following this discussion, a number of popular microprocessors and microcomputer systems are described.

7.1. MICROPROCESSOR SELECTION

The selection of a suitable microprocessor depends primarily on the particular application. Since the characteristics of the various processors are quite different, a number of factors must be considered in making a good choice. From the standpoint of the designer, the selection process involves investigating the software, hardware, and system design of a candidate processor [1]. Software design investigation requires examination of many features, including architecture (e.g., word length and speed) and programming flexibility. Hardware design investigation includes examining completeness (amount of support hardware necessary), and system design considers available design aids (both hardware and software).

Word length is the first feature usually considered [2]. The determining requirements include analog resolution, computational accuracy, character length, and width of parallel inputs or outputs. Also, when specifying word size, one should remember that ease of programming, not the efficiency with which the application is performed, is affected.

Other important architectural features include the number of CPU registers, type of return stack, interrupt capability, interface structures, and memory types. The number of registers in the processor is obviously an important feature of its architecture. These registers can reduce references to main storage, which may conserve both external memory and time. CPU registers generally consist of ALU, index, and general-purpose (scratch-pad) registers.

The return stack is used for nesting of subroutines, processing interrupts, and for temporary storage of data. Hardware stacks are implemented as on-chip (CPU) pushdown stacks. Software stacks are stored in RAM, with an on-chip stack pointer maintained in the CPU. The hardware stack is faster, but its size is limited by the number of registers in the CPU stack. The software stack, on the other hand, is restricted only by the size of external RAM.

The speed of the microprocessor has been gauged using numerous measures. Some include cycle time, state time, minimum instruction time, register-to-register addition time, and interrupt response time. Register-to-register addition time is a popular estimate of the computing speed because nearly every processor has an add instruction. These measures should not be the only criteria used in timing estimation since they do not measure the power of the instruction set.

The degree of programming flexibility can be assessed by an examination of the processor instruction set [3]. Multiple addressing modes (Sec. 4.4) conserve memory, simplify programming, and increase speed by using one-word memory reference instructions. Other important capabilities include arithmetic instructions (e.g., binary and BCD arithmetic, multiply and divide, and double-precision arithmetic) and logical and I/O control instructions.

The number of additional IC packages required for a microcomputer system is an indication of the completeness of the microcomputer set. Support hardware is often required for clock generation and timing, memory and I/O control, data and address buffers, multiplexer inputs, interrupt control, and power supply voltages.

Hardware and software support from the manufacturer are both important considerations. Software support includes documented manuals and applications literature. Both of these are an important measure of the manufacturer's commitment to servicing the needs of the user. Another system design consideration is the availability of a prototyping system which is essential to develop and debug hardware and software for a given application. Such a system usually includes a microcomputer system with extended memory capability, interface for an I/O device such as a teletypewriter, a control console, pROM programming capability, and software support. The software support should include, as a minimum, a monitor, an editor, and an assembler.

The following microprocessor checklist is very useful in the evaluation of a candidate processor.

7.2. INTEL 4004

The Intel 4004 was the first commercially available microprocessor. It is a parallel, 4-bit, p-channel MOS device with an addressing structure which is that of a Harvard class computer [1]. The system operates from a two-phase clock (750 kHz, maximum) and has a basic cycle time (eight clock periods) of 10.8 μs.

A microcomputer using the 4004 CPU has a unique architecture. Program storage is entirely in ROM and an I/O port is provided on each ROM. RAM is used for data storage and an output port is provided on each RAM. Initially, the system

MICROPROCESSOR CHECKLIST*

COST CONSIDERATIONS

Normally chip cost is not the largest factor, but it could be in a simple system. The major cost is usually in the circuitry needed to support the microprocessor. The engineering cost to put your system together, however, can be greatly influenced by the amount of quality of support the chip supplier has available.

Support circuitry
☐ Clock circuitry and clock drivers—how many phases?
☐ Power supplies—common or special?
☐ Buffers—MOS to TTL input/output?
☐ How much control logic (i.e., address and data latches, etc.)?
☐ Memory—standard or special?
☐ Power of the instruction set (a good instruction set can reduce memory requirements by 40%).
☐ Support requirements (the larger these are, the more expensive the PCB or the greater the number of PCB's required).
☐ Ease of checkout (test vs purchased card).
☐ Processor card availability (small production and preproduction will use off-the-shelf cards).

Support from supplier
☐ Hardware support
    prototyping system
    mechanical hardware
    processor cards
    memory cards
    interface cards and cables
☐ Software support
    high level languages
    assemblers
    utility programs—debug and edit
    loaders—absolute and relocatable
    peripheral drivers (TTY, card reader, line printer, floppy disc, etc.)
    special subroutines (BCD to binary and binary to BCD, floating point math package, etc.)

Literature

How well written the hardware and software manuals are determines how much time is spent in learning the system.
☐ Technical manuals
☐ Software manuals
☐ Application notes
☐ Special interfaces—D/A, A/D peripherals

Technical support
This can reduce the engineering time and cost required to get the new product designed and into production.
☐ Area system specialist
☐ Field application engineer
☐ Plant applications and engineering groups

PERFORMANCE

Speed
☐ Efficiency of the instruction set—how many instructions are needed to solve a particular problem (a math problem, a process control problem, data handling, etc.)?
☐ Execution time of each instruction.
☐ Microprogrammability—can the instruction set be changed?

Interface
☐ Input/output flexibility and capability
    How many peripherals can be handled?
    How many commands to each peripheral?
    How large is the subroutine to handle any of the peripherals?
    How much logic is required?
☐ Interrupt flexibility and capability
    Can vectored interrupts and/or polled interrupts be handled by the processor?
    How many interrupts can be handled by the processor?
☐ Special control features
    Enable signals (single line control where fast response or ease of interface is important).
    Sense inputs (test a single input and respond accordingly).

*Reprint from "Primer on Microprocessors." *Electronic Products*, Vol. 17, No. 9 (February, 1975), p. 41.

may be somewhat difficult to understand. However, once any difficulties are resolved, the system offers a powerful tool for the designer.

Architecture

A microcomputer based on the 4004 consists of a set of IC devices whose operation is usually described in negative logic (Sec. 2.2). A system is possible with a 4004 CPU and one or more 4001 ROMs when combined with I/O devices and a clock, but it will usually also include one or more 4002 RAMs and 4003 shift registers. A microcomputer employing these devices is the Intel MCS-4 shown in Fig. 7.1 [4]. Each device of this system will now be described.

A.   4004 CPU

A block diagram of the 4004 CPU is shown in Fig. 7.2. The functional sections of the processor are the address stack, index (scratch-pad) registers, 4-bit ALU, instruction register/decoder and control, and peripheral circuitry. These sections are internally connected via a 4-bit bus.

The address stack is a 4×12-bit dynamic RAM array. It contains a 12-bit program counter and three 12-bit stack registers. The 12-bit program counter permits addressing 4K of ROM, and the three register stack allows three levels of subroutine nesting. The address is stored in an address buffer and demultiplexed onto the internal bus in three 4-bit slices. The address is incremented by a 4-bit incrementer after each slice is sent out on the bus.

The index (scratch-pad) register is a 16×4-bit dynamic RAM array. This array may be directly addressed as sixteen 4-bit registers for immediate computation or control. The array may also be used as eight 8-bit registers (eight 4-bit pairs) for addressing RAM and ROM and storing data fetched from ROM.

A 4-bit ALU performs addition on data from the internal bus and the accumulator and carry flip-flop. This sum is then transferred to the accumulator and carry flip-flops. Decimal arithmetic is implemented using a Decimal Adjust Accumulator (DAA) instruction. The accumulator is provided with a shifter to perform shift instructions. It also communicates with the command control register which holds a 3-bit code used for CM-RAM line switching.

The instruction register consists of 4-bit registers OPR and OPA. It is loaded from the internal bus through a multiplexer and holds the instruction fetched from ROM. These instructions are decoded by the instruction decoder and gated with timing signals to generate the control signals for the various functional blocks.

Peripheral circuitry includes a data bus I/O buffer with input/output terminals D_0–D_3, a timing and SYNC generator, and a ROM command control (CM-ROM) and four RAM command control (CM-RAM$_i$) output buffers.

The 4004 is fabricated in a 16-pin dual in-line package (DIP). TEST is a terminal used in conjunction with a Jump On Condition instruction (JCN). RESET is a terminal used to clear all registers and flip-flops. Other terminals include two-phase clock inputs ϕ_1 and ϕ_2, and SYNC output.

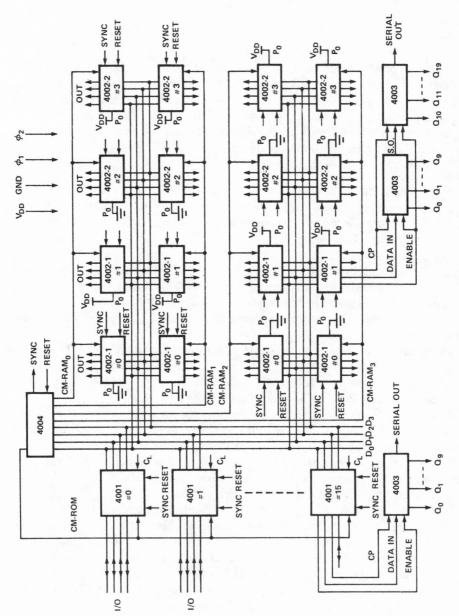

Fig. 7.1. INTEL MCS-4 microcomputer (Courtesy of INTEL Corporation).

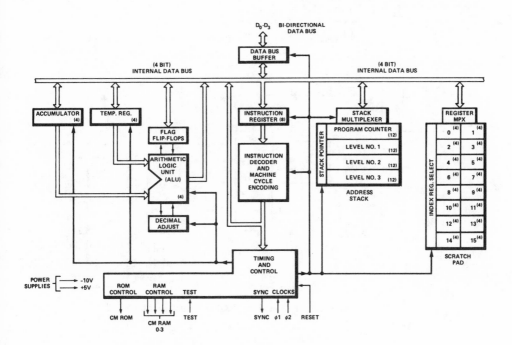

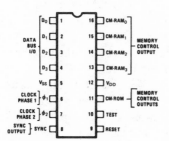

Fig. 7.2. Block diagram of a 4004 CPU (Courtesy of INTEL Corporation).

B.   4001 ROM

The 4001 contains a 256 × 8-bit mask-programmable ROM and 4-bit I/O port. A block diagram of this device is shown in Fig. 7.3. Data and addresses are transferred to the CPU via the 4-bit bidirectional data bus I/O buffer (D_0–D_3). The address register and decoder receives an address in three 4-bit slices. The address is decoded to select 1 of 256 8-bit words in 1 of 16 ROMs (4K bytes total). This word is multiplexed onto the internal bus in two 4-bit slices and transferred to the CPU. A Command Line (CM) terminal is provided to enable the ROM.

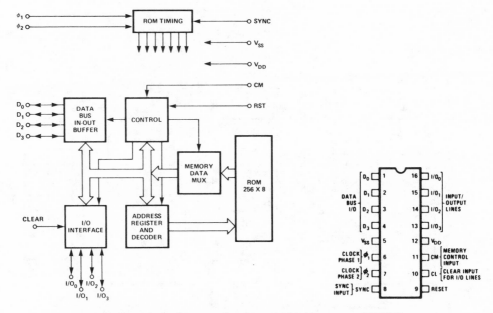

Fig. 7.3. Block diagram of a 4001 ROM (Courtesy of INTEL Corporation).

The ROM may also function as an I/O control device. The ROM can transfer information between the data bus lines and four external I/O lines (I/O_i). The operations are Read ROM Port (RDR) and Write ROM Port (WRR). The RDR instruction transfers data on the I/O terminals to the internal bus. If a WRR instruction is received, the data present on the internal bus is latched in the output flip-flops associated with the I/O lines. Each I/O line may be uniquely dedicated as either an input or an output in the mask-programming process.

The 4001 is contained in a 16-pin DIP. The CL terminal is used to asynchronously clear the output register and RESET is used to reset all internal flip-flops, including the output register. ϕ_1 and ϕ_2 are two-phase clock inputs, and SYNC is a signal supplied by the 4004 at the start of each instruction cycle, which is used to synchronize the memory.

C. 4002 RAM

The 4002 RAM (Fig. 7.4) contains a dynamic array of 320 bits arranged in four registers of twenty 4-bit characters each. The twenty characters consist of sixteen 4-bit main memory characters and four 4-bit status characters. The device also provides four output lines to perform output operations. Data and addresses between the 4002 and 4004 are provided via the bidirectional data bus I/O buffer using terminals D_0–D_3. The 4004 can access sixteen 4002 RAMs for a total of 1280 4-bit characters and sixteen 4-bit output ports.

In addressing RAM the 4004 executes a Send Register Control (SRC) instruction to send out the contents of a designated index register pair as an address to a main

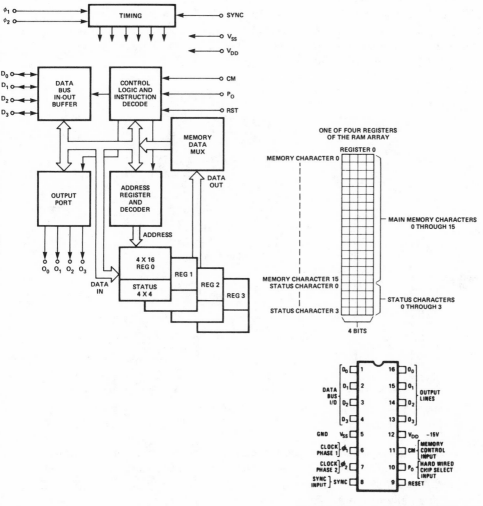

Fig. 7.4. Block diagram of a 4002 RAM (Courtesy of INTEL Corporation).

memory character in RAM. This also activates the CM terminal via the appropriate CM-RAM$_i$ line. The CM-RAM$_i$ line is selected by a Designated Command Line (DCL) instruction. The status character locations are selected by use of the I/O and RAM instructions.

All communications with the system are through the data bus. The 4-bit output port (O_0–O_3) permits data out from the system. An external RESET signal is used to clear the memory and all static flip-flops including output registers.

The 4002 is contained in a 16-pin DIP available in two metal options. The P_0 terminal is used for chip selection in conjunction with the option. ϕ_1 and ϕ_2 are external clock inputs and SYNC is provided by the 4004.

D. 4003 Shift Register

The 4003 is a static 10-bit shift register with serial-in (DATA IN), parallel-out (Q_0–Q_9), and serial-out (SERIAL OUT) data, as shown in Fig. 7.5. It is employed to increase the number of output lines for interfacing I/O devices such as keyboards, displays, TTYs, and A/D converters.

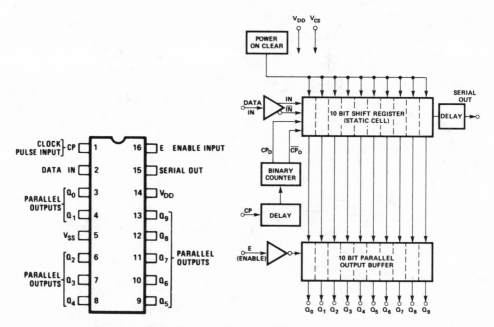

Fig. 7.5. Block diagram of a 4003 Shift Register (Courtesy of INTEL Corporation).

Data is loaded serially and the ten parallel outputs are enabled by the enable (E) terminal. The SERIAL OUT is not affected by E. Data shifting is controlled by the Clock Pulse input (CP). DATA IN and CP can be simultaneous; however, CP is delayed internally to avoid race conditions.

The 4003, like the previous devices, is packaged in a 16-pin DIP.

Instruction Cycle

An instruction cycle for the 4004 consists of eight clock periods, or states, denoted by A_1, A_2, A_3, M_1, M_2, X_1, X_2, and X_3 (Fig. 7.6). In states A_1 through A_3, an address from the program counter in the CPU is sent to ROM. The CM-ROM line is enabled during A_3. In states M_1 and M_2, the selected 4001 sends an instruction to the CPU. The op code (OPR) is sent during M_1 and the modifier or operand (OPA) during M_2. If the CPU receives an I/O instruction, it will activate the CM-ROM and the appropriate CM-RAM$_i$ line during M_2 to permit the ROMs and RAMs to receive the OPA portion of the I/O instruction. The DCL instruction selects the desired CM-RAM$_i$.

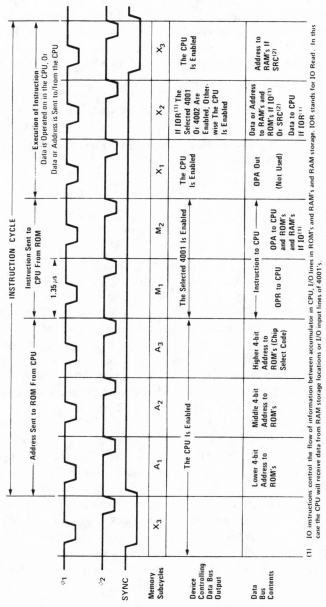

Fig. 7.6. MCS-4 Basic Instruction Cycle (Courtesy of INTEL Corporation).

(1) IO instructions control the flow of information between accumulator in CPU, I/O lines in ROM's and RAM's and RAM storage. In this case the CPU will receive data from RAM storage locations or I/O input lines of 4001's.

(2) The SRC instruction designates the chip number and address for a following IO instruction.

Execution of the instruction occurs during states X_1, X_2, and X_3. Data is operated upon by the CPU, or data (or address) is sent out or received by the CPU. When a Send Register Control (SRC) instruction is executed, the CPU transmits eight bits of data during X_2 and X_3 and activates the CM-ROM and the appropriate CM-RAM$_i$ line at X_2. The 4001 interprets data at X_2, when simultaneous with CM-ROM, as the chip number of the ROM that should later perform the I/O operation. Data at X_3 is ignored. In the case of the 4002, the data at X_2 and X_3 satisfies the following format:

X_2				X_3			
D_3 D_2		D_1 D_0		D_3	D_2	D_1	D_0
Chip No. (0 through 3)		Register No. (0 through 3)		Main Memory Character No. (0 through 15)			

After an SRC instruction, only one 4001 and one 4002 will be ready to execute a following I/O instruction.

Instruction Set

The instruction set of the 4004 consists of 45 instructions in three groups (Appendix A). The first group contains sixteen machine instructions. Eleven of these are one-word (8-bit) instructions divided into two 4-bit fields. In this case, the upper four bits (OPR) contain the op code for the operation (e.g., add, subtract, load, etc.) and the lower four bits (OPA) contain the modifier or operand (e.g., register address, data, or instruction modifier). The remaining five instructions of the group are two-word instructions for jump, skip, and fetch-immediate operations. As in one-word instructions, the OPR of the first word contains the op code and the OPA contains a register address, upper part of a ROM address, or a condition for jumping. The second word contains either the middle and lower portions in OPR and OPA, respectively, of another ROM address or eight bits of data.

A second group contains fifteen I/O and RAM instructions. The OPR contains a 4-bit code for the I/O group, and the OPA identifies the I/O operation. This group includes instructions for enabling I/O ROM ports and output RAM ports, and for reading out of and writing into individual RAM main memory and status characters. A third group consists of fourteen accumulator group instructions. As in the second group, the OPR contains a 4-bit code for the accumulator group, and the OPA identifies the particular operation. This group includes Clear, Increment, Decrement, Rotate, and Decimal Adjust Accumulator instructions. Also available is a Keyboard Process instruction (KBP) which converts the contents of the accumulator from a 1-of-4 to a binary code.

Prototyping Systems

The microcomputer of Fig. 7.1 is a production model of a system which is usually developed using a prototyping system. It cannot be used for prototyping because the 4001 ROM, in which the program is stored, is mask-programmed. A basic MCS-4

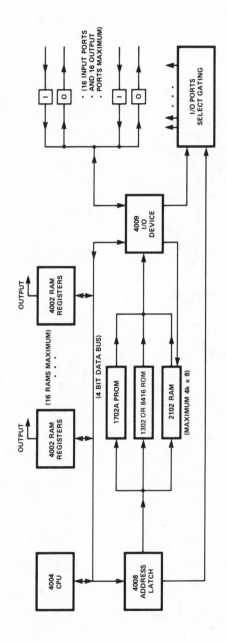

Fig. 7.7. Basic MCS-4 system using the 4008/4009 (Courtesy of INTEL Corporation).

207

prototyping system is shown in Fig. 7.7 [5]. In this figure, the 4008 and 4009 which are used in conjunction with any combination of RAM (2102), pROM (1720A), and/or ROM (1301) replace the 4001 of Fig. 7.1. All activity remains under the control of the 4004. A set of 4008/4009 and several TTL decoders are sufficient to interface 4K words of program memory, sixteen 4-bit input ports, and sixteen 4-bit output ports. Program memory is arranged in *pages*, where a page is 256 bytes.

The 4008 is an address latch chip which latches the 8-bit program address sent by the 4004 during A_1 and A_2 (Fig. 7.6) for word selection within a page. During A_3 it latches the address for a memory page (ROM chip number). These four bits are decoded externally and one page of program memory is chosen. The 4009 transfers the 8-bit instruction from program memory to the CPU, four bits at a time, at M_1 and M_2. The 4008/4009 also provide I/O operations under the control of the 4004.

The use of pROM and RAM allows program changes during system development. For a 1702A pROM, changes require erasing and reprogramming the memory using a pROM programmer. In the case of the 2102 RAM, the program may be altered under software control. A forty-sixth instruction, Write Program Memory (WPM), exists in the 4004 for writing instructions into the RAM program memory. This RAM memory is distinct from the 4002 RAM and is organized in 8-bit words and 256-word pages. This is identical to the 4001 memory organization.

Available in the MCS-4 microcomputer set are numerous hardware modules for the designer. Four which are very useful are a CPU, a Memory Control, a RAM Memory, and a pROM Programmer module. The CPU module is a functional microcomputer itself. It contains a 4004 microprocessor, four 4002 RAMs, a 4008/4009 interface set, a two-phase crystal clock, four input ports and eight output ports (including a TTY interface), and sockets to accommodate four 1702A pROMs (1K bytes). The Control Memory module is used to interface the CPU module and RAM Memory module and allows the RAM memory of the latter module to be used as both executable program memory and data storage. The RAM Memory module consists of 4K bytes (sixteen pages) of RAM implemented with the 2102 static RAM elements. The pROM Programmer module, a useful function in a prototyping system, is used to program the 1702A pROMs.

A popular prototyping system using the above modules is the Intel INTELLEC 4/MOD 4 [6]. The standard system provides 320 4-bit characters (4002 RAM) of data storage, 4K bytes (2102 RAM) of program memory, and a standard set of software.

The standard software includes a resident monitor and an assembler [7]. The assembler is provided on paper tape and loaded into and executed from the RAM program memory. In addition to the standard software, a cross-assembler and simulator written in FORTRAN IV are available. These software products are also available on General Electric, Tymshare, and United Computing Systems time-sharing computer networks.

Comments

A microcomputer based on the 4004 is a calculator-oriented system. The 4002 RAM, which is used for data storage, is designed to operate on 4-bit quantities. This is ideal for manipulating BCD numbers. The four-register stack which allows three levels of subroutine nesting is sufficient for most numeric applications, but it may be inadequate in more generalized applications.

The method of addressing the 4002 is somewhat unconventional. First, the program must issue instructions (DCL and SRC) to select the desired character. Finally, the specific storage read or write is issued. Another idiosyncracy is that the input and output ports are physically located on the memory chips. Since the I/O operation in no way interferes with storage, the best policy for the programmer is to forget that memory and I/O share the same chip [8].

The 4004 does not have a halt or interrupt capability. The TEST terminal, however, is available to permit a conditional jump (JCN) in response to an important external event. Other instructions which are not available in the processor's repertoire are logical operations AND, OR, and EXCLUSIVE-OR. These functions must be generated in software.

A distinct advantage of this microcomputer set is that each of the 4001, 4002, 4003, and 4004 operate from a single 15-volt power supply. In addition, Intel Corporation has developed numerous supporting ICs including a two-phase clock generator (4201) and a standard memory interface (4289) to replace the 4008/4009 combination.

7.3. INTEL 4040

The Intel 4040 is a 4-bit, parallel MOS device which is an enhanced version of the 4004. It retains all of the functional capability of its predecessor and provides several significant improvements in both hardware and software [9]. The 4040 software contains the entire 4004 instruction set plus fourteen additional instructions which include logical operations and an interrupt and stop capability.

The hardware design features an expanded address stack and index register array. Also, separate power supply terminals are provided for the output buffers which permit direct interfacing to other circuit types. The 4040, like the 4004, is a Harvard class computer which operates from a two-phase clock (750 kHz, maximum) and has a basic cycle time (eight clock periods) of 10.8 μs.

Architecture

A microcomputer employing the 4040 CPU can be formed by replacing the 4004 of Fig. 7.1 by the 4040 processor. A block diagram of the 4040 is shown in Fig. 7.8. The major functional areas of the processor are the address stack and address incrementer, index (scratch-pad) register array, ALU, instruction register/decoder and control logic, hardware interrupt and stop control, and peripheral circuits. Comparing these to the functional areas of the 4004, we see that the hardware interrupt and stop control are added features in the 4040 architecture.

The address register is a dynamic RAM array of 8 × 12 bits operating as a pushdown stack. It functions in a manner identical to that of the 4 × 12-bit address register of the 4004. It contains a 12-bit program counter and seven 12-bit stack

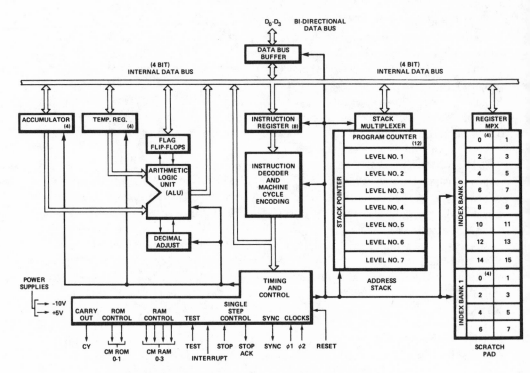

Fig. 7.8. Block diagram of the 4040 CPU (Courtesy of INTEL Corporation).

registers. The seven-register stack allows seven levels of subroutine nesting. The contents of the selected address register are stored in an address buffer and multiplexed onto the internal bus in three 4-bit segments. The contents of the address buffer are incremented by a 4-bit carry-look-ahead circuit following the transfer of each 4-bit segment, and this value is written back into the selected address register via the address buffer.

The index register is a 12 × 8-bit dynamic RAM array organized in three groups of 4 × 8 bits. Two groups (registers 0–7 in banks 0 and 1) must be individually selected with SB0 and SB1 instructions, whereas the third group (registers 8–15) are always available for use. Two modes of operation are possible for the two register banks. In one mode, 24 directly addressable 4-bit storage locations are available for intermediate computations or control purposes. In the second mode, twelve 4-bit pairs of storage locations are provided for addressing RAM, ROM, and I/O ports or for storing data fetched from ROM.

The ALU performs 4-bit addition on data from the internal bus and the accumulator and carry flip-flop. The sum is then transferred to the accumulator and carry flip-flop. The accumulator is provided with a shifter to implement shift-left and shift-right operations. The accumulator also communicates with the command register, special ROMs, condition logic, and the internal bus. The command register holds a

3-bit code used for CM-RAM line switching which permits direct addressing of sixteen 4002's (1280 × 4 bits). A fourth bit in the command register is used for CM-ROM switching to allow the selection of two 4K banks of ROM for a total 8K bytes of memory. The special ROMs perform Decimal Adjust Accumulator (DAA) and Process Keyboard (KBP) instructions.

The instruction register consists, as in the case of the 4004, of 4-bit registers OPR and OPA. It is loaded from the internal bus during an instruction cycle through a multiplexer, and it holds the fetched instruction. The instructions are decoded in the instruction decoder to provide the control signals for the various functional areas.

The INTERRUPT and STOP terminals are provided to override the normal processor operation. The interrupt logic acknowledges the presence of an interrupt signal and forces the processor to execute a Jump to Subroutine (JMS) instruction to ROM, page 0, location 3. The interrupt is acknowledged via the INTERRUPT ACKNOWLEDGE terminal. The stop control logic operates in a similar manner by detecting and acknowledging the presence of a stop signal. The processor is forced to execute a No-Operation (NOP) instruction and remains in a stopped condition until the stop signal is removed. The stop state is acknowledged via the STOP ACKNOWLEDGE terminal.

The peripheral circuits include the data bus I/O buffers for communicating between data terminals $(D_0 - D_3)$ and the internal bus, a timing and SYNC generator, CM-ROM and CM-RAM lines, and a power-on-clear flip-flop. The 4040 is packaged in a 24-pin DIP as shown in Fig. 7.9.

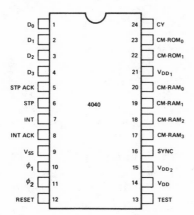

Fig. 7.9. 4040 24-pin DIP (Courtesy of INTEL Corporation).

Instruction Cycle

The basic system timing for the 4040 is identical to that of the 4004, as shown in Fig. 7.10. The reader is referred to Sec. 7.2 for a description of the 4004 instruction cycle. The data bus contents at various times during the instruction cycle are defined as in the 4004, with the exception of the data at X_1 and the carry output (CY) during X_3 of a NOP instruction. The 4040 outputs the contents of the accumulator at X_1

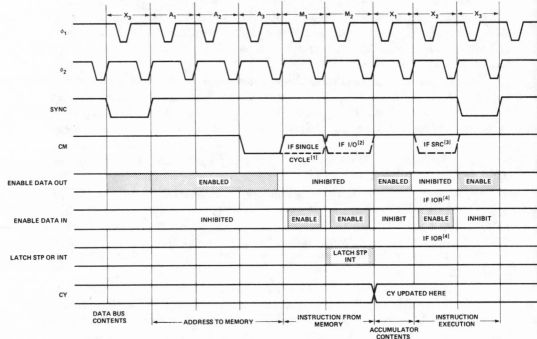

NOTES:

1. CM-ROM, RAM SIGNALS WILL BE PRESENT AT M_1 FOR ANY SINGLE CYCLE INSTRUCTION OR FOR THE FIRST CYCLE OF A DOUBLE CYCLE INSTRUCTION.
2. CM-ROM, RAM SIGNALS WILL BE PRESENT AT M_2 FOR ANY OF THE SIXTEEN I/O GROUP INSTRUCTIONS.
3. CM-ROM, RAM SIGNALS WILL BE PRESENT AT X_2 DURING EXECUTION OF AN SRC INSTRUCTION.
4. IOR MEANS ONE OF THE I/O READ INSTRUCTIONS: SBM, ROM, RDR, ADM, RDϕ, RD1, RD2, RD3.

Fig. 7.10. 4040 basic timing cycle (Courtesy of INTEL Corporation).

for program debugging, whereas the 4004 simply copies the data which is received at M_2.

A timing feature not present in the 4004 is the generation of the CM-ROM and CM-RAM signals at M_1. This occurs for all single-cycle instructions and for the first cycle of all double-cycle instructions. This feature allows external logic to distinguish between instruction information and address or data at M_1 and M_2.

Instruction Set

The instruction set of the 4040 contains 60 instructions: the 46 instructions of the 4004 and 14 new instructions (Appendix A). The instruction format is identical to that of the 4004. These new instructions include a Halt (HLT) to inhibit the program counter and data buffers and logical OR and AND instructions. A Branch Back from Interrupt and Restore the Previous SRC (BBS) instruction is used in processing interrupts to restore the program counter and SRC to their pre-interrupt values.

Enable Interrupt (EIN), Disable Interrupt (DIN), and Transfer Contents of the Command Register to the Accumulator (LCR) instructions are also provided for processing interrupts. The LCR instruction is used to store the CM-RAM and CM-ROM status prior to processing an interrupt.

Other instructions are the Designate ROM Banks (DB0 and DB1) which enable CM-ROM$_0$ and CM-ROM$_1$ lines. Each line enables 4K bytes of ROM allowing a total of 8K words. Also provided are Select Index Register Banks 0 and 1 (SB0 and SB1) instructions for selecting the index register banks within the processor.

Microcomputer Systems

The system shown in Fig. 7.7 will function as a microcomputer with the 4004 replaced by the 4040 processor. An alternate system, using several Intel MCS-40 components, is shown in Fig. 7.11. In this system, the 4201 is an IC clock system requiring an external crystal. The 4308 ROM is a mask-programmed 1024 × 8-bit memory with four I/O ports (sixteen lines) which is functionally identical to four 4001 chips. The 4207, 4209, and 4211 are general-purpose I/O devices which expand the I/O capability of the 4040. One of these devices has the same I/O capacity as a 4308. In a minimum configuration (4201, 4040, and a 4308), 1K of memory and sixteen I/O lines are available in this system.

A microcomputer using standard memory components is shown in Fig. 7.12. The 4289 memory and I/O interface device replaces the 4008/4009 devices of Fig. 7.7 for interfacing pROMs (1702A), RAMs (2102), and/or ROMs to facilitate system development. The 4316 is a mask-programmed 2048 × 8-bit ROM, and the 4101 is a 256 × 4-bit static RAM. The 3216/26 are 4-bit parallel bidirectional bus drivers.

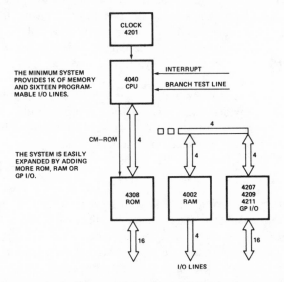

Fig. 7.11. Block diagram of a typical MCS-40 microcomputer (Courtesy of INTEL Corporation).

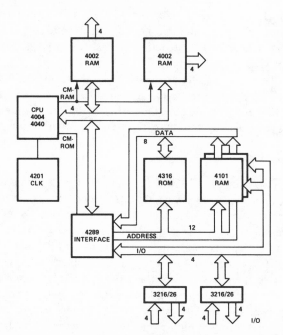

Fig. 7.12. Microcomputer using standard memory components (Courtesy of INTEL Corporation).

A popular prototyping system based on the 4040 processor is the Intellec 4/MOD 40. This system, which is similar to the Intellec 4/MOD 4 described in the previous section, contains a CPU, a RAM Memory, a Memory Control, and a pROM Programmer module. It provides 320 4-bit characters (4002 RAM) of data storage and 4K bytes (2102) of program memory. The data storage and program memory are expandable to 2560 characters and 12K bytes, respectively. Program memory can consist of pROM, RAM, and/or ROM.

Standard software for the system includes a resident monitor and an assembler [7]. The assembler is provided on paper tape for loading into and executing from the RAM program memory. A cross-assembler and simulator written in FORTRAN IV are also available. These are provided on national time-sharing systems (see Sec. 7.2).

Comments

Microcomputers employing the 4040 processor are both hardware- and software-compatible with those using the 4004. The additional instructions of the 4040 permit logical AND and OR operations, and the expanded address register stack to eight registers permits subroutine nesting to seven levels. If interrupts are to be serviced, however, one level should be left unused for this purpose.

The program memory has been extended to two 4K-byte banks which are selected by DB0 and DB1 instructions. The use of subroutines in one bank by programs in another presents a software problem because a memory bank is not selected by an address in the 12-bit address register. Special provisions must be made to select the proper memory bank for the return address [1].

The index register array has been increased and divided into two banks, selected by SB0 and SB1 instructions. Registers 0 through 7 are duplicated in each bank, which permits the programmer to employ one set of registers 0–7 for use of subroutines in one bank of program ROM. The other register set can then be used with subroutines in the other bank of ROM.

Single-level interrupts are processed by the 4040, and the INTERRUPT ACKNOWLEDGE signal is used to inhibit other interrupts until the first is completely serviced. Interrupt enable and disable instructions are provided for protecting sequences of instructions from being interrupted. When an interrupt occurs, the processor vectors the program counter to page 0, location 3 of the currently selected ROM bank. For this reason, Intel suggests duplicating the initial portions of the interrupt software in each bank of program storage.

7.4. NATIONAL IMP-4

The IMP-4 is a microprogrammable microprocessor (Sec. 4.4) which is made up of parts from the GPC/P parts set [1]. The microprocessor consists of three ICs, a register and arithmetic logic unit (RALU), a 4-bit interface logic unit (FILU), and a control and read-only-memory unit (CROM). The instruction set of the machine may be determined by mask-programming the CROM according to the user's specifications. This approach is not feasible in many cases; therefore, National provides a standard CROM which is suitable for many applications. We will confine our discussion to the IMP-4 with the standard instruction set.

Architecture [10]

The RALU contains a 4-bit ALU and seven general-purpose 4-bit registers. A 4-bit status register (overflow, link, carry, general flag) and a 16-word stack are also included. In the standard IMP-4, three of the seven general-purpose registers are used for internal housekeeping. The remaining four are used as accumulators (AC0–AC3). A block diagram and a terminal diagram for the RALU are illustrated in Fig. 7.13.

Any of the seven general-purpose registers (R1–R7) may be loaded on the A or B bus for processing by the ALU. The ALU will perform AND, OR, ADD, and EXCLUSIVE-OR operations. The shifter provides a 1-bit left or right shift and transfers the shifted information in and out of terminals 11 and 14. The 16-word LIFO stack can be accessed over the A and R buses. When the stack is full, a stack-full signal (STFL) is provided at terminal 3.

The link flag may be included in the shift operation and the overflow and carry flags are set or reset as a result of ADD operations. The general flag may be used for interrupt enable. The link, carry, and overflow operations may be disabled and any

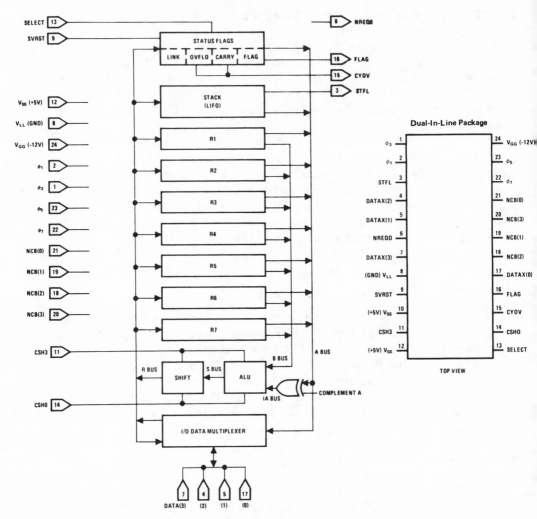

Fig. 7.13. RALU (a) Block diagram, (b) Terminal diagram (Courtesy of National Semiconductor Corporation, USA).

of the flags used under program control. Communication between the RALU and other parts of the system is provided by the I/O data multiplexer.

The CROM provides the microprogrammable control section for the microprocessor. A 100 × 23-bit ROM stores the microprogram. In the standard IMP-4, the ROM is programmed with a standard instruction set. Associated with the ROM is the circuitry to execute the microinstructions. The microprogram executes macroprogram instructions, which are stored in the system memory. The microprogram contains an instruction-fetch routine which reads a macroinstruction from the system

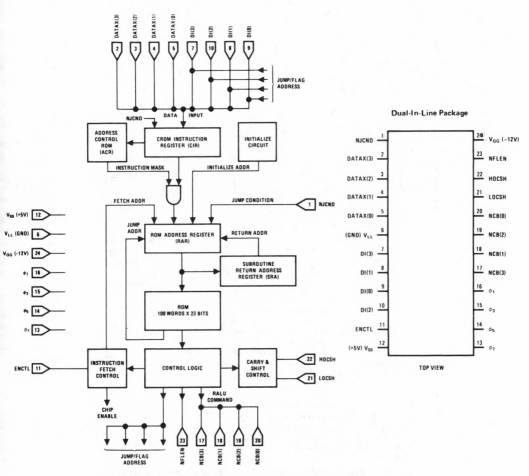

Fig. 7.14. CROM (a) Block diagram, (b) Terminal diagram (Courtesy of National Semiconductor Corporation, USA).

memory and causes a branch to the appropriate microprogram routine which implements the macroinstruction. A block diagram and a terminal diagram of the CROM are illustrated in Fig. 7.14.

The FILU provides the logic to interface the CROM and RALU to external memory and peripheral devices. It provides the microprocessor with sixteen flags, an 8-jump-condition multiplexer, an address register, a program counter, and a 6-level program counter stack. A 12-bit address bus and a 4-bit bidirectional data bus are provided for interfacing to memory and peripherals. The program counter points to the location in main memory of the next instruction to be read into the microprocessor. The 12-bit program counter (PC) may directly address 4096 bytes of memory. The program counter stack allows six levels of subroutine nesting. The address register

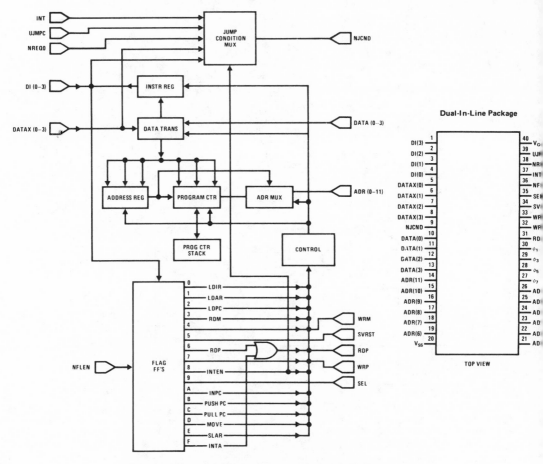

Fig. 7.15. FILU (a) Block diagram, (b) Terminal diagram (Courtesy of National Semiconductor Corporation, USA).

(AR) points to the location of data referred to in memory reference instructions. A block diagram and a terminal diagram of the FILU are illustrated in Fig. 7.15 A typical system diagram illustrating the interconnection of the RALU, CROM, and FILU with memory and I/O to form a microcomputer is illustrated in Fig. 7.16. During an instruction fetch, the contents of the memory location addressed by the PC are loaded into the IR in the FILU. After the first four bits are loaded into the IR, the PC is incremented and the next four bits of the instruction are fetched from memory. These four bits are sent directly to the CROM via the DATAX lines. At the same time, the four bits which were loaded into the IR in the FILU are also transmitted to the CROM over the DI lines, and the latched output of the jump condition multiplexer in the FILU is sent to the CROM. If the instruction contains a memory address, the microprogram will load the memory address into the AR in

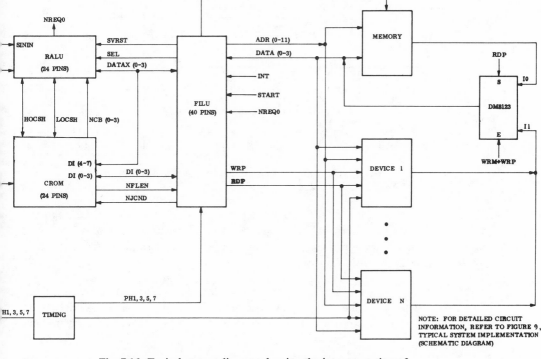

Fig. 7.16. Typical system diagram showing the interconnection of IMP-4 components (Courtesy of National Semiconductor Corporation, USA).

the FILU. The address is fetched from memory and formed in the AR by the memory address formation routine in the following manner:

1. The memory data addressed by the PC is loaded into bits 0–3 of AR.

2. PC is incremented, and the data addressed is loaded into bits 4–7 of AR.

3. PC is again incremented, and the data addressed is loaded into bits 8–11 of the AR.

4. Data addressed by the AR is loaded into the memory data register in the RALU.

Figure 7.17 illustrates a Load Accumulator, LD, instruction as it would appear in assembler notation, the hexadecimal equivalent as it would appear in memory, and the bit positions loaded into the CROM instruction register (CIR) and the AR.

The op code for the LD AC3 instruction is 74_{16} (Appendix B). The least significant four bits of the instruction are loaded first; therefore, the 4 appears in memory location 100 and the 7 in location 101. The address is stored in consecutive memory locations following the instruction, with the least significant hexadecimal word immediately following the op code in location 102.

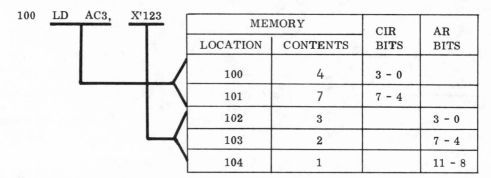

100 LD AC3, X'123				
MEMORY			**CIR**	**AR**
LOCATION	CONTENTS		**BITS**	**BITS**
100	4		3 – 0	
101	7		7 – 4	
102	3			3 – 0
103	2			7 – 4
104	1			11 – 8

Fig. 7.17. A load accumulator instruction for the IMP-4 (Courtesy of National Semiconductor Corporation, USA).

Interrupts enter the system through the jump condition multiplexer. During each instruction fetch, the interrupt line is tested. If an interrupt is sensed, a branch is executed to an interrupt processing routine in the microprogram (in CROM). This routine performs the following steps:

1. The interrupt enable flag is cleared to prevent additional interrupts from occurring until the first one is processed. The flag may be set under direct macroprogram control or upon execution of a Return from Interrupt instruction.

2. The contents of the PC are pushed onto the PC stack. This provides a return address when the interrupt routine is completed.

3. The program counter is cleared.

4. Using the zero address of the PC, device 0 (which must be an interrupt handler) is addressed and requested to scan all other devices in order to locate the interrupting device. Device 0 performs a hardware polling to locate the interrupting device.

5. When the interrupting device is located, the AR is loaded with an address (associated with the interrupting device). This is the starting address of the macroinstruction service routine.

System Timing

A timing diagram for the IMP-4 system is illustrated in Fig. 7.18. The basic machine cycle consists of the execution of one microprogram step. This cycle is composed of eight time periods, T1–T8. A pulse occurs on one of the four clock lines during the odd time intervals, T1, T3, T5, and T7.

Primary control of the RALU by the CROM is accomplished over the 4-bit control bus, NCB (Fig. 7.13). During T1, the three least significant control bits [NCB(0)–NCB(2)] specify the address of the register (R1–R7) to be loaded on the A bus. The fourth control bit enables stack operations. During T3, the address of the register to be loaded on the B bus is specified by NCB(0)–NCB(2). The most signifi-

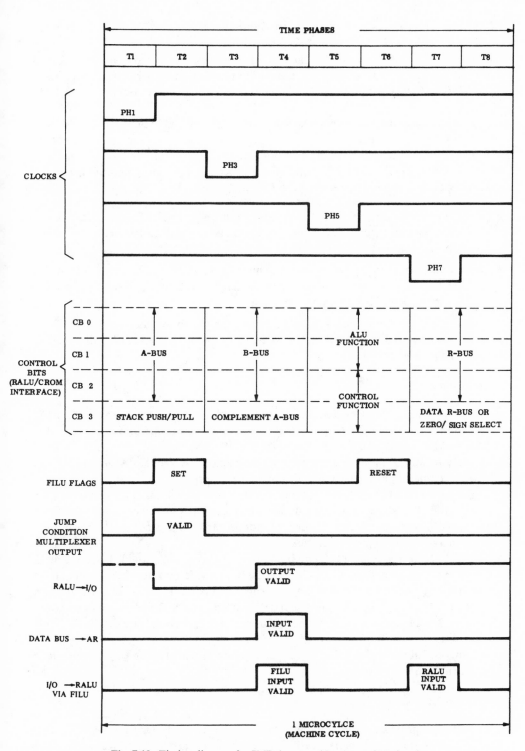

Fig. 7.18. Timing diagram for IMP-4 system (Courtesy of National Semiconductor Corporation, USA).

cant bit, NCB(3), indicates whether the A bus is to be complemented as it is transferred to the IA bus (Fig. 7.13). During T5, the ALU operation to be performed is specified by NCB(0)–NCB(1). NCB(2)–NCB(3) specify the shift and provide bus control for the R bus.

A unique flag address is established during each machine cycle. At T2 the flag may be set, and at T6 the flag may be reset. Therefore, a flag may be set, reset, or pulsed during a single machine cycle. If a conditional jump is being performed, the condition is tested during T2. Data transfer between the processor and main memory or peripherals may occur during T4 in one of the following ways:

1. The data present on the A bus is sent out through the FILU and is held on the terminal pins through T1. This information is output data destined for memory or an external device.

2. Data from memory or peripherals may be gated into the AR of the FILU. This occurs if either the RDM or INTA flag is set. If this is the case, no output from the RALU to memory can occur.

3. Data is read into the FILU if neither of the two previous cases occurs. This data is stored in a latch and is gated to the RALU during T7 if directed by the microprogram.

Instruction Set

The standard IMP-4 instruction set provides 42 instructions. A complete list is included in Appendix B. The typical arithmetical and logical operations are provided —binary ADD, AND, OR, and EXCLUSIVE-OR. The operands for these instructions may be any of the four accumulators or memory. A decimal ADD of any two of the accumulators using excess-3 arithmetic is also provided.

Data associated with the four accumulators can be shifted, rotated, pushed, or popped from the stack, and loaded from memory or a peripheral using a single instruction. The flags may be pushed or popped from the stack and the address register may be loaded from the stack.

Conditional and unconditional branch instructions are provided. The branch instructions include a Branch on Condition (BOC) which allows the transfer to be determined by one of eight conditions. Among these conditions are four which allow a branch to be based on an individual bit in accumulator 0 (AC0). Accumulators 0, 1, and 3 may be incremented and a conditional branch executed with a single instruction.

Jump to Subroutine and Return instructions are provided along with two methods for return from an interrupt.

Development Systems

National provides a prototyping system, the IMP-4P Development System, which consists of a control panel, a CPU card, a memory card, an interface card, power supplies, and a teletypewriter interface. Standard monitor debug programs are provided in ROM. A teletypewriter provides keyboard and paper tape input and output for the system. The basic system contains 8K words of read/write memory in addition to the ROM.

A cross-assembler and a pROM paper tape generator, both compatible with the General Electric Information Service time-share system, are also provided.

Companion Systems

Using the same basic building blocks, National also has an 8-bit machine, IMP-8, and a 16-bit machine, IMP-16. The IMP-8 uses two RALUs, a CROM, and a 4-bit control bus. The IMP-16 uses four RALUs, one or two CROMs, and a 4-bit control bus.

Comments

The IMP series of microcomputers was the first microprogrammable micro-computers. Microprogramming provides the capability of tailoring the instruction set to the user's particular application. It provides significant advantages for some systems with large production runs.

For many users, microprogramming simply introduces an additional complexity. In addition to microprogramming the machine, the user must generate his own support software—a formidable task for the novice. For this reason, National supplies a CROM, programmed with a standard instruction set, for each of the IMP series computers. By means of this CROM, macroprogramming is performed in the same fashion as it is for other microprocessors.

A single-chip version of the IMP-16, which is called PACE, is also available. It is described in Sec. 7.11.

7.5. ROCKWELL PPS-4 [11–15]

The PPS-4 is a monolithic, p-channel, 4-bit, parallel processing system. The microprocessor was originally developed as a single-chip calculator. The instruction set is extremely powerful for this class of operations [1].

The system employs a pair of timing signals which are generated from a clock circuit using a standard 3.58-MHz color-television crystal. User-selected wiring options allow the division of the frequency by 18 or 14 to provide a clock frequency of 199 kHz or 256 kHz, respectively. Thus, the basic cycle time is 5.029 μs or 3.911 μs. The system is faster than this cycle time indicates, however, because the machine cycles overlap.

Architecture

A block diagram of the CPU of the PPS-4 is shown in Fig. 7.19.

The CPU contains an instruction decoder, program counter, accumulator, and ALU to perform the basic functions of a microprocessor (Sec. 4.1). A carry flip-flop

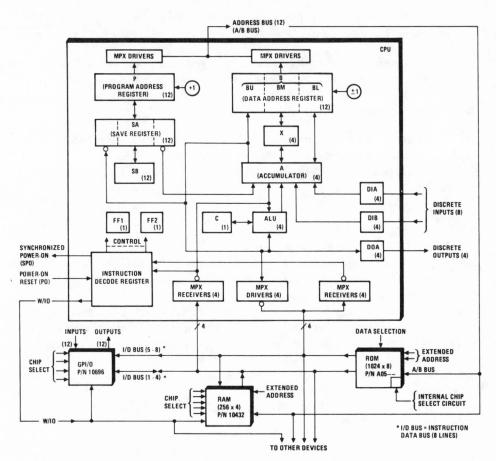

Fig. 7.19. Block diagram of the PPS-4 CPU (Courtesy of Rockwell International Corporation).

and two individual control flip-flops are provided to control conditional branching [11].

1. Memory Addressing

Program words and data words are addressed via a 12-bit address bus. The program address is held in the *program address register* (P register) which consists of two 6-bit registers. The six lower-order bits are automatically incremented following each instruction. The six higher-order bits must be set from the program. Execution of subroutines is facilitated by the provision of a two-level stack (SA and SB registers) within the microprocessor. For programs which require more than two levels of return address storage, an instruction (CYS) is provided to allow the stack to be extended into RAM.

Thus, virtually unlimited nesting is available, although software must be written to set up and access the portion of the stack in RAM.

The *data address register* (B register) is made up of three 4-bit registers BU (upper four bits), BM (middle four bits), and BL (lower four bits). BL may be incremented under program control to allow sequencing through the RAM registers. BU and BM may be set to any value with the software. Numerous memory-access instructions are provided which also perform modification of BU or BM. These instructions make the PPS-4 extremely efficient in handling arrays of data words. For example, a 16-digit, fixed-point, decimal add can be performed with only eight instructions.

A 4-bit *X register* is provided to facilitate temporary storage of the accumulator or BM. Using the accumulator and the X register, the upper eight bits of B (BU and BM) may be temporarily stored during the retrieval of a new data address from RAM.

2. Word Transfers

Data words or program words from RAM or ROM are multiplexed on the 8-bit instruction/data (I/D) bus (Fig. 7.20). Program words are transferred to the instruction decoder. Four-bit data words are passed to the accumulator on bit lines 1–4 of the I/D bus. At the same time, the contents of the accumulator are placed on bit lines 5–8 of the I/D bus. This allows the single-cycle exchange of information between the accumulator and RAM.

3. ALU/Accumulator

The ALU and accumulator are the center of the information-processing system. The accumulator is the primary working register and is the central data-interchange point for almost all data transfer operations. Since the accumulator is the focal point of all processing, the X register is made available for temporary storage of the accumulator. Arithmetic and logical operations are performed by the ALU. The ALU implements several ADD instructions. Some of these include conditional branching as a result of the add operation and decimal correction for implementing decimal addition. Logical operations include AND, OR, EXCLUSIVE-OR, and COMPLEMENT.

4. Input/Output

Input/output operations may be performed via the I/D bus or the set of three 4-bit discrete terminals. Two 4-bit discrete inputs (group A and group B) are provided for inputting special signals, switch positions, or flags from external circuitry. The discrete inputs are internally synchronized and will change states between -2.5 V and 7 V (for a 17-V power supply). The discrete outputs (four bits) may be used to output the accumulator directly to external circuits. The output driver is an open-drain MOS transistor to ground. In the ON state, the output is driven to ground with a maximum resistance of 1.25 kΩ and a maximum current of 1.25 mA. In the OFF state, the output is floating ($\geq$ 5 MΩ).

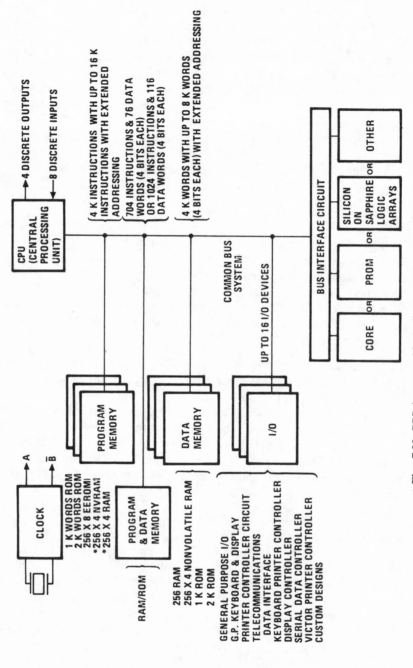

Fig. 7.20. PPS-4 system block diagram (Courtesy of Rockwell International Corporation).

The basic input/output instruction uses the I/D bus (Fig. 7.19). Two machine cycles are required for this instruction. During the first cycle, the first eight bits from the program memory merely inform the microprocessor that an I/O operation is in progress. The CPU then ignores the second byte of the instruction. The first eight bits also cause the WI/O signal to be available to the I/O devices. This signal is used to inhibit the memory elements and enable the I/O devices for the next cycle.

The second byte of the instruction is passed directly to the I/O devices. In the standard PPS devices, bits 5–8 identify the particular I/O device and bits 1–4 contain an operation code which is interpreted by the device. During the next data-transfer phase of the cycle, information may pass from the device to the accumulator on bits 1–4, and in the reverse direction on bits 5–8. Rockwell provides a variety of standard interface elements which are compatible with the PPS-4 system.

5. Control

The control section supplies a Write signal and I/O enable (WI/O) to a terminal for use in controlling memory write commands and the basic I/O operations on the I/D bus.

During power turn-on, the CPU requires an external signal to initialize the P register. A negative pulse on the POWER ON RESET terminal must be supplied. The microprocessor then generates a sychronized power-on output signal which may be used to initialize external circuits.

Although the PPS-4 does not have a true interrupt capability, limited interrupt behavior may be provided using software or the POWER ON RESET terminal.

6. Machine Cycle

The clock signals received by the microprocessor are logically divided into four phases. The internal signals are operated on at four times the frequency of the A clock. Figure 7.21 shows a typical machine cycle.

During the first and third phases, ϕ_1 and ϕ_3, the data and address buses are cleared. During ϕ_2 the ROM address is placed on the address bus, and during ϕ_4 the program word from ROM is read into the CPU. The timing sequence enables the system to drive high capacitive loads, e.g., as many as thirty PPS devices can share the bus without additional buffering or drive circuitry.

In the PPS-4 system, the machine cycles overlap. While the program word is being read from ROM on the I/D bus, during ϕ_4, the RAM address (from the B register) is placed on the address bus to address the appropriate data word. Then the address of the next instruction is placed on the address bus while the data word from RAM is being read and operated on.

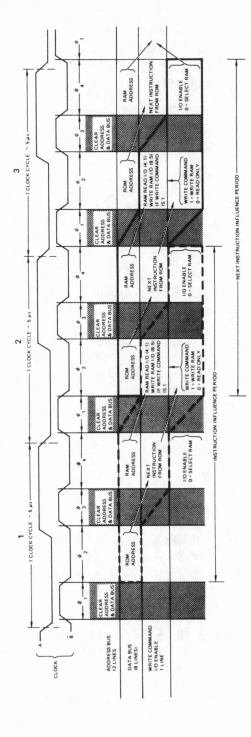

Fig. 7.21. Basic bus timing for PPS-4 (Courtesy of Rockwell International Corporation).

Organization of Memory

The 12-bit address lines allow 4K of RAM and 4K of ROM to be addressed directly. An additional 4K of RAM may be addressed by using one of the discrete output lines as a chip-select. Figure 7.22 illustrates the organization of the data memory. The data memory is composed of a maximum of sixteen 256×4 RAMs. The BU register specifies the chip which is being addressed. BM specifies the column and BL the row of the data word. A Special Address Generation (SAG) instruction allows access to any data word in the first column of the first RAM (BM $= 0$, BU $= 0$) without altering the contents of the B register [12].

Program memory is organized into 4×16-byte pages. Page 0 contains memory addresses 000–03F, page 1 contains 040–07F, page 2 contains 080–0BF, etc. Program address word organization is shown in Fig. 7.23. The program address word is a 14-bit word with twelve bits provided by the P register. The remaining two bits (BANK ADDRESS) are generally provided via the discrete output port.

The design of the PPS-4 gives special significance to certain program memory locations. Location 000 is always the location of the first instruction to be executed after the power is turned on. The initialization routine generally is contained on pages 1 and 2. Page 3 contains pointers. The first sixteen words (0C0–0CF) of page 3 contain data address pointers for the Load B Indirect instructions, and the remaining forty-eight locations (0D0–0FF) contain pointers to subroutine entry addresses selected by the Transfer and Mark instruction. These subroutine entry addresses may be any address on pages 4–15 of ROM 0. The remainder of the ROM memory has no special significance. It is used for program storage. Figure 7.24 shows the basic organization of the ROM memory.

Instruction Set

The PPS-4 instruction set includes fifty 1- and 2-byte instructions (Appendix C). These instructions may be categorized functionally as data transfer, arithmetic, logical, data address modification, internal register manipulation, program address modification, and input/output instructions. Many of the instructions are multi-faceted, i.e., more than one operation is performed by a single instruction. For example, some instructions will automatically test and modify the program sequence while performing another function such as moving or adding data [13].

The *data transfer instructions* include immediate loading of the accumulator and loading the accumulator from RAM. Instructions are also provided to exchange the accumulator with a word in RAM. Three of the four instructions in this category also provide for modification of the data address register (B). One of these single-byte instructions exchanges the accumulator and RAM, modifies three bits of BM, decrements BL, and skips the next ROM word if the new value of BL is 1111_2.

The *arithmetic instructions* consist of five add instructions and a decimal correction which facilitates decimal arithmetic. Three of these provide for skipping the next ROM word if the carry out is 1. AND, OR, EXCLUSIVE-OR, and COMPLEMENT form the *logical instructions*.

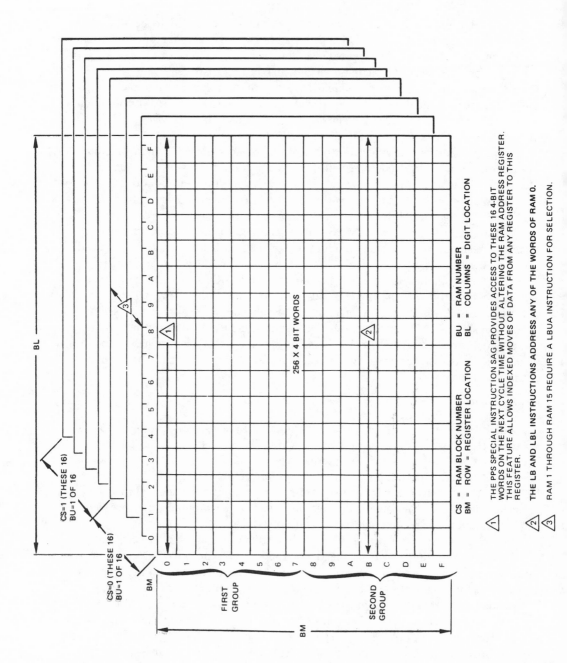

256 X 4 BIT WORDS

FIRST GROUP

SECOND GROUP

CS=0 (THESE 16)
BU=1 OF 16

CS=1 (THESE 16)
BU=1 OF 16

CS = RAM BLOCK NUMBER   BU = RAM NUMBER
BM = ROW = REGISTER LOCATION   BL = COLUMNS = DIGIT LOCATION

△1 THE PPS SPECIAL INSTRUCTION SAG PROVIDES ACCESS TO THESE 16 4-BIT
WORDS ON THE NEXT CYCLE TIME WITHOUT ALTERING THE RAM ADDRESS REGISTER.
THIS FEATURE ALLOWS INDEXED MOVES OF DATA FROM ANY REGISTER TO THIS
REGISTER.

△2 THE LB AND LBL INSTRUCTIONS ADDRESS ANY OF THE WORDS OF RAM 0.

△3 RAM 1 THROUGH RAM 15 REQUIRE A LBUA INSTRUCTION FOR SELECTION.

230

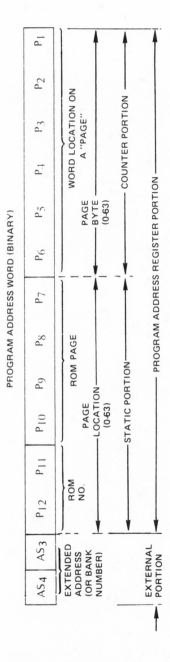

PROGRAM ADDRESS WORD (BINARY)

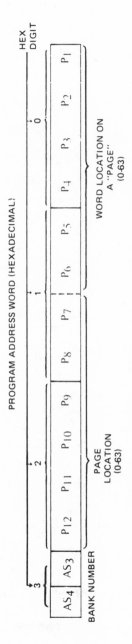

PROGRAM ADDRESS WORD (HEXADECIMAL)

Fig. 7.23. Program address word (Courtesy of Rockwell International Corporation).

231

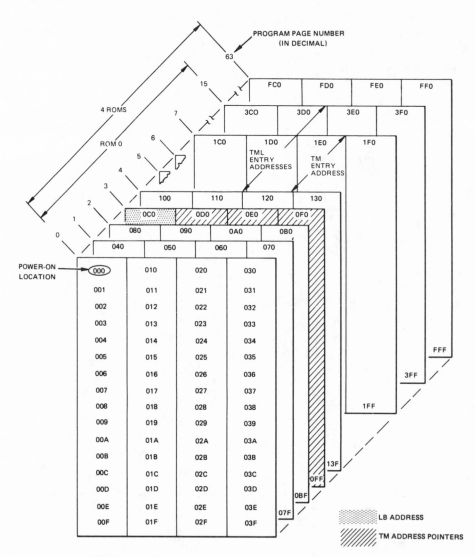

Fig. 7.24. Program memory organization (Courtesy of Rockwell International Corporation).

The *data address modification instructions* include several methods for loading the B register. The X register, accumulator, and ROM may be used to alter all or part of the contents of the B register. An interesting and useful characteristic of the Load B Indirect (LB) and Load B Long (LBL) instructions is that only the first occurrence of an LB or LBL instruction in a consecutive string of LB and LBL will be executed.

Unconditional and conditional transfer instructions are available for *program address modification*. In addition to those discussed in connection with other categories, instructions are provided for transferring within the same memory page and to other pages. A Transfer and Mark instruction provides transfer to a memory area containing the pointer address of a subroutine (page 3). When this instruction is executed, the return address is stored in the SA register. Conditional and unconditional Return instructions are available. Several conditional skip instructions allow the skip to be based on the carry flip-flop, condition flip-flop, and zero in the accumulator.

Internal register manipulation including transfers between the A, X, SA, SB, and B registers may be accomplished. In addition, all flags may be set or reset directly under program control. Finally, four input/output instructions are provided. The basic I/O instruction allows exchange of the accumulator and the contents of the data bus. Two discrete input and a discrete output instruction are also included.

Support Hardware

Two clock signals are required by the PPS-4. These are supplied by a single-chip clock generator. An external crystal is required. This is typically a standard 3.6-MHz color-television crystal. Clock *A* is a square wave and clock *B* consists of a train of pulses occurring at each phase of the *A* clock.

ROM, RAM, and I/O devices are designed to operate directly from the buses. Therefore, no additional hardware is needed to configure a typical system. Rockwell supplies a number of special-purpose interface ICs which are compatible with the system. These include a General-Purpose Keyboard and Display Device, Telecommunications Data Interface, and Serial Data Controller circuit. For communication with static MOS and TTL devices over the buses, a Bus Interface Circuit is also available.

The PPS-4 uses a single 17-V power supply from which 75–250 mW per package is required.

Microcomputer Systems

Evaluation and development may be facilitated by the use of modules to breadboard a proposed system. Rockwell provides CPU, RAM, pROM, and General-Purpose I/O modules among others [14].

The CPU module typically contains the CPU, clock with crystal, two 256×4 RAMs, and two GPI/O devices. The RAM module contains eight 256×4 RAMS ($2K \times 4$) and may also be configured as $1K \times 8$ bits for ROM emulation. The pROM module provides sockets for sixteen 1702A pROMs, two Bus Interface devices, and associated decoding logic. Forty-eight TTL buffered inputs and forty-eight buffered TTL outputs are provided by the General-Purpose I/O module.

The development of prototype systems is greatly simplified by the use of the PPS-4MP Assemulator. The basic configuration of the assemulator contains the CPU,

256 words of data memory, and 1K of program memory. A text editor, resident ROM assembler, and debugging programs are provided to assist the programmer. An interface is provided for the ASR 33 Teletype and the TI 733-ASR terminals. The system is packaged in a rack-mounted chassis which contains a variety of switches and indicators to assist in initialization and debugging. Optional equipment includes a pROM programmer and a high-speed paper tape reader.

A cross-assembler and simulator program is available in FORTRAN IV. It is also available on Tymshare and General Electric time-sharing network [15].

Comments

The PPS-4 has an extremely powerful instruction set for performing precision arithmetic. Many of the instructions perform two or more functions. The provision of a large variety of special-purpose interface components has broadened the applicability of the system from its calculator beginnings.

One shortcoming of the system is its lack of interrupt capability. A simulated interrupt can be provided by software, or the POWER ON RESTART terminal may be used to obtain a form of interrupt. Considerable external hardware or software will be necessary if interrupt capability is necessary.

The system is designed to require minimal support hardware. The special-purpose and general-purpose interface circuits are designed for direct connection to the microprocessor buses. In addition, only one power supply is required.

7.6.   INTEL 8008/8008-1

The Intel 8008 was the first 8-bit, monolithic microprocessor to be developed [8]. It is a p-channel MOS device whose addressing structure is that of a von Neumann class computer. The device requires a two-phase clock operating at 500 kHz (maximum) and has a basic cycle time (ten clock periods) of 20 μs. A selected version, the 8008-1, operates at a clock frequency of 800 kHz (maximum) and has a basic cycle time of 12.5 μs.

Architecture

A block diagram of the 8008/8008-1 is shown in Fig. 7.25. The four functional areas of the processor consist of the instruction register and control section, internal memory, ALU, and I/O buffers [16]. These areas communicate with one another over an internal 8-bit data bus. The role and structure of each area are now described.

1.   Instruction Register and Control Section
The instruction register is the heart of the processor control. Instructions are fetched from memory, stored in the instruction register, and decoded for control of both the internal memory and the ALU. The timing and cycle control sections provide two input terminals (READY and INTERRUPT) and four output terminals (S_0, S_1, S_2, and SYNC) for internal and external control, respectively.

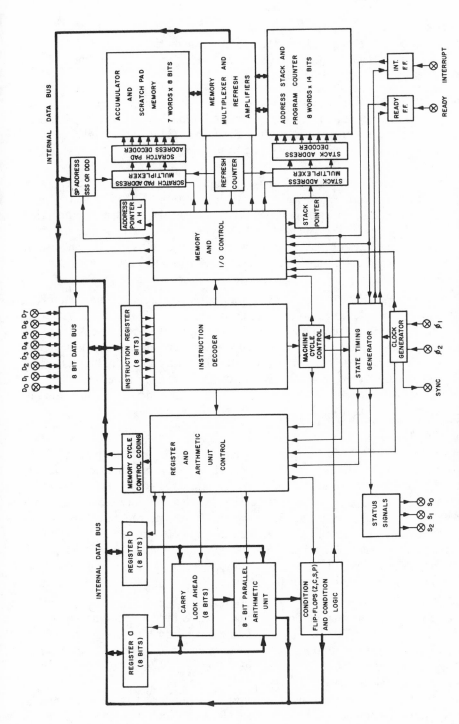

Fig. 7.25. Block diagram of the 8008/8008-1 (Courtesy of INTEL Corporation).

235

2. Internal Memory

Dynamic RAM is employed for two internal memories: a pushdown address stack and a scratch-pad array. These memories are automatically refreshed—in the worst case every eighty clock periods.

(a) *Address Stack.* The address stack consists of eight 14-bit registers which provide storage for eight lower-order and six high-order address bits in each register. A 14-bit address permits the direct addressing of 16K words of memory. Memory, in this case, can be any combination of RAM, ROM, or shift registers.

One register of the stack is used as a program counter and the remaining seven allow address storage for nesting of subroutines up to seven levels. The stack, an LIFO array, stores the content of the program counter when a Call instruction is executed and restores the program counter upon the execution of a Return. A 3-bit address pointer is used to indicate the location of the program counter. When the capacity of the stack is exceeded, the deepest-level register of the stack is lost, as described in Sec. 4.4.

(b) *Scratch-Pad Memory.* The scratch-pad memory contains an 8-bit accumulator (A) and six additional 8-bit data registers (B, C, D, E, H, and L). All arithmetic operations use the accumulator as one of the operands. All registers are independent and may be used for temporary storage. For instructions which address external memory, registers H and L are required for a register-indirect addressing mode. Register L contains the eight lower-order bits and register H contains the six higher-order bits of the address. In this case, bits 6 and 7 of H are "don't cares."

3. ALU

All arithmetic and logical operations are performed in the 8-bit parallel binary arithmetic unit which includes look-ahead carry logic. Registers a and b are temporary registers (inaccessible to the programmer) used to store the contents of the accumulator and the operand for ALU operations. They are also used for temporary address and data storage during intraprocessor transfers. Four control (status) bits—carry flip-flop, zero flip-flop, sign flip-flop, and parity flip-flop—are set as the result of an arithmetical or logical operation. These bits provide conditional branching capability through Call, Jump, or Return on Condition instructions (Sec. 4.4). The carry bit is required for multiple-precision arithmetic.

4. I/O Buffer

The I/O buffer controls the flow of data between the internal data bus of the processor and the external data bus (D_0–D_7). Signals from the timing and control sections are used for time-multiplexing of the data bus to allow control information, 14-bit addresses, and data to be transmitted between the processor and external memory or I/O devices.

The processor is packaged in an 18-pin dual in-line package, as shown in Fig. 7.26. ϕ_1 and ϕ_2 are inputs for the two-phase clock, and power supply voltages V_{CC}

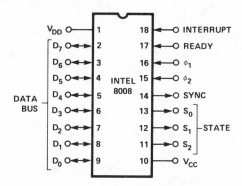

Fig. 7.26. 8008/8008-1 18-pin DIP.

and V_{DD} are $+5$ V and -9 V, respectively. At 25°C, the IC dissipates 1W of power. All inputs are TTL-compatible, and all outputs are low-power TTL-compatible.

Machine Cycle

Typically, a machine cycle consists of five states, with each state requiring two clock periods; see Fig. 7.27. Two states, T1 and T2, are required to send an address to external memory, and state T3 is needed to fetch the instruction or data. States T4 and T5 are employed for the execution of the instruction. If the processor is used with slow memories, the READY line is used to synchronize the processor with these memories. In this case, the processor enters a WAIT state until the memory byte is available. A READY is acknowledged by T3.

Upon the receipt of an INTERRUPT, the T1 state is replaced by the T1I state at the beginning of a machine cycle. This avoids aborting any instruction in progress when an INTERRUPT is requested. The program counter is not incremented during T1I, as it normally would be in T1. When the INTERRUPT is acknowledged, external logic is required to disable the memory from the memory data bus and jam an 8-bit instruction word directly onto the bus during T3. Finally, if a halt (HLT) instruction is fetched, the processor enters a STOP state at the end of T3. An INTERRUPT is then required to restart the machine. A state-transition diagram describing the processor cycle is shown in Fig. 7.28.

The processor controls the use of the data bus and determines whether it will be sending or receiving data. State signals S_0, S_1, and S_2, along with SYNC, inform the peripheral circuitry of the state of the processor. A table of the binary state codes is shown in Table 7.1.

Instructions for the 8008 require one, two, or three machine cycles for complete execution. The first cycle is always an instruction fetch cycle (PCI). The second and third cycles are data reading (PCR), data writing (PCW), or I/O operations (PCC).

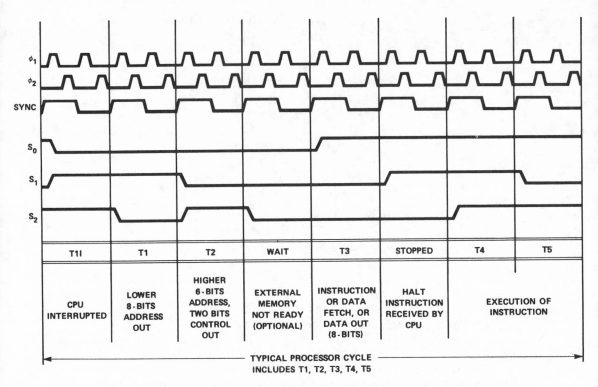

Fig. 7.27. Basic 8008 machine cycle (Courtesy of INTEL Corporation).

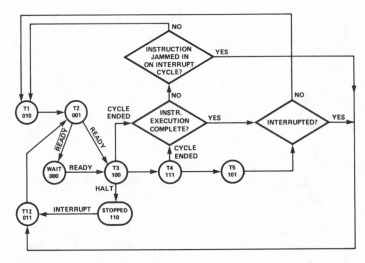

Fig. 7.28. CPU state transition diagram (Courtesy of INTEL Corporation).

Table 7.1 BINARY STATE CODES.

S_0	S_1	S_2	State
0	1	0	T1
0	1	1	T1I
0	0	1	T2
0	0	0	WAIT
1	0	0	T3
1	1	0	STOPPED
1	1	1	T4
1	0	1	T5

Table 7.2 CYCLE CODES.

D_6	D_7	Cycle	Function
0	0	PCI	Designates the address is for a memory read (first byte of instruction).
0	1	PCR	Designates the address is for a memory read data (additional bytes of instruction or data).
1	0	PCC	Designates the data as a command I/0 operation.
1	1	PCW	Designates the address is for a memory write data.

The cycle types are coded with two bits, D_6 and D_7, as shown in Table 7.2, and are only present on the data bus during T2. Many instructions for the processor do not require the two execution states T4 and T5. In this case, these states are omitted.

Instruction Set

The instruction set of the 8008 consists of forty-eight instructions in four logical groups (Appendix D). Instructions in the various groups are either one, two, or three bytes in length. The first byte contains the op code, and the second and third bytes, if necessary, give the data or the address. One-byte instructions include register-to-register, memory reference, I/O, arithmetical or logical, rotate, and return instructions. Two-byte and three-byte instructions include immediate mode and jump or call instructions, respectively.

The first group consists of seven so-called index (scratch-pad) register instructions (these registers are not index registers by the conventional definition; see Sec. 4.4). Five allow data transfers between individual registers and between registers and external memory. The remaining two instructions permit incrementing and decrementing all index (scratch-pad) registers, excluding register A.

Twenty-eight instructions are accumulator group instructions for arithmetical and logical operations. Twenty-four ALU instructions divided into three groups of eight each are: (a) operations that reference index registers, (b) operations that reference external memory via the H and L registers, and (c) operations that reference immediate data. ALU operations in each category allow for addition and subtraction with or without carry or borrow, AND, OR, and EXCLUSIVE-OR operations, and equality tests involving the accumulator. Four shift instructions permit shifting the accumulator left or right, through or around the carry bit.

A third group consists of ten stack control instructions for jumps, calls, and returns, both unconditional and based upon tests of the four status bits. A special one-word call, Restart (RST), is provided for use with interrupts or frequently used subroutines.

The final group contains two I/O instructions. IN permits transferring an 8-bit word to the accumulator from one of eight input ports implied in the instruction field. OUT causes the contents of the accumulator to be output to one of twenty-four implicit output addresses.

Also included in the instruction set are two machine instructions: the Halt (HLT) and No Operation (NOP). The NOP is a register-to-register transfer where the source and destination registers are the same (e.g., MOV A, A).

Support Hardware

One of the primary shortcomings of the 8008 is the large amount of peripheral logic necessary to form a microcomputer as a consequence of the single 8-bit data bus. This requires the implementation of a multiplexer and a complex timing network for control of the system. Approximately twenty MSI packages are required in order to interface the processor to external memory and I/O devices.

To form a microcomputer system, the processor typically requires the external circuitry shown in Fig. 7.29 [17]. In this figure, the CPU unit consists of the processor, a two-phase clock, control logic, registers I_1 and I_2, and decoders for cycle, phase, and state decoding. The 8-bit bidirectional data bus connects the processor to external memory and registers I_1 and I_2 (address and status latches). The control section determines the direction of data flow on the bus to and from the processor and strobes data into registers I_1 and I_2. It also decides when the memory reads or writes, and it activates the I/O channels.

External registers I_1 and I_2 supply addresses to memory, as well as data bytes and pointers to I/O channels. Data from the two MSB positions of I_2 are transferred to the cycle decoder to produce PCI, PCR, PCW, and PCC (Table 7.2). This coordinates the internal operation of the processor with the external circuitry. The state decoder is a 1-of-8 decoder which supplies the control logic with the state of the CPU (Table 7.1), whereas the phase decoder supplies clock phase information.

For a detailed discussion of the timing signals and circuits of an 8008 microcomputer system, refer to Reference [18].

Microcomputer Systems

A popular microcomputer set available for the system designer is the Intel MCS-8. Numerous hardware modules are available in this set. Several which are very useful are a CPU, an Input/Output, an Output, a RAM Memory, and a pROM Memory module.

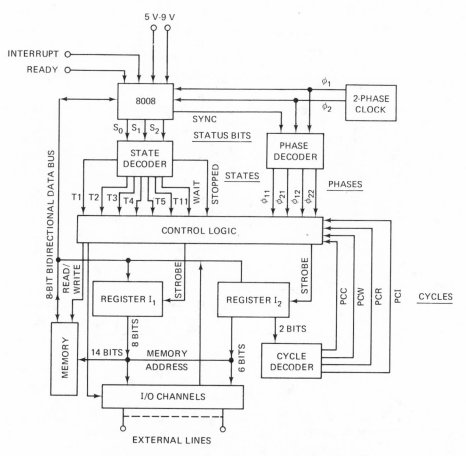

Fig. 7.29. Typical microcomputer system using the 8008.

The CPU module includes all the circuitry of Fig. 7.29, excluding the memory and I/O channels sections. The Input/Output module provides an I/O facility having four 8-bit individually addressable ports at both the input and the output. Two of these at both the input and output are used for TTY interfacing and control. The heart of the TTY communication circuit is the Universal Asynchronous Receiver Transmitter (UART), as described in Sec. 6.6. The Output module provides eight 8-bit individually addressable output ports which are TTL-compatible.

The RAM Memory module is a 4K byte, n-channel MOS memory system employing thirty-two 1024-bit 2102 static RAMs. The pROM Memory module accommodates up to sixteen 1702A pROMs. For volume requirements, the mask-programmed 1302 ROMs can be used. Address and data latches and module select decoding are provided on both memory modules.

A useful prototyping system employing the above modules is the Intellec 8/MOD 8. A block diagram of this system is shown in Fig. 7.30. In addition to these modules,

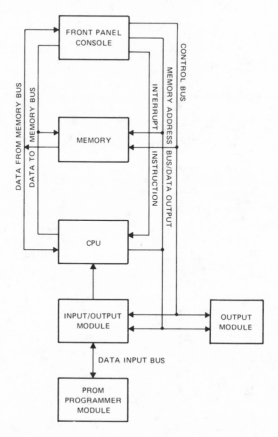

Fig. 7.30. Block diagram of the Intellec 8/MOD 8 (Courtesy of INTEL Corporation).

the system includes a console and a pROM programmer module for programming the 1702A. 8K bytes of RAM and a set of standard software are supplied.

The standard software includes a resident system monitor, an assembler (three-pass), and a text editor [19–20]. The assembler and text editor may be loaded from paper tape via an ASR 33 TTY. In addition to the standard software, a PL/M compiler, cross-assembler, and simulator are available in FORTRAN IV (provided on national time-sharing systems) [21].

Numerous companies are marketing microcomputers using the 8008 or 8008-1 processor providing, in many instances, both hardware and software support.

Comments

A system designer considering the use of a microcomputer based on the 8008 or 8008-1 processor should be aware of several properties. The 8008 operates from a 500-kHz asymmetrical two-phase clock, whereas the 8008-1 employs an 800-kHz symmetrical two-phase clock. For this reason, the 8008-1 is often used even in cases where the additional speed is of no advantage [1].

The microprocessor does not have instructions with direct addresses since two CPU (H and L) registers must be used to reference main storage. In fetching an operand from storage, these two registers must be loaded with the desired address. This requires at least three instructions to refer to arbitrarily placed data. In addition, some operations, such as moving data from one place in storage to another, are somewhat awkward.

Another problem area is that associated with an interrupt. When an interrupt occurs, the processor inhibits incrementing the program counter (PC), acknowledges the interrupt, and proceeds with an instruction fetch cycle. External hardware is used to jam an instruction on the data bus (usually a Restart) which pushes the PC onto the stack and initiates an interrupt-service routine. When the interrupt routine is complete, a Return pops the stack, restoring the PC. To commence execution at the state immediately prior to the interrupt, all scratch-pad registers and status bits which are being used in the main program must be restored to their original values. Since H and L are required to address memory during the interrupt, the programmer must reserve two of the scratch-pad registers as interrupt registers. This reduces the effective number of the registers in the scratch-pad file from seven to five.

Finally, the single 8-bit bus into the processor requires a large amount of support hardware. If a single IC is produced which will replace these components, this processor will be valuable in many more applications.

7.7. INTEL 8080

The Intel 8080, an 8-bit, monolithic, n-channel MOS device, is a second-generation microprocessor with many improvements over its predecessor, the 8008 [22]. These improvements include thirty additional instructions, a tenfold improvement in speed with a basic cycle time of 2 μs, and separate address and data buses. Most of the external logic required to support the 8008 is on the 8080 CPU, and all the important interfacing signals are generated on designated processor pins.

Although the architecture of the 8080 is significantly different from that of the 8008, there is a major software compatibility designed for upgrading to the newer processor.

Architecture

A block diagram of the 8080 CPU is shown in Fig. 7.31. The four functional areas of the CPU are the register array and address logic, ALU, instruction register and control section, and the data bus buffer [23]. The structure and role of each area are described as follows.

1. Register Array and Address Logic
    The register array consists of a static RAM array organized in six 16-bit registers:

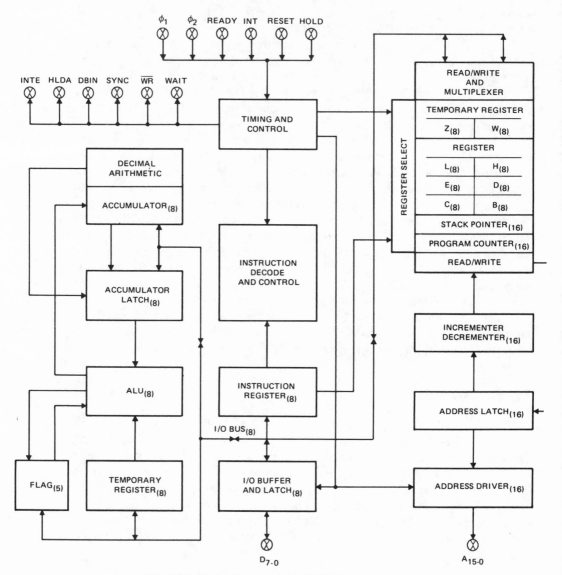

Fig. 7.31. Block diagram of the 8080 (Courtesy of INTEL Corporation).

(a) *Program Counter (PC)*. The 16-bit PC maintains the memory address of the current program instruction and increments upon every instruction fetch.

(b) *Stack Pointer (SP)*. The 16-bit SP maintains the address of the next stack location in memory. The SP is decremented when data is pushed on the stack and incremented when data is popped. The SP can be initialized to use any portion of RAM. This allows a virtually unlimited subroutine nesting capability.

(c) *Register Pairs* (*B-C, D-E, H-L,* and *W-Z*). Register pairs *B-C, D-E,* and *H-L* are six 8-bit scratch-pad registers which can be used as six single registers (8-bit) or as three register pairs (16-bit). The temporary register pair *W-Z* is used for internal instructions and is not accessible to the programmer.

The 16-bit address latch receives data from any of the three scratch-pad register pairs and permits 65K bytes of memory to be directly addressed via the address buffers (A_0–A_{15}). The incrementer/decrementer receives data from the address latch and transfers it to the register array. During the transfer, the data may be incremented or decremented. Data bytes are multiplexed between the internal bus and the register array, and 16-bit transfers are permitted between the register array and the address latch or incrementer/decrementer circuit.

2. Arithmetic and Logic Unit

The ALU performs arithmetical, logical, and rotate operations. Registers which function with the ALU include an 8-bit accumulator, an 8-bit temporary accumulator, an 8-bit temporary register, and a 5-bit flag register (zero, carry, sign, parity, and auxiliary carry).

Decimal correction of the accumulator is accomplished by the DAA instruction using the auxiliary carry. The flag bits provide a conditional branching capability via instructions such as Call and Jump on Condition (Sec. 4.4).

In the design of the processor, the inclusion of the accumulator into the arithmetic and logic unit area has avoided the use of the internal bus for data transfers between the scratch-pad memory and the ALU during arithmetical and logical operations. This is a significant improvement over the 8008 which requires sharing the internal bus for these transfers.

3. Instruction Register and Control Section

The instruction register is an 8-bit register which transfers information from the internal bus to the instruction decode and control section. The output of the decoder, combined with timing signals from the timing and state control section, provides the control signals for the memory, ALU, and data bus buffer.

Outputs from the instruction decoder and external control signals feed the timing and state control section. Inputs into the timing section include clock inputs ϕ_1 and ϕ_2 (the inputs of a two-phase external clock) and four internal control inputs READY, Interrupt (INT), RESET, and HOLD. Six state and cycle outputs provide Interrupt Enable (INTE), Hold Acknowledge (HLDA), Data Bus In (DBIN), SYNC, Write (WR), and WAIT signals for external control of memory and I/O devices.

4. Data Bus Buffer

The data bus buffer is an 8-bit, bidirectional, tri-state buffer used to isolate the internal bus of the processor from the external data bus (D_0–D_7). In the output mode, the content of the internal bus is transferred into an 8-bit latch. This latch drives the data bus output buffers. These buffers are switched off during input or nontransfer operations. In the input mode, data from the external data bus is transferred to the internal bus.

The 8080 is packaged in a 40-pin dual in-line package, as shown in Fig. 7.32.

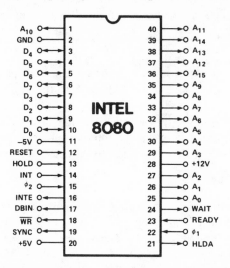

Fig. 7.32. 8080 40-pin DIP (Courtesy of INTEL Corporation).

Instruction Cycle

A machine cycle in the 8080 consists of three, four, or five states, where each state is equal to the time interval of one period of the two-phase clock. Typically, the clock frequency is 2 MHz, which results in a state of 0.5-μs duration. An instruction cycle is composed of one to five machine cycles.

The nine different machine cycles which may occur in the processor are the FETCH, MEMORY READ, MEMORY WRITE, STACK READ, STACK WRITE, INPUT, OUTPUT, INTERRUPT, and HALT cycles. No instruction cycle will consist of more than five of these cycles. The machine cycles that occur depend on the particular instruction being executed; however, the first machine cycle of any instruction cycle is always a FETCH. The processor identifies the machine cycle being executed by placing an 8-bit status signal on the data lines (D_0–D_7) during the SYNC interval, as shown in Table 7.3. This data may be latched and decoded for use in the control of external circuitry.

A typical timing diagram for a FETCH machine cycle is shown in Fig. 7.33. All machine cycles have the three states T_1, T_2, and T_3. If the processor has to wait for a response from a peripheral, then the cycle may contain one or more wait states T_w. During these first three states, data is transferred to or from the processor. After the T_3 state, execution of the T_4 and T_5 states depends on the type of instruction being processed. The activities of the different states are summarized in Table 7.4.

A state transition diagram for the processor is shown in Fig. 7.34. In addition to the T_1–T_5 and T_w states, the diagram also shows how the READY, HOLD, and INTERRUPT lines are sampled during a machine cycle, and how the conditions on these lines may modify the basic transition sequence.

Table 7.3 8080 STATUS BIT DEFINITIONS.

Symbols	Data Bus Bit	Definition
INTA*	D_0	Acknowledge signal for Interrupt request. Signal should be used to gate a Restart instruction onto the data bus when DBIN is active.
$\overline{\text{WO}}$	D_1	Indicates that the operation in the current machine cycle will be a WRITE MEMORY or OUTPUT function ($\overline{\text{WO}}$ = 0). Otherwise, a READ MEMORY or INPUT operation will be executed.
STACK	D_2	Indicates that the address bus holds the pushdown stack address from the stack pointer.
HLTA	D_3	Acknowledge signal for Halt instruction.
OUT	D_4	Indicates that the address bus contains the address of an output device, and the data bus will contain the output data when WR is active.
M_1	D_5	Provides a signal to indicate that the CPU is in the FETCH cycle for the first byte of an instruction.
INP*	D_6	Indicates that the address bus contains the address of an input device, and the input data should be placed on the data bus when DBIN is active.
MEMR*	D_7	Designates that the data bus will be used for memory read data.

*These three status bits can be used to control the flow of data onto the 8080 data bus.

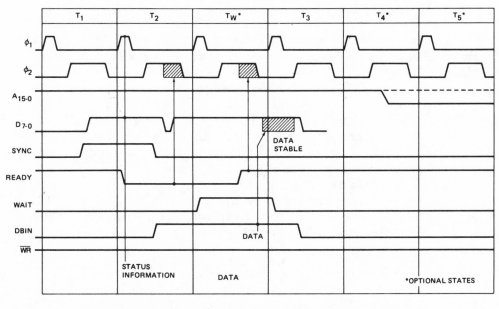

Fig. 7.33. Typical FETCH machine cycle (Courtesy of INTEL Corporation).

Table 7.4 8080 STATE DEFINITIONS.

State	Associated Activities
T_1	A memory address or I/O device number is placed on the address bus; status information is placed on the data bus.
T_2	The CPU samples the READY and HOLD inputs and checks for Halt instruction.
T_w (optional)	Processor enters WAIT state if READY is low or if Halt instruction has been executed.
T_3	An instruction byte (FETCH cycle), data byte (MEMORY READ, STACK READ, or INPUT cycle), or Interrupt instruction (INTERRUPT cycle) is input to the CPU from the data bus; or a data byte (MEMORY WRITE, STACK WRITE, or OUTPUT cycle) is output onto the data bus.
T_4, T_5 (optional)	States T_4 and T_5 are available if the execution of a particular instruction requires them; if not, the CPU may skip one or both of them. T_4 and T_5 are used only for internal processor operations.

When an INTERRUPT request occurs and the INTE is high, the INT flip-flop is set during the last state of the machine cycle in which the request occurs. This ensures that the current cycle completes execution. The INTERRUPT cycle proceeds as a FETCH cycle with the INTA status bit acknowledging the request. The contents of the PC are latched on the address lines at T_1, but the PC is not incremented during the cycle. At T_3, an 8-bit interrupt instruction is jammed onto the data bus. This requires external logic to temporarily disconnect the memory from the processor and allow the interrupting device to command the data bus. A special 1-byte call (RST) is generally used in processing interrupts. This instruction addresses one of eight fixed memory locations and allows the formulation of a program for saving the contents of the PC, flag bits, and scratch-pad memory in the stack. After servicing the interrupt, an orderly return to the interrupted instruction is easily accomplished.

A HOLD request is applied to the processor when a direct memory access (DMA) is desired. A HOLD is acknowledged by placing a high on the HLDA output pin and by floating the address and data outputs. The address and data buses are then under the control of the peripheral which made the request, enabling it to conduct memory transfers without processor intervention.

When a halt instruction (HLT) is executed, the processor enters the T_{WH} after T_2 of the next machine cycle (Fig. 7.33). In order to exit this state, a RESET, HOLD, or INTERRUPT must be executed. In the case of a HOLD, however, when the HOLD is terminated the processor returns to the halt state.

Instruction Set

The 8080 instruction set consists of 78 instructions which include the 48 instructions of the 8008 and 30 new instructions (Appendix E). The new instructions give the 8080 much more flexibility in operations involving data manipulation, memory addressing, and the processing of interrupts.

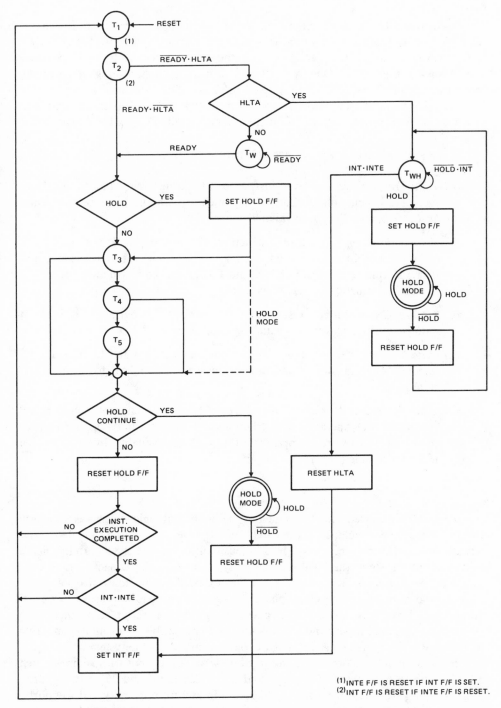

RESET

T_1
(1)

T_2
(2)

$\overline{READY} \cdot HLTA$

READY $\cdot \overline{HLTA}$

HLTA — YES

NO

T_W

READY — $\overline{READY}$

INT $\cdot$ INTE — T_{WH} — $\overline{HOLD} \cdot \overline{INT}$

HOLD

HOLD — YES — SET HOLD F/F

NO

SET HOLD F/F

T_3

T_4

HOLD MODE

HOLD MODE — HOLD

$\overline{HOLD}$

RESET HOLD F/F

T_5

HOLD CONTINUE — YES

NO

RESET HOLD F/F

RESET HLTA

HOLD MODE — HOLD

INST. EXECUTION COMPLETED — NO

YES

$\overline{HOLD}$

RESET HOLD F/F

INT $\cdot$ INTE — NO

YES

SET INT F/F

(1) INTE F/F IS RESET IF INT F/F IS SET.
(2) INT F/F IS RESET IF INTE F/F IS RESET.

Fig. 7.34. 8080 state transition diagram (Courtesy of INTEL Corporation).

249

As in the 8008, all instructions are either one, two, or three bytes in length. Multiple-byte instructions are stored in successive memory locations. The first byte of the instruction gives the op code, whereas the second and third bytes, if required, give the data or the address. One-byte instructions include register-to-register, memory reference, arithmetic, logical, Rotate, Return, Push, Pop, and Enable or Disable Interrupt instructions. Two-byte instructions include immediate mode and I/O instructions. Three-byte instructions include Jump, Call, Direct, Load, and Store instructions.

The instruction set consists of five groups:

(a) *Data Transfer Group*. Eleven instructions for transferring data to and from memory. Instructions for addressing memory via the three register pairs (*B-C*, *D-E*, and *H-L*) are available.

(b) *Arithmetic Group*. Fourteen instructions for performing arithmetic operations on data in registers and memory. Instructions for incrementing and decrementing register pairs (INX and DCX) and an instruction permitting decimal arithmetic (DAA) are available.

(c) *Logical Group*. Fifteen instructions for performing logical operations on data in registers and memory and on condition flags.

(d) *Branch Group*. Twenty-nine instructions for performing conditional and unconditional transfers. Conditional transfers are permitted for eight conditions.

(e) *Stack, I/O, and Machine Control Group*. Nine instructions for performing stack and I/O operations. Instructions for pushing and popping register pairs and status words to and from the stack are available. Interrupt enable (EI) and disable (DI) are also available.

Support Hardware

The 8080 is designed such that much of the peripheral logic which was necessary for the 8008 has been included in the CPU. The use of separate address and data buses has also eliminated the necessity of the data bus multiplexer of the 8008. In forming a microcomputer system, the 8080 requires only six external TTL packages. This is illustrated in Fig. 7.35 [22]. In this figure, an external crystal-controlled oscillator supplies two nonoverlapping clock phases, ϕ_1 and ϕ_2. Buffers interface to external address and data buses, and a NAND gate and eight latches set up status bits at the appropriate time. All inputs and outputs are TTL-compatible. A memory consisting of ROM, RAM, or shift registers, and I/O devices completes the system.

External signals are organized on three buses: an address bus with 16 lines which addresses up to 65K bytes of memory and up to 256 input and 256 output ports; a bidirectional 8-bit data bus which carries data to and from memory and I/O ports; and a control bus which synchronizes the processor, external memory, and I/O devices.

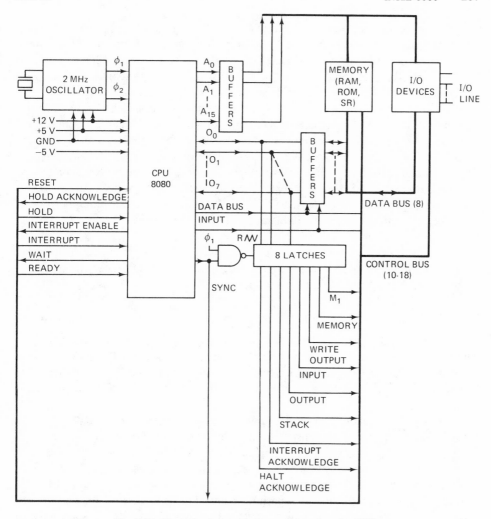

Fig. 7.35. Typical microcomputer system using the 8080.

The control bus also handles interrupts, direct memory access (DMA) controls, and processor status information.

Microcomputer Systems

A popular microcomputer set available for the system designer, based on the 8080, is the Intel MCS-80 [23]. This set is an outgrowth of the MCS-8. The hardware available in this set is essentially the same as that which was developed for its predecessor. This includes a CPU, an Input/Output, an Output, a RAM Memory and a pROM Memory module. Since all modules, excluding the CPU module, are similar to those of the MCS-8, the reader is referred to Sec. 7.6. The CPU module for the

MCS-80, of course, replaces the 8008 with the 8080. In addition to these modules, Intel offers numerous other peripheral support components in the MCS-80 family.

A useful prototyping system in the MCS-80 series is the Intellec 8/MOD 80 [24], which utilizes the additional features of the 8080 processor to achieve superior performance characteristics over its predecessor, the MOD 8. Another useful microcomputer is the Intellec MDS, which consists of two systems: a basic facility that controls a general-purpose set of development resources (similar to the Intellec 8), and a specialized in-circuit emulator. The emulator tailors the programming, emulation, and diagnostic functions to a particular class of microcomputers.

The standard software, like the MOD 8, includes a resident system monitor, an assembler (three-pass) [25], and a text editor. The assembler and text editor may be loaded from paper tape via an ASR 33 TTY. In addition, a PL/M compiler, cross-assembler, and simulator are available in FORTRAN IV (provided on national time-sharing systems).

As in the case of 8008-based microcomputers, numerous manufacturers are marketing microcomputers using the 8080 processor. In most instances, these vendors provide both hardware and software support.

Comments

The 8080 is designed so that microcomputers using this processor are software-compatible with systems based on the 8008. However, because the 8080 has such different CALL and I/O procedures, one often rewrites the 8008 programs from the beginning [26]. This, depending on the particular program, may or may not be the case.

The basic instruction cycle of the 8080 requires 2 μs as compared to 12.5 μs for the 8008-1. The thirty new instructions include an entire class of storage-referencing instructions in which three register pairs are available for addressing memory. The additional instructions often reduce the memory requirements from 95% to 70% of that needed in an 8008-based system. The stack is located in RAM and is limited only by the storage capacity. This permits a nesting of subroutines which is almost unlimited. In addition, instructions are available which allow status bits and register pairs to be stored in the stack for the processing of interrupts.

The 8080 is packaged in a 40-pin DIP and has separate address and data buses having tri-state outputs. This allows direct memory access by use of external circuitry when the processor is placed in a HOLD condition. As a result of the separate data and address buses, a microcomputer is formed with as few as six TTL packages. A disadvantage, however, is that the 8080 requires three separate power supplies.

7.8. Motorola 6800 [27–30]

The 6800 is an 8-bit, monolithic, NMOS microprocessor. Associated with the microprocessor is a family of compatible components which include programmable interfaces. All of these devices utilize a single 5-V power supply. Each of the 6800 family components can be connected directly to the microprocessor address and data buses. The buses are capable of driving a TTL load plus several 6800 family components without buffering. A two-phase external clock (1 MHz, maximum) must be externally supplied.

Architecture

The basic architecture of the microprocessor is illustrated in Fig. 7.36. Data flow to and from the CPU occurs over the 8-bit data bus (D0–D7). Addresses are sent over the 16-bit address bus (A0–A15). Both of the buses are connected to the CPU through tri-state devices to allow DMA operations. The microprocessor does not distinguish between memory and peripheral addresses. Therefore, some of the 65K addresses must be reserved for peripheral addresses. The 6800 includes the ALU, 16-bit program

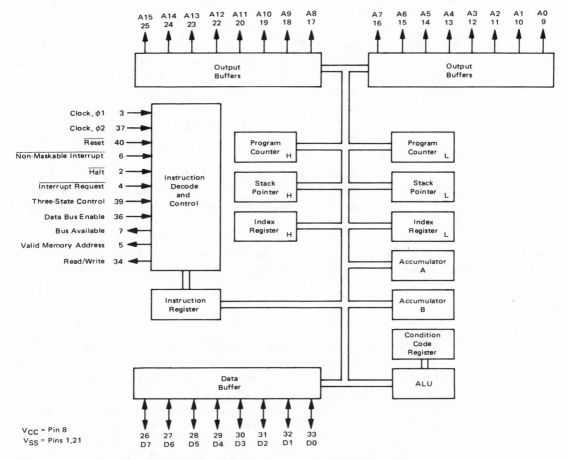

Fig. 7.36. Architecture of the 6800 microprocessor (Courtesy of Motorola Semiconductor Products, Inc.).

counter (PC), 16-bit stack pointer, 16-bit index or general-purpose register, two 8-bit accumulators, and a condition code register.

The stack pointer allows an LIFO stack to be implemented at any address in memory and to be limited in size only by the memory space. The index register may be used to store data or a 16-bit memory address for use in the indexed mode of addressing. The condition code register indicates the results of an ALU operation: negative (N), zero (Z), overflow (V), carry from bit 7 (C), and half carry from bit 3 (H). These bits are used with the conditional branch instructions.

The ALU performs arithmetical and logical operations including AND, OR, EXCLUSIVE-OR, NEGATE, COMPARE, ADD, SUBTRACT, and DECIMAL ADJUST which allows BCD arithmetic to be performed.

The 6800 architecture allows DMA in a block-transfer mode, or a cycle-stealing mode. If the $\overline{\text{Halt}}$ terminal is placed in the low state, all activity of the machine will be halted at the completion of the current instruction. The buses are floated in the HALT mode and address and/or data may be externally supplied to communicate directly with memory.

The Three-State Control (TSC) terminal may be used to implement DMA on a cycle-stealing basis. If TSC is placed in a high state, the address bus and the Read/ Write line (which controls the direction of information flow on the data bus) go to a high-impedance state 500 ns later. The data bus is not effected by TSC and has its own enable (Data Bus Enable). This approach assures rapid response to the DMA request. Since the internal memories of the 6800 are dynamic, however, the TSC terminal cannot be held in the high state for longer than 5 μs if loss of data in the microprocessor is to be avoided.

Interrupts may be requested by signaling the CPU via the $\overline{\text{Interrupt}}$ $\overline{\text{Request}}$ terminal. At the termination of execution of the current instruction, the system will respond (if the interrupt mask bit in the condition code register is not set) by pushing the index register, accumulators, condition code register, and program counter onto the stack. The interrupt mask bit will also be set to inhibit further interrupts. Program control then branches to the address specified in memory locations FFF8 and FFF9. The address contained in these locations is the starting address of the interrupt-service routine.

Timing

Instructions are executed within the microprocessor in units consisting of one ϕ_1 clock period and one ϕ_2 clock period. Using a 1-MHz clock, each cycle is 1 μs long. A minimum of two cycles are required to execute a single instruction.

During ϕ_1 of a FETCH cycle, the memory address is placed on the address bus, and during ϕ_2 the instruction or data byte is loaded into an internal register. The execution of the associated internal operation is performed during the next ϕ_1 cycle. In this manner, an instruction may be completed in as few as two cycles or as many as twelve cycles. If an instruction requires more than two cycles, the functions may overlap, i.e., a fetch may be performed while the preceding instruction is being executed.

Instruction Set

Immediate, direct (1-, 2-, or 3-byte instructions), indexed, and relative addressing modes are all used in the 6800. In the indexed addressing mode, the address contained in the second byte of the instruction is added to the lowest eight bits of the index register. The carry is then added to the highest-order eight bits of the index register. The result is used to address memory.

In relative addressing, the address contained in the second byte of the instruction is added to the lowest eight bits of the PC. To this result is added 2, which allows the user to address data within a range of -125 to $+129$ bytes of the present instruction.

The 6800 has a set of seventy-two different instructions. A complete listing is included in Appendix F. They may be categorized as data-handling, arithmetic, logic, control and transfer, data test, condition codes, address maintenance, and interrupt handling. The data-handling instructions include several instructions for moving data between the two accumulators, memory, and the stack. Data may be altered with Clear, Increment, Decrement, Complement (1's and 2's), Rotate, and Shift instructions.

The arithmetic instructions include Add, Subtract, and Decimal Adjust Accumulator. AND, OR, and EXCLUSIVE-OR comprise the logical instructions. The control transfer instructions include unconditional Branch, Jump, and Jump-to-Subroutine. The Branch instruction uses relative addressing, while the Jump instruction uses direct or indexed addressing. A number of conditional branches are available which test the condition of one or more bits of the condition codes register.

The data test instructions set the condition codes without altering the data. They include Bit Test (for comparing individual bits of accumulator A or B with a memory word), Compare, and Test (for determining the sign of a number). Condition code instructions are provided which enable the programmer to set or reset directly the Carry, Interrupt, or Overflow flags. The entire contents of the condition code register may be moved to or from accumulator A with a single instruction. Eleven instructions are provided for address maintenance. These instructions allow operations on the index register, e.g., Compare, Increment, Decrement, and Transfer to or from memory or the stack pointer. Similar instructions are available for operation on addresses stored in the stack pointer.

Finally, the interrupt-handling instructions include a software interrupt (SWI) which stores the status of the processor in the stack before processing the interrupt and a Return from Interrupt (RTI) instruction which restores the status of the microprocessor after an interrupt is processed. A Wait for Interrupt (WAI) instruction causes the status to be stored in the stack and places the machine in a halt condition until a hardware interrupt occurs ($\overline{\text{IRQ}} = 1$).

Support Hardware

In addition to memory components, several programmable interface circuits are available in the 6800 family. Among these are the Peripheral Interface Adapter (PIA) and Asynchronous Communications Interface Adapter (ACIA).

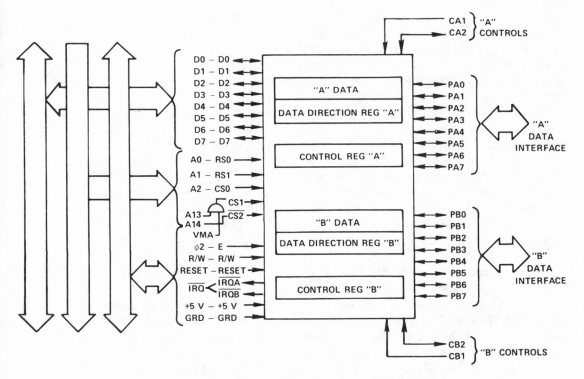

Fig. 7.37. Diagram of PIA (Courtesy of Motorola Semiconductor Products, Inc.).

Each PIA provides sixteen bits of I/O at two addressable locations in memory. A diagram of the PIA is shown in Fig. 7.37. Interface with the microprocessor is provided by eight data input lines, five address lines consisting of two register-select lines and three chip-select lines, and control lines. The control lines include a RESET, read/write (R/W), and interrupt request ($\overline{IRQ}$), which is used to signal the microprocessor that an interrupt is desired. On the peripheral side of the interface are two complete ports (*A* and *B*), each of which has eight data lines and two control lines. The PIA itself contains an 8-bit data register, 8-bit data direction register, and an 8-bit control register for ports *A* and *B*. The data direction register allows the direction of flow for each bit to be determined independently. A 1 in a bit indicates that the corresponding bit is an output, and a 0 causes the corresponding peripheral data line to act as an input.

Addressing of registers in the PIA is accomplished using the register select inputs (RS0 and RS1) along with bit 2 in the control register (CRA-2 or CRB-2) according to Table 7.5. The operation of the peripheral control lines (CA1, CA2, CB1, CB2) is controlled by the control register. The format of the control register is illustrated in Fig. 7.38.

Table 7.5 INTERNAL ADDRESSING OF PIA.

RS1	RS0	Control Register Bit		Register Selected
		CRA-2	CRB-2	
0	0	1	—	Peripheral Interface Register *A*
0	0	0	—	Data Direction Register *A*
0	1	—	—	Control Register *A*
1	0	—	1	Peripheral Interface Register *B*
1	0	—	0	Data Direction Register *B*
1	1	—	—	Control Register *B*

	7	6	5	4	3	2	1	0
CRA	IRQA1	IRQA2	CA2 Control			DDRA Access	CA1 Control	

	7	6	5	4	3	2	1	0
CRB	IRQB1	IRQB2	CB2 Control			DDRB Access	CB1 Control	

Fig. 7.38. Control word format for PIA (Courtesy of Motorola Semiconductor Products, Inc.).

Bit 0 is used to enable the microprocessor interrupt lines (IRQA or IRQB) and bit 1 determines the transition which will set the Interrupt flag. If bit 1 is a 0, the flag will be set on a 1 → 0 transition, and vice versa if the bit is a 1. Bits 3–5 provide control for lines CA2 or CB2. In addition to the controls available for CA1 and CB1, CA2 and CB2 may be designated as output control lines. Bits 6 and 7 are Interrupt Request flags which may be interrogated by the microprocessor.

The ACIA is a programmable interface which provides the data formatting and control to interface serial asynchronous data communications information to the 6800. A diagram of the ACIA is provided in Fig. 7.39. The parallel data of the bus system is serially transmitted and received with proper formatting and error-checking. A programmable control register provides variable word lengths, clock division ratios, transmit control, receive control, and interrupt control.

Internally, there are four registers in the ACIA, two read-only and two write-only registers. The read-only registers are Status and Receive Data; the write-only registers are Control and Transmit Data. Data to be transmitted serially is placed in the transmit data register, and data which has been received is read from the receive data register. The status register provides information on the status of the interface such as Receive Data Register Full, Transmit Data Register Empty, Parity Error, Framing Error, and Modem Status signals. The control register allows, for example, word length, stop bits, and parity to be altered by the microprocessor. The interface functions similarly to a UART (described in Sec. 6.6). A modem may be directly connected to the ACIA to allow transmission of data over telephone lines.

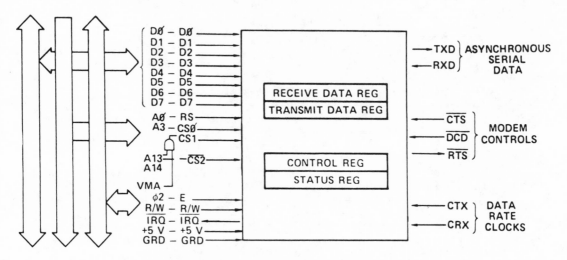

Fig. 7.39. Diagram of the ACIA (Courtesy of Motorola Semiconductor Products, Inc.).

Microcomputer System

A small, but functional, microcomputer can be built using only four 6800 family components consisting of a microprocessor, ROM, RAM, and PIA. In addition, a two-phase clock and a single 5-V power supply are required. A block diagram of such a system is illustrated in Fig. 7.40. The system shown employs 1K bytes of ROM for storing the program and a 128-byte RAM for data storage. The PIA provides two independently programmable 8-bit I/O ports for communicating with two peripheral devices.

Motorola supplies a 6800 Evaluation module as a means of evaluating the 6800 in a particular application. This system consists of a microprocessor, six 128×8 RAMS, a 1024×8 ROM, two PIAs, data and address buffers, and a variable master clock (100 kHz to 1 MHz). The module interfaces directly with a TTY which communicates with the MIKBUG program that is stored in ROM. This program allows data in memory or registers to be read and altered from the keyboard. The system is supplied on a single PC board. A RAM module, which provides 2K bytes of RAM, is also available. It has bus drivers/receivers and address selection switches for interface to the 6800 bus. An I/O module card supplies two PIA circuits plus the option of constructing customized interface circuits. Switches are provided to enable the user to select the base memory address for each PIA.

A prototyping system which consists of the MPU module, Debug module, Baud Rate module, power supply, and chassis is also supplied by Motorola. The Debug module provides the capability for debugging and evaluating a user's program. It contains a program in ROM and scratch-pad memory (RAM) for the debug program. The Baud Rate module provides eight selectable Baud rates between 110 and 9600. This module interfaces with a TTY- or an RS-232C-compatible terminal.

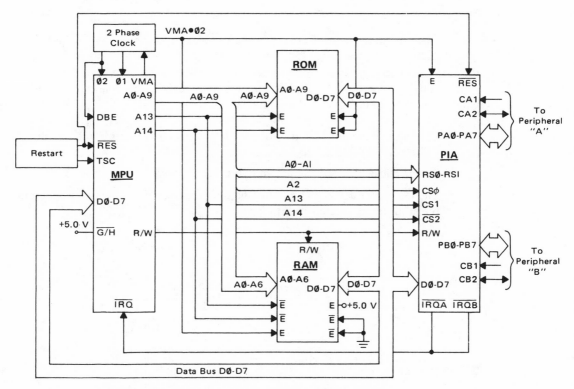

Fig. 7.40. Block diagram of a microcomputer using the 6800 micro-processor (Courtesy of Motorola Semiconductor Products, Inc.).

Comments

The 6800 is a second-generation, 8-bit microprocessor which utilizes numerous addressing modes. An effort has been made to assure minimum parts count for small systems. A single 5-V power supply, for example, is required for all 6800 family components, and buffering is not required for most systems. The NMOS processor will execute instructions in 2 to 12 μs with a 1-MHz clock.

7.9. RCA COSMAC

The RCA COSMAC is a parallel, 8-bit, CMOS microprocessor which is implemented in two IC packages [31–34]. The CMOS technology provides a high noise immunity that allows the processor to operate in electrically hostile environments. COSMAC is completely static, permitting the system clock to be controlled to facilitate interface with very slow memories or I/O devices. The processor operates from a single-phase clock having a frequency which is variable from dc to 2 MHz.

Architecture

A block diagram of the COSMAC microprocessor is shown in Fig. 7.41. The system features a register array (R) consisting of sixteen 16-bit scratch-pad registers. Individual registers in the array are selected by a 4-bit code from one of the three registers labeled N, P, and X. The contents of any R register can be directed, via the buffer register A, to any one of the following:

1. The external memory (multiplexed onto eight memory address lines for direct addressing of 65,536 bytes).

2. The D register (either of the two bytes can be gated to D).

3. The increment/decrement circuit where it is increased or decreased by 1 and replaced in the selected 16-bit register.

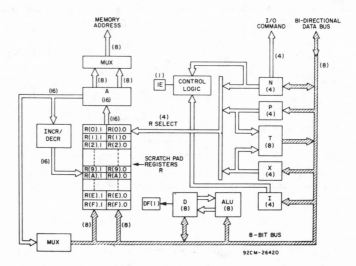

Fig. 7.41. Block diagram of the RCA COSMAC (Courtesy of RCA Solid State Division).

The three paths may operate independently or in various combinations in the same machine cycle.

Every COSMAC instruction consists of two 8-clock-pulse machine cycles (Fig. 7.42). The first cycle is a FETCH cycle, and the second is the EXECUTE cycle. In a FETCH cycle, the P register selects register $R(P)$ as the current program counter. $R(P)$ contains the memory address from which the instruction is to be fetched. When the instruction is read from memory, the higher-order four bits of the instruction byte are loaded into the I register and the lower-order four bits into the N register. The content of the program counter $R(P)$ is automatically incremented to point to the next byte in the memory.

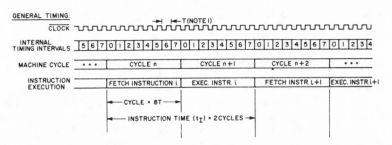

Fig. 7.42. Timing diagram for the RCA COSMAC (Courtesy of RCA Solid State Division).

The X register selects one of the sixteen registers $R(X)$ to point to the memory for an operand (or data).

The N register can perform the following, depending on the type of instruction fetched:

1. Designate one of sixteen registers in R to be acted upon during register operations.

2. Indicate to the I/O devices a command code or device-selection code for peripherals.

3. Indicate specific operations for ALU instructions, types of tests to be performed during branch instructions, or operating modes of interrupt-handling instructions.

4. Indicate the value of P to designate a new register to be used as the program counter $R(P)$.

5. Indicate the value of X to designate a new register to be used as the data pointer $R(X)$.

The R registers can be assigned by a programmer in three ways: as program counters, as data pointers, or as scratch-pad registers for storing two bytes of data.

A. Program Counters

Any register can be the main program counter where the address of the selected register is held in the P register. Other R registers can be used as subroutine program counters. By a single instruction, the contents of P can be changed to effect a call to a subroutine. During an interrupt, register $R(1)$ is used as the program counter for the interrupt-service routine. At all other times, any register can be designated as the program counter.

B. Data Pointers

Registers in R may be used as data pointers to indicate where data is located in memory. The register designated by X [i.e., $R(X)$] points to the data for the following instructions (see Appendix G):

1. ALU operations F0 through F7
2. Output instructions 60 through 67
3. Input instructions 68 through 6F

The register $R(N)$, designated by N, points to the operand for instruction $4N$ (load D from memory) and instruction $5N$ (store D). The register $R(P)$ (the program counter) is used as the data pointer for ALU instructions F8 through FF. During these instruction executions, the operation is referred to as *data immediate*.

Another important function of R as a data pointer occurs in a DMA operation. When a DMA-in or DMA-out request is received, one machine cycle is "stolen" at the end of the EXECUTE machine cycle of the current instruction. Register $R(0)$ is always used as the data pointer in a DMA operation (hardwired). At the end of each transfer, $R(0)$ is incremented so that the processor is ready for the next DMA request. The DMA channel provides a simple method for entering data or programs into memory.

C. Data Registers

When registers in R are used to store data, four instructions are provided which allow D to receive from or write into either the higher-order- or lower-order-byte portions of $R(N)$, the register designated by N. By this mechanism (together with loading by data immediate), the program pointer and data pointer designations are initiated. Also, this technique allows scratch-pad registers in R to hold general data.

D. Interrupt Servicing

Register $R(1)$ is used as the program counter whenever interrupt servicing is performed. Following an interrupt request (when the interrupt enable, IE, is activated), the current EXECUTE machine cycle of an instruction is completed, the contents of P and X are stored in temporary register T, and P and X are set to new values. These values are hex digits 1 and 2 in P and X, respectively. The interrupt enable is automatically deactivated to inhibit other interrupts. The contents of T are saved by instruction 78 in the memory location pointed to by $R(X)$, where $X = 2$. At the conclusion of the interrupt, the routine restores the pre-interrupt values of P and X via a single instruction. The interrupt-enable flip-flop is enabled by the programmer if further interrupts are desired.

A register summary of the COSMAC is given in Table 7.6. The processor is fabricated in two dual in-line packages, as shown in the terminal assignment diagram of Fig. 7.43.

Instruction Set

The COSMAC instruction set given in Appendix G consists of fifty-nine instructions. Six instructions are provided for register operations which include Increment and Decrement R, and register exchanges between R and D. Two memory reference

Table 7.6 COSMAC REGISTER SUMMARY

Register	No. of Bits	Function
D	8	Data register (accumulator)
DF	1	Data flag (ALU carry)
R	16	1-of-16 scratch-pad registers
P	4	Designates program counter $R(P)$
X	4	Designates data pointer $R(X)$
N	4	Low-order instruction digit
I	4	High-order instruction digit
T	8	Temporary register; holds old X and P after interrupt
IE	1	Interrupt enable

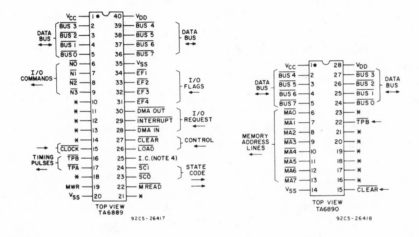

Package Interconnections

TA6889 Pin No.	1	2	3	4	5	10	11	12	13	14	16	18	21	27	36	37	38	39	40
TA6890 Pin No.	1	27	26	25	24	17	18	19	20	23	22	21	16	15	5	4	3	2	28

* These pins are for interchip connections only.

Fig. 7.43. Terminal assignment diagrams for the COSMAC (Courtesy of RCA Solid State Division).

instructions permit data exchanges between D and memory. Fifteen ALU instructions include Addition, Subtraction, Shift, Load, and logical (AND, OR, EXCLUSIVE-OR) operations. Fourteen branching instructions allow Skip and conditional and unconditional branching. Six control instructions consist of Idle (halt), Set P

or X, Return, Disable Interrupt, and Save (contents of T). Sixteen input/output byte transfer instructions complete the instruction set.

Microcomputer Systems

A typical microcomputer system employing the COSMAC microprocessor is shown in Fig. 7.44. Support hardware necessary for the CPU includes a bus separator, I/O control circuits, clock, and an address latch. Memory, consisting of ROM and/or RAM, can be provided to a maximum of 65, 536 bytes.

A prototyping system based on the COSMAC processor is the RCA Microprocessor Hardware Support Kit (COSMAC Microkit). The Microkit consists of a CPU, clock and control, bus separator, address latch, 512-byte RAM and pROM, I/O decoder, terminal, and byte I/O printed circuit cards. These cards are housed in a 19-in. rack having a power supply and front panel configured with basic controls. The pROM card contains a utility program which performs commonly required functions: program loading, memory dump, modification of memory locations, paper tape punch, saving of registers, and start of program execution at a specified location. Additional memory can be added to the basic system.

Software support for the Microkit includes an editor, assembler, and simulator/debugger. The software support system is available in two forms. It is supplied as a 9-track, 800-bpi, IBM-compatible tape, written in standard FORTRAN IV for installation on a variety of computers. It is also available on the General Electric Information Services International Network for use by time-sharing customers.

Comments

The COSMAC processor is a static CMOS device which offers the advantages of high noise immunity and operation from a single-phase clock. The clock frequency is variable from dc to 2 MHz. The processor can be operated from a single power supply having a voltage range of 4 to 12 V. The internal voltage supply (V_{DD}) is isolated from the I/O supply (V_{cc}) so that the processor may operate at maximum speed ($V_{DD} = 10$ V) while interfacing with various IC families such as TTL.

The CPU has sixteen 16-bit R registers, each of which may be used for data-holding, as an index register, or as a program counter. The depth of an on-chip pushdown stack is therefore limited by other uses of these registers, as specified by the user. Since the program counter in one program can be treated as an operand in another, the pushdown stack of return addresses can be extended by storing register contents into main storage.

The processor has four I/O flag inputs (EF1 through EF4) to enable the I/O controllers to transfer status information to the CPU. These levels can be tested by conditional branch instructions and can be used to establish priorities for interrupt. The processor also has a useful on-chip DMA facility. Interfaces for communications networks, keyboards, TV displays, and floppy disks have been constructed utilizing the interrupt and DMA capabilities of the device [34].

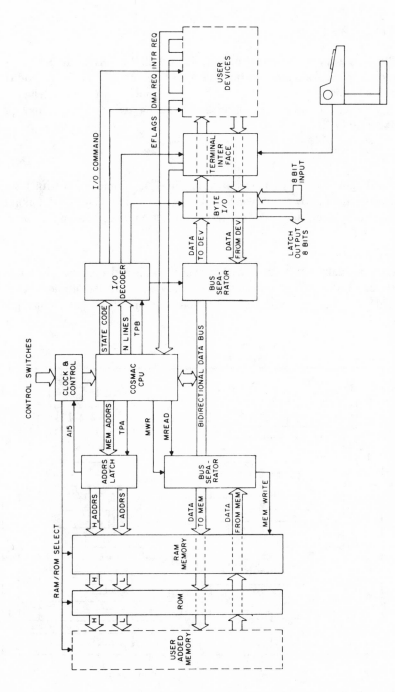

Fig. 7.44. Block diagram of a typical microcomputer (Courtesy of RCA Solid State Division).

7.10. ROCKWELL PPS-8

The PPS-8 is a more powerful version of the PPS-4 described in Sec. 7.5. The first and most obvious difference is that the PPS-8 is an 8-bit machine. Additional instructions and capability (e.g., interrupt) have been included in the system.

The PPS-8 uses the same clock circuit as the PPS-4 and retains the single power supply voltage (−17 V).

Architecture [35]

A block diagram of the CPU is shown in Fig. 7.45. Comparison with Fig. 7.19 clearly illustrates the family resemblance of the two machines. The CPU contains an ALU, program counter, address registers, instruction decoder, and scratch-pad registers.

1. Memory Addressing

Program and data words are addressed via a 14-bit address bus. The addresses are multiplexed on the address bus and the memory elements demultiplex them. The program address is held in the P register which is composed of two 7-bit registers,

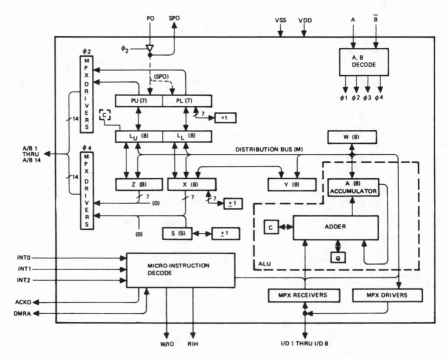

Fig. 7.45. Block diagram of PPS-8 CPU (Courtesy of Rockwell International Corporation).

PL and *PU*. *PL*, the least-significant seven bits of *P*, is incremented automatically during the execution of an instruction and may be altered during the execution of branch-type instructions.

Upon the execution of a subroutine call (Branch and Link, BL), the contents of the *P* register are saved in the 16-bit *L register*, and the contents of the *L* register are transferred to a 32-byte stack in RAM. The *S* register serves as an address pointer to the stack. It is automatically incremented or decremented when data or the *L* register is pushed or popped from the stack.

The 14-bit address of a data word is held in the *Z* and *X* registers. The most-significant seven bits are held in the *Z register*. The least-significant seven bits are held in the *X register*. The most significant bit of the *X* register controls the upper seven bits of the address. If the MSB is:

1—the *Z* register contents are output for the seven MSBs of the address.

0—logic zero is output for the seven MSBs of the address.

In addition, the *Y* register may be used to provide the lower RAM address.

2.   Word Transfers

A block diagram of a PPS-8 system is illustrated in Fig. 7.46. Data and instructions are multiplexed on the Instruction/Data (I/D) bus. During clock phase ϕ_4 the information on the I/D bus is treated as a program instruction, and during ϕ_2 it is treated as a RAM word or I/O data.

3.   ALU/Accumulator

The accumulator is the primary working register, as it is in the PPS-4. It serves as the central data-exchange point for most data transfer instructions. An 8-bit adder is equipped with a carry flag (*C*) and an intermediate carry flag (*Q*) to facilitate BCD arithmetic.

4.   Input/Output

All input/output is accomplished on the I/D bus. The basic input and output instructions simply cause the transfer of information from the I/D bus to the accumulator, and vice versa. An additional I/O instruction (IO4) causes only four bits of information to be exchanged between the accumulator and the I/O device. In this instruction, bits 5–8 of the accumulator are transferred to the device and bits 1–4 are transferred from the device to the accumulator. The IO4 instruction provides compatibility between the PPS-4 and PPS-8 systems.

All I/O commands are two-byte instructions which require two machine cycles for execution. The first byte indicates that an I/O instruction is in progress, while the second byte is interpreted by the I/O devices. Up to sixteen devices can be addressed, and commands can be sent to each device during the second byte of the instruction.

5.   Control

The control section provides signals for controlling the operation of the system. The Read Inhibit (RIH) line and the Write Command I/O Enable (W/IO) line are used to control the direction of data transfer on the I/D bus. During ϕ_2, a 1 on the

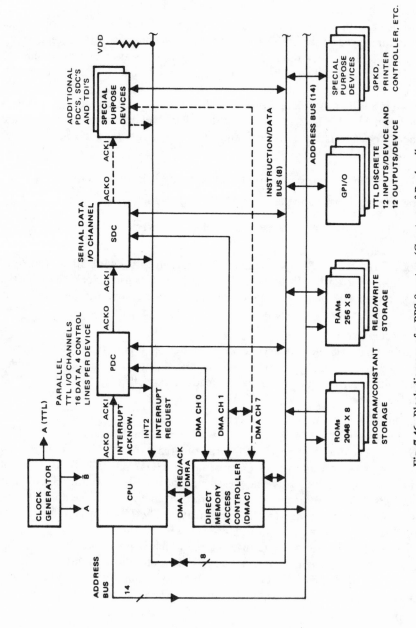

Fig. 7.46. Block diagram of a PPS-8 system (Courtesy of Rockwell International Corporation).

W/IO is interpreted as a write enable and a word on the I/D bus is written into the RAM address which was specified in the preceding ϕ_4. The CPU and system are initialized using the power-on (PO) signal in the same manner as for the PPS-4.

6. Machine Cycle

The clock signals are divided into four phases in the same manner as for the PPS-4. Comparison of the timing diagram of the PPS-4 (Fig. 7.21) with that of the PPS-8, shown in Fig. 7.47, reveals the basic similarities in their operations.

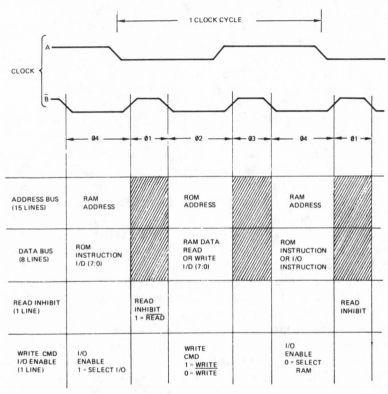

Fig. 7.47. Timing diagram for the PPS-8 (Courtesy of Rockwell International Corporation).

The buses are cleared on phases ϕ_1 and ϕ_3, and data and addresses are transferred during phases ϕ_2 and ϕ_4. Unlike the PPS-4, the PPS-8 has a Read Inhibit line which is used to inhibit the READ operation during a WRITE or I/O cycle. This line is interpreted during ϕ_1 of the cycle. The instruction fetch and the data fetch overlap, i.e., the RAM address is sent out on the address bus while the previously addressed instruction from ROM is being transferred via the I/D bus.

Organization of Memory

The 14-bit address lines allow 16K of ROM and 16K of RAM to be directly addressed by the processor. Additional memory can be addressed via an output port using one of the chip select inputs to the RAM circuit. Both program and data memory are organized on a page basis. Each page consists of 128 bytes.

The seven LSBs of the Z register normally contain the page address for data memory access, while the byte address on the page is specified by the seven LSBs of the X register. Several alternatives to this arrangement are available, however. For example, the L register may be used to provide the RAM address. The byte address may be provided by the Y register instead of the X register, and page 0 can be addressed at any time independently of the contents of Z. The first 32 bytes of page 0 (0–31) are reserved for the LIFO stack.

The page address for a program memory access is held in the most-significant seven bits of the P register, PU. The byte address is held in the seven least-significant bits of P, PL. Certain locations in memory are normally set aside for data pools. A *data pool* is a reservoir of common words (bytes) which may be shared by many instructions. The PPS-8 contains three such pools, a Command pool, a Literal pool, and a Subroutine Entry pool.

The Command pool occupies the first 64 program memory locations of page 0. The first four of these bytes (0–3) are reserved for power-on initialization. The remaining locations may be used to supply the second byte of the two-byte instructions LX, LY, LZ, LXL, LYL, LZL, LAL, PSHX, PSHY, PSHZ, PSHA, POPX, POPY, POPZ, POPA, SB, RB (Appendix H). Each of the above instructions, except SB and RB, has a predetermined second byte. The second byte of SB and RB contains a "bit" designator to point to one of eight bits of a memory word. Therefore, 16 different combinations of the second byte are possible for these two instructions. This 16, together with the 15 second bytes required to handle the other two-byte instructions listed above, means that 31 locations are required for the Command pool in addition to the four required for power-on initialization.

The effect of the Command pool is to allow a two-byte instruction to be referenced by one byte, as illustrated in Fig. 7.48. There are six three-byte instructions, LAI, LXI, LYI, LZI, AISK, and ANI, which can use the Command pool. These instructions are of the immediate class. The first two bytes define the instruction

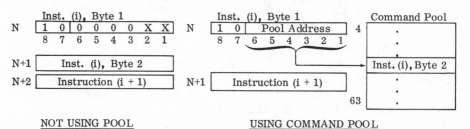

Fig. 7.48. Format of a two-byte instruction (Courtesy of Rock-well International Corporation).

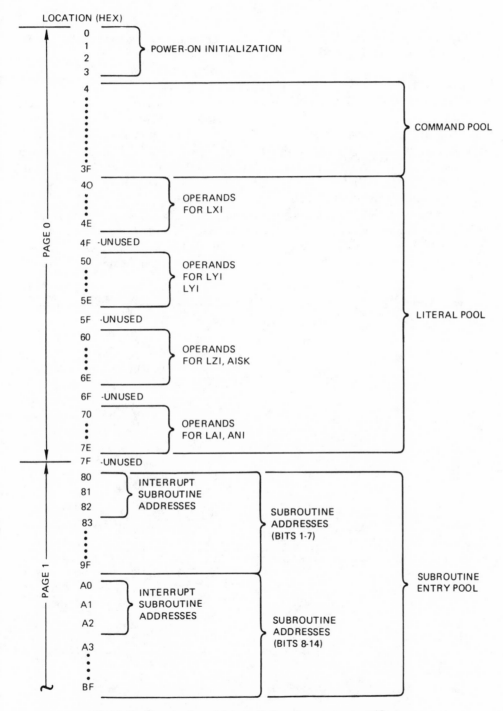

Fig. 7.49. Organization of data pools in program memory (Courtesy of Rockwell International Corporation).

and the third provides the data which is to be used. If the second byte of the instruction is obtained from the Command pool, then the three-byte instruction can be reduced to a two-byte instruction, with the second byte containing the literal operand (immediate data).

The six three-byte instructions listed above can also be reduced to two-byte instructions by sharing the literal operand in a *Literal pool*. The Literal pool occupies 64 words of ROM on page 0, locations 64–127, as illustrated in Fig. 7.49. The three-byte instructions can be reduced to one-byte instructions by using both the Command and Literal pools with the instruction. Figure 7.50 illustrates the application of the Literal pool.

Subroutine calls are accomplished using a Branch and Link (BL) instruction which points to a Subroutine Entry pool containing the subroutine entry address. The Subroutine Entry pool occupies the first 64 bytes of page 1 in program memory (Fig. 7.49). The first 32 bytes specify the lower seven bits of the subroutine address, and the second 32 bytes specify the corresponding upper seven address bits. The use

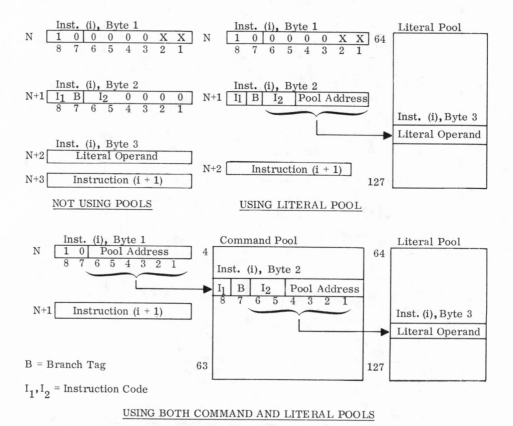

Fig. 7.50. Application of the literal pool (Courtesy of Rockwell International Corporation).

of the pool allows a subroutine anywhere in memory to be called using a single-byte instruction. The first three subroutine addresses are reserved for processing interrupts. Figure 7.51 illustrates the format for a BL instruction.

Access to the pools is automatic if the PPS assembler is used. The programmer may assign data to the pools or use a standard pool assignment.

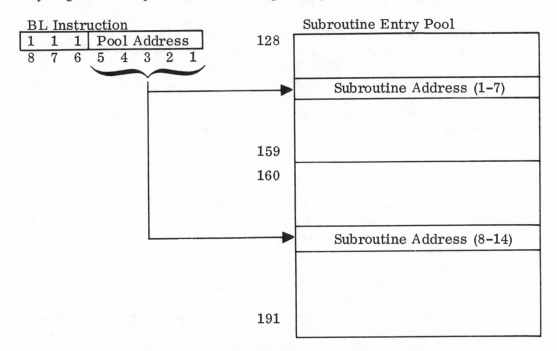

Fig. 7.51. Format for a BRANCH AND LINK instruction using the subroutine entry pool (Courtesy of Rockwell International Corporation).

Interrupt

The PPS-8 has a three-level priority interrupt. The highest level is normally dedicated to power-failure detection. The second level of interrupt is intended for use as a real-time clock. The third level is a general interrupt which uses a daisy-chain technique for achieving a priority for general interrupts [36]. In Fig. 7.46 the connection of interrupting devices is illustrated. The INTERRUPT ACKNOWLEDGE terminal is wired to the ACKI terminal of the highest-priority device. An INTERRUPT REQUEST line from each device is wire-ORed to the CPU on the common INTERRUPT REQUEST line. The CPU acknowledges the request on the INTERRUPT ACKNOWLEDGE. When the interrupting device receives the acknowledgment, it identifies itself to the CPU on the I/D bus and does not pass the ACKNOWLEDGE signal to the next device. The CPU then takes control to process the interrupting device.

Instruction Set

An extensive set of powerful one-, two-, and three-byte instructions is provided. As with the PPS-4, many instructions are multifaceted. A complete list of the PPS-8 instructions is given in Appendix H.

Capability is provided for transferring data between the CPU and memory and to move data from register to register in the CPU. Data from the CPU may be pushed onto the stack and retrieved when needed. The usual arithmetical and logical operations are available in addition to two decimal correction instructions which are valuable in performing BCD arithmetic. Individual bits in RAM may be set or reset by the programmer without calling the word from memory with the SB and RB instructions.

Numerous conditional branch and skip instructions are also provided. The instruction set is extremely powerful for applications requiring the processing of strings of data words.

Support Hardware

The PPS-8 requires a minimum of support hardware to build a functioning system. The basic building blocks (CPU, RAM, ROM, I/O) are all directly compatible, i.e., they may be connected directly together. The system uses a single 17-V power supply, and a clock circuit is available which requires only a crystal, such as a color-television crystal, to establish the frequency.

A number of input/output ICs are available to allow a wide variety of devices to be interfaced to the PPS-8. In addition to the General-Purpose I/O circuit, there is a programmable Parallel Data Controller (PDC). The PDC provides a variety of programmable functions including interrupt and DMA processing. A Direct Memory Access Controller provides all of the hardware necessary to perform DMA transfers. The Telecommunications Data Interface circuit contains the circuitry to make serial-to-parallel data conversions, and vice versa. It also contains a modem and may be used with unconditioned voice-grade telephone lines.

Comments

The PPS-8 bears a strong family resemblance to the PPS-4. In addition to the longer word length, interrupt capability is provided and additional instructions to facilitate high-speed data processing are included. Rockwell provides a large variety of support circuits which can be directly placed on the system buses.

The Rockwell microcomputers are unique in the use of numerous standard interface ICs which are designed especially for the PPS-4/8. Many of these interface ICs are programmable and are capable of performing certain tasks related to the peripheral with a minimum of CPU intervention.

The PPS-8 system is a very powerful system which bears little resemblance to other microcomputers. With the large amount of support hardware provided by Rockwell, it is possible to minimize package count and hold power requirements to a minimum. The versatility of the system and the complexity of the instruction set complicate the programming task, however.

7.11. NATIONAL PACE [37, 38]

The PACE is a 16-bit, monolithic, PMOS microprocessor. PACE is an acronym for Processing and Control Element. It is fundamentally a single-chip version of the IMP-16 microprocessor. The similarity is readily apparent from Fig. 7.52 when com-

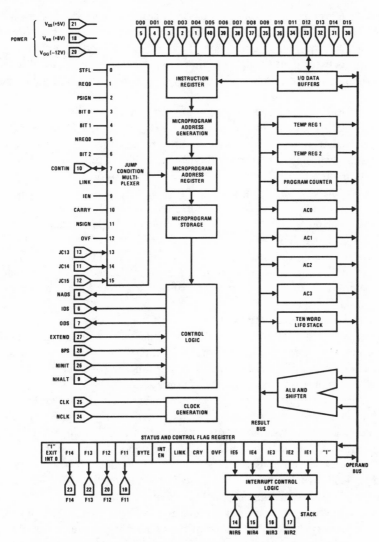

Fig. 7.52. Block diagram of the PACE (Courtesy of National Semiconductor Corporation, USA).

pared with the RALU and CROM in Sec. 7.4. The PACE combines the four RALUs and one CROM required for the IMP-16 along with a jump condition multiplexer, control flag, multilevel vectored interrupt, and multiphase clock generator on a single chip. Power requirements are $+5$ V and -12 V for the PMOS unit. Although it is slower than NMOS circuitry, the 16-bit word length allows the system to compete speedwise with 8-bit NMOS systems in certain applications.

Architecture

The PACE retains the unified bus-oriented architecture of the IMP series machines. The microprogram, which defines the macroinstructions, is fixed, i.e., unlike the IMP series it is not possible for the user to specify a microprogram for PACE. The processor contains an ALU, data storage registers, control logic, status and control flag register, multilevel priority interrupt logic, and jump condition multiplexer.

The data registers include four accumulators, AC0–AC3. AC0 is the principal working register, AC1 is the secondary working register, and AC2 and AC3 are page pointers or auxiliary data registers. Three other registers include a program counter and two temporary registers used by the control logic to implement the instruction set. In addition a ten-word LIFO stack is provided for storage of the program counter (during subroutine or interrupt execution), status flags, or data. Provision of a stack full or stack empty interrupt facilitates the extension of the stack into RAM.

The ALU provides AND, OR, EXCLUSIVE-OR, Complement, Shift, binary ADD, and BCD (four digits per word) ADD operations. Either 8- or 16-bit data may be operated on by the processor by setting a status flag (BYTE). This allows character-oriented applications to be implemented and executed using an 8-bit peripheral data bus and memory, while address formation and instruction storage are implemented in 16-bit words.

The control logic of the PACE implements the microprogram execution in a manner similar to the IMP series (Sec. 7.4). A microcycle requires 2 μs for execution, and a typical machine instruction requires 4–5 microcycles. The control section also controls the operation of a conditional jump multiplexer which specifies sixteen conditions for the Branch on Condition (BOC) instruction.

The status and control flag register may be loaded from or loaded to any accumulator or the stack. This allows testing, masking, and storage of the status. The function of each bit in the status flag register is given in Table 7.7. The BYTE flag is used to specify an 8-bit data length. In the 8-bit data mode, modifications of the carry, overflow, and link flags are based on the eight least-significant bits. Four flags (11–14) may be assigned by the programmer. These flags drive output pins and may be used to directly control system functions or as software status flags.

A six-level, vectored priority interrupt is provided. Figure 7.53 illustrates the interrupt control logic. When an interrupt request occurs, the interrupt request latch will be set if the corresponding interrupt is enabled. If the master interrupt enable is true, then an interrupt will be generated.

Table 7.7 STATUS FLAG REGISTER BIT FUNCTION
(Courtesy of National Semiconductor Corp., USA.)

Register Bit	Flag Name	Function
0	"1"	Not used-always logic 1
1	IE1	Interrupt enable level 1
2	IE2	Interrupt enable level 2
3	IE3	Interrupt enable level 3
4	IE4	Interrupt enable level 4
5	IE5	Interrupt enable level 5
6	OVF	Overflow
7	CRY	Carry
8	LINK	Link
9	IEN	Master interrupt enable
10	BYTE	8-bit data length
11	F11	Flag 11
12	F12	Flag 12
13	F13	Flag 13
14	F14	Flag 14
15	"1"	Always logic 1, addressed for Interrupt 0 exit

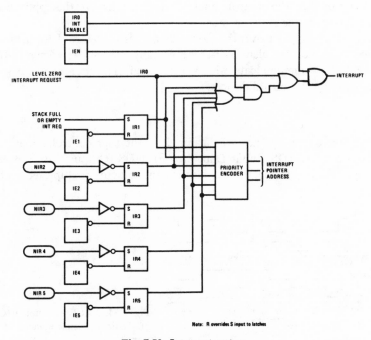

Note: R overrides S input to latches

Fig. 7.53. Interrupt system.

During the interrupt sequence, an address is provided by the output of the priority encoder and is used to access the pointer for the highest-priority interrupt request. The pointers are stored in locations 2–7 of memory (Table 7.8). The pointer specifies the starting address of the interrupt-service routine for that particular level. Prior to executing the interrupt-service routine, the program counter is pushed onto the stack and the master interrupt enable (IEN) is set FALSE. The interrupt enables for each level may be set or reset using the Set Flag (SFLG) and Pulse Flag (PFLG) instructions.

Table 7.8   INTERRUPT POINTER TABLE

8	Int 0 program
7	Int 0 PC pointer
6	Int 5 pointer
5	Int 4 pointer
4	Int 3 pointer
3	Int 2 pointer
2	Int 1 pointer
1	Not assigned
Loc 0	Initialization inst.

The highest-priority (zero) level cannot be disabled. The program counter is not pushed onto the stack in this level interrupt but is stored in memory. Location 7 points to the PC. The zero-level interrupt-service routine begins in location 8. This interrupt level is typically used by the control panel in order to interrupt the application program without affecting the system status.

Data transfers take place over the sixteen data lines D00–D15. Peripheral devices are referenced like memory elements; therefore, any memory reference instruction can be employed to communicate with a peripheral. The user must assign some memory addresses to peripheral devices.

Timing

Data transfer operations are synchronized by the four control signals, NADS (Address Data Strobe), IDS (Input Data Strobe), ODS (Output Data Strobe), and EXTEND, as illustrated in Fig. 7.54. Addresses and data are multiplexed on the six-

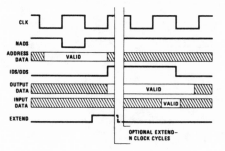

Fig. 7.54. PACE I/O timing (Courtesy of National Semiconductor Corporation, USA).

teen data lines. An NADS is provided in the center of the address data and may be used to strobe the address into an address latch. The IDS and ODS indicate the type of data transfer and may be used to enable tri-state I/O buffers and gate data into registers or memory. The EXTEND input allows the I/O cycle time to be extended by integral numbers of clock cycles to adapt to a variety of memory and peripheral devices or for DMA bus interfacing.

Instruction Set

The instruction set includes instructions which use direct and indirect memory addressing. Three modes of direct addressing are available: base page, program counter relative, and index register relative. The mode of addressing is specified by the XR field of the instruction, as illustrated in Fig. 7.55. When the XR field is 00, base

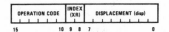

Fig. 7.55. Memory reference instruction format.

page addressing is used. Two different types of base page addressing are available. One is selected by the base page select (BPS) input. If BPS = 0, then the memory address is formed by setting bits 8–15 to zero. This permits addressing the first 256 locations in memory. If BPS = 1, the address is formed by setting bits 8–15 to the value of bit 7. This permits addressing the first 128 ($0-7F_{16}$) and the last 128 (FF80–$FFFF_{16}$) words in memory. The latter technique is useful for splitting the base page memory between ROM and RAM or peripherals.

Addressing relative to the PC is specified when the XR field is 01. In this case the 8-bit displacement (treated as a 2's complement number) is added to the contents of the PC. This allows referencing memory locations from 127 below to 128 above the contents of the PC.

With the index register relative mode of addressing, any memory location may be referenced. The 8-bit displacement field is treated in the same manner as in PC relative addressing. The memory address is formed by adding the displacement to the contents of AC2 (when $XR = 10$) or AC3 (when $XR = 11$).

Indirect addressing consists of first establishing an address in the same fashion as with direct addressing. The 16-bit contents of the memory location at this address are then used as the address of the operand.

The instruction set includes forty-five instructions which may be divided into eight categories, as shown in Appendix I. The seven branch instructions provide the capability to transfer control anywhere within the 16-bit addressing space. Conditional branches may be accomplished using the BOC instruction, which allows testing of the sixteen conditions listed in Table 7.9.

Additional branching capability is provided by the skip instructions which permit memory- or peripheral-to-register comparisons without altering data. The memory data transfer instructions provide data transfer between memory or peripherals and the accumulators.

Table 7.9 BRANCH CONDITIONS

Number	Mnemonic	Condition
0	STFL	Stack full
1	REQ0	(AC0) equal to zero[1]
2	PSIGN	(AC0) has positive sign[2]
3	BIT 0	Bit 0 of AC0 true
4	BIT 1	Bit 1 of AC0 true
5	NREQ0	(AC0) is nonzero[1]
6	BIT 2	Bit 2 of AC0 is true
7	CONTIN	CONTIN (continue) input is true
8	LINK	LINK is true
9	IEN	IEN is true
10	CARRY	CARRY is true
11	NSIGN	(AC0) has negative sign[2]
12	OVF	OVF is true
13	JC13	JC13 input is true
14	JC14	JC14 input is true
15	JC15	JC15 input is true

Note 1: If the selected data length is eight bits, only bits 0–7 of AC0 are tested.

Note 2: Bit 7 is the sign bit (instead of bit 15) if the selected data length is eight bits.

The memory data operating instructions provide operations between AC0 (principal accumulator) and memory or peripheral data. This includes both binary and 4-digit BCD arithmetic. The register data class provides operations which include transfer capabilities between accumulators, flag register, and stack. Instructions in the register data operate class allow logical and arithmetical operations between data in the accumulators. They may be used for address and data modification and to reduce the number of memory references in a program. The shift and rotate instructions allow eight different operations which are useful for multiply, divide, bit scanning, and serial I/O operations. In the miscellaneous category are instructions which allow any of the sixteen bits of the status flag register to be set or reset (pulsed) individually.

Figure 7.56 illustrates a 16-bit binary multiply routine using the PACE instruction set. The 16-bit value in AC2 is multiplied by the 16-bit value in AC1, and the 32-bit

```
                Binary Multiply Routine
CONST:    WORD  X'FFFF      ; CONSTANT FOR DOUBLE PREC. ADD
START:    LI    R1, 0       ; CLEAR RESULT REGISTER
          LI    R3, 16      ; LOOP COUNT TO AC3
          CAI   R0, 0       ; COMPLEMENT MULTIPLIER
LOOP:     RADD  R1, R1      ; SHIFT RESULT LEFT INTO CARRY
          RADC  R0,R0       ; SHIFT CARRY INTO MULTIPLIER
                            ; AND MULTIPLIER INTO CARRY

          BOC  CARRY, TEST  ; TEST FOR ADD
          RADD R2, R1       ; ADD MULTIPLICAND TO RESULT
          SUBB R0, CONST    ; ADD CARRY TO H.O. RESULT
TEST:     AISZ R3, -1       ; DECREMENT LOOP COUNT
          JMP LOOP          ; REPEAT LOOP
```

Fig. 7.56. Binary multiply routine (Courtesy of National Semicondutor Corporation, USA).

result is placed in AC0 (high-order sixteen bits) and AC1 (low-order sixteen bits). Worst-case execution time is under one millisecond.

Support Hardware

The support hardware required to implement a microcomputer system is illustrated in Fig. 7.57. In order to reduce power dissipation and chip size, the output buffers were designed to drive current sense amplifiers with tri-state capability. PACE is supported by an extensive array of software and hardware products, many of them shared with the IMP-16.

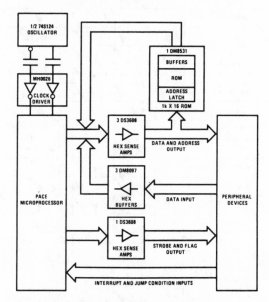

Fig. 7.57. A microcomputer using the PACE microprocessor (Courtesy of National Semiconductor Corporation, USA).

Software support includes assemblers, loaders, a debug program, an editor, diagnostics, and pROM programmer. Hardware support includes ROMs, RAMs, tri-state buffers, sense amplifiers, latches, clock oscillators/drivers, dc-dc converters, parallel interface buffers, and asynchronous communications interfaces.

A prototyping system is also offered which provides a means of developing and debugging applications hardware and software.

Comments

The PACE is a monolithic, fixed-instruction-set version of the IMP-16, with which it is fully compatible. The microprocessor has a powerful instruction set which, with its 16-bit word length, makes it a strong contender for applications requiring significant numerical computations. The vector interrupt feature allows rapid location

MICROPROCESSOR SCORECARD

	CLASSIFICATION	TECHNOLOGY	PARTS FAMILY							FEATURES						WORD SIZE (Data/Instruction)	ADDRESS CAPACITY (Program Words)	CLOCK (kHz/Phases)
			Clock Driver	I/O Interface	UART/USRT	RAM	ROM/PROM	Interface	Interrupts	One-chip CPU	Microprogrammed	Accessible Stack	DMA Ability	BCD Arithmetic	0...70° C. Avail			
ELECTRONIC ARRAYS	8-Bit CPU	NMOS		✓		✓	✓		✓	✓		✓	✓	✓		8/8	64K	1000/2
FAIRCHILD F-8	8-Bit CPU	NMOS	✓	✓	✓	✓	✓	✓	✓	✓		✓	✓	✓		8/8	64K	2000/0
GENERAL INSTRUMENTS CP-1600	16-Bit CPU	NMOS		✓	✓	✓	✓		✓	✓	✓	✓	✓	✓		16/10	64K	5000/2
GENERAL INSTRUMENTS LP8000	8-Bit CPU	PMOS				✓	✓		✓		✓			✓		8/8	2K	800/2
INTEL 3002	2-Bit Slice	TTL			✓	✓	✓	✓	✓		✓		✓			2N/18+	512	6061/1
INTEL 4004	4-Bit CPU	PMOS	✓	✓		✓	✓	✓	✓		✓			✓		4/8	4K	740/2
INTEL 4040	4-Bit CPU	PMOS	✓	✓		✓	✓	✓	✓		✓			✓		4/8	4K	740/2
INTEL 8008-1	8-Bit CPU	PMOS	✓	✓	✓	✓	✓	✓	✓						✓	8/8	16K	800/2
INTEL 8080	8-Bit CPU	NMOS	✓	✓	✓	✓	✓	✓	✓	✓		✓	✓	✓	✓	8/8	64K	2083/2
INTERSIL 6100	12-Bit CPU	CMOS	✓			✓			✓	✓		✓			✓	12/12	4K	4000/0
MONOLITHIC MEMORIES 6701	4-Bit Slice	TTL								✓				✓		4/17		6606/1
MOS TECHNOLOGY 6501	8-Bit CPU	NMOS		✓		✓	✓		✓	✓		✓		✓		8/8	64K	1000/2
MOSTEK 5065	8-Bit CPU	PMOS				✓	✓		✓	✓		✓	✓			8/8	32K	1400/3
MOTOROLA 6800	8-Bit CPU	NMOS		✓	✓	✓	✓	✓	✓	✓		✓	✓	✓		8/8	64K	1000/2
NATIONAL CMP-8	8-Bit CPU	NMOS		✓	✓	✓	✓	✓	✓	✓		✓	✓			8/8	64K	/2
NATIONAL GPC/P	4-Bit Slice	PMOS								✓	✓	✓	✓			4N/23	100	715/4
NATIONAL IMP-4	4-Bit CPU	PMOS						✓	✓		✓		✓			4/4	4096	500/4
NATIONAL IMP-8	8-Bit CPU	PMOS						✓		✓	✓	✓				8/8	64K	715/4
NATIONAL IMP-16	16-Bit CPU	PMOS						✓		✓	✓	✓				16/16	64K	715/4
NATIONAL PACE	16-Bit CPU	PMOS	✓			✓	✓	✓	✓	✓		✓	✓			16/16	64K	2000/2
RCA COSMAC	8-Bit CPU	CMOS				✓	✓		✓	✓		✓	✓		✓	8/8	64K	2670/1
ROCKWELL PPS-4	4-Bit CPU	PMOS	✓	✓	✓	✓	✓			✓		✓		✓		4/8	4K	200/2
ROCKWELL PPS-8	8-Bit CPU	PMOS	✓	✓	✓	✓	✓		✓	✓		✓		✓		8/8	16K	256/2
SIGNETICS 2650	8-Bit CPU	NMOS					✓	✓				✓				8/8	32K	1200/1
TEXAS INSTRUMENTS SBP0400	4-Bit Slice	IIL								✓			✓			4N/9+		1000/1
TEXAS INSTRUMENTS TMS1000	4-Bit CPU	PMOS							✓	✓			✓			4/8	1K	500/1
TOSHIBA TLCS-12	12-Bit CPU	NMOS		✓		✓	✓		✓	✓	✓			✓		12/12	4K	1000/3
TRANSITRON 1601	4-Bit Slice	TTL					✓		✓	✓	✓					16/16	32K	
WESTERN DIGITAL 1600	16-Bit CPU	NMOS		✓	✓	✓		✓		✓	✓	✓				16/16	64K	3300/4

Fig. 7.58. MICROPROCESSOR SCORECARD (Extracted from *New Logic Notebook*, published by Microcomputer Technique, Inc., Reston, Va.).

Register Add Time (μ sec per Data Word)	ALU	XR	GP	Return-Stack Size (Nr x Bits)	Voltages Required	Power Dissipation	Package Sizes (DIP Pins)	Price Range (approx.; 100 qty.; CPU)	First Samples	First Deliveries	Remarks
	1	1	15	7 x 16			40		3Q75		16-Byte String Operations
2	65			(RAM)	+5, +12	.6	40	$ 75	1Q75	2Q75	Clock on Chip
2.4	6			(RAM)	−3, +5, +12	.6	40	$ 200	3Q75	3Q75	
5	1		48	3 x 11	−12, +5	.5	40	$ 35	2Q75	3Q75	16K Program Space in 8 Banks
.165	2		10	(NONE)	5	.8	28,40	$ 25	3Q74	3Q74	Second Source: Signetics
10.8	1		16	3 x 12	15 or (−10,+5)	1.0	16	$ 30	2Q71	4Q71	Second Source: National
10.8	1		24	7 x 12	15 or (−10,+5)	1.0	16,24	$ 40	4Q74	4Q74	8K Program Space in Two Banks
12.5	1		6	7 x 14	−9, +5	1.0	18	$ 60	4Q71	1Q72	
2	1		6	(RAM)	−5, +5, +12	1.0	40	$ 150	4Q73	2Q74	Second Source: AMD, TI
5	1		1	Modifies Program	5	.01	28,40	$ 240	2Q75	3Q75	PDP-8 Code; Clock on Chip
.2	3		16	(NONE)	5	1.0	40	$ 95	1Q74	2Q74	Similar to AMD 2901
2	1	1		(RAM)	5	.25	40	$ 20	3Q75	4Q75	Similar to Motorola 6800
10	3			(RAM)	−12, −5, +5	.7	40	$ 100	1Q74	3Q74	3-State CPU
2	2	1		(RAM)	5	.25	24,40	$ 150	2Q74	4Q74	Second Source: AMI
1.6	2	2		(RAM)			40		3Q75		
1.4	8			16 x 4N	−12, +5	.7	22,24	$ 150	1Q73	3Q73	$1 \leqslant N \leqslant 6$
12	4			7 x 12	−12, +5	1.0	24,40	$ 150	3Q74	4Q74	16 x 4 Data Stack
4.6	3	1		16 x 8	−12, +5	1.0	22,24	$ 230	4Q73	1Q74	
4.6	2	2		16 x 16	−12, +5	1.4	22,24	$ 310	1Q73	3Q73	
8	2	2		10 x 16	−12, +5, +8	.7	40	$ 132	1Q75	2Q75	
6	1		p	r x 16	5 ~ 12	.01	28,40	$ 300	4Q74	2Q75	$(p + 2r) \leqslant 30$
5	1		1	2 x 12	17	.225	42	$ 45	1Q72	3Q72	8K Program Space in Two Banks
4	1	1	2	(RAM)	17	.3	42	$ 47	4Q74	1Q75	
4.8	7			8 x 15	5	.5	40	$ 120	1Q75	2Q75	
1	10				> .85	.13	40	$ 40	4Q74	3Q75	
12	1		1	1 x 6	15	.1	28,40		1Q75	2Q75	Clock, RAM, ROM in Chip
13	4		6	(RAM)	−5, +5	.8	16,24,26,42	$ 215	2Q74	3Q74	
.4	u	v		(RAM)			40		3Q75	4Q75	$(u + v) \leqslant 8$
.6	x	y		(RAM)	−5, +5, +12	1.2	40	$ 250	3Q75	3Q75	$(x + y) \approx 16$

Fig. 7.58. (Continued)

283

and service of interrupting devices. All instructions are one word (16 bits) long which simplifies the programming task.

7.12. MICROPROCESSOR SUMMARY

The previous sections include descriptions of first- and second-generation microprocessors whose architectures vary greatly. In choosing the processors that have been described, an attempt was made to select not only the more popular devices, but also those whose architecture, considered in combination, include the most important operational features. A number of microprocessors are available which are not described. Since these devices have features which are similar to those described, the reader should easily understand their operation by referring to the manufacturer's literature.

In Fig. 7.58, a summary of the characteristics of a number of processors (including those described in the previous sections) is shown.

REFERENCES

1. OGDIN, J. and S. McPHILLIPS, "Microprocessor Scoreboard." *New Logic Notebook*, Vol. I, No. 1, Microcomputer Technique, Inc. (September, 1974).

2. WEISSBERGER, ALAN J., "MOS/LSI Microprocessor Selection." *Electronic Design*, Vol. 22, No. 12 (June 7, 1974).

3. WEISS, D., "Software for MOS/LSI Microprocessors" (three part series). *Electronic Design* (April 1, 1974).

4. *MCS-4 Microcomputer Set Users Manual*, Rev. 5. Intel Corp., Santa Clara, Calif., March, 1974.

5. *Data Catalog*. Intel Corp., Santa Clara, Calif., February, 1973.

6. *Intellec 4 and Microcomputer Modules Reference Manual*. Intel Corp., Santa Clara, Calif., 1974.

7. *4004 and 4040 Microcomputer System Assembly Language Programming Manual*. Intel Corp., Santa Clara, Calif., November, 1974.

8. OGDIN, J. L., "Microcomputers: Promises and Practices." IEEE Intercon 74, Session 17, N.Y., March, 1974.

9. *Intel MCS-40 User's Manual for Logic Designers*. Intel Corporation, Santa Clara, Calif., November, 1974.

10. *IMP-4 Technical Description*. Publication No. 4200017A, National Semiconductor Corp., November, 1974.

11. *PPS-4 Microcomputer Program Library*. Rockwell International Corp., November, 1974.

12. *PPS-4 Microcomputer Programming Manual*. Rockwell International Corp., October, 1974.

13. *MOS/LSI Parallel Processing System Programmers Reference Manual for Micropro-gramming*. Rockwell International Corp., May, 1973.

14. *PPS-4 Evaluation and Development Modules*, Rev. 1. Rockwell International Corp., June, 1974.

15. *Operating Manual for PPS-4 Microprogram Development Using the Time-sharing Option of the IBM Operating System 360 (TSO)*. Rockwell International Corp., May, 1974.

16. *MCS-8 Microcomputer Set 8008 Users Manual*, Rev. 4. Intel Corp., Santa Clara, Calif., November, 1973.

17. LEWIS, D. R. and W. R. SIENA, "How to Build a Microcomputer." *Electronic Design*, Vol. 19 (Sept. 13, 1973).

18. *Intellec 8 Reference Manual*. Intel Corp., Santa Clara, Calif., 1974.

19. *Intellec 8 Microcomputer System Operators Manual*. Intel Corp., Santa Clara, Calif., November, 1973.

20. *MCS-8 Assembly Language Programming Manual*. Intel Corp., Santa Clara, Calif., November, 1973.

21. *A Guide To PL/M Programming*. Intel Corp., Santa Clara, Calif., September, 1973.

22. SHIMA, M. and F. FAGGIN, "In Switch to n-MOS Microprocessor Gets a 2-μs cycle time." *Electronics* (April 18, 1974).

23. *Intellec 8/MOD 80 Reference Manual*. Intel Corp., Santa Clara, Calif., 1974.

24. *Intellec 8/MOD 80 Operators Manual*. Intel Corp., Santa Clara, Calif., June, 1974.

25. *Programming Manual for the 8080 Microcomputer System*. Intel Corp., Santa Clara, Calif., May, 1974.

26. CUSHMAN, R. H., "The Intel 8080: First of the Second-Generation Microprocessors." EDN, Vol. 19, No. 9 (May 5, 1974).

27. *M6800 Systems Reference and Data Sheets*. Motorola Semiconductor Products, Inc., Phoenix, Ariz., 1974.

28. *M6800 Benchmark Family for Microcomputer Systems*. Motorola Semiconductor Products, Inc., Phoenix, Ariz., 1975.

29. *Programming Manual M6800 Microprocessor*. Motorola Semiconductor Products, Inc., Phoenix, Ariz., 1974.

30. YOUNG, LINK, TOM BENNETT, and JEFF LAVELL, "n-channel MOS Technology Yields New Generation of Microprocessors." *Electronics* (April 18, 1974).

31. *RCA COS/MOS Microprocessor (COSMAC)*. RCA Solid State Division, Somerville, N.J., February, 1975.

32. *User Manual for the COSMAC Microprocessor—MPM-101*. RCA Solid State Division, Somerville, N.J.

33. *Program Development Guide for the COSMAC Microprocessor—MPM-102*. RCA Solid State Division, Somerville, N.J.

34. RUSSO, PAUL M. and MICHAEL D. LIPPMAN, "Case History: Store and Forward." *IEEE Spectrum* (September, 1974).

35. *Introduction and Description Parallel Processing System (PPS-8)*. Document No. 20164 N40, Rev. 2, Rockwell International Corp., October, 1974.

36. BASS, J. E., "A Microcomputer-Based CRT Terminal." Rockwell International Corp., 1975.

37. *Pace Users Manual*. National Semiconductor Corp., December, 1974.

38. FOX, WILLIAM A. and GEORGE F. REYLING, JR., "A Single Chip 16-bit Microprocessor for General Application." National Semiconductor Corp., 1974.

EXERCISES

7.1. Determine the class (Harvard or Princeton) of the following microprocessors.
  (a) National IMP-4
  (b) Rockwell PPS-4
  (c) Motorola 6800
  (d) RCA COSMAC
  (e) Rockwell PPS-8
  (f) National PACE

7.2. Which of the processors of Exercise 7.1 are microprogrammable? Discuss the advantages and disadvantages of microprogrammable microprocessors.

7.3. Which of the processors in Exercise 7.1 have multiple accumulators? Discuss the advantages of machines having two or more accumulators.

7.4. Discuss and compare the interrupt capabilities of the National IMP-4 and the Intel 4040.

7.5. Repeat Exercise 7.4 for the Intel 8080 and the Motorola 6800.

7.6. Repeat Exercise 7.4 for the RCA COSMAC and the Rockwell PPS-8.

7.7. Discuss the advantages that the National PACE offers in handling interrupts.

7.8. Discuss and compare the DMA capabilities of the Intel 8080 and the RCA COSMAC.

7.9. Repeat Exercise 7.8 for the Motorola 6800 and the Rockwell PPS-8.

7.10. Repeat Exercise 5.4 using the instruction sets for each of the processors listed in Exercise 7.1.

7.11. Repeat Example 5.5 (Sec. 5.6) for the processors listed in Exercise 7.1.

8 DESIGN METHODOLOGY AND APPLICATIONS

The design of digital systems using microprocessors requires a different perspective from that of random logic design [1]. Hardware and software requirements are integrally related. Many tasks may be performed in either hardware or software, and numerous tradeoffs must be made during the design process. The description of some popular microprocessors in Chapter 7 clearly indicates the variety of architecture and capability in the microcomputer field. For many applications, the selection of an appropriate microcomputer for a particular application is a nontrivial task.

In this chapter we will describe and illustrate some typical steps in a design procedure. Following the design procedure, several additional applications which illustrate various parts of the procedure will be presented.

8.1. DESIGN METHODOLOGY

Microcomputers have been successfully applied to three classes of applications. The first of these are in systems which previously employed a minicomputer. In some systems where a mini is employed, its full capability is not utilized. Under these circumstances, a micro might be used to economic advantage. The second class of applications includes systems that formerly employed random logic (combinational and sequential networks). Microcomputers are replacing hardwired logic in many systems. The resulting systems are more flexible and often cheaper. A common characteristic of successful applications is the ability to customize the system via software changes. It has been suggested that any digital system employing more than fifty gates is a candidate for application of a microcomputer. The major handicap in using microcomputers to replace random logic is decreased speed. The increased generality of the microcomputer usually means that more time is required to perform a given function.

The third class of applications consists of new applications of digital techniques. The inexpensive computing power of the microcomputer has led to many original

287

applications in which digital processing has not been previously employed. Examples of such systems are games, kitchen appliances, and "smart" measuring instruments.

The design of microcomputer systems proceeds through six phases: (1) problem definition, (2) evaluation, (3) design, (4) breadboarding of a prototype, (5) testing of the prototype, and (6) simplification of the final system.

As an example of the steps in a design procedure, we will consider the interface for an IBM Selectric typewriter to allow communication with a computer or calculator which has the capability of carrying out a "handshake" (asynchronous) transfer with the interface. This example provides an interesting case in which random logic can be effectively replaced by a microcomputer.

Problem Definition

The beginning of every application project must be a well-conceived definition of the task to be performed. The characteristics of external devices which will link the microcomputer to the real world must be clearly defined. This step brings into focus the functions which are to be performed by the microcomputer and the timing relationships to be satisfied. The amount of data to be stored in the system should also be evaluated to estimate the memory requirements. Once this information is clearly defined, we proceed to evaluate the applicability of a microcomputer and to select some candidate microprocessors.

For the Selectric interface, the inputs and outputs shown in Fig. 8.1 will appear at the interface. The inputs from the calculator or computer are TTL-compatible. In order to avoid confusion, we will refer to the input device as a calculator. The interface lines consist of eight lines carrying an ASCII code and four control lines. The I/O line indicates whether the calculator is requesting an input or output operation. CONTROL provides an indication that the bus contains data for the interface. In an input operation, it signals the interface to place data on the bus. FLAG is set by the interface to

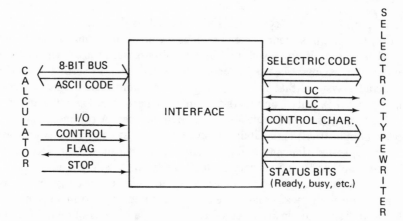

Fig. 8.1. Input/output functions for a Selectric interface.

indicate the availability of the interface for data transfer, and the *STOP* line provides a signal from the calculator to halt the Selectric. STOP serves to interrupt the printing and may be used to reset the interface. The timing of the signals for a typical input operation from the calculator is illustrated in Fig. 8.2. FLAG is tested by the calculator, and when FLAG is LO a transfer may occur. CONTROL is then brought HI by the calculator, and the data is read by the interface.

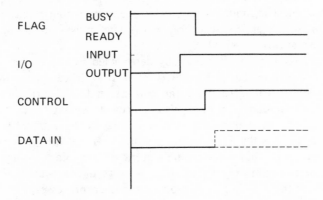

Fig. 8.2. Timing relationship for the calculator side of the interface for an input operation.

The 8-bit ASCII code which is read by the interface must then be converted to the Selectric character code (Fig. 8.3). The Selectric code is a 7-bit code in which the seventh bit is a parity bit. It has no resemblence to ASCII or any other standard code [2].

Each of the output lines to the Selectric must drive a magnet which controls the tilt and rotation of the printing ball. Each character is selected by tilting and rotating the ball and then striking the paper with the ball. In addition, separate lines are available for uppercase and lowercase. This is achieved by rotating the ball 180°. The shift operation must be completed before the character is output to the typewriter.

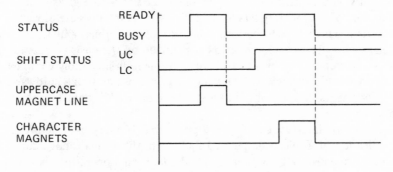

Fig. 8.3. Typical output operation to the typewriter.

Additional typewriter functions such as carriage return, index (line feed), backspace, space, tab, and keyboard lock are each controlled by a separate output line which drives a magnet. A READY/BUSY indication for the typewriter can be logically derived from the status lines of the Selectric. This indicator is used to control an asynchronous transfer to the typewriter. Prior to the transmission of a character to the typewriter, the shift position—which may be read from two status lines—should be determined to assure that the ball is in the proper position for an uppercase (or lowercase) character. The timing of an output operation is illustrated in Fig. 8.3 for the transmission of an uppercase character. Magnet pulses are terminated at the transition of the status from READY to BUSY.

The memory requirement is essentially determined by the memory required to make the code conversion. The 7- bit ASCII input from the calculator will require at most 128 memory locations to make the conversion to Selectric character code. Essentially the same amount of memory will be needed to make the conversion in the reverse direction. This transformation table should be stored in ROM because it will be permanent data. Thus the ROM memory requirements will be approximately 256 bytes plus the memory required for program storage. Temporary storage of words to be transmitted will require only a few words, and we may assume that this storage will be available in the scratch-pad memory of the microprocessor.

Evaluation

Once the problem is defined, the applicability of one or more microcomputers is examined. During this phase of the evaluation, some general topics of importance are [1]:

1. Functions to be performed.
2. Hardware requirements.
3. Timing limitations.
4. Memory requirements.

Frequently, consideration of the functions to be performed gives a clear view of the applicability of microcomputers to the task. Microcomputers are especially applicable to systems which have to perform complicated logical manipulations. They are also effective when frequent decisions must be made on the basis of past or present information. A microcomputer is capable of implementing incredibly complex logical operations. With random logic, logical complexity means additional hardware. Applications which suggest a bus input/output structure offer additional advantages to the microcomputer.

In the Selectric interface example, the presence of a data-bus structure is natural to the application of a microcomputer. In addition, the asynchronous data transfer requires the frequent testing of status bits and conditional operations based on these status bits. This is easily performed with the microcomputer. The code conversion

(ASCII to Selectric code) may also be performed efficiently in the microcomputer. From a functional standpoint, therefore, it is clear that the microcomputer is a candidate for this application.

The physical size and cost of a system are governed by the amount of hardware required. Hardware requirements for microcomputers are determined to a great extent by the input/output operations required. An estimate of the hardware requirements can be formulated by considering the following questions [1]:

1. How many I/O channels are required for data acquisition and transmission?

2. Do all I/O channels use the same data rates?

3. Are all I/O channels handling equal amounts of data flow?

4. Do I/O channels operate serially or in parallel?

5. Are the I/O channels randomly selected or do they operate in some predetermined sequence?

6. What word length will the I/O data have?

The hardware requirements are a function of the microcomputer system chosen. At this point, therefore, some candidate microcomputers may be evaluated on the basis of the hardware requirements. In the desire to minimize hardware, designers often overlook the cost of software development. A system which requires more hardware may have significantly simpler software requirements. To evaluate this tradeoff, it is valuable to consider a typical I/O operation and draw a flow chart of the steps required to perform this operation. A program can then be written for the candidate microcomputers. Such a program, which is used to compare different systems, is called a *benchmark*. A benchmark program is valuable in comparing the power of the instruction sets of the microprocessors. In some applications, internal data manipulations may be more significant than the I/O operations. In these cases, the benchmark program should include the most often repeated or most critical (from a timing standpoint) operations to be performed.

As an illustration of this approach, we will consider the operation of the Selectric interface in controlling the printing of a single character on the typewriter. Assume that the character has been read from the calculator in ASCII, converted into Selectric code, and is stored in the scratch-pad memory of the processor. Figure 8.4 is a flow chart of the software needed to perform this transfer.

The interface must intially check the status of the typewriter. If it is in a READY condition, then the uppercase/lowercase status should be read and compared with the shift required for the character being printed. If the shift status is not as desired, then a pulse must be applied to the proper magnet to cause the shift to take place. The appropriate shift magnet (UC or LC) must be held while the BUSY status is checked. When a BUSY condition is obtained, the magnet is released and the READY status is read until a READY is obtained. At this point the 7-bit Selectric code for the character is outputted to the typewriter to drive the appropriate character-selection magnets.

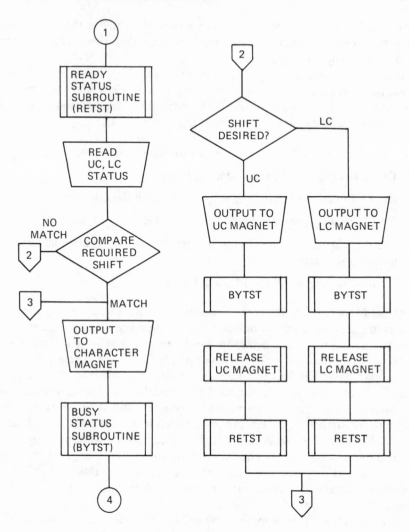

Fig. 8.4. Flow chart of benchmark for printing a character on the typewriter.

The magnets are released when a BUSY status is read, and the interface then waits until a READY is obtained before proceeding with the next operation.

We will now develop a benchmark program for the Intel MCS-40 (Sec. 7.3).

Benchmark for MCS-40 (Example 8.1)

Figure 8.5 illustrates a block diagram of the elements required to design an interface using the MCS-40 components. The 4289 interface circuit provides the required fourteen 4-bit I/O ports plus the multiplexing required to enable the program developer to use the 4702A pROM. The 4702A is a reprogrammable pROM. It offers distinct advantages over mask-programmed ROMs or fusible link pROMs during the

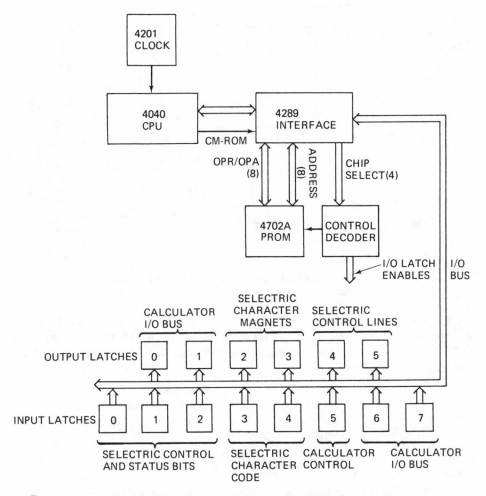

Fig. 8.5. Block diagram of interface using MCS-40 system.

development stages. Once a system is proven, it may be desirable to replace the 4289 and 4702A (1702A) with the standard ROM (4001) and general I/O interface circuits 4207/09/11.

The Control Decoder decodes the chip select lines $(C_0–C_3)$ from the 4289 to enable the pROM or appropriate I/O port. Latches are shown at each of the I/O ports, but they may not be required in all cases. This can be determined during the design stage.

Figure 8.6 illustrates the hardware involved in the benchmark program. In the course of developing this benchmark, three output ports and one input port will be required. Appropriate individual bits are identified in Fig. 8.6. It is assumed that READY (R) and BUSY (B) signals are available for input to input port 0. External logic or software is required to generate these indicators from the signals available at the terminals of the Selectric.

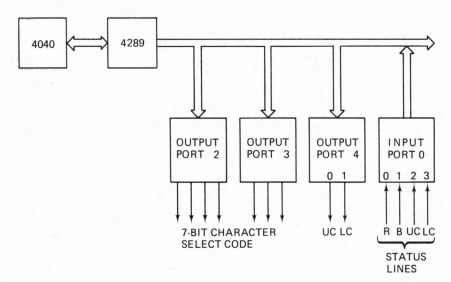

Fig. 8.6. Block diagram of a portion of the I/O system required for the benchmark program.

The testing of the READY and BUSY lines are recurring operations. This suggests the use of a subroutine for testing these inputs. For the READY test, a subroutine RETST is shown below. The subroutine assumes that an SRC command has been processed to address port 0.

```
RETST  : RDR              ; Read input port 0
         RAR              ; Rotate bit 0 into carry
         JCN 0AH, RETST   ; Jump if carry = 0
         BBL       0
```

The subroutine causes the input port to be read repeatedly until the READY line is 1. A similar routine can be written to test for a BUSY.

```
BYTST  : RDR              ; Read input port 0
         RAR
         RAR              ; Rotate bit 1 into carry
         JCN 0AH, BYTST   ; Jump if carry = 0
         BBL       0
```

With the availability of these two subroutines, a program may be written to follow the flow chart of Fig. 8.4. Such a program is (IR register assignments employed are shown in Fig. 8.10):

```
; TEST READY STATUS AND DETERMINE SHIFT STATUS
         FIM   4, 00H     ; Load IR pair 4 with 00
         SRC   4          ; Select input port 0
         JMS   RETST      ; Call subroutine to test ready
         RDR              ; Read shift status of typewriter
         AN6              ; IR#6 contains the desired shift
```

```
                              ;  Bit 2 = 1 if UC desired
                              ;  Bit 3 = 1 if LC desired
                              ;  AND actual status with desired status
          JCN  0CH, LAST  ;  Jump if match
;  If shift status is not as desired then address the uppercase or lowercase
;  magnets appropriately
          FIM  8, 40H
          SRC  8          ;  Address port 4
          LD   6          ;  Recall desired status
          RAL
          JCN  2, UPER    ;  Jump if UC is desired
;  Load the appropriate bit into accumulator
;  Bit 1 for lowercase, bit 0 for uppercase
          LDM  2          ;  Load data for lowercase
          JUN  SHIFT
UPER  :   LDM  1          ;  Set bit 0 for uppercase
SHIFT :   WRR             ;  Excite appropriate shift magnet
          SRC  4          ;  Select port 0
          JMS  BYTST      ;  Check for busy
          SRC  8          ;  Address port 4
          LDM  0
          WRR             ;  Release magnets
          SRC  4          ;  Select port 0
          JMS  RETST      ;  Check for ready
;  IR3 and bits 0-2 of IR2 contain the selectric code for character to
;  be printed
LAST  :   FIM  10, 20H
          SRC  10         ;  Select port 2
          LD   3          ;  Load 4 bits of code
          WRR
          INC  10
          SRC  10         ;  Select port 3
          LD   2          ;  Load remainder of code
          WRR
          SRC  4          ;  Select port 0
          JMS  BYTST      ;  Check for busy
          FIM  10, 20H
          SRC  10
          LDM  0
          WRR             ;  Release character selection magnets
          INC  10
          SRC  10
          WRR             ;  Release remaining character select magnets
          .
          .
          .
```

The same procedure may also be used to write the benchmark program for competing microprocessors. The benchmark may be used to assess the ease of programming the operations required, the execution time, memory requirements, and hardware interfacing requirements. After the benchmark is written for all candidate microcomputers, a suitable one is selected and the design is undertaken. Many factors must be considered in making the system selection. These include [3]:

1. Word size.

2. Memory size and return address stack size.

3. Arithmetic modes.

4. Interface requirements.

5. Interrupt capability.

6. DMA capability.

7. Power requirements.

8. Number of packages required.

9. Component prices.

10. Familiarity with candidate microprocessor.

For many applications an off-the-shelf microcomputer or microcomputer development system is valuable during the initial design and breadboarding phases. In the discussion which follows, we will assume that a development system, in this case the INTELLEC 40 (Sec. 7.3), is available for the initial software development and interface design.

Design

During the design phase, hardware design and software development take place concurrently. Hardware design generally consists of solving interfacing problems and designing the hardware necessary to perform the I/O functions. Close coordination is required at this stage because the hardware design impacts the software development. During the design, provisions should be made for system testing [4]. This generally requires some additional hardware. It will certainly require some special software to aid in debugging the system. If properly planned, such programs can be a valuable asset in the debugging phase.

In this example, we will use an INTELLEC 40 development system for the MCS-40 system. Some powerful debugging capabilities are included in the development system. To simplify the explanation, it will be assumed that the development system contains adequate testing facilities. At the completion of the testing phase, the components of the development system may be selectively replaced to obtain a production model.

For the example system (Selectric interface), the hardware design begins with the system diagram shown in Fig. 8.5. The Control Decoder of Fig. 8.5 must decode the

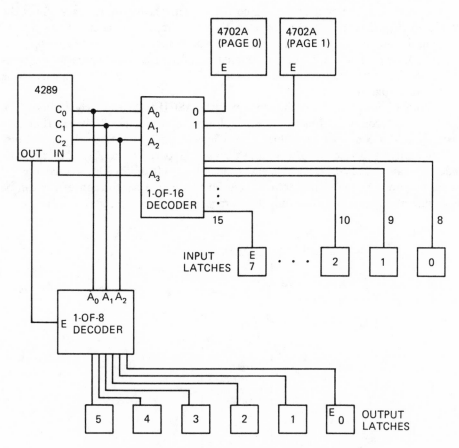

Fig. 8.7. Decoding and control of I/O and memory addresses.

chip select outputs of the 4289 interface to enable the proper input or output port. Figure 8.7 illustrates the hardware required for this task. The 4289 provides a 4-bit CHIP SELECT (C_0–C_3) signal which serves as the page number (highest four bits) for program memory addresses. During input or output operations the device code appears at C_0–C_2 along with an appropriate level on the IN and OUT terminals. In Fig. 8.7, the 1-of-16 decoder is used to address the program memory and the input ports. If an INPUT instruction is executing, the IN terminal will be 1 and the eight input ports are enabled by lines 8–15 of the decoder. Lines 0–7 can be used to address up to eight pROMs for program memory storage. If an output instruction is executing, the OUT terminal will be 1 and the 1-of-8 decoder will be enabled. Latches are provided at the input and output ports to ensure that timing is compatible. The latches are not, of course, capable of driving the relays for the Selectric. Thus, high-current drivers (such as the National DH0006) will be required to drive the Selectric magnets from the output latches (output ports 2, 3, 4, and 5).

The software development must be correlated with the hardware design. Since the interface design has a definite impact on the software, a flow chart of the general program should be written first. The program may be subdivided into small tasks such as an input or output routine or a manipulation of internal data words. In the typewriter interface example, one output routine has already been written as a part of the benchmark program.

Another important part of the program is the ASCII-to-Selectric code conversion. This may be accomplished using a table look-up procedure. The 8-bit ASCII code is basically a 7-bit code with an eighth bit serving as a parity bit. Suppose that we first test the parity of the incoming word and then set the parity bit to zero. The resulting code will range from 00–7F (2^7 memory locations). If this code is used for the memory address of the equivalent character in Selectric code, the conversion can be made directly. Figure 8.8 illustrates the storage of the Selectric codes in memory.

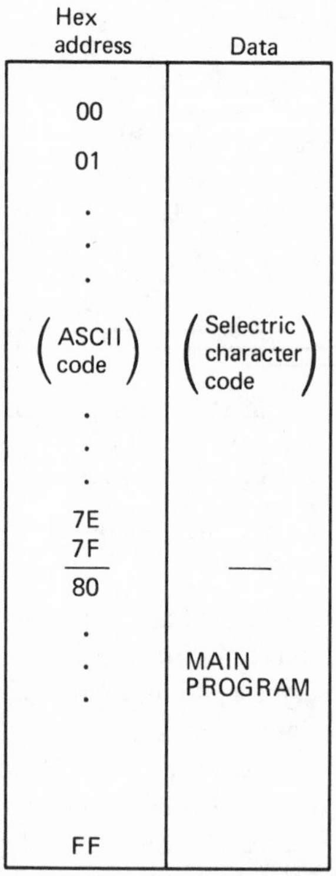

```
          Hex
        address              Data
       ┌──────────────┬──────────────────┐
       │     00       │                  │
       │              │                  │
       │     01       │                  │
       │      .       │                  │
       │      .       │                  │
       │      .       │                  │
       │   ⎛ASCII⎞    │    ⎛Selectric⎞   │
       │   ⎝code ⎠    │    ⎜character⎟   │
       │              │    ⎝code     ⎠   │
       │      .       │                  │
       │      .       │                  │
       │      .       │                  │
       │     7E       │                  │
       │     7F       │                  │
       │    ─────     │       ───        │
       │     80       │                  │
       │      .       │                  │
       │      .       │      MAIN         │
       │      .       │    PROGRAM        │
       │              │                  │
       │              │                  │
       │     FF       │                  │
       └──────────────┴──────────────────┘
```

Fig. 8.8. Memory map of ROM 0 for typewriter interface example.

The Selectric character code corresponds only to the character selection magnets of the typewriter. Carriage return for example, requires the excitation of a separate magnet. One of the seven bits of the Selectric code is a parity bit. If this bit is temporarily omitted, two bits may be used to flag the entries which require magnets other than the character-selection magnets to be driven. The format of the Selectric code, as it appears in memory, is shown in Fig. 8.9.

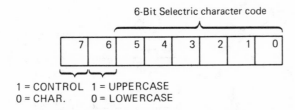

Fig. 8.9. Selectric code word in memory.

When the Selectric code is read from memory, bit 7 is examined. If it is a 1, then the 6-bit code in bits 0–5 represents a control magnet which is to be excited (such as line feed or carriage return). If a 0 is found in bit 7, the 6-bit code represents the code of a character to be printed. The parity bit must be generated and placed in the LSB position before the character code is outputted to the typewriter. Figure 8.10 shows a *register map* of the internal registers of the 4040. Such maps aid in accounting for the data stored. In systems requiring RAM memory, a *memory map* (showing location of data stored in RAM) is also invaluable.

A flow chart of the conversion subprogram is illustrated in Fig. 8.11. The program begins after the ASCII character has been read from the calculator and has been stored in register pair 0 (IR 0 and IR 1). A program to implement the flow chart begins with the conversion of the ASCII code to Selectric code. First the parity bit is stripped from the ASCII code and then a Fetch Indirect (FIN) instruction is employed to read the Selectric code. FIN causes the 8-bit content of the 0 index register pair

0 ASCII CODE	1
2 SELECTRIC CODE	3
4 I/O PORT ADDRESS (CHARACTER)	5
6 DESIRED STATUS OF TYPEWRITER	7
8 I/O PORT ADDRESS (UC/LC MAGNETS)	9
10 I/O PORT ADDRESS (SELECTRIC CHARACTERS)	11
12	13
14	15

Fig. 8.10. Map of 4040 internal registers.

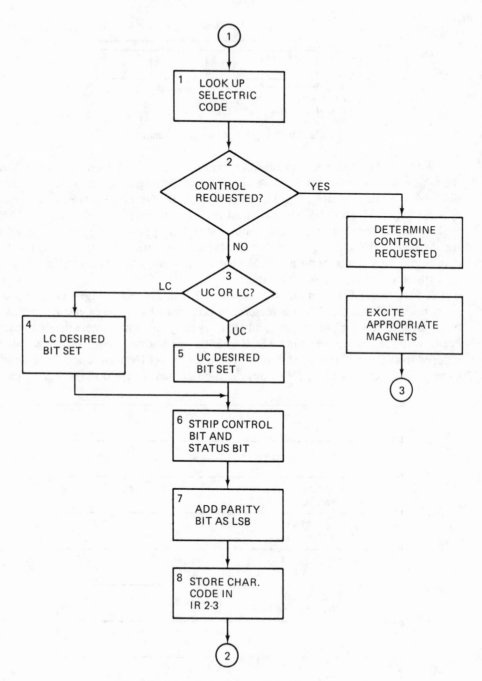

Fig. 8.11. Flow chart of conversion subprogram.

(IR 0 and IR 1) to be sent out as an address in the same page as the FIN instruction is located. The 8-bit word at that location is loaded into the designated register pair. For our example, FIN must be located on page 0 of the program memory. The flow chart may be implemented as follows:

```
; BLOCK 1 OF FIGURE 8.11
            LD 0            ; ACC ← IR 0
            RAL             ; SHIFT PARITY BIT INTO CARRY
            CLC             ; STRIP PARITY BIT
            RAR             ; RESTORE CODE W/O PARITY
            XCH 0           ; IR 0 ← ACC
            FIN  2          ; MOVE SELECTRIC CODE TO REGISTER
                            ; PAIR 2.
;  ***      BLOCK 2    ****
            LD 2
            RAL             ; ROTATE CONTROL BIT INTO CARRY
            JCN  2, CTRL  ; JUMP TO CTRL IF CODE REQUIRES A
                            ; CONTROL OPERATION
;  CTRL IS A SUBROUTINE TO EXCITE CONTROL MAGNETS
;  CTRL WILL NOT BE LISTED
;  ***      BLOCK 3    ****
            RAL             ; ROTATE SHIFT BIT INTO CARRY
            JCN  2, SETUP
;  ***      BLOCK 4    ****
            LDM 8
            XCH 6           ; SET LOWERCASE BIT
            JUN  SET
;  ***      BLOCK 5    ***
   SETUP :  LDM 4
            XCH 6           ; SET UPPERCASE BIT
;  ***      BLOCK 6    ***
     SET :  LD 2            ; REPLACE UPPER BITS OF SELECTRIC CODE
            CLC
            RAL
            CLC             ; STRIP CONTROL BIT
            RAL
            CLC             ; STRIP SHIFT BIT
            RAR             ; TWO UPPERMOST BITS IN SELECTRIC CODE
                            ; ARE CONTAINED IN BITS 1 AND 2 OF
                            ; ACCUMULATOR
            XCH 2
;  SHIFT MSB OF IR 3 INTO LSB OF IR 2
            CLB
            XCH 5           ; CLEARS IR 5
            XCH 3
```

```
          RAL                ; SHIFT MSB OF IR 3 INTO CARRY
          XCH 3
          XCH 2
          ADD 5              ; ADD CARRY INTO LSB OF SELECTRIC CODE
                             ; IN IR 2
          XCH 2
; ***     BLOCK 7     ****
; DETERMINE THE PARITY OF THE 6 BIT SELECTRIC CODE
; IR 9 WILL BE USED TO HOLD RESULT OF ADDING 1'S
; IR 11 WILL BE USED AS AN INDEX
          CLB
          XCH 9
          JMS  CBIT     ; COUNT BITS WHICH ARE ONE
          XCH 2
          XCH 3
          XCH 2
          JMS  CBIT     ; COUNT BITS WHICH ARE ONE
; ***     BLOCK 8     ****
          LD 9
          RAR
          JNC  2, END8  ; CHECK TO DETERMINE PARITY BIT
          CMC           ; SET CARRY TO 1
          XCH 3
          XCH 2
          XCH 3
          ADD 5         ; MOVE PARITY BIT INTO LSB
          XCH 3         ; COMPLETE INTERPRETATION
    END8 :  NOP
```

The program is a straightforward implementation of the flow chart. Subroutine CBIT (count bits), which counts the number of 1's in a 4-bit word, is used to determine the parity (odd) bit of the code in BLOCK 8. CBIT may be implemented by the following program.

```
   CBIT  :  LDM 0CH
            XCH 11       ; INITIALIZE INDEX REGISTER
            LD  2        ; BRING IN IR 2
   RPET  :  RAR
            JCN  2, ADD1 ; JUMP IF 1
            ISZ  11, RPET ; INCREMENT INDEX
            BBL  0
   ADD1  :  INC 9
            ISZ  11, RPET
            BBL  0
```

The rest of the program is written in a similar manner. Each task is identified and then a program is written to implement the operation.

Breadboarding

It is advantageous to breadboard the design using a development system such as the INTELLEC 40. Such a system contains a complete microcomputer along with some valuable testing and debugging software. The external equipment and necessary interfaces are built and integrated with the development system.

The software package, which is partially debugged on an assembler, is executed on the prototype hardware and the real debugging then begins. At this stage of the development, most problems will be solved by modification of the software because hardware redesign is too expensive [4]. The breadboard testing first concentrates on verifying the operation for one or two specific tasks. It is helpful to store the program in RAM while developing the breadboard system. This allows rapid changes to be made in the program during testing.

Testing

After the system is breadboarded, the testing begins. A test plan should be conceived which allows each function of the application to be tested. Insight into the operation of the system is necessary to locate potential troubles and devise methods of testing. Changes in the program are usually implemented in machine language. The correct machine code is placed directly into the RAM in place of the erroneous code. The development system is especially valuable in this case because the software is available to accomplish the correction process from a terminal or teletypewriter.

Care is required in correcting the machine language program if a single-byte instruction must be replaced by a multibyte instruction, or vice versa. It may be necessary to make corrections in the addresses associated with branch or subroutine call instructions. Detailed documentation of all programming changes is absolutely essential. If pROMs are used for program storage during the testing phase, it is necessary to reprogram a pROM each time a change is made in the program.

No matter how detailed and well-conceived the testing program, it is probable that some bugs will remain in a complex program after the testing is completed. As a result, field-programmable ROMs are frequently used in the early production models of a system. As confidence in the software grows, a mask-programmable ROM may be substituted with economic benefits.

Simplification of the Final System

When the system has been satisfactorily tested using the development system, it may be simplified. Simplification is generally accomplished systematically on a step-by-step basis. One part of the system at a time is simplified until a system suitable for production is obtained. This simplification also applies to software. During the initial design phase, the most important goal is to write a program to accomplish the specified task. In other words, the initial goal is to get the system working. Although efficient programming is always desirable, inordinate amounts of time should not be spent in writing "optimum" programs during the initial design. During simplification, the program should be carefully examined to determine methods of improving the speed of execution or minimizing the memory space required to store and implement the program.

8.2. EXAMPLES OF MICROCOMPUTER APPLICATIONS

In the remainder of the chapter, several system applications will be presented. The examples illustrate the many application areas for microcomputers. Some examples will emphasize hardware and others, software. In some, the formulation of an algorithm is stressed, while in others, details of a portion of the assembly language program are presented.

Data Acquisition System (Example 8.2)

Microcomputers are very useful in processing analog signals which commonly occur in instrumentation systems. In a manufacturing process, for example, such signals can be readily monitored and decisions made for precise process control. These decisions and the resulting sequence of events are completely specified by user-supplied software. A common task is the monitoring of a number of voltages or currents in a systematic fashion [5].

A system for monitoring eight analog voltages is shown in Fig. 8.12. A prototype system is illustrated employing an INTELLEC 80 (8080 microprocessor) development system, an 8-channel analog multiplexer (MUX), and an 8-bit analog-to-digital (A/D) converter. In operation, the processor issues a command to select 1-of-8 channels via bit lines 0–2 of output port 3. Following the channel selection, the processor issues a start conversion pulse on bit line 4, which initiates the A/D conversion of the selected analog channel. At the start of the conversion, the end-of-conversion (E.O.C.) line is driven to a TRUE state. When the conversion is completed, the E.O.C. returns to the FALSE state.

The E.O.C. is connected to bit 0 of input port 2. The microcomputer continues to read port 2 until a FALSE is read on the E.O.C. line. The digital value of the analog voltage is then transferred into memory through input port 3.

A flow chart of the program required to read the eight analog voltages is illustrated in Fig. 8.13.

A program to implement the flow chart is:

```
LBI  0F8H      ;  Initialize index and channel select
LXI  D,DSTOR   ;  Pointer to data storage
               ;  DSTOR must be previously defined
```

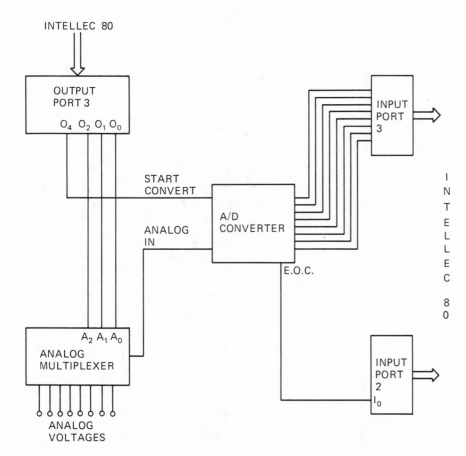

Fig. 8.12. Diagram of a Data Acquisition System.

NEXTC :	MOV	A,B	; Load accumulator with the
			; complement of channel no.
	ANI	0EFH	; Insert start convert bit
	OUT	3	; Reset A/D, select channel
	MOV	A,B	; RESET start convert bit
	OUT	3	; Start conversion
STATUS :	IN	2	; Read E.O.C. on bit 0
	RAR		; Shift into carry
	JNC	STATUS	; Check E.O.C.
	IN	3	; Input data
	STAX	D	; Store data
	DCX	D	; Decrement data address
	INR	B	; Decrement channel
	JNZ	NEXTC	

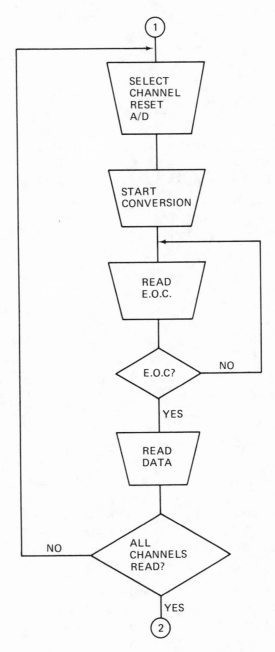

Fig. 8.13. Flow chart of Data Acquisition Program.

The INTELLEC 80 input and output ports invert the data presented to them. For this reason, the complement of the desired output is output by the software. The timing diagram for the A/D converter is illustrated in Fig. 8.14. The converter is reset on a HI-to-LO transition, and the conversion is initiated on a LO-to-HI transition on the START CONVERT line of the A/D converter. Completion of the conversion is signaled by a LO level on the E.O.C. line.

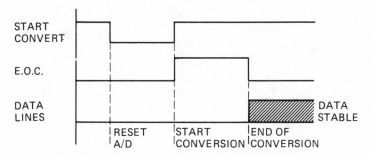

Fig. 8.14. Timing diagram for A/D converter.

Data Concentrator (Example 8.3)

In many computer systems it is necessary to transfer information from a terminal such as a teletypewriter or CRT to a large computer (e.g., an IBM 360) over telephone wires. A typical data-transmission system of this type is shown in Fig. 8.15.

Typically, the terminal device is capable of transmission at 110–300 Baud, while the modem is capable of handling up to 4800 Baud. A modem is therefore capable of handling a number of terminals over the same phone line.

A data concentrator receives data from several low-speed lines and transmits the data over a single high-speed line, and vice versa [6]. Microcomputers are well suited to this task. Figure 8.16 illustrates a data concentrator using the National IMP-8.

The interface between the modem and the microcomputer is serial. Therefore, data input from the modem may be made through the TEST terminal on the micro-

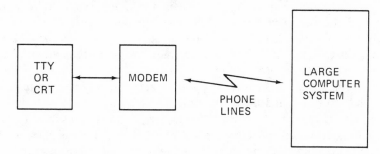

Fig. 8.15. Data transmission system from a terminal to a large computer.

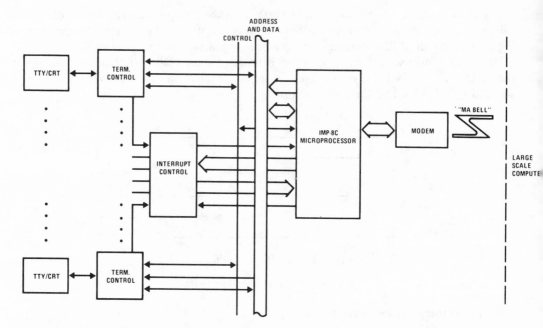

Fig. 8.16. Data concentrator (Courtesy of National Semiconductor Corporation, U.S.A.).

processor. Data can be read serially by testing the TEST terminal periodically with a conditional branch instruction. A time delay must be implemented in software to determine the bit time interval. Output to the modem is made via a software-controlled FLAG terminal.

Each terminal must have a terminal controller to interface it to the microprocessor. The controller will contain a UART to convert the serial data from the terminal-to-parallel data for storage and subsequent input to the microcomputer over the data bus. Input and output buffers provide storage of the data waiting to be transferred. A status register in the interface is checked by the microcomputer to determine whether or not the interface is ready to receive data from the computer. When data is waiting at the interface to be transferred to the computer, an interrupt request is generated by the terminal controller. The request goes to the interrupt controller which resolves conflicts caused by multiple interrupt requests. A functional block diagram of the terminal controller is provided in Fig. 8.17.

The interrupt controller is basically a priority encoder. All interrupt requests are directed to the controller, and the address of the requesting device with the highest priority is passed to the computer. All of the interrupt request lines from the devices are ORed to provide a single interrupt request which is passed to the microcomputer. An illustration of the function and input/output information for the interrupt controller is shown in Fig. 8.18.

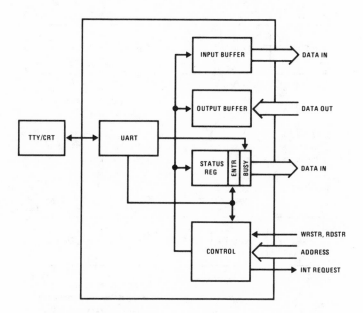

Fig. 8.17. Terminal controller (Courtesy of National Semiconductor Corporation, U.S.A.).

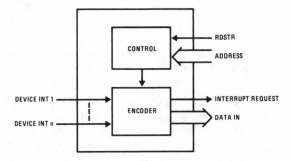

Fig. 8.18. Interrupt controller (Courtesy of National Semiconductor Corporation, U.S.A.).

Data flow between the terminals and the large computer is under the control of the microcomputer. Each character which is transferred to or from the modem is accompanied by a control character. The output control character (microcomputer $\rightarrow$ modem) has the form shown in Fig. 8.19(a). Every time the large computer receives a character pair from the modem, it will send a character pair from its output buffer. Bit 5 of the output control character indicates to the computer whether the microcomputer will accept the character pair it has sent. If this bit is 0, the large computer must restore this character pair to its output buffer. Figure 8.19(b) illustrates the input control character. The input control character specifies the destination terminal of the

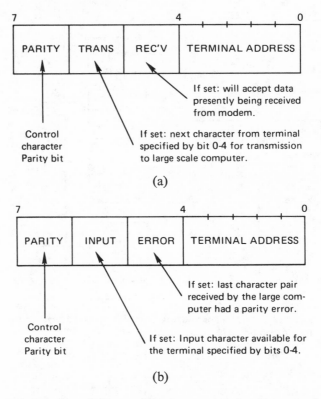

Fig. 8.19. Control characters for data transmission (Courtesy of National Semiconductor Corporation, U.S.A.).

next character to be transmitted. Bit 5 of this control character is set if the large computer found a parity error in the last character pair it received.

A flow chart of the program required to implement the data concentrator is illustrated in Fig. 8.20.

Capacitance Bridge (Example 8.4)

An example of a microprocessor application to instruments is the Boonton 76A automatic capacitance bridge. A block diagram of the bridge is illustrated in Fig. 8.21 [7].

In this unit, the microcomputer, an MCS-4 system, controls the front panel display and I/O. It also controls the bridge balance and determines the capacitance, conductance, Q factor, and dissipation of the capacitor connected to the output terminals. In addition, it automatically corrects predictable bridge errors and autoranges from 0 to 2000 pF.

One of the most important facets of any application involves the input/output functions. A careful tradeoff of hardware versus software design must be made in every application. In this application, the relationship between the microcomputer and the front panel will be described.

The front panel of the bridge is illustrated in Fig. 8.22. The switch circuitry senses the switch closures and provides switch status information by lighting an LED above each switch that is closed. Twenty switches are read and eighteen status indicators are controlled by the MCS-4.

A schematic of the switching circuitry is shown in Fig. 8.23. Study of the circuitry and the software required to control the circuitry provides valuable insight into application of the MCS-4 system.

Switch data is transferred in parallel to the 5-bit shift registers by pulsing of the LOAD line. This is accomplished by addressing the I/O address 14. At this point, switch-closure information is contained in the 7496 shift registers. The first four bits of switch data are read by pulsing of the READ line. This is accomplished by a Read instruction (RDR). Next, a pulse is applied to the RESTORE line to shift the status information from the CPU back to the shift registers. At the same time, the pulse on the RESTORE line starts a gated clock which provides four clock pulses to the shift registers to shift the next four bits into position for reading. As the switch bits are being read, status bits replace them in the register. After five of these operations, all of the switch data will have been moved to the MCS-4 (stored in RAM), and status bits from the RAM will be located in the 7476's. The program steps required to implement these tasks are illustrated in Fig. 8.24.

Instructions 1 and 2 and subroutine BLE (22–25) simply enable the panel I/O functions by setting the appropriate BLOCK ENABLE (1 in this case). Instructions 3 and 4 initialize the index register pairs to the address of the status/switch bits in the RAM and the I/O address for LOAD (14). Register 13 is also set as an index to provide for five repetitions of instructions 8–19 in order to read the five blocks of switch data and restore the status bits.

Instruction 5 informs the microprocessor that register 12 contains the address to which an output is to be made. Thus, when a WRR (write to ROM port) occurs, the LOAD pulse is generated at address 14 (content of IR 12 is 14). Instruction 7 increments register 12 so that upon the next WRR a pulse will be applied to the RESTORE line. Instructions 8–11 cause the status bits to be read from RAM, complemented, and temporarily saved in register 0. Four bits of switch data are read by step 12 and then complemented and written into the RAM. Steps 15–17 cause the four status bits in register 0 to be placed in the shift register and the shift register to be shifted four places to present the next data to be read. Instructions 18 and 19 increment the memory address to the address of the next status/switch word in RAM and test to determine if the loop is complete. Following these steps, the switch data has replaced the status data in RAM, and the status bits have been shifted to the shift registers where they are displayed by the LEDs.

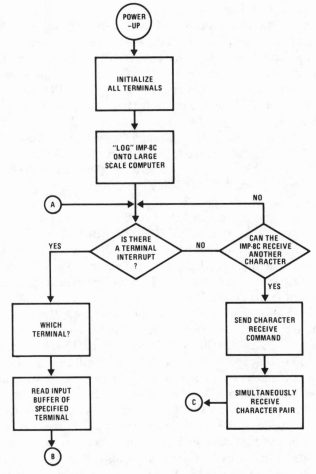

Fig. 8.20. Flow chart for data concentrator (Courtesy of National Semiconductor Corporation, U.S.A.).

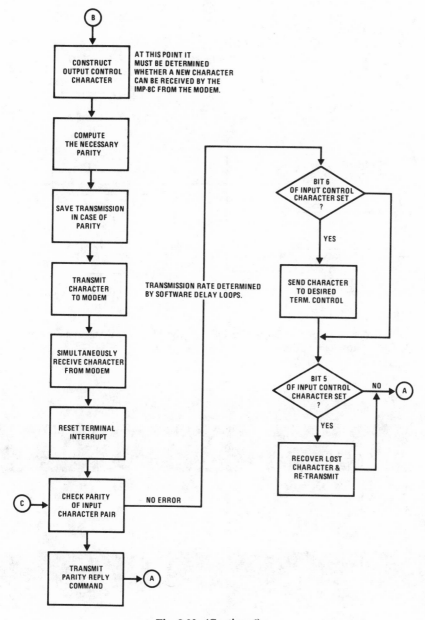

Fig. 8.20. (Continued)

313

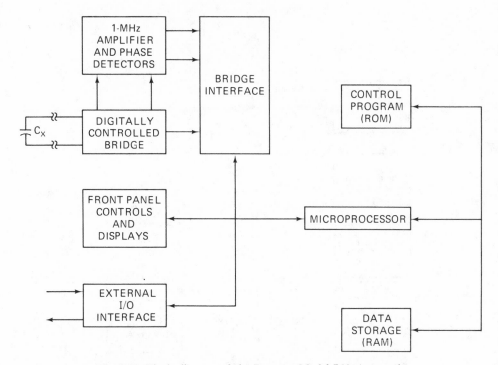

Fig. 8.21. Block diagram of the Boonton Model 76A Automatic Capacitance Bridge.

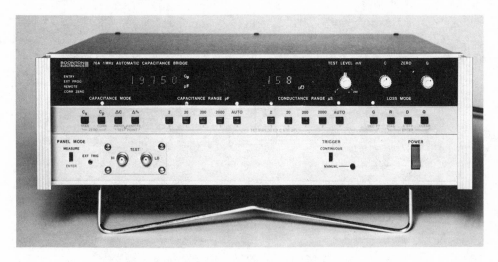

Fig. 8.22. Boonton Model 76A 1MHz Automatic Capacitance Bridge.

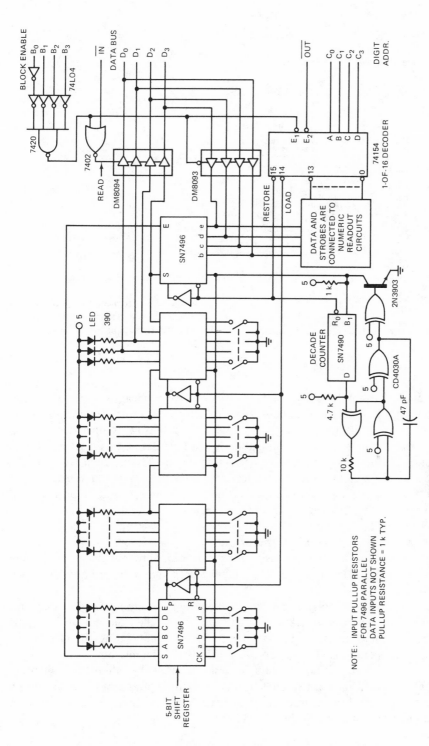

Fig. 8.23. Function of the switch circuitry of the Boonton Bridge.

315

```
MNEMONIC                 COMMENTS
INSTRUCTION

    LDM 1         /LOAD 1 TO ACC; BLOCK ENABLE FOR PANEL
    JMS BLE       /JUMP TO SR AND WRITE 1 TO RAM PORT Ø

    FIM 14 96     /INIT. REG 14,15 TO ADDRESS DIGIT Ø

    FIM 12 235    /INIT. REG 12 = 14 FOR WRR, REG 13 = 11

    SRC 13        /PREPARE FOR WRR WITH DIGIT ADDR. = 14
    WRR           /CREATE SWITCH LOAD PULSE
    INC 12        /INCREMENT REG 12 FROM 14 TO 15
SWL, SRC 14       /PREPARE TO READ DIGIT FROM RAM
    RDM           /READ DIGIT (STATUS DATA) TO ACC.
    CMA           /COMPLEMENT; LAMP ON FOR LOGIC ZERO
    XCH Ø         /SAVE TEMPORARILY IN REG Ø
    RDR           /READ SWITCH DATA
    CMA           /COMPLEMENT; SWITCH CLOSURE = LOGIC Ø
    WRM           /WRITE SWITCH DATA IN PLACE OF STATUS
    LD Ø          /GET STATUS DATA FROM REG Ø
    SRC 12        /PREPARE TO RESTORE STATUS INDICATION
    WRR           /RESTORE STATUS AND SHIFT 4 PLACES
    INC 15        /CHANGE RAM ADDRESS TO NEXT DIGIT
    ISZ 13 SWL    /INCR. REG 13; JUMP TO SWL IF NOT Ø

    LDM 15        /LOAD 15 TO ACCUMULATOR
    JMS BLE       / JUMP TO SR AND WRITE 15 TO RAM PORT Ø

BLE, FIM Ø Ø      /ADDRESS RAM Ø

    SRC Ø         /SEND ADDRESS TO RAM
    WMP           /WRITE BLOCK ENABLE CODE
    BBL Ø         /RETURN TO CALLING POINT
```

Fig. 8.24. Program listing for reading switches and restoring status information to front panel.

An Electronic Lock (Example 8.5)

As another example of a possible microcomputer application, consider an electronic lock [8]. This device is a buzzer type of the form in use in apartments, banks, and other areas. In the normal state, the lock is closed. In order to open it, a button is pressed which initiates a sequence of light flashes. A light flashes on for several seconds and then goes off. This pattern is repeated three times. During each ON period, a button is pressed a certain number of times corresponding to the combination of the lock. If, for example, the combination is 7–3–4, the button would be pressed seven times during the first ON period, three times during the second ON period, and four times during the last period.

A flow chart of the algorithm is illustrated in Fig. 8.25.

A flow chart for the microprocessor program required to implement this example is illustrated in Fig. 8.26. An 8-second period has been chosen for the light (4 seconds on and 4 seconds off).

The program is a straightforward combination of delay loops (4-second timer subroutine) and counting operations. The lamp is switched on and off at regular intervals, and each time the lamp is turned off, the count during the ON cycle is examined. All operations may be controlled directly by the microprocessor.

As it is presented, the above example could be adapted to almost any microprocessor. The reader will obtain valuable insight by writing programs to implement this example using several of the microprocessors described in Chapter 7 and comparing the resulting programs and hardware required.

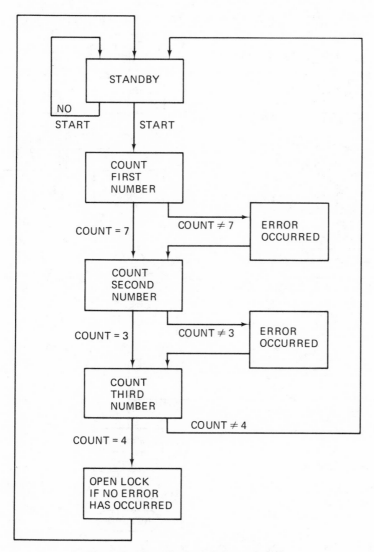

Fig. 8.25. Flow diagram of electronic lock.

CRT Terminal (Example 8.6)

A microcomputer may be used to control a CRT terminal [9]. Some of the first microprocessors were designed with the application to a CRT terminal in mind. These "smart" terminals reduce the load on large central computing centers and allow the operator the capability of editing input data in an off-line mode.

A basic CRT terminal which uses the Rockwell PPS-8 microprocessor is shown in

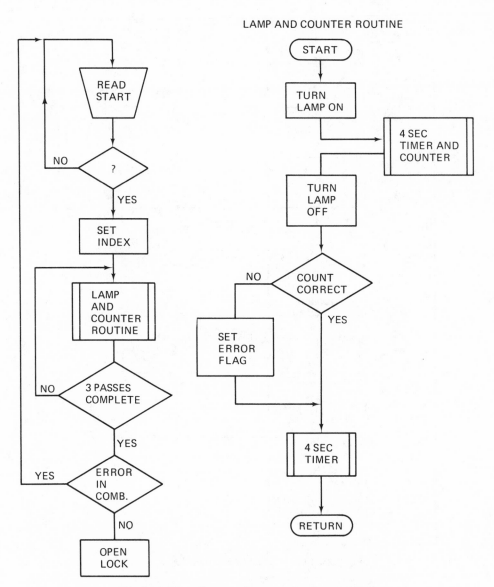

Fig. 8.26. Flow diagram of program for electronic lock.

the block diagram of Fig. 8.27 [10]. A CRT monitor is used to display twenty-four lines of characters. A line may consist of up to eighty characters. The display is generated from a standard television raster. Eleven scans are required for each line of characters (Fig. 8.28).

The display is refreshed periodically on a line-by-line basis. The system uses two line buffers in the refreshing operation. As one line of characters is being refreshed

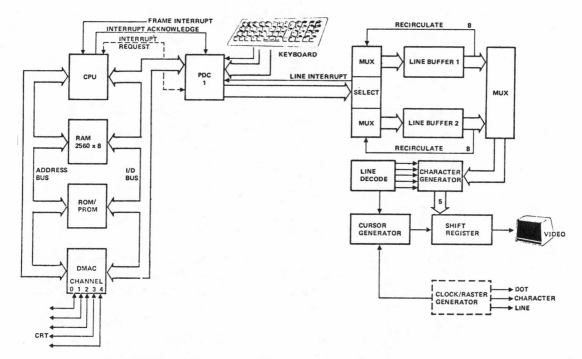

Fig. 8.27. Block diagram of CRT system (Courtesy of Rockwell International Corporation).

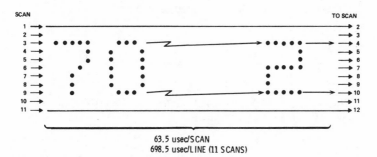

Fig. 8.28. Character display (Courtesy of Rockwell International Corporation).

from line buffer 1, line buffer 2 is being loaded from RAM memory by a DMA transfer. Line buffer 1 drives the character generator and shift register to generate the characters on the CRT face. Data in line buffer 1 must be recirculated eleven times to provide information for the eleven scan lines required to generate each line of characters (Fig. 8.29). When a line is refreshed, the next line is available in buffer 2. As buffer 2 is used to refresh a line, buffer 1 is loaded from RAM.

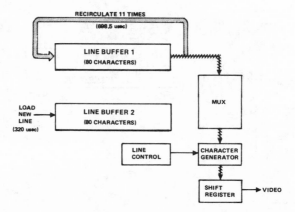

Fig. 8.29. CRT system refreshing operation from line buffer 1 (Courtesy of Rockwell International Corporation).

The CRT must be refreshed sixty times per second, or every 16.67 ms. Since there are twenty-four lines of characters, 698 μs may be used to complete the eleven scan lines required for each character line. Loading the line buffer for the next line of characters requires 320 μs (4 μs/character). The remaining time, 380 μs per line, may be used to service the modem or perform editing and system control functions. Figure 8.30 illustrates the timing associated with refreshing the CRT.

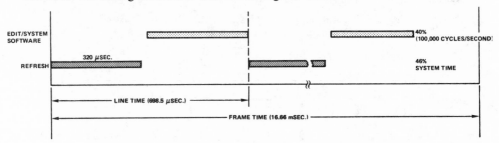

Fig. 8.30. Timing associated with CRT refresh (Courtesy of Rockwell International Corporation).

Summary

A number of applications have been discussed in this chapter to illustrate the wide variety of applications and to provide insight into feasible microcomputer applications. Many aspects of the design procedure have also been illustrated in the examples.

The use of microprocessors in digital systems typically reduces the hardware complexity at the expense of software complexity. The software for a well-defined task requiring 2000 instructions may be expected to require 4–6 weeks of effort with 30–40% of this time spent in design and documentation, 10–20% in coding, and 40–60% in debugging [11].

REFERENCES

1. LEWIS, DONALD R. and W. RALPH SIENA, "Microprocessor or Random Logic." *Electronic Design* (Sept. 1, 1973), pp. 106–10.

2. *IBM Selectric Input/Output Typewriter*. IBM Corp., Industrial Products, N. Y.

3. OGDIN, J. and S. MCPHILLIPS, *New Logic Notebook*. Vol. I, No. 1, Microcomputer Technique, Inc. (September, 1974).

4. OGDIN, J. L., "Getting Started in Microprocessors and Microcomputers." *Instrumentation Technology* (January, 1975), pp. 35–43.

5. ROSE, C. W. and J. D. SCHOEFFLER, "Microcomputers for Data Acquisition." *Instrumentation Technology* (September, 1974), pp. 65–69.

6. THOMPSON, ROGER, "The IMP-8C As a Data Concentrator." AN-113, National Semiconductor Corp., May, 1974.

7. LEE, RICHARD, "Microprocessor ICs Improve Instruments." *Electronic Design*, Vol. 22, No. 9, pp. 150–54.

8. GLADSTONE, BRUCE, "Designing With Microprocessors Instead of Wired Logic Asks More of Designers." *Electronics* (Oct. 11, 1973), pp. 91–104.

9. CROPPER, L. C. and J. W. WHITING, "Microprocessors in CRT Terminals." *Computer*, Vol. 7, No. 8, pp. 48–53.

10. BASS, J. E., "A Microcomputer-Based CRT Terminal." Rockwell International Corp., April, 1975.

11. CASSELLS, DOUGLAS A., "Microcomputer Programming." *Modern Data* (January, 1975), pp. 49–51.

EXERCISES

8.1. List some important considerations in microprocessor selection.

8.2. How long will the conversion subprogram which implements the flow chart of Fig. 8.11 require for execution? Refer to Sec. 7.3 and Appendix A for information.

8.3. Write the conversion subprogram in Fig. 8.11 for the Rockwell PPS-4.

8.4. Repeat Exercise 8.3 for the National IMP-4.

8.5. Repeat Exercise 8.3 for the National PACE.

8.6. Repeat Example 8.2 using the Intellec 40 (Intel 4040) system.

8.7. Repeat Example 8.2 using the Rockwell PPS-4 system.

8.8. Repeat Example 8.2 using the Motorola 6800 system.

8.9. Repeat Example 8.2 using the RCA COSMAC.

8.10. Design an electronic lock for Example 8.5 using the Intel 4040.

8.11. Repeat Exercise 8.10 for the National IMP-4.

8.12. Repeat Exercise 8.10 for the Rockwell PPS-4.

8.13. Consider a system to aid in the completion of an income-tax short form (1040A) by automatically spacing to the next blank, performing all arithmetic operations, and computing the tax. Discuss the system requirements and draw a flow chart of the program.

8.14. Suppose one wishes to read an analog voltage into an INTELLEC 40 system. Minimal hardware is a requirement and the microcomputer is to perform the A/D conversion.

    (a) Draw a block diagram of the system and discuss the hardware requirements.

    (b) Draw a flow chart of the program required to perform the A/D conversion.

    (c) Write an assembly language program to perform the transfer.

INSTRUCTION SET FOR INTEL 4004 AND 4040

(Courtesy of Intel Corp.)

BASIC INSTRUCTION SET

The basic instruction set of the 4040 and 4004 (CPU) are shown below. The following section will describe each instruction in detail.

[Those instructions preceded by an asterisk (*) are 2 word instructions that occupy 2 successive locations in ROM]

MACHINE INSTRUCTIONS (Logic 1 = Low Voltage = Negative Voltage; Logic 0 = High Voltage = Ground)

MNEMONIC	OPR $D_3 D_2 D_1 D_0$	OPA $D_3 D_2 D_1 D_0$	DESCRIPTION OF OPERATION
NOP	0 0 0 0	0 0 0 0	No operation.
*JCN	0 0 0 1 $A_2 A_2 A_2 A_2$	$C_1 C_2 C_3 C_4$ $A_1 A_1 A_1 A_1$	Jump to ROM address $A_2 A_2 A_2 A_2$, $A_1 A_1 A_1 A_1$ (within the same ROM that contains this JCN instruction) if condition $C_1 C_2 C_3 C_4$[1] is true, otherwise skip (go to the next instruction in sequence).
*FIM	0 0 1 0 $D_2 D_2 D_2 D_2$	R R R 0 $D_1 D_1 D_1 D_1$	Fetch immediate (direct) from ROM Data D_2, D_1 to index register pair location RRR.[2]
SRC	0 0 1 0	R R R 1	Send register control. Send the address (contents of index register pair RRR) to ROM and RAM at X_2 and X_3 time in the Instruction Cycle.
FIN	0 0 1 1	R R R 0	Fetch indirect from ROM. Send contents of index register pair location 0 out as an address. Data fetched is placed into register pair location RRR.
JIN	0 0 1 1	R R R 1	Jump indirect. Send contents of register pair RRR out as an address at A_1 and A_2 time in the Instruction Cycle.
*JUN	0 1 0 0 $A_2 A_2 A_2 A_2$	$A_3 A_3 A_3 A_3$ $A_1 A_1 A_1 A_1$	Jump unconditional to ROM address A_3, A_2, A_1.
*JMS	0 1 0 1 $A_2 A_2 A_2 A_2$	$A_3 A_3 A_3 A_3$ $A_1 A_1 A_1 A_1$	Jump to subroutine ROM address A_3, A_2, A_1, save old address. (Up 1 level in stack.)
INC	0 1 1 0	R R R R	Increment contents of register RRRR.[3]
*ISZ	0 1 1 1 $A_2 A_2 A_2 A_2$	R R R R $A_1 A_1 A_1 A_1$	Increment contents of register RRRR. Go to ROM address A_2, A_1 (within the same ROM that contains this ISZ instruction) if result $\neq 0$, otherwise skip (go to the next instruction in sequence).
ADD	1 0 0 0	R R R R	Add contents of register RRRR to accumulator with carry.
SUB	1 0 0 1	R R R R	Subtract contents of register RRRR to accumulator with borrow.
LD	1 0 1 0	R R R R	Load contents of register RRRR to accumulator.
XCH	1 0 1 1	R R R R	Exchange contents of index register RRRR and accumulator.
BBL	1 1 0 0	D D D D	Branch back (down 1 level in stack) and load data DDDD to accumulator.
LDM	1 1 0 1	D D D D	Load data DDDD to accumulator.

NEW 4040 INSTRUCTIONS

MNEMONIC	OPR $D_3 D_2 D_1 D_0$	OPA $D_3 D_2 D_1 D_0$	DESCRIPTION OF OPERATION
HLT	0 0 0 0	0 0 0 1	Halt — inhibit program counter and data buffers.
BBS	0 0 0 0	0 0 1 0	Branch Back from Interrupt and restore the previous SRC. The Program Counter and send register control are restored to their pre-interrupt value.
LCR	0 0 0 0	0 0 1 1	The contents of the COMMAND REGISTER are transferred to the ACCUMULATOR.
OR4	0 0 0 0	0 1 0 0	The 4 bit contents of register #4 are logically "OR-ed" with the ACCUM.
OR5	0 0 0 0	0 1 0 1	The 4 bit contents of index register #5 are logically "OR-ed" with the ACCUMULATOR.
AN6	0 0 0 0	0 1 1 0	The 4 bit contents of index register #6 are logically "AND-ed" with the ACCUMULATOR
AN7	0 0 0 0	0 1 1 1	The 4 bit contents of index register #7 are logically "AND-ed" with the ACCUMULATOR.
DB0	0 0 0 0	1 0 0 0	DESIGNATE ROM BANK 0. CM-ROM$_0$ becomes enabled.
DB1	0 0 0 0	1 0 0 1	DESIGNATE ROM BANK 1. CM-ROM$_1$ becomes enabled.
SB0	0 0 0 0	1 0 1 0	SELECT INDEX REGISTER BANK 0. The index registers 0 - 7.
SB1	0 0 0 0	1 0 1 1	SELECT INDEX REGISTER BANK 1. The index registers 0* - 7*.
EIN	0 0 0 0	1 1 0 0	ENABLE INTERRUPT.
DIN	0 0 0 0	1 1 0 1	DISABLE INTERRUPT.
RPM	0 0 0 0	1 1 1 0	READ PROGRAM MEMORY.

INPUT/OUTPUT AND RAM INSTRUCTIONS

(The RAM's and ROM's operated on in the I/O and RAM instructions have been previously selected by the last SRC instruction executed.)

MNEMONIC	OPR $D_3 D_2 D_1 D_0$	OPA $D_3 D_2 D_1 D_0$	DESCRIPTION OF OPERATION
WRM	1 1 1 0	0 0 0 0	Write the contents of the accumulator into the previously selected RAM main memory character.
WMP	1 1 1 0	0 0 0 1	Write the contents of the accumulator into the previously selected RAM output port.
WRR	1 1 1 0	0 0 1 0	Write the contents of the accumulator into the previously selected ROM output port. (I/O Lines)
WPM	1 1 1 0	0 0 1 1	Write the contents of the accumulator into the previously selected half byte of read/write program memory (for use with 4008/4009 only)
WRϕ [4]	1 1 1 0	0 1 0 0	Write the contents of the accumulator into the previously selected RAM status character 0.
WR1 [4]	1 1 1 0	0 1 0 1	Write the contents of the accumulator into the previously selected RAM status character 1.
WR2 [4]	1 1 1 0	0 1 1 0	Write the contents of the accumulator into the previously selected RAM status character 2.
WR3 [4]	1 1 1 0	0 1 1 1	Write the contents of the accumulator into the previously selected RAM status character 3.
SBM	1 1 1 0	1 0 0 0	Subtract the previously selected RAM main memory character from accumulator with borrow.
RDM	1 1 1 0	1 0 0 1	Read the previously selected RAM main memory character into the accumulator.
RDR	1 1 1 0	1 0 1 0	Read the contents of the previously selected ROM input port into the accumulator. (I/O Lines)
ADM	1 1 1 0	1 0 1 1	Add the previously selected RAM main memory character to accumulator with carry.
RDϕ [4]	1 1 1 0	1 1 0 0	Read the previously selected RAM status character 0 into accumulator.
RD1 [4]	1 1 1 0	1 1 0 1	Read the previously selected RAM status character 1 into accumulator.
RD2 [4]	1 1 1 0	1 1 1 0	Read the previously selected RAM status character 2 into accumulator.
RD3 [4]	1 1 1 0	1 1 1 1	Read the previously selected RAM status character 3 into accumulator.

ACCUMULATOR GROUP INSTRUCTIONS

CLB	1 1 1 1	0 0 0 0	Clear both. (Accumulator and carry)
CLC	1 1 1 1	0 0 0 1	Clear carry.
IAC	1 1 1 1	0 0 1 0	Increment accumulator.
CMC	1 1 1 1	0 0 1 1	Complement carry.
CMA	1 1 1 1	0 1 0 0	Complement accumulator.
RAL	1 1 1 1	0 1 0 1	Rotate left. (Accumulator and carry)
RAR	1 1 1 1	0 1 1 0	Rotate right. (Accumulator and carry)
TCC	1 1 1 1	0 1 1 1	Transmit carry to accumulator and clear carry.
DAC	1 1 1 1	1 0 0 0	Decrement accumulator.
TCS	1 1 1 1	1 0 0 1	Transfer carry subtract and clear carry.
STC	1 1 1 1	1 0 1 0	Set carry.
DAA	1 1 1 1	1 0 1 1	Decimal adjust accumulator.
KBP	1 1 1 1	1 1 0 0	Keyboard process. Converts the contents of the accumulator from a one out of four code to a binary code.
DCL	1 1 1 1	1 1 0 1	Designate command line.

NOTES: [1] The condition code is assigned as follows:

$C_1 = 1$ Invert jump condition $C_2 = 1$ Jump if accumulator is zero $C_4 = 1$ Jump if test signal is a 0

$C_1 = 0$ Not invert jump condition $C_3 = 1$ Jump if carry/link is a 1

[2] RRR is the address of 1 of 8 index register pairs in the CPU.

[3] RRRR is the address of 1 of 16 index registers in the CPU.

[4] Each RAM chip has 4 registers, each with twenty 4-bit characters subdivided into 16 main memory characters and 4 status characters. Chip number, RAM register and main memory character are addressed by an SRC instruction. For the selected chip and register, however, status character locations are selected by the instruction code (OPA).

Appendix

B INSTRUCTION SET FOR THE NATIONAL IMP-4

(Courtesy of National Semiconductor Corporation, Inc.)

2.1   NOTATION AND SYMBOLS USED IN IMP-4 INSTRUCTION DESCRIPTIONS

Refer to table 3 for definitions of the notation and symbols used in the IMP-4 instruction descriptions. The notations are given in alphabetical order followed by the symbols. Upper-case mnemonics refer to fields in the instruction word; lower-case mnemonics refer to the numerical value of the corresponding fields. In cases where both lower- and upper-case mnemonics are composed of the same letters, only the lower-case mnemonic is given in table 3. The use of lower-case notation designates variables.

Table 3. Notations Used in Instruction Set

Notation	Definition
ACr	Denotes a specific working register (AC0, AC1, AC2, or AC3), where r is the number of the accumulator referenced in the instruction.
AR	Denotes the address register in the FILU used for addressing memory or peripheral devices.
b	Denotes a bit whose value depends upon the contents of a field whose value is variable.
BNKCTL	Denotes Bank Control Register.
cc	Denotes the 4-bit condition code value for conditional branch instructions.
CY	Indicates that the Carry flag is set if there is a carry due to the instruction.
disp	Stands for displacement value and it represents an operand in a nonmemory reference instruction or an address field in a memory reference instruction.
dr	Denotes the number of a destination working register that is specified in the instruction-word field.

Table 3. Notations Used in Instruction Set (Continued)

Notation	Definition
EA	Denotes the effective address.
fc	Denotes the number of the referenced flag.
L	Denotes 1-bit Link (L) flag.
OV	Indicates that the overflow flag is set if there is an overflow due to the instruction.
PC	Denotes the 12-bit Program Counter in the FILU.
PC Stack	Denotes top word of Program Counter Stack.
r	Denotes the number of a working register that is specified in the instruction-word field.
SEL	Denotes the Select control flag. It is used to select the carry or overflow for output on the carry and overflow (CYOV) line of the CPU, and to include the link bit (L) in shift operations.
sr	Denotes the number of a source working register that is specified in the instruction-word field.
STK	Denotes the register at the top of the general purpose stack in the RALU.
( )	Denotes the contents of the item within the parentheses. (ACr) is read as "the contents of ACr." (EA) is read as "the contents of EA."
(( ))	Denotes the contents of the item addressed by ( ).
$\sim$	Indicates the logical complement (ones complement) of the value on the right-hand side of $\sim$.
$\leftarrow$	Item on left is replaced by item on right.
$\rightarrow$	Item on left replaces item on right.
$\rightleftarrows$	Items are exchanged.
$\wedge$	Denotes an AND operation.
$\vee$	Denotes an OR operation.
$\triangledown$	Denotes an EXCLUSIVE OR operation.

2.2 INSTRUCTION DESCRIPTIONS

Each class and subclass of instruction is introduced by a table that lists and summarizes the instructions. The word format is illustrated.

2.3   8-BIT INSTRUCTIONS

2.3.1   Register-to-Register Operations

Op Code	Mnemonic	Description
bbbb1000	RADD	(ACdr) ← (ACdr) + (ACsr); Binary Register Add. CY, OV
bbbb1001	RAND	(ACdr) ← (ACdr) ∧ (ACsr); Logical Register AND
bbbb1010	RXOR	(ACdr) ← (ACdr) ▽ (ACsr); Logical Register EXCLUSIVE OR
bbbb1100	RCPY	(ACdr) ← (ACsr); Register Copy
bbbb1101	RXCH	(ACdr) ⇄ (ACsr); **Register Exchange**
bbbb1110	DADD	(ACdr) ← (ACdr) + (ACsr); Decimal Add. excess-3 addition with carry-in/carry-out

2.3.2   Flag Operations

Op Code	Mnemonic	Description
bbbb1011	SFLG	Set Flag (See table 4)
bbbb1111	PFLG	Pulse Flag (See table 4)

Table 4. Flag Codes

Flag Code (fc)		Flag Mnemonic Used	Description
Binary	Hexadecimal		
0000	0	LDIR	Load Instruction Register
0001	1	LDARF	Load Address Register
0010	2	LDPCF	Load Program Counter
0011	3	RDM	Read Memory → AR
0100	4	WRM	Write into Memory
0101	5	SVRST	Save/Restore RALU flags
0110	6	RDP	Read Peripheral Data
0111	7	WRP	Write Peripheral Data
1000	8	INTEN	Enable Interrupts
1001	9	SEL	Select use of link bit in shift
1010	A	INPC	Increment PC
1011	B	PUSHPC	Push PC Stack
1100	C	PULLPC	Pull PC Stack
1101	D	MOVE	Transfer (AR) → (PC)
1110	E	SLAR	(AR) → ADR Bus
1111	F	INTA	Interrupt Acknowledge

Notes: 1.   All jump conditions are tested at PH 2 time; however, INTR is generated at PH 3 time of the previous cycle.

2.   Only flags 8 through 13 apply for macroprogramming. Use of other flags could result in undesired looping.

2.3.3   Single Register Operations

Op Code	Mnemonic	Description
00bb0010	PUSH	(STK) ◄— (ACr)
01bb0010	PULL	(ACr) ◄— (STK)
10bb0010	SHL	Shift (ACr) Left*
11bb0010	SHR	Shift (ACr) Right*
00bb0011	RINTAR	(ACr) ◄— Peripherals as addressed by AR; Register In Through AR
01bb0011	ROUTAR	(ACr) —► Peripherals as addressed by AR; Register Out Through AR
00bb0100	LDTAR	(ACr) ◄— ((AR)); Load Through AR
11bb0100	STTAR	((AR)) ◄— (ACr); Store Through AR
11bb0101	ROL	Rotate (ACr) Left*

*   The link bit is included in the shift if the SEL Flag is set. Selecting the link makes the register
appear as if it were 5 bits wide (with the link in the most significant bit position).

2.3.4   Miscellaneous Operations

Op Code	Mnemonic	Description
00000000	------	Not used
00010000	PUSHF	(STK) ◄— (FLAGS); Push RALU flags
00100000	PULLF	(FLAGS) ◄— (STK); Pull RALU flags
00110000	LDAR	Top 3 words STK —► (AR); Load AR
01000000	RTS	(PC) ◄— (PC Stack); Return from Subroutine
01010000	RTI	Set INTEN Flag, (BNKCTL) ◄— (STK), (PC) ◄— (PC Stack); Return from Interrupt
01100000	------	Not used
01110000	RITA	Set INTEN Flag, (BNKCTL) ◄— (STK), (PC) ◄— (PC Stack), (PC) ◄— (AR); Return from Interrupt Through AR

2.4   12-BIT INSTRUCTIONS

2.4.1   Immediate Operations

Op Code	Mnemonic	Description
10bb0011	LI	(ACr) ◄— data; Load Immediate
11bb0011	AI	(ACr) ◄— (ACr) + data; Add Immediate. CY, OV

2.5   16-BIT INSTRUCTIONS

2.5.1   Register Index Operation

Op Code	Mnemonic	Description
10bb0110	RIND	Memory Register Index. Used to form 12-bit address as follows:

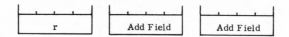

2.6   20-BIT INSTRUCTIONS

Note: Low order 12 bits are used for absolute address.

2.6.1   Memory Reference Arithmetic Operation

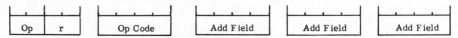

Op Code	Mnemonic	Description
01bb0100	LD	(ACr) ← (EA); Load
10bb0100	ST	(EA) ← (ACr); Store
00bb0101	ADD	(ACr) ← (ACr) + (EA); Binary Add. CY, OV
01bb0101	SUB	(ACr) ← (EA) + ∼ (ACr) +1; Subtract. CY, OV
10bb0101	OR	(ACr) ← (ACr) ∨ (EA); Logical OR

2.6.2   Branch On Test and Jump Instructions

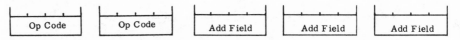

Op Code	Mnemonic	Description
10000000	BRGE	Branch if: ABS(AC0) ≥ ABS(AC1); Branch if Greater than or Equal to. CY, OV
10100000	BRNE	Branch if: (AC0) ≠ (AC1); Branch if Not Equal. CY, OV
11000000	JSR	Jump to Subroutine direct
11100000	JMP	Jump to absolute address direct

2.6.3 Branch On Condition

Op Code	Mnemonic	Description
bbbb0001	BOC	Branch occurs if Condition Code (cc) is true (See table 5)

Table 5. Condition Codes

Condition Code (cc)		Mnemonic Used	Description
Binary	Hexadecimal		
0000	0	INTR	Interrupt Request
0001	1	BIT0	Bit 0 of (AC0) is a '1'
0010	2	BIT1	Bit 1 of (AC0) is a '1'
0011	3	BIT2	Bit 2 of (AC0) is a '1'
0100	4	BIT3	Bit 3 of (AC0) is a '1'
0101	5	REQ0	(AC0) = 0
0110	6	NREQ0	(AC0) $\neq$ 0
0111	7	UJMPC	User defined Jump Condition

2.6.4 Miscellaneous

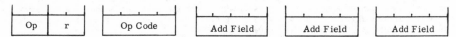

Op Code	Mnemonic	Description
00bb0110	-----	Not Used
01bb0110	DLD	(EA) ← (EA) - 1; (ACr) ← (EA); Decrement and Load
11bb0110	ILD	(EA) ← (EA) + 1; (ACr) ← (EA); Increment and Load
00bb0111	RIN	Input Peripheral Data → (ACr); Register In
01bb0111	ROUT	(ACr) → Peripheral; Register Out
10bb0111	INCBC	Increment (ACr), Compare to AC2, Branch if Not Equal; Increment Branch on Condition
11bb0111	DCBC	Decrement (ACr), Compare to AC2, Branch if Not Equal; Decrement Branch on Condition

331

Appendix

INSTRUCTION SET FOR THE
ROCKWELL PPS-4

(Courtesy Rockwell International Corp.)

INSTRUCTION LIST

The following pages provide a listing of the 50 instructions which can be used to control generation of ROM and RAM address as well as manipulation and transfer of data between the CPU and RAM and I/O. Definitions of symbology used in the instruction list is also provided such that a programmer can easily understand the instruction list and begin to visualize how the PPS may be used for a given application.

DEFINITIONS OF SYMBOLIC NOTATION

Symbols

A	Accumulator Register, A(4:1)
A/Bn	Line n of Address Bus
B	RAM Address Register, B(12:1)
C	Carry Link Flip-Flop
FF_1, FF_2	General Flip-Flop 1, General Flip-Flop 2
I	Instruction (Typically 8-bit Field)
I/Dn	Line n of Instruction/Data Bus
In	Byte n of Long Instruction (i.e. I_1 = 1st byte, I_2 = 2nd byte)
M	RAM Memory Contents Designated by Register B
m	General Numeric Designator, m = 1, 2, 3, . . .
n	General Numeric Designator, n = 1, 2, 3, . . .
P	ROM Program Counter Register, P (12:1)
BL	Lower Field of Register B (4:1)
BM	Middle Field of B Register B (8:5)
BU	Upper Field of B Register, B (12:9)
R(n)	Bit n of General Register R
R(m:n)	Bits m thru n of General Register R inclusive [e.g., R(12:7)]
SA	Upper Stack of Save Registers, SA(12:1)
SB	Lower Stack of Save Registers, SB(12:1)
W/IO	Write Command and I/O Enable Line

DEFINITIONS OF SYMBOLIC NOTATION

Symbols

X	Secondary Accumulator Register, X(4:1)
Digit	Four Bit Field (sometimes referred to as Data or Character)
Byte	Eight Bit Field
Page	ROM Block of 64 Bytes (*)
← →	Replaces
←→	Exchange
‾	1's Complement (e.g., $\overline{A}$ is 1's complement of A)
V	Logical Inclusive OR
⩛	Logical Exclusive OR
Λ	Logical and
+	Algebraic Add
-	Algebraic Subtract

*A page is defined in the PPS as 64 ROM address locations. The page number is specified by the six (6) most significant bits of the 12-bit P register. The locations within a page are defined by the six (6) least significant bits.

P REGISTER

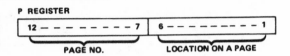

ARITHMETIC INSTRUCTIONS

Mnemonics	I/D Bus OP Code Hex & Binary	Name	Description	Symbolic Equation
AD	OB 0000 1011	Add (1 cycle)	The result of binary addition of contents of accumulator and 4-bit contents of the RAM currently addressed by B register, replaces the contents of accumulator. The resulting carry-out is loaded into C flip-flop.	C, A ← A+M
ADC	OA 0000 1010	Add with carry-in (1 cycle)	Same as AD except the C flip-flop serves as a carry-in to the adder.	C,A ← A+M+C
ADSK	O9 0000 1001	Add and skip on carry-out (1 cycle)	Same as AD except the next ROM word will be skipped (ignored) if a carry-out is generated.	C, A ← A+M Skip if C = 1
ADCSK	O8 0000 1000	Add with carry-in and skip on carry-out (1 cycle)	Same as ADSK except the C flip-flop serves as a carry-in to the adder.	C, A ← A+M+C Skip if C = 1
ADI	60-6E *0110 xxxx Except 65	Add immediate and skip on carry-out (1 cycle)	The result of binary addition of contents of accumulator and 4-bit immediate field of instruction word replaces the contents of accumulator. The next ROM word will be skipped (ignored) if a carry-out is generated. This instruction does not use or change the C flip-flop. The immediate field I(4:1) of this instruction may not be equal to binary 0000 or 1010 (See CYS and DC)	A ← A+[I(4:1)] Skip if carry-out = one I(4:1) ≠ ˙0000 I(4:1) ≠ 1010 See Note 3
DC	65 0110 0101	Decimal Correction (1 cycle)	Binary 1010 is added to contents of accumulator. Result is stored in accumulator. Instruction does not use or change carry flip-flop or skip.	A ← A+1010

333

LOGICAL INSTRUCTIONS

AND	OD 0000 1101	Logical AND (1 cycle)	The result of logical AND of accumulator and 4-bit contents of RAM currently addressed by B register replaces contents of accumulator.	$A \leftarrow A \wedge M$
OR	OF 0000 1111	Logical OR (1 cycle)	The result of logic OR of accumulator and 4-bit contents of RAM currently addressed by B register replaces contents of accumulator.	$A \leftarrow A \vee M$
EOR	OC 0000 1100	Logical Exclusive-OR (1 cycle)	The result of logic exclusive-OR of accumulator and 4-bit contents of RAM currently addressed by B register replaces contents of accumulator.	$A \leftarrow A \veebar M$
COMP	OE 0000 1110	Complement (1 cycle)	Each bit of the accumulator is logically complemented and placed in accumulator.	$A \leftarrow \bar{A}$

*xxxx Indicates restrictions on bit patterns allowable in immediate field as specified in the symbolic equation description.

DATA TRANSFER INSTRUCTIONS

Mnemonics	I/D Bus OP Code Hex & Binary	Name	Description	Symbolic Equation
SC	20 0010 0000	Set Carry flip-flop (1 cycle)	The C flip-flop is set to 1.	$C \leftarrow 1$
RC	24 0010 0100	Reset Carry flip-flop (1 cycle)	The C flip-flop is set to 0.	$C \leftarrow 0$
SF1	22 0010 0010	Set FF1 (1 cycle)	Flip-flop 1 is set to 1.	$FF1 \leftarrow 1$
RF1	26 0010 0110	Reset FF1 (1 cycle)	Flip-flop 1 is set to 0.	$FF1 \leftarrow 0$
SF2	21 0010 0001	Set FF2 (1 cycle)	Flip-flop 2 is set to 1.	$FF2 \leftarrow 1$
RF2	25 0010 0101	Reset FF2 (1 cycle)	Flip-flop 2 is set to 0.	$FF2 \leftarrow 0$
LD	30-37 0011 0 . . .	Load Accumulator from Memory (1 cycle)	The 4-bit contents of RAM currently addressed by B register are placed in the accumulator. The RAM address in the B register is then modified by the result of an exclusive-OR of the 3-bit immediate field I(3:1) and B(7:5).	$A \leftarrow M$; $B(7:5) \leftarrow B(7:5) \veebar$ $[I(3:1)]$ See Note 3
EX	38-3F 0011 1 . . .	Exchange Accumulator and Memory (1 cycle)	Same as LD except the contents of accumulator are also placed in currently addressed RAM location.	$A \leftrightarrow M$ $B(7:5) \leftarrow B(7:5) \veebar$ $[I(3:1)]$ See Note 3
EXD	28-2F 0010 1 . . .	Exchange Accumulator and Memory and decrement BL (1 cycle) See Note 3	Same as EX except RAM address in B register is further modified by decrementing BL by 1. If the new contents of BL is 1111, the next ROM word will be ignored.	$A \leftrightarrow M$ $B(7:5) \leftarrow B(7:5) \veebar$ $[I(3:1)]$; $BL \leftarrow BL-1$ Skip on BL=1111
LDI	70-7F 0111	Load Accumulator Immediate (1 cycle)	The 4-bit contents, immediate field I(4:1), of the instruction are placed in accumulator. (See Note below)	$A \leftarrow [I(4:1)]$ See Note 3

NOTE

Only the first occurrence of an LDI in a consecutive string of LDI's will be executed. The program will ignore the remaining LDI's and execute next valid instruction.

Mnemonics	I/D Bus OP Code Hex & Binary	Name	Description	Symbolic Equation
LAX	12 0001 0010	Load Accumulator from X register (1 cycle)	The 4-bit contents of the X register are placed in the accumulator.	$A \leftarrow X$
LXA	1B 0001 1011	Load X Register from Accumulator (1 cycle)	The contents of the accumulator are transferred to the X register.	$X \leftarrow A$
LABL	11 0001 0001	Load Accumulator with BL (1 cycle)	The contents of BL register are transferred to the accumulator.	$A \leftarrow BL$
LBMX	10 0001 0000	Load BM with X (1 cycle)	The contents of X register are transferred to BM register.	$BM \leftarrow X$
LBUA	04 0000 0100	Load BU with A (1 cycle)	The contents of accumulator are transferred to BU register. Also, the contents of currently addressed RAM are transferred to accumulator.	$BU \leftarrow A, A \leftarrow M$
XABL	19 0001 1001	Exchange Accumulator and BL (1 cycle)	The contents of accumulator and BL register are exchanged.	$A \leftrightarrow BL$
XBMX	18 0001 1000	Exchange BM and X (1 cycle)	The contents of BM register and X register are exchanged.	$X \leftrightarrow BM$
XAX	1A 0001 1010	Exchange Accumulator and X (1 cycle)	The contents of accumulator and X register are exchanged.	$A \leftrightarrow X$
XS	06 0000 0110	Exchange SA and SB (1 cycle)	The 12-bit contents of SA register and SB register are exchanged.	$SA \leftrightarrow SB$
CYS	6F 0110 1111	Cycle SA register and accumulator. (1 cycle)	A 4-bit right shift of the SA register takes place with the four bits which are shifted off the end of SA being transferred into the accumulator. The contents of the accumulator are placed in the left end of SA register.	$A \leftarrow SA(4:1)$ $SA(4:1) \leftarrow SA(8:5)$ $SA(8:5) \leftarrow SA(12:9)$ $SA(12:9) \leftarrow A$
LB **	C0-CF 1st word 1100 . . . . 2nd word from page 3	Load B Indirect (2 cycles)	Sixteen consecutive locations on ROM page 3 (I_2) contain data which can be loaded into the eight least significant bits of the B register by use of any LB instruction. The four most significant bits of B register will be loaded with zeros. The contents of the SB register will be destroyed. This instruction takes two cycles to execute but occupies only one ROM word. (Automatic return) (See Note below.)	$SB \leftarrow SA, SA \leftarrow P$ $P(12:5) \leftarrow 0000\,1100$ $P(4:1) \leftarrow I1(4:1)$ $BU \leftarrow 0000$ $B(8:1) \leftarrow [I2(8:1)]$ $P \leftarrow SA, SA \leftrightarrow SB$ See Notes 3 and 4
LBL	00 1st word 0000 0000 2nd word	Load B Long (2 cycles)	This instruction occupies two ROM words, the second of which will be loaded into the eight least significant bits of the B register. The four most significant bits of B (BU) will be loaded with zeros. (See Note below)	$BU \leftarrow 0000$ $B(8:1) \leftarrow [I2(8:1)]$ See Note 3
INCB	17 0001 0111	Increment BL (1 cycle)	BL register (least significant four bits of B register) is incremented by 1. If the new contents of BL is 0000, then the next ROM word will be ignored.	$BL \leftarrow BL+1$ Skip on BL=0000
DECB	1F 0001 1111	Decrement BL (1 cycle)	BL register is decremented by 1. If the new contents of BL is 1111, then the next ROM word will be ignored.	$BL \leftarrow BL-1$ Skip on BL = 1111

NOTE

Only the first occurrence of an LB or LBL instruction in a consecutive string of LB or LBL will be executed. The program will ignore the remaining LB or LBL and execute the next valid instruction. Within subroutines the LB instruction must be used with caution because the contents of SB have been modified.

Mnemonics	I/D Bus OP Code Hex & Binary	Name	Description	Symbolic Equation
T *	80-BF 10-- ----	Transfer (1 cycle)	An unconditional transfer to a ROM word on the current page takes place. The least significant 6-bits of P register P(6:1) are replaced by six bit immediate field I(6:1).	$P(6:1) \leftarrow I(6:1)$
TM**	DO-FF * 1st word 11xx .... 2nd word from page 3	Transfer and Mark Indirect (2 cycles)	48 Consecutive locations on ROM page 3 contains pointer data which identify subroutine entry addresses. These subroutine entry addresses are limited to pages 4 through 7. This TM instruction will save the address of the next ROM word in the SA register after loading the original contents of SA into SB. A transfer then occurs to one of the subroutine entry addresses. This instruction occupies one ROM word but takes two cycles for execution.	$SB \leftarrow SA, SA \leftarrow P$ $P(12:7) \leftarrow 000011$ $P(6:1) \leftarrow I1(6:1)$ $P(12:9) \leftarrow 0001$ $P(8:1) \leftarrow I2(8:1)$ See Note 4 Note: $I1(6:5) \neq 00$
TL	50-5F 1st word 0101 .... 2nd word	Transfer Long (2 cycles)	This instruction executes a transfer to any ROM word on any page. It occupies two ROM words and requires two cycles for execution. The first byte loads P(12:9) with field I1(4:1) and then the second byte I2(8:1) is placed in P(8:1).	$P(12:9) \leftarrow I1(4:1);$ $P(8:1) \leftarrow I2(8:1)$
TML	01-03 * 1st word 0000 00xx 2nd word	Transfer and Mark Long (2 cycles)	This instruction executes a transfer and mark to any location on ROM pages 4 through 15. It occupies two ROM words and requires two cycle times for execution.	See Note 4 $SB \leftarrow SA, SA \leftarrow P$ $P(12:9) \leftarrow I1(4:1)$ $P(8:1) \leftarrow I2(8:1)$ Note $I1(2:1) \neq 00$
SKC	15 0001 0101	Skip on Carry flip-flop (1 cycle)	The next ROM word will be ignored if C flip-flop is 1.	Skip if C = 1
SKZ	1E 0001 1110	Skip on Accumulator Zero (1 cycle)	The next ROM word will be ignored if accumulator is zero.	Skip if A = 0
SKBI	40-4F 0100	Skip if BL Equal to Immediate (cycle)	The next ROM word will be ignored if the least significant four bits of B register (BL) is equal to the 4-bit immediate field I(4:1) of instruction.	Skip if BL = I(4:1)
SKF1	16 0001 0110	Skip if FF1 Equals 1 (1 cycle)	The next ROM word will be ignored if FF2 is 1.	Skip if FF1 = 1
SKF2	14 0001 0100	Skip if FF2 Equals 1 (1 cycle)	The next ROM word will be ignored if FF1 is 1.	Skip if FF2 = 1
RTN **	05 0000 0101	Return (1 cycle)	This instruction executes a return from subroutine by loading contents of SA register into P register and interchanges the SB and SA registers.	$P \leftarrow SA, SA \leftrightarrow SB$

*xx   Indicates restrictions on bit patterns allowable in the designated bit positions in the instruction field as specified in the symbolic equation description.

**   These instructions, with the exception of T * +1, cannot be used in ROM location 0000.

Mnemonics	I/D Bus OP Code Hex & Binary	Name	Description	Symbolic Equation
RTNSK **	07 0000 0111	Return and Skip (1 cycle)	Same as RTN except the first ROM word encountered after the return from subroutine is skipped.	$P \leftarrow SA$, $SA \leftrightarrow SB$ $P \leftarrow P+1$

INPUT/OUTPUT INSTRUCTIONS

Mnemonics	I/D Bus OP Code Hex & Binary	Name	Description	Symbolic Equation
IOL	1C 1st word 0001 1100 2nd word ---- ----	Input/Output Long (2 cycles)	This instruction occupies two ROM words and requires two cycles for execution. The first ROM word is received by the CPU and sets up the I/O Enable signal. The second ROM word is then received by the I/O devices and decoded for address and command. The contents of the accumulator inverted are placed on the data lines for acceptance by the I/O. At the same time, input data received by the I/O device is transferred to the accumulator inverted.	$\overline{A} \rightarrow$ Data Bus $A \leftarrow \overline{\text{Data Bus}}$ $I2 \rightarrow$ I/O Device
DIA	27 0010 0111	Discrete Input Group A (1 cycle)	Data at the inputs to discrete. Group A is transferred to the accumulator.	$A \leftarrow DIA$
DIB	23 0010 0011	Discrete Input Group B (1 cycle)	Data at the inputs to discrete. Group B is transferred to the accumulator.	$A \leftarrow DIB$
DOA	1D 0001 1101	Discrete Output (1 cycle)	The contents of the accumulator are transferred to the discrete output register.	$DOA \leftarrow A$

SPECIAL INSTRUCTION

| SAG | 13 0001 0011 | Special Address Generation (1 cycle) | This instruction causes the eight most significant bits of the RAM address output to be zeroed during the next cycle only. Note that this instruction does not alter the contents of the B register. | A/B Bus (12:5) $\leftarrow$ 0000 0000 A/B Bus (4:1) $\leftarrow$ BL (4:1) Contents of "B" remain unchanged |

GENERAL NOTES

(1) The word "skip" or "ignore" as used in this instruction set means the instruction will be read from memory but not executed. Each skipped or ignored word will require one clock cycle time.

(2) The reference to ROM pages and locations are defined as the ROM address appearing on the A/B bus. During initial Power On the starting address is Page 0 Location 0 and is automatically incremented each clock cycle.

(3) Instruction ADI, LD, EX, EXD, LDI, LB and LBL have a numeric value coded as part of the instruction in the immediate field. This numeric value must be in complementary form on the bus. All of these immediate fields which are inverted are shown in brackets.

For example: ADI 1, as written by the programmer who wishes to add one to the value in the accumulator, is converted to $6E_{(16)} = 0110 \lfloor 1110 \rfloor$; the bracketed binary value is the value as seen on the data bus.

If the programmer is using the Rockwell Assembler he does not have to manually determine the proper inverted value as the assembler does this for him.

(4) On all instructions which transfer the contents of P into SA, the P register has already been advanced to the next instruction location.

Appendix

 INSTRUCTION SET FOR INTEL 8008

(Courtesy Intel Corp.)

Basic Instruction Set

Data and Instruction Formats

Data in the 8008 is stored in the form of 8-bit binary integers. All data transfers to the system data bus will be in the same format.

$$\boxed{D_7\ D_6\ D_5\ D_4\ D_3\ D_2\ D_1\ D_0}$$

DATA WORD

The program instructions may be one, two, or three bytes in length. Multiple byte instructions must be stored in successive words in program memory. The instruction formats then depend on the particular operation executed.

One Byte Instructions

$\boxed{D_7\ D_6\ D_5\ D_4\ D_3\ D_2\ D_1\ D_0}$ OP CODE

Two Byte Instructions

$\boxed{D_7\ D_6\ D_5\ D_4\ D_3\ D_2\ D_1\ D_0}$ OP CODE

$\boxed{D_7\ D_6\ D_5\ D_4\ D_3\ D_2\ D_1\ D_0}$ OPERAND

Three Byte Instructions

$\boxed{D_7\ D_6\ D_5\ D_4\ D_3\ D_2\ D_1\ D_0}$ OP CODE

$\boxed{D_7\ D_6\ D_5\ D_4\ D_3\ D_2\ D_1\ D_0}$ LOW ADDRESS

$\boxed{X\ \ X\ \ D_5\ D_4\ D_3\ D_2\ D_1\ D_0}$ HIGH ADDRESS*

TYPICAL INSTRUCTIONS

Register to register, memory reference, I/O arithmetic or logical, rotate or return instructions

Immediate mode instructions

JUMP or CALL instructions

*For the third byte of this instruction, D_6 and D_7 are "don't care" bits.

For the MCS-8 a logic "1" is defined as a high level and a logic "0" is defined as a low level.

Index Register Instructions

The load instructions do not affect the flag flip-flops. The increment and decrement instructions affect all flip-flops except the carry.

MNEMONIC	MINIMUM STATES REQUIRED	INSTRUCTION CODE			DESCRIPTION OF OPERATION
		$D_7\ D_6$	$D_5\ D_4\ D_3$	$D_2\ D_1\ D_0$	
(1) MOV r_1, r_2	(5)	1 1	D D D	S S S	Load index register r_1 with the content of index register r_2.
(2) MOV r, M	(8)	1 1	D D D	1 1 1	Load index register r with the content of memory register M.
MOV M, r	(7)	1 1	1 1 1	S S S	Load memory register M with the content of index register r.
(3) MVI r	(8)	0 0	D D D	1 1 0	Load index register r with data B . . . B.
		B B	B B B	B B B	
MVI M	(9)	0 0	1 1 1	1 1 0	Load memory register M with data B . . . B.
		B B	B B B	B B B	
INR r	(5)	0 0	D D D	0 0 0	Increment the content of index register r (r ≠ A).
DCR r	(5)	0 0	D D D	0 0 1	Decrement the content of index register r (r ≠ A).

Accumulator Group Instructions

The result of the ALU instructions affect all of the flag flip-flops. The rotate instructions affect only the carry flip-flop.

Mnemonic	States	D7 D6	D5 D4 D3	D2 D1 D0	Description
ADD r	(5)	1 0	0 0 0	S S S	Add the content of index register r, memory register M, or data
ADD M	(8)	1 0	0 0 0	1 1 1	B . . . B to the accumulator. An overflow (carry) sets the carry
ADI	(8)	0 0	0 0 0	1 0 0	flip-flop.
		B B	B B B	B B B	
ADC r	(5)	1 0	0 0 1	S S S	Add the content of index register r, memory register M, or data
ADC M	(8)	1 0	0 0 1	1 1 1	B . . . B from the accumulator with carry. An overflow (carry)
ACI	(8)	0 0	0 0 1	1 0 0	sets the carry flip-flop.
		B B	B B B	B B B	
SUB r	(5)	1 0	0 1 0	S S S	Subtract the content of index register r, memory register M, or
SUB M	(8)	1 0	0 1 0	1 1 1	data B . . . B from the accumulator. An underflow (borrow)
SUI	(8)	0 0	0 1 0	1 0 0	sets the carry flip-flop.
		B B	B B B	B B B	
SBB r	(5)	1 0	0 1 1	S S S	Subtract the content of index register r, memory register M, or data
SBB M	(8)	1 0	0 1 1	1 1 1	data B . . . B from the accumulator with borrow. An underflow
SBI	(8)	0 0	0 1 1	1 0 0	(borrow) sets the carry flip-flop.
		B B	B B B	B B B	

Basic Instruction Set

MNEMONIC	MINIMUM STATES REQUIRED	D7 D6	D5 D4 D3	D2 D1 D0	DESCRIPTION OF OPERATION
ANA r	(5)	1 0	1 0 0	S S S	Compute the logical AND of the content of index register r,
ANA M	(8)	1 0	1 0 0	1 1 1	memory register M, or data B . . . B with the accumulator.
ANI	(8)	0 0	1 0 0	1 0 0	
		B B	B B B	B B B	
XRA r	(5)	1 0	1 0 1	S S S	Compute the EXCLUSIVE OR of the content of index register
XRA M	(8)	1 0	1 0 1	1 1 1	r, memory register M, or data B . . . B with the accumulator.
XRI	(8)	0 0	1 0 1	1 0 0	
		B B	B B B	B B B	
ORA r	(5)	1 0	1 1 0	S S S	Compute the INCLUSIVE OR of the content of index register
ORA M	(8)	1 0	1 1 0	1 1 1	r, memory register m, or data B . . . B with the accumulator.
ORI	(8)	0 0	1 1 0	1 0 0	
		B B	B B B	B B B	
CMP r	(5)	1 0	1 1 1	S S S	Compare the content of index register r, memory register M,
CMP M	(8)	1 0	1 1 1	1 1 1	or data B . . . B with the accumulator. The content of the
CPI	(8)	0 0	1 1 1	1 0 0	accumulator is unchanged.
		B B	B B B	B B B	
RLC	(5)	0 0	0 0 0	0 1 0	Rotate the content of the accumulator left.
RRC	(5)	0 0	0 0 1	0 1 0	Rotate the content of the accumulator right.
RAL	(5)	0 0	0 1 0	0 1 0	Rotate the content of the accumulator left through the carry.
RAR	(5)	0 0	0 1 1	0 1 0	Rotate the content of the accumulator right through the carry.

Program Counter and Stack Control Instructions

Mnemonic	States	D7 D6	D5 D4 D3	D2 D1 D0	Description
(4) JMP	(11)	0 1	X X X	1 0 0	Unconditionally jump to memory address B3 . . . B3B2 . . . B2.
		B2 B2	B2 B2 B2	B2 B2 B2	
		X X	B3 B3 B3	B3 B3 B3	
(5) JNC, JNZ, JP, JPO	(9 or 11)	0 1	0 C4 C3	0 0 0	Jump to memory address B3 . . . B3B2 . . . B2 if the condition
		B2 B2	B2 B2 B2	B2 B2 B2	flip-flop c is false. Otherwise, execute the next instruction in sequence.
		X X	B3 B3 B3	B3 B3 B3	
JC, JZ JM, JPE	(9 or 11)	0 1	1 C4 C3	0 0 0	Jump to memory address B3 . . . B3B2 . . . B2 if the condition
		B2 B2	B2 B2 B2	B2 B2 B2	flip-flop c is true. Otherwise, execute the next instruction in sequence.
		X X	B3 B3 B3	B3 B3 B3	
CALL	(11)	0 1	X X X	1 1 0	Unconditionally call the subroutine at memory address B3 . . .
		B2 B2	B2 B2 B2	B2 B2 B2	B3B2 . . . B2. Save the current address (up one level in the stack).
		X X	B3 B3 B3	B3 B3 B3	
CNC, CNZ, CP, CPO	(9 or 11)	0 1	0 C4 C3	0 1 0	Call the subroutine at memory address B3 . . . B3B2 . . . B2 if the
		B2 B2	B2 B2 B2	B2 B2 B2	condition flip-flop c is false, and save the current address (up one
		X X	B3 B3 B3	B3 B3 B3	level in the stack.) Otherwise, execute the next instruction in sequence.
CC, CZ, CM, CPE	(9 or 11)	0 1	1 C4 C3	0 1 0	Call the subroutine at memory address B3 . . . B3B2 . . . B2 if the
		B2 B2	B2 B2 B2	B2 B2 B2	condition flip-flop c is true, and save the current address (up one
		X X	B3 B3 B3	B3 B3 B3	level in the stack). Otherwise, execute the next instruction in sequence.
RET	(5)	0 0	X X X	1 1 1	Unconditionally return (down one level in the stack).
RNC, RNZ, RP, RPO	(3 or 5)	0 0	0 C4 C3	0 1 1	Return (down one level in the stack) if the condition flip-flop c is false. Otherwise, execute the next instruction in sequence.
RC, RZ RM, RPE	(3 or 5)	0 0	1 C4 C3	0 1 1	Return (down one level in the stack) if the condition flip-flop c is true. Otherwise, execute the next instruction in sequence.
RST	(5)	0 0	A A A	1 0 1	Call the subroutine at memory address AAA000 (up one level in the stack).

Input/Output Instructions

IN	(8)	0 1	0 0 M	M M 1	Read the content of the selected input port (MMM) into the accumulator.
OUT	(6)	0 1	R R M	M M 1	Write the content of the accumulator into the selected output port (RRMMM, RR ≠ 00).

Machine Instruction

HLT	(4)	0 0	0 0 0	0 0 X	Enter the STOPPED state and remain there until interrupted.
	(4)	1 1	1 1 1	1 1 1	

NOTES:

(1) SSS = Source Index Register ⎤ These registers, r$_i$, are designated A(accumulator–000),
      DDD = Destination Index Register ⎦ B(001), C(010), D(011), E(100), H(101), L(110).

(2) Memory registers are addressed by the contents of registers H & L.

(3) Additional bytes of instruction are designated by BBBBBBBB.

(4) X = "Don't Care".

(5) Flag flip-flops are defined by C$_4$C$_3$: carry (00-overflow or underflow), zero (01-result is zero), sign (10-MSB of result is "1"), parity (11-parity is even).

340

Appendix

E INSTRUCTION SET FOR INTEL 8080

(Courtesy Intel Corp.)

SILICON GATE MOS 8080

INSTRUCTION SET

The accumulator group instructions include ARITHMETIC and LOGICAL OPERATORS with DIRECT, INDIRECT, AND IMMEDIATE addressing modes.

MOVE, LOAD, and STORE instruction groups provide the ability to move either 8 or 16 bits of data between memory, the six working registers and the accumulator using DIRECT, INDIRECT, and IMMEDIATE addressing modes.

The ability to branch to different portions of the program is provided with JUMP, JUMP CONDITIONAL, and COMPUTED JUMPS. Also the ability to CALL to and RETURN from subroutines is provided both conditionally and unconditionally. The RESTART (or single byte call instruction) is useful for interrupt vector operation.

Double precision operators such as STACK manipulation and DOUBLE ADD instructions extend both the arithmetic and interrupt handling capability of the 8080. The ability to INCREMENT

and DECREMENT memory, the six general registers and the accumulator is provided as well as EXTENDED INCREMENT and DECREMENT instructions to operate on the register pairs and stack pointer. Further capability is provided by the ability to ROTATE the accumulator LEFT or RIGHT through or around the carry bit.

Input and output may be accomplished using memory addresses as I/O ports or the directly addressed I/O provided for in the 8080 instruction set.

The following special instruction group completes the 8080 instruction set: the NO-OP instruction, HALT to stop processor execution and the DAA instructions provide decimal arithmetic capability. STC allows the carry flag to be directly set, and the CMC instruction allows it to be complemented. CMA complements the contents of the accumulator and XCHG exchanges the contents of two 16-bit register pairs directly.

Data and Instruction Formats

Data in the 8080 is stored in the form of 8-bit binary integers. All data transfers to the system data bus will be in the same format.

$$D_7 \; D_6 \; D_5 \; D_4 \; D_3 \; D_2 \; D_1 \; D_0$$
DATA WORD

The program instructions may be one, two, or three bytes in length. Multiple byte instructions must be stored in successive words in program memory. The instruction formats then depend on the particular operation executed.

One Byte Instructions

| $D_7 \; D_6 \; D_5 \; D_4 \; D_3 \; D_2 \; D_1 \; D_0$ | OP CODE |

TYPICAL INSTRUCTIONS

Register to register, memory reference, arithmetic or logical, rotate return, PUSH, POP, ENABLE or DISABLE
INTERRUPT INSTRUCTIONS

Two Byte Instructions

| $D_7 \; D_6 \; D_5 \; D_4 \; D_3 \; D_2 \; D_1 \; D_0$ | OP CODE |
| $D_7 \; D_6 \; D_5 \; D_4 \; D_3 \; D_2 \; D_1 \; D_0$ | OPERAND |

Immediate mode or I/O instructions

Three Byte Instructions

$D_7 \; D_6 \; D_5 \; D_4 \; D_3 \; D_2 \; D_1 \; D_0$	OP CODE
$D_7 \; D_6 \; D_5 \; D_4 \; D_3 \; D_2 \; D_1 \; D_0$	LOW ADDRESS OR OPERAND 1
$D_7 \; D_6 \; D_5 \; D_4 \; D_3 \; D_2 \; D_1 \; D_0$	HIGH ADDRESS OR OPERAND 2

JUMP, CALL or DIRECT LOAD
AND STORE INSTRUCTIONS

For the 8080 a logic "1" is defined as a high level and a logic "0" is defined as a low level.

SILICON GATE MOS 8080
INSTRUCTION SET

Summary of Processor Instructions

Mnemonic	Description	D7	D6	D5	D4	D3	D2	D1	D0	Clock[2] Cycles
MOV r1,r2	Move register to register	0	1	D	D	D	S	S	S	5
MOV M,r	Move register to memory	0	1	1	1	0	S	S	S	7
MOV r,M	Move memory to register	0	1	D	D	D	1	1	0	7
HLT	Halt	0	1	1	1	0	1	1	0	7
MVI r	Move immediate register	0	0	D	D	D	1	1	0	7
MVI M	Move immediate memory	0	0	1	1	0	1	1	0	10
INR r	Increment register	0	0	D	D	D	1	0	0	5
DCR r	Decrement register	0	0	D	D	D	1	0	1	5
INR M	Increment memory	0	0	1	1	0	1	0	0	10
DCR M	Decrement memory	0	0	1	1	0	1	0	1	10
ADD r	Add register to A	1	0	0	0	0	S	S	S	4
ADC r	Add register to A with carry	1	0	0	0	1	S	S	S	4
SUB r	Subtract register from A	1	0	0	1	0	S	S	S	4
SBB r	Subtract register from A with borrow	1	0	0	1	1	S	S	S	4
ANA r	And register with A	1	0	1	0	0	S	S	S	4
XRA r	Exclusive Or register with A	1	0	1	0	1	S	S	S	4
ORA r	Or register with A	1	0	1	1	0	S	S	S	4
CMP r	Compare register with A	1	0	1	1	1	S	S	S	4
ADD M	Add memory to A	1	0	0	0	0	1	1	0	7
ADC M	Add memory to A with carry	1	0	0	0	1	1	1	0	7
SUB M	Subtract memory from A	1	0	0	1	0	1	1	0	7
SBB M	Subtract memory from A with borrow	1	0	0	1	1	1	1	0	7
ANA M	And memory with A	1	0	1	0	0	1	1	0	7
XRA M	Exclusive Or memory with A	1	0	1	0	1	1	1	0	7
ORA M	Or memory with A	1	0	1	1	0	1	1	0	7
CMP M	Compare memory with A	1	0	1	1	1	1	1	0	7
ADI	Add immediate to A	1	1	0	0	0	1	1	0	7
ACI	Add immediate to A with carry	1	1	0	0	1	1	1	0	7
SUI	Subtract immediate from A	1	1	0	1	0	1	1	0	7

Mnemonic	Description	D7	D6	D5	D4	D3	D2	D1	D0	Clock[2] Cycles
RZ	Return on zero	1	1	0	0	1	0	0	0	5/11
RNZ	Return on no zero	1	1	0	0	0	0	0	0	5/11
RP	Return on positive	1	1	1	1	0	0	0	0	5/11
RM	Return on minus	1	1	1	1	1	0	0	0	5/11
RPE	Return on parity even	1	1	1	0	1	0	0	0	5/11
RPO	Return on parity odd	1	1	1	0	0	0	0	0	5/11
RST	Restart	1	1	A	A	A	1	1	1	11
IN	Input	1	1	0	1	1	0	1	1	10
OUT	Output	1	1	0	1	0	0	1	1	10
LXI B	Load immediate register Pair B & C	0	0	0	0	0	0	0	1	10
LXI D	Load immediate register Pair D & E	0	0	0	1	0	0	0	1	10
LXI H	Load immediate register Pair H & L	0	0	1	0	0	0	0	1	10
LXI SP	Load immediate stack pointer	0	0	1	1	0	0	0	1	10
PUSH B	Push register Pair B & C on stack	1	1	0	0	0	1	0	1	11
PUSH D	Push register Pair D & E on stack	1	1	0	1	0	1	0	1	11
PUSH H	Push register Pair H & L on stack	1	1	1	0	0	1	0	1	11
PUSH PSW	Push A and Flags on stack	1	1	1	1	0	1	0	1	11
POP B	Pop register pair B & C off stack	1	1	0	0	0	0	0	1	10
POP D	Pop register pair D & E off stack	1	1	0	1	0	0	0	1	10
POP H	Pop register pair H & L off stack	1	1	1	0	0	0	0	1	10
POP PSW	Pop A and Flags off stack	1	1	1	1	0	0	0	1	10

Mnemonic	Description	D7	D6	D5	D4	D3	D2	D1	D0	Clock[2] Cycles
SBI	Subtract immediate from A with borrow	1	1	0	1	1	1	1	0	7
ANI	And immediate with A	1	1	1	0	0	1	1	0	7
XRI	Exclusive Or immediate with A	1	1	1	0	1	1	1	0	7
ORI	Or immediate with A	1	1	1	1	0	1	1	0	7
CPI	Compare immediate with A	1	1	1	1	1	1	1	0	7
RLC	Rotate A left	0	0	0	0	0	1	1	1	4
RRC	Rotate A right	0	0	0	0	1	1	1	1	4
RAL	Rotate A left through carry	0	0	0	1	0	1	1	1	4
RAR	Rotate A right through carry	0	0	0	1	1	1	1	1	4
JMP	Jump unconditional	1	1	0	0	0	0	1	1	10
JC	Jump on carry	1	1	0	1	1	0	1	0	10
JNC	Jump on no carry	1	1	0	1	0	0	1	0	10
JZ	Jump on zero	1	1	0	0	1	0	1	0	10
JNZ	Jump on no zero	1	1	0	0	0	0	1	0	10
JP	Jump on positive	1	1	1	1	0	0	1	0	10
JM	Jump on minus	1	1	1	1	1	0	1	0	10
JPE	Jump on parity even	1	1	1	0	1	0	1	0	10
JPO	Jump on parity odd	1	1	1	0	0	0	1	0	10
CALL	Call unconditional	1	1	0	0	1	1	0	1	17
CC	Call on carry	1	1	0	1	1	1	0	0	11/17
CNC	Call on no carry	1	1	0	1	0	1	0	0	11/17
CZ	Call on zero	1	1	0	0	1	1	0	0	11/17
CNZ	Call on no zero	1	1	0	0	0	1	0	0	11/17
CP	Call on positive	1	1	1	1	0	1	0	0	11/17
CM	Call on minus	1	1	1	1	1	1	0	0	11/17
CPE	Call on parity even	1	1	1	0	1	1	0	0	11/17
CPO	Call on parity odd	1	1	1	0	0	1	0	0	1H/17
RET	Return	1	1	0	0	1	0	0	1	10
RC	Return on carry	1	1	0	1	1	0	0	0	5/11
RNC	Return on no carry	1	1	0	1	0	0	0	0	5/11

Mnemonic	Description	D7	D6	D5	D4	D3	D2	D1	D0	Clock[2] Cycles
STA	Store A direct	0	0	1	1	0	0	1	0	13
LDA	Load A direct	0	0	1	1	1	0	1	0	13
XCHG	Exchange D & E, H & L Registers	1	1	1	0	1	0	1	1	4
XTHL	Exchange top of stack, H & L	1	1	1	0	0	0	1	1	18
SPHL	H & L to stack pointer	1	1	1	1	1	0	0	1	5
PCHL	H & L to program counter	1	1	1	0	1	0	0	1	5
DAD B	Add B & C to H & L	0	0	0	0	1	0	0	1	10
DAD D	Add D & E to H & L	0	0	0	1	1	0	0	1	10
DAD H	Add H & L to H & L	0	0	1	0	1	0	0	1	10
DAD SP	Add stack pointer to H & L	0	0	1	1	1	0	0	1	10
STAX B	Store A indirect	0	0	0	0	0	0	1	0	7
STAX D	Store A indirect	0	0	0	1	0	0	1	0	7
LDAX B	Load A indirect	0	0	0	0	1	0	1	0	7
LDAX D	Load A indirect	0	0	0	1	1	0	1	0	7
INX B	Increment B & C registers	0	0	0	0	0	0	1	1	5
INX D	Increment D & E registers	0	0	0	1	0	0	1	1	5
INX H	Increment H & L registers	0	0	1	0	0	0	1	1	5
INX SP	Increment stack pointer	0	0	1	1	0	0	1	1	5
DCX B	Decrement B & C	0	0	0	0	1	0	1	1	5
DCX D	Decrement D & E	0	0	0	1	1	0	1	1	5
DCX H	Decrement H & L	0	0	1	0	1	0	1	1	5
DCX SP	Decrement stack pointer	0	0	1	1	1	0	1	1	5
CMA	Compliment A	0	0	1	0	1	1	1	1	4
STC	Set carry	0	0	1	1	0	1	1	1	4
CMC	Compliment carry	0	0	1	1	1	1	1	1	4
DAA	Decimal adjust A	0	0	1	0	0	1	1	1	4
SHLD	Store H & L direct	0	0	1	0	0	0	1	0	16
LHLD	Load H & L direct	0	0	1	0	1	0	1	0	16
EI	Enable Interrupts	1	1	1	1	1	0	1	1	4
DI	Disable interrupt	1	1	1	1	0	0	1	1	4
NOP	No-operation	0	0	0	0	0	0	0	0	4

NOTES: 1. DDS or SSS – 000 B – 001 C – 010 D – 011 E – 100 H – 101 L – 110 Memory – 111 A.

2. Two possible cycle times, (5/11) indicate instruction cycles dependent on condition flags.

F INSTRUCTION SET FOR THE MOTOROLA 6800

(Courtesy Motorola Semiconductor Products, Inc.)

MPU INSTRUCTION SET

The XC6800 has a set of 72 different instructions that have been designed for use in point-of-sale terminals, data communications, and peripheral control. Included are binary and decimal arithmetic, logical, shift, rotate, load, store, conditional or unconditional branch, interrupt and stack manipulation instructions (Tables 2 thru 6).

MPU ADDRESSING MODES

The XC6800 eight-bit microprocessing unit has seven address modes that can be used by a programmer, with the addressing mode a function of both the type of instruction and the coding within the instruction. A summary of the addressing modes for a particular instruction can be found in Table 7 along with the associated instruction execution time that is given in machine cycles. With a clock frequency of 1 MHz, these times would be microseconds.

Accumulator (ACCX) Addressing — In accumulator only addressing, either accumulator A or accumulator B is specified. These are one-byte instructions.

Immediate Addressing — In immediate addressing, the operand is contained in the second byte of the instruction except LDS and LDX which have the operand in the second and third bytes of the instruction. The MPU addresses this location when it fetches the immediate instruction for execution. These are two or three-byte instructions.

Direct Addressing — In direct addressing, the address of the operand is contained in the second byte of the instruction. Direct addressing allows the user to directly

address the lowest 256 bytes in the machine i.e., locations zero through 255. Enhanced execution times are achieved by storing data in these locations. In most configurations, it should be a random access memory. These are two-byte instructions.

Extended Addressing — In extended addressing, the address contained in the second byte of the instruction is used as the higher eight-bits of the address of the operand. The third byte of the instruction is used as the lower eight-bits of the address for the operand. This is an absolute address in memory. These are three-byte instructions.

Indexed Addressing — In indexed addressing, the address contained in the second byte of the instruction is added to the index register's lowest eight bits in the MPU. The carry is then added to the higher order eight bits of the index register. This result is then used to address memory. The modified address is held in a temporary address register so there is no change to the index register. These are two-byte instructions.

Implied Addressing — In the implied addressing mode the instruction gives the address (i.e., stack pointer, index register, etc.). These are one-byte instructions.

Relative Addressing — In relative addressing, the address contained in the second byte of the instruction is added to the program counter's lowest eight bits plus two. The carry or borrow is then added to the high eight bits. This allows the user to address data within a range of –125 to +129 bytes of the present instruction. These are two-byte instructions.

TABLE 2 – MICROPROCESSOR INSTRUCTION SET – ALPHABETIC SEQUENCE

ABA	Add Accumulators	CLR	Clear	PUL	Pull Data
ADC	Add with Carry	CLV	Clear Overflow	ROL	Rotate Left
ADD	Add	CMP	Compare	ROR	Rotate Right
AND	Logical And	COM	Complement	RTI	Return from Interrupt
ASL	Arithmetic Shift Left	CPX	Compare Index Register	RTS	Return from Subroutine
ASR	Arithmetic Shift Right	DAA	Decimal Adjust		
BCC	Branch if Carry Clear	DEC	Decrement	SBA	Subtract Accumulators
BCS	Branch if Carry Set	DES	Decrement Stack Pointer	SBC	Subtract with Carry
BEQ	Branch if Equal to Zero	DEX	Decrement Index Register	SEC	Set Carry
BGE	Branch if Greater or Equal Zero			SEI	Set Interrupt Mask
BGT	Branch if Greater than Zero	EOR	Exclusive OR	SEV	Set Overflow
BHI	Branch if Higher	INC	Increment	STA	Store Accumulator
BIT	Bit Test	INS	Increment Stack Pointer	STS	Store Stack Register
BLE	Branch if Less or Equal	INX	Increment Index Register	STX	Store Index Register
BLS	Branch if Lower or Same			SUB	Subtract
BLT	Branch if Less than Zero	JMP	Jump	SWI	Software Interrupt
BMI	Branch if Minus	JSR	Jump to Subroutine	TAB	Transfer Accumulators
BNE	Branch if Not Equal to Zero	LDA	Load Accumulator	TAP	Transfer Accumulators to Condition Code Reg.
BPL	Branch if Plus	LDS	Load Stack Pointer	TBA	Transfer Accumulators
BRA	Branch Always	LDX	Load Index Register	TPA	Transfer Condition Code Reg. to Accumulator
BSR	Branch to Subroutine	LSR	Logical Shift Right	TST	Test
BVC	Branch if Overflow Clear	NEG	Negate	TSX	Transfer Stack Pointer to Index Register
BVS	Branch if Overflow Set	NOP	No Operation	TXS	Transfer Index Register to Stack Pointer
CBA	Compare Accumulators	ORA	Inclusive OR Accumulator	WAI	Wait for Interrupt
CLC	Clear Carry				
CLI	Clear Interrupt Mask	PSH	Push Data		

TABLE 3 – ACCUMULATOR AND MEMORY INSTRUCTIONS

		ADDRESSING MODES															BOOLEAN/ARITHMETIC OPERATION	COND. CODE REG.					
		IMMED			DIRECT			INDEX			EXTND			IMPLIED			(All register labels	5	4	3	2	1	0
OPERATIONS	MNEMONIC	OP	~	#	OP	~	#	OP	~	#	OP	~	#	OP	~	#	refer to contents)	H	I	N	Z	V	C
Add	ADDA	8B	2	2	9B	3	2	AB	5	2	BB	4	3				$A + M \rightarrow A$	↕	•	↕	↕	↕	↕
	ADDB	CB	2	2	DB	3	2	EB	5	2	FB	4	3				$B + M \rightarrow B$	↕	•	↕	↕	↕	↕
Add Acmltrs	ABA													1B	2	1	$A + B \rightarrow A$	↕	•	↕	↕	↕	↕
Add with Carry	ADCA	89	2	2	99	3	2	A9	5	2	B9	4	3				$A + M + C \rightarrow A$	↕	•	↕	↕	↕	↕
	ADCB	C9	2	2	D9	3	2	E9	5	2	F9	4	3				$B + M + C \rightarrow B$	↕	•	↕	↕	↕	↕
And	ANDA	84	2	2	94	3	2	A4	5	2	B4	4	3				$A \cdot M \rightarrow A$	•	•	↕	↕	R	•
	ANDB	C4	2	2	D4	3	2	E4	5	2	F4	4	3				$B \cdot M \rightarrow B$	•	•	↕	↕	R	•
Bit Test	BITA	85	2	2	95	3	2	A5	5	2	B5	4	3				$A \cdot M$	•	•	↕	↕	R	•
	BITB	C5	2	2	D5	3	2	E5	5	2	F5	4	3				$B \cdot M$	•	•	↕	↕	R	•
Clear	CLR							6F	7	2	7F	6	3				$00 \rightarrow M$	•	•	R	S	R	R
	CLRA													4F	2	1	$00 \rightarrow A$	•	•	R	S	R	R
	CLRB													5F	2	1	$00 \rightarrow B$	•	•	R	S	R	R
Compare	CMPA	81	2	2	91	3	2	A1	5	2	B1	4	3				$A - M$	•	•	↕	↕	↕	↕
	CMPB	C1	2	2	D1	3	2	E1	5	2	F1	4	3				$B - M$	•	•	↕	↕	↕	↕
Compare Acmltrs	CBA													11	2	1	$A - B$	•	•	↕	↕	↕	↕
Complement, 1's	COM							63	7	2	73	6	3				$\overline{M} \rightarrow M$	•	•	↕	↕	R	S
	COMA													43	2	1	$\overline{A} \rightarrow A$	•	•	↕	↕	R	S
	COMB													53	2	1	$\overline{B} \rightarrow B$	•	•	↕	↕	R	S
Complement, 2's	NEG							60	7	2	70	6	3				$00 - M \rightarrow M$	•	•	↕	↕	①	②
(Negate)	NEGA													40	2	1	$00 - A \rightarrow A$	•	•	↕	↕	①	②
	NEGB													50	2	1	$00 - B \rightarrow B$	•	•	↕	↕	①	②
Decimal Adjust, A	DAA													19	2	1	Converts Binary Add. of BCD Characters into BCD Format	•	•	↕	↕	↕	③
Decrement	DEC							6A	7	2	7A	6	3				$M - 1 \rightarrow M$	•	•	↕	↕	④	•
	DECA													4A	2	1	$A - 1 \rightarrow A$	•	•	↕	↕	④	•
	DECB													5A	2	1	$B - 1 \rightarrow B$	•	•	↕	↕	④	•
Exclusive OR	EORA	88	2	2	98	3	2	A8	5	2	B8	4	3				$A \oplus M \rightarrow A$	•	•	↕	↕	R	•
	EORB	C8	2	2	D8	3	2	E8	5	2	F8	4	3				$B \oplus M \rightarrow B$	•	•	↕	↕	R	•
Increment	INC							6C	7	2	7C	6	3				$M + 1 \rightarrow M$	•	•	↕	↕	⑤	•
	INCA													4C	2	1	$A + 1 \rightarrow A$	•	•	↕	↕	⑤	•
	INCB													5C	2	1	$B + 1 \rightarrow B$	•	•	↕	↕	⑤	•
Load Acmltr	LDAA	86	2	2	96	3	2	A6	5	2	B6	4	3				$M \rightarrow A$	•	•	↕	↕	R	•
	LDAB	C6	2	2	D6	3	2	E6	5	2	F6	4	3				$M \rightarrow B$	•	•	↕	↕	R	•
Or, Inclusive	ORAA	8A	2	2	9A	3	2	AA	5	2	BA	4	3				$A + M \rightarrow A$	•	•	↕	↕	R	•
	ORAB	CA	2	2	DA	3	2	EA	5	2	FA	4	3				$B + M \rightarrow B$	•	•	↕	↕	R	•

OPERATIONS	MNEMONIC	IMMED OP	~	#	DIRECT OP	~	#	INDEX OP	~	#	EXTND OP	~	#	IMPLIED OP	~	#	BOOLEAN/ARITHMETIC OPERATION (All register labels refer to contents)	H	I	N	Z	V	C
Push Data	PSHA													36	4	1	$A \rightarrow M_{SP}$, $SP - 1 \rightarrow SP$	•	•	•	•	•	•
	PSHB													37	4	1	$B \rightarrow M_{SP}$, $SP - 1 \rightarrow SP$	•	•	•	•	•	•
Pull Data	PULA													32	4	1	$SP + 1 \rightarrow SP$, $M_{SP} \rightarrow A$	•	•	•	•	•	•
	PULB													33	4	1	$SP + 1 \rightarrow SP$, $M_{SP} \rightarrow B$	•	•	•	•	•	•
Rotate Left	ROL							69	7	2	79	6	3				M ⟩	•	•	↑	↑	⑥	↑
	ROLA													49	2	1	A ⟩	•	•	↑	↑	⑥	↑
	ROLB													59	2	1	B ⟩	•	•	↑	↑	⑥	↑
Rotate Right	ROR							66	7	2	76	6	3				M ⟩	•	•	↑	↑	⑥	↑
	RORA													46	2	1	A ⟩	•	•	↑	↑	⑥	↑
	RORB													56	2	1	B ⟩	•	•	↑	↑	⑥	↑
Shift Left, Arithmetic	ASL							68	7	2	78	6	3				M ⟩	•	•	↑	↑	⑥	↑
	ASLA													48	2	1	A ⟩	•	•	↑	↑	⑥	↑
	ASLB													58	2	1	B ⟩	•	•	↑	↑	⑥	↑
Shift Right, Arithmetic	ASR							6/	7	2	77	6	3				M ⟩	•	•	↑	↑	⑥	↑
	ASRA													47	2	1	A ⟩	•	•	↑	↑	⑥	↑
	ASRB													57	2	1	B ⟩	•	•	↑	↑	⑥	↑
Shift Right, Logic	LSR							64	7	2	74	6	3				M ⟩	•	•	R	↑	⑥	↑
	LSRA													44	2	1	A ⟩	•	•	R	↑	⑥	↑
	LSRB													54	2	1	B ⟩	•	•	R	↑	⑥	↑
Store Acmltr.	STAA				97	4	2	A7	6	2	B7	5	3				$A \rightarrow M$	•	•	↑	↑	R	•
	STAB				D7	4	2	E7	6	2	F7	5	3				$B \rightarrow M$	•	•	↑	↑	R	•
Subtract	SUBA	80	2	2	90	3	2	A0	5	2	B0	4	3				$A - M \rightarrow A$	•	•	↑	↑	↑	↑
	SUBB	C0	2	2	D0	3	2	E0	5	2	F0	4	3				$B - M \rightarrow B$	•	•	↑	↑	↑	↑
Subtract Acmltrs.	SBA													10	2	1	$A - B \rightarrow A$	•	•	↑	↑	↑	↑
Subtr. with Carry	SBCA	82	2	2	92	3	2	A2	5	2	B2	4	3				$A - M - C \rightarrow A$	•	•	↑	↑	↑	↑
	SBCB	C2	2	2	D2	3	2	E2	5	2	F2	4	3				$B - M - C \rightarrow B$	•	•	↑	↑	↑	↑
Transfer Acmltrs	TAB													16	2	1	$A \rightarrow B$	•	•	↑	↑	R	•
	TBA													17	2	1	$B \rightarrow A$	•	•	↑	↑	R	•
Test, Zero or Minus	TST							6D	7	2	7D	6	3				$M - 00$	•	•	↑	↑	R	R
	TSTA													4D	2	1	$A - 00$	•	•	↑	↑	R	R
	TSTB													5D	2	1	$B - 00$	•	•	↑	↑	R	R
																		H	I	N	Z	V	C

LEGEND:

OP	Operation Code (Hexadecimal);	+	Boolean Inclusive OR;
~	Number of MPU Cycles;	⊙	Boolean Exclusive OR;
#	Number of Program Bytes;	$\overline{M}$	Complement of M;
+	Arithmetic Plus;	→	Transfer Into;
−	Arithmetic Minus;	0	Bit = Zero;
·	Boolean AND;	00	Byte = Zero;
M_{SP}	Contents of memory location pointed to be Stack Pointer;		

Note – Accumulator addressing mode instructions are included in the column for IMPLIED addressing

CONDITION CODE SYMBOLS:

H	Half-carry from bit 3;
I	Interrupt mask
N	Negative (sign bit)
Z	Zero (byte)
V	Overflow, 2's complement
C	Carry from bit 7
R	Reset Always
S	Set Always
↑	Test and set if true, cleared otherwise
•	Not Affected

TABLE 4 – INDEX REGISTER AND STACK MANIPULATION INSTRUCTIONS

POINTER OPERATIONS	MNEMONIC	IMMED OP	~	#	DIRECT OP	~	#	INDEX OP	~	#	EXTND OP	~	#	IMPLIED OP	~	#	BOOLEAN/ARITHMETIC OPERATION	H	I	N	Z	V	C
Compare Index Reg	CPX	8C	3	3	9C	4	2	AC	6	2	BC	5	3				$X_H - M$, $X_L - (M+1)$	•	•	⑦	↑	⑦	•
Decrement Index Reg	DEX													09	4	1	$X - 1 \rightarrow X$	•	•	•	↑	•	•
Decrement Stack Pntr	DES													34	4	1	$SP - 1 \rightarrow SP$	•	•	•	•	•	•
Increment Index Reg	INX													08	4	1	$X + 1 \rightarrow X$	•	•	•	↑	•	•
Increment Stack Pntr	INS													31	4	1	$SP + 1 \rightarrow SP$	•	•	•	•	•	•
Load Index Reg	LDX	CE	3	3	DE	4	2	EE	6	2	FE	5	3				$M \rightarrow X_H$, $(M+1) \rightarrow X_L$	•	•	⑨	↑	R	•
Load Stack Pntr	LDS	8E	3	3	9E	4	2	AE	6	2	BE	5	3				$M \rightarrow SP_H$, $(M+1) \rightarrow SP_L$	•	•	⑨	↑	R	•
Store Index Reg	STX				DF	5	2	EF	7	2	FF	6	3				$X_H \rightarrow M$, $X_L \rightarrow (M+1)$	•	•	⑨	↑	R	•
Store Stack Pntr	STS				9F	5	2	AF	7	2	BF	6	3				$SP_H \rightarrow M$, $SP_L \rightarrow (M+1)$	•	•	⑨	↑	R	•
Indx Reg → Stack Pntr	TXS													35	4	1	$X - 1 \rightarrow SP$	•	•	•	•	•	•
Stack Pntr → Indx Reg	TSX													30	4	1	$SP + 1 \rightarrow X$	•	•	•	•	•	•

TABLE 5 – JUMP AND BRANCH INSTRUCTIONS

OPERATIONS	MNEMONIC	RELATIVE OP	~	#	INDEX OP	~	#	EXTND OP	~	#	IMPLIED OP	~	#	BRANCH TEST	5 H	4 I	3 N	2 Z	1 V	0 C
Branch Always	BRA	20	4	2										None	•	•	•	•	•	•
Branch If Carry Clear	BCC	24	4	2										C = 0	•	•	•	•	•	•
Branch If Carry Set	BCS	25	4	2										C = 1	•	•	•	•	•	•
Branch If = Zero	BEQ	27	4	2										Z = 1	•	•	•	•	•	•
Branch If ≥ Zero	BGE	2C	4	2										N⊕V = 0	•	•	•	•	•	•
Branch If > Zero	BGT	2E	4	2										Z + (N⊕V) = 0	•	•	•	•	•	•
Branch If Higher	BHI	22	4	2										C + Z = 0	•	•	•	•	•	•
Branch If ≤ Zero	BLE	2F	4	2										Z + (N⊕V) = 1	•	•	•	•	•	•
Branch If Lower Or Same	BLS	23	4	2										C + Z = 1	•	•	•	•	•	•
Branch If < Zero	BLT	2D	4	2										N⊕V = 1	•	•	•	•	•	•
Branch If Minus	BMI	2B	4	2										N = 1	•	•	•	•	•	•
Branch If Not Equal Zero	BNE	26	4	2										Z = 0	•	•	•	•	•	•
Branch If Overflow Clear	BVC	28	4	2										V = 0	•	•	•	•	•	•
Branch If Overflow Set	BVS	29	4	2										V = 1	•	•	•	•	•	•
Branch If Plus	BPL	2A	4	2										N = 0	•	•	•	•	•	•
Branch To Subroutine	BSR	8D	8	2											•	•	•	•	•	•
Jump	JMP				6E	4	2	7E	3	3				} See Special Operations	•	•	•	•	•	•
Jump To Subroutine	JSR				AD	8	2	BD	9	3					•	•	•	•	•	•
No Operation	NOP										02	2	1	Advances Prog. Cntr. Only	•	•	•	•	•	•
Return From Interrupt	RTI										3B	10	1		⑩					
Return From Subroutine	RTS										39	5	1	} See Special Operations	•	•	•	•	•	•
Software Interrupt	SWI										3F	12	1		•	•	•	•	•	•
Wait for Interrupt	WAI										3E	9	1		•	⑪	•	•	•	•

TABLE 6 – CONDITION CODE REGISTER MANIPULATION INSTRUCTIONS

OPERATIONS	MNEMONIC	IMPLIED OP	~	#	BOOLEAN OPERATION	5 H	4 I	3 N	2 Z	1 V	0 C
Clear Carry	CLC	0C	2	1	0 → C	•	•	•	•	•	R
Clear Interrupt Mask	CLI	0E	2	1	0 → I	•	R	•	•	•	•
Clear Overflow	CLV	0A	2	1	0 → V	•	•	•	•	R	•
Set Carry	SEC	0D	2	1	1 → C	•	•	•	•	•	S
Set Interrupt Mask	SEI	0F	2	1	1 → I	•	S	•	•	•	•
Set Overflow	SEV	0B	2	1	1 → V	•	•	•	•	S	•
Acmltr A → CCR	TAP	06	2	1	A → CCR	⑫					
CCR → Acmltr A	TPA	07	2	1	CCR → A	•	•	•	•	•	•

CONDITION CODE REGISTER NOTES:

(Bit set if test is true and cleared otherwise)

1	(Bit V)	Test: Result = 10000000?
2	(Bit C)	Test: Result = 00000000?
3	(Bit C)	Test: Decimal value of most significant BCD Character greater than nine? (Not cleared if previously set.)
4	(Bit V)	Test: Operand = 10000000 prior to execution?
5	(Bit V)	Test: Operand = 01111111 prior to execution?
6	(Bit V)	Test: Set equal to result of N ⊕ C after shift has occurred.
7	(Bit V)	Test: Sign bit of most significant (MS) byte = 1?
8	(Bit V)	Test: 2's complement overflow from subtraction of MS bytes?
9	(Bit N)	Test: Result less than zero? (Bit 15 = 1)
10	(All)	Load Condition Code Register from Stack. (See Special Operations)
11	(Bit I)	Set when interrupt occurs. If previously set, a Non-Maskable Interrupt is required to exit the wait state.
12	(ALL)	Set according to the contents of Accumulator A.

TABLE 7 — INSTRUCTION ADDRESSING MODES AND ASSOCIATED EXECUTION TIMES

(Times in Machine Cycles)

	(Dual Operand)	ACCX	Immediate	Direct	Extended	Indexed	Implied	Relative
ABA		•	•	•	•	•	2	•
ADC	x	•	2	3	4	5	•	•
ADD	x	•	2	3	4	5	•	•
AND	x	•	2	3	4	5	•	•
ASL		2	•	•	6	7	•	•
ASR		2	•	•	6	7	•	•
BCC		•	•	•	•	•	•	4
BCS		•	•	•	•	•	•	4
BEA		•	•	•	•	•	•	4
BGE		•	•	•	•	•	•	4
BGT		•	•	•	•	•	•	4
BHI		•	•	•	•	•	•	4
BIT	x	•	2	3	4	5	•	•
BLE		•	•	•	•	•	•	4
BLS		•	•	•	•	•	•	4
BLT		•	•	•	•	•	•	4
BMI		•	•	•	•	•	•	4
BNE		•	•	•	•	•	•	4
BPL		•	•	•	•	•	•	4
BRA		•	•	•	•	•	•	4
BSR		•	•	•	•	•	•	8
BVC		•	•	•	•	•	•	4
BVS		•	•	•	•	•	•	4
CBA		•	•	•	•	•	2	•
CLC		•	•	•	•	•	2	•
CLI		•	•	•	•	•	2	•
CLR		2	•	•	6	7	•	•
CLV		•	•	•	•	•	2	•
CMP	x	•	2	3	4	5	•	•
COM		2	•	•	6	7	•	•
CPX		•	3	4	5	6	•	•
DAA		•	•	•	•	•	2	•
DEC		2	•	•	6	7	•	•
DES		•	•	•	•	•	4	•
DEX		•	•	•	•	•	4	•
EOR	x	•	2	3	4	5	•	•

	(Dual Operand)	ACCX	Immediate	Direct	Extended	Indexed	Implied
INC		2	•	•	6	7	•
INS		•	•	•	•	•	4
INX		•	•	•	•	•	4
JMP		•	•	•	3	4	•
JSR		•	•	•	9	8	•
LDA	x	•	2	3	4	5	•
LDS		•	3	4	5	6	•
LDX		•	3	4	5	6	•
LSR		2	•	•	6	7	•
NEG		2	•	•	6	7	•
NOP		•	•	•	•	•	2
ORA	x	•	2	3	4	5	•
PSH		•	•	•	•	•	4
PUL		•	•	•	•	•	4
ROL		2	•	•	6	7	•
ROR		2	•	•	6	7	•
RTI		•	•	•	•	•	10
RTS		•	•	•	•	•	5
SBA		•	•	•	•	•	2
SBC	x	•	2	3	4	5	•
SEC		•	•	•	•	•	2
SEI		•	•	•	•	•	2
SEV		•	•	•	•	•	2
STA	x	•	•	4	5	6	•
STS		•	•	5	6	7	•
STX		•	•	5	6	7	•
SUB	x	•	2	3	4	5	•
SWI		•	•	•	•	•	12
TAB		•	•	•	•	•	2
TAP		•	•	•	•	•	2
TBA		•	•	•	•	•	2
TPA		•	•	•	•	•	2
TST		2	•	•	6	7	•
TSX		•	•	•	•	•	4
TSX		•	•	•	•	•	4
WAI		•	•	•	•	•	9

NOTE: Interrupt time is 12 cycles from the end of the instruction being executed, except following a WAI instruction. Then it is 4 cycles.

349

Appendix

G INSTRUCTION SET FOR THE RCA COSMAC

(Courtesy of RCA Semiconductor Division.)

Instruction Set

The COSMAC instruction summary is given in Table I. Hexadecimal notation is used to refer to the 4-bit binary codes. Many of the instructions have been discussed in the Architecture section. Symbols used are:

R(W): Register designated by W, where
W = N, or X, or P
R(W).0: Lower-order byte of R(W)
R(W).1: Higher-order byte of R(W)

Operation Notation

$$M(R(N)) \rightarrow D; R(N) + 1$$

This notation means: The memory byte pointed to by R(N) is loaded into D, and R(N) is incremented by 1.

Table I — Instruction Summary

Register Operations

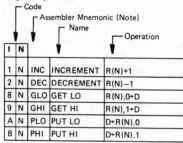

I	N			
1	N	INC	INCREMENT	R(N)+1
2	N	DEC	DECREMENT	R(N)−1
8	N	GLO	GET LO	R(N).0→D
9	N	GHI	GET HI	R(N).1→D
A	N	PLO	PUT LO	D→R(N).0
B	N	PHI	PUT HI	D→R(N).1

N=0,1,2, . . .,9,A,B, . . .,E,F (Hexadecimal Notation)

Memory Reference

I	N			
4	N	LDA	LOAD ADV	M(R(N))→D;R(N)+1
5	N	STR	STORE	D→M(R(N))

Table I — Instruction Summary

Branching

I	N			
3	0	BR	UNCOND.BR.	M(R(P))→R(P).0
3	2	BZ	BR.IF D=00	M(R(P))→R(P).0 IF D=00/R(P)+1
3	3	BDF	BR.IF DF=1	M(R(P))→R(P).0 IF DF=1/R(P)+1
3	4	B1	BR.IF EF1=1	M(R(P))→R(P).0 IF EF1=1/R(P)+1
3	5	B2	BR.IF EF2=1	M(R(P))→R(P).0 IF EF2=1/R(P)+1
3	6	B3	BR.IF EF3=1	M(R(P))→R(P).0 IF EF3=1/R(P)+1
3	7	B4	BR.IF EF4=1	M(R(P))→R(P).0 IF EF4=1/R(P)+1
3	8	SKP	SKIP	R(P)+1
3	A	BNZ	BR.IF D≠00	M(R(P))→R(P).0 IF D≠00/R(P)+1
3	B	BNF	BR.IF DF=0	M(R(P))→R(P).0 IF DF=0/R(P)+1
3	C	BN1	BR.IF EF1=0	M(R(P))→R(P).0 IF EF1=0/R(P)+1
3	D	BN2	BR.IF EF2=0	M(R(P))→R(P).0 IF EF2=0/R(P)+1
3	E	BN3	BR.IF EF3=0	M(R(P))→R(P).0 IF EF3=0/R(P)+1
3	F	BN4	BR.IF EF4=0	M(R(P))→R(P).0 IF EF4=0/R(P)+1

ALU Operations

I	N			
F	0	LDX	LOAD BY X	M(R(X))→D
F	1	OR	OR	M(R(X)) ∨ D→D
F	2	AND	AND	M(R(X)) · D→D
F	3	XOR	EXCL.OR	M(R(X)) ⊕ D→D
* F	4	ADD	ADD	M(R(X))+D→D;C→DF
* F	5	SD	SUBTRACT D	M(R(X))−D→D;C→DF
* F	6	SHR	SHIFT RIGHT	SHIFT D RIGHT; LSB→DF;0→MSB
* F	7	SM	SUBTRACT M	D−M(R(X))→D;C→DF
F	8	LDI	LOAD IMM	M(R(P))→D;R(P)+1
F	9	ORI	OR IMM	M(R(P)) ∨ D→D;R(P)+1
F	A	ANI	AND IMM	M(R(P)) · D→P;R(P)+1
F	B	XRI	EXCL.OR IMM	M(R(P)) ⊕ D→D; R(P)+1
* F	C	ADI	ADD IMM	M(R(P))+D→D; C→DF;R(P)+1
* F	D	SDI	SUBT D IMM	M(R(P))−D→D; C→DF;R(P)+1
* F	F	SMI	SUBT M IMM	D−M(R(P))→D; C→DF;R(P)+1

Control

I	N			
0	0	IDL	IDLE	WAIT FOR INTERRUPT/ DMA-IN/ DMA-OUT
D	N	SEP	SET P	N→P
E	N	SEX	SET X	N→X
7	0	RET	RETURN	M(R(X))→ X, P; R(X)+1;1→IE
7	1	DIS	DISABLE	M(R(X))→X, P; R(X)+1;0→IE
7	8	SAV	SAVE	T→M(R(X))

Table I — Instruction Summary

Input-Output Byte Transfer

I	N			
6	0	OUT 0	OUTPUT 0	M(R(X))→BUS; R(X)+1;N=0
6	1	OUT 1	OUTPUT 1	M(R(X))→BUS; R(X)+1;N=1
6	2	OUT 2	OUTPUT 2	M(R(X))→BUS; R(X)+1;N=2
6	3	OUT 3	OUTPUT 3	M(R(X))→BUS; R(X)+1;N=3
6	4	OUT 4	OUTPUT 4	M(R(X))→BUS; R(X)+1;N=4
6	5	OUT 5	OUTPUT 5	M(R(X))→BUS; R(X)+1;N=5
6	6	OUT 6	OUTPUT 6	M(R(X))→BUS; R(X)+1;N=6
6	7	OUT 7	OUTPUT 7	M(R(X))→BUS; R(X)+1;N=7
6	8	INP 0	INPUT 0	BUS→M(R(X)); N=8
6	9	INP 1	INPUT 1	BUS→M(R(X)); N=9
6	A	INP 2	INPUT 2	BUS→M(R(X)); N=A
6	B	INP 3	INPUT 3	BUS→M(R(X)); N=B
6	C	INP 4	INPUT 4	BUS→M(R(X)); N=C
6	D	INP 5	INPUT 5	BUS→M(R(X)); N=D
6	E	INP 6	INPUT 6	BUS→M(R(X)); N=E
6	F	INP 7	INPUT 7	BUS→M(R(X)); N=F

*These are the only operations that modify DF. DF is set or reset by an ALU carry during add or subtract. Subtraction is by 2's complement: $A-B = A+\bar{B}+1$.

Note: This type of abbreviated nomenclature is used when programs are designed with the aid of the COSMAC Assembler Simulator/Debugger System, which is available on commercial timesharing systems. Refer to "Program Development Guide for the COSMAC Microprocessor" for details.

Test and Branch

The Test and Branch instructions can branch unconditionally, test for D=0 or D=1, test for DF=0 or DF=1, or can test the status of the four I/O flags. A "successful" branch loads the byte following the instruction into the lower-order byte position of the current program counter, effecting a branch within the current 256-byte "page" of memory. If the test to branch is not successful, the next instruction in sequence is executed.

352

INSTRUCTION SET FOR THE
ROCKWELL PPS-8

(Courtesy of Rockwell International Corp.)

Table 3-1. List of Instructions

MNEMONIC	NAME	BYTES	CYCLES	DESCRIPTION	
				VERBAL	SYMBOLIC
L	Load A	1	1	The current RAM operand is placed in the accumulator	A ◄─ M
LN	Load A, Increment Address	1	1	Same as L. Additionally, the X register is incremented	A ◄─ M X ◄─ X+1, skip if X=0
LD	Load A, Decrement Address	1	1	Same as L. Additionally, the X register is decremented	A ◄─ M X ◄─ X-1, skip if X=127
LNXL	Load A, Increment Address, Exchange L	1	1	Same as LN. Additionally, the contents of the L register and the Z & X registers are exchanged	A ◄─ M X ◄─ X+1, skip if X=0 Z, X ◄►L
LDXL	Load A, Decrement Address, Exchange L	1	1	Same as LD. Additionally, the contents of the L register and the Z & X registers are exchanged	A ◄─ M X ◄─ X-1, skip if X=127 Z,X ◄►L
LNCX	Load A, Increment & Compare Address, Exchange L	1	1	Same as LNXL. Additionally, the next instruction is skipped if X = Y	A ◄─ M X ◄─ X+1 Skip if X=0 or X=Y Z,X ◄►L
LDCX	Load A, Decrement & Compare Address, Exchange L	1	1	Same as LDXL. Additionally, the next instruction is skipped if X = Y	A ◄─ M X ◄─ X-1 Skip if X=127 or X=Y Z,X ◄►L
LNXY	Load A, Increment Address, Exchange Y	1	1	Same as LN. Additionally, the contents of the X & Y registers are exchanged	A ◄─ M X ◄─ X+1, skip if X=0 X ◄►Y
S	Store A	1	1	The contents of the accumulator are stored in the current RAM operand address	M ◄─ A
SN	Store A, Increment Address	1	1	Same as S. Additionally, the X register is incremented	M ◄─ A X ◄─ X+1, skip if X=0

Table 3-1. List of Instructions (Continued)

MNEMONIC	NAME	BYTES	CYCLES	DESCRIPTION	
				VERBAL	SYMBOLIC
SD	Store A, Decrement Address	1	1	Same as S. Additionally, the X register is decremented	M ← A X ← X-1, skip if X=127
SNXL	Store A, Increment Address, Exchange L	1	1	Same as SN. Additionally, the contents of the L register and the Z & X registers are exchanged	M ← A X ← X+1, skip if X=0 Z,X ←→ L
SDXL	Store A, Decrement Address, Exchange L	1	1	Same as SD. Additionally, the contents of the L register and the Z & X registers are exchanged	M ← A X ← X-1, skip if X=127 Z,X ←→ L
SNCX	Store A, Increment & Compare Address, Exchange L	1	1	Same as SNXL. Additionally, the next instruction is skipped if X = Y	M ← A X ← X+1 Skip if X=0 or X=Y Z,X ←→ L
SDCX	Store A, Decrement & Compare Address, Exchange L	1	1	Same as SDXL. Additionally, the next instruction is skipped if X = Y	M ← A, X ← X-1 Skip if X=127 or X=Y Z,X ←→ L
SNXY	Store A, Increment Address, Exchange Y	1	1	Same as SN. Additionally, the contents of the X and Y registers are exchanged	M ← A X ← X+1, skip if X=0 X ←→ Y
X	Exchange	2	2	These instructions are identical to the corresponding store instructions except that the accumulator and the current RAM operand are exchanged	A ←→ M
XN	Exchange, Increment Address	2	2		A ←→ M X ← X+1, skip if X=0
XD	Exchange, Decrement Address	2	2		A ←→ M X ← X-1, skip if X=127
XNXL	Exchange, Increment Address, Exchange L	2	2		A ←→ M X ← X+1, skip if X=0 Z,X ←→ L
XDXL	Exchange, Decrement Address, Exchange L	2	2		A ←→ M X ← X-1, skip if X=127 Z,X ←→ L
XNCX	Exchange, Increment & Compare Address, Exchange L	2	2		A ←→ M X ← X+1 Skip if X=0 or X=Y Z,X ←→ L
XDCX	Exchange, Decrement & Compare Address, Exchange L	2	2	These instructions are identical to the corresponding store instructions except that the accumulator and the current RAM operand are exchanged	A ←→ M X ← X-1 Skip if X=127 or X=Y Z,X ←→ L

Table 3-1. List of Instructions (Continued)

MNEMONIC	NAME	BYTES	CYCLES	DESCRIPTION	
				VERBAL	SYMBOLIC
XNXY	Exchange, Increment Address, Excahnge Y	2	2	These instructions are identical to the corresponding store instructions except that the accumulator and the current RAM operand are exchanged	A↔M X←X+1, skip if X=0 X↔Y
LX	Load X	1,2	2	The current RAM operand is placed in the X register	X←M
LY	Load Y	1,2	2	The current RAM operand is placed in the Y register	Y←M
LZ	Load Z	1,2	2	The current RAM operand is placed in the Z register	Z←M
LAI	Load A Immediate	1-3	3	The specified literal operand is placed in the accumulator	A←I3
LXI	Load X Immediate	1-3	3	The specified literal operand is placed in the X register	X←I3
LYI	Load Y Immediate	1-3	3	The specified literal operand is placed in the Y register	Y←I3
LZI	Load Z Immediate	1-3	3	The specified literal operand is placed in the Z register	Z←I3
LAL	Load A through Link	1,2	3	The ROM operand addressed by the L register is placed in the accumulator	W←A, A←(L) L←L+1
LXL	Load X through Link	1,2	3	The ROM operand addressed by the L register is placed in the X register	X←(L) L←L+1
LYL	Load Y through Link	1,2	3	The ROM operand addressed by the L register is placed in the Y register	Y←(L) L←L+1
LZL	Load Z through Link	1,2	3	The ROM operand addressed by the L register is placed in the Z register	Z←(L) L←L+1
LXA	Load X from A	1	1	The contents of the accumulator are placed in the X register	X←A
LYA	Load Y from A	1	1	The contents of the accumulator are placed in the Y register	Y←A
LZA	Load Z from A	1	1	The contents of the accumulator are placed in the Z register	Z←A

355

Table 3-1. List of Instructions (Continued)

MNEMONIC	NAME	BYTES	CYCLES	DESCRIPTION	
				VERBAL	SYMBOLIC
LLA	Load L from A	1	1	The contents of the accumulator are placed in the upper 8 bits of the L register	L(16:9)◄─ A
XY	Exchange Y	1	1	The contents of the X and Y register are exchanged	X◄►Y
XL	Exchange L	1	1	The contents of the L register and the Z & X registers are exchanged	L◄►Z,X
XAX	Exchange A and X	1	1	The contents of the X register and the accumulator are exchanged	A◄►X
XAY	Exchange A and Y	1	1	The contents of the Y register and the accumulator are exchanged	A◄►Y
XAZ	Exchange A and Z	1	1	The contents of the Z register and the accumulator are exchanged	A◄►Z
XAL	Exchange A and L	1	1	The contents of the upper half of the L register and the accumulator are exchanged	A◄►L(16:9)
INCX	Increment X	1	1	The X register is incremented by one	X◄─ X+1 Skip if X=0
DECX	Decrement X	1	1	The X register is decremented by one	X◄─ X-1√ Skip if X=127
INXY	Increment X, Exchange Y	1	1	The X register is incremented and the contents of the X and Y registers are exchanged	X◄─ X+1, skip if X=0 X◄►Y
DEXY	Decrement X, Exchange Y	1	1	The X register is decremented and the contents of the X and Y registers are exchanged	X◄─ X-1, skip if X=127 X◄►Y
INCY	Increment Y	2	2	The Y register is incremented by one	Y◄─ Y+1 Skip if Y=0
DECY	Decrement Y	2	2	The Y register is decremented by one	Y◄─ Y-1 Skip if Y=127
PSHA	Push A	1,2	2	The contents of the accumulator are pushed into the stack	A─► (S) S◄─S+1
PSHX	Push X	1,2	2	The contents of the X register pushed into the stack	X─►(S) S◄─S+1
PSHY	Push Y	1,2	2	The contents of the Y register are pushed into the stack	Y─► (S) S◄─S+1
PSHZ	Push Z	1,2	2	The contents of the Z register are pushed into the stack	Z─► (S) S◄─S+1

Table 3-1. List of Instructions (Continued)

MNEMONIC	NAME	BYTES	CYCLES	DESCRIPTION VERBAL	DESCRIPTION SYMBOLIC
PSHL	Push L	1	3	The contents of the L register are pushed into the stack and replaced by the contents of the A and W registers	$L \rightarrow (S+1,S)$ $A,W \rightarrow L$ $S \leftarrow S+2$
POPA	Pop A	1,2	2	The uppermost byte is popped from the stack and placed in the accumulator	$S \leftarrow S-1$ $A \leftarrow (S)$ Skip if S=31
POPX	Pop X	1,2	2	The uppermost byte is popped from the stack and placed in the X register	$S \leftarrow S-1$ $X \leftarrow (S)$ Skip if S=31
POPY	Pop Y	1,2	2	The uppermost byte is popped from the stack and placed in the Y register	$S \leftarrow S-1$ $Y \leftarrow (S)$ Skip if S=31
POPZ	Pop Z	1,2	2	The uppermost byte is popped from the stack and placed in the Z register	$S \leftarrow S-1$ $Z \leftarrow (S)$ Skip if S=31
POPL	Pop L	1	3	The uppermost 2 bytes are popped from the stack and placed in the L register	$S \leftarrow S-2$ $L \leftarrow (S+1,S)$
A	Add	1	1	The sum of the accumulator and the current RAM operand are placed in the accumulator	$C,A \leftarrow A+M$ $Q \leftarrow IC$
AC	Add with Carry	1	1	Same as A except the carry flip-flop, C, is used as a carry-in	$C,A \leftarrow A+M+C$ $Q \leftarrow IC$
ASK	Add, Skip on Carry	1	1	Same as A. Additionally, the next instruction is skipped if a carry-out is generated	$C,A \leftarrow A+M$ $Q \leftarrow IC$ Skip if C=1
ACSK	Add with Carry, Skip on Carry	1	1	Same as AC. Additionally, the next instruction is skipped if a carryout is generated	$C,A \leftarrow A+M+C$ Skip if C=1
AISK	Add Immediate, Skip on Carry	1-3	3	The sum of the accumulator and the specified literal operand is placed in the accumulator	$A \leftarrow A+I3$ $Q \leftarrow IC$ Skip if carry-out
INCA	Increment A	1	1	The accumulator is incremented by one	$A \leftarrow A+1$ $Q \leftarrow IC$
DC	Decimal Correct (1)	1	1	The hexadecimal value 66 is added to the accumulator	$A \leftarrow A+66_{16}$ $Q \leftarrow IC$
DCC	Decimal Correct (2)	1	1	The accumulator is modified based on the states of the C&Q flip-flops	$\overline{C,Q}$ 0,0 $\quad A \leftarrow A+(9A)_{16}$ 0,1 $\quad A \leftarrow A+(A0)_{16}$ 1,0 $\quad A \leftarrow A+(FA)_{16}$ 1,1 $\quad$ No change

Table 3-1. List of Instructions (Continued)

MNEMONIC	NAME	BYTES	CYCLES	DESCRIPTION	
				VERBAL	SYMBOLIC
AN	Logical AND	1	1	The logical product of the accumulator and the current RAM operand is placed in the accumulator	$A \leftarrow A \wedge M$
ANI	Logical AND Immediate	1-3	3	The logical product of the accumulator and the specified literal operand is placed in the accumulator	$A \leftarrow A \wedge I3$
OR	Logical OR	1	1	The logical sum of the accumulator and the current RAM operand is placed in the accumulator	$A \leftarrow A \vee M$
EOR	Logical Exclusive OR	1	1	The logical exclusive or (addition without carry) of the accumulator and the current RAM operand is placed in the accumulator	$A \leftarrow A \triangledown M$
COM	Complement	1	1	The one's complement of the accumulator is placed in the accumulator	$A \leftarrow \bar{A}$
SC	Set Carry	1	1	The carry flip-flop, C, is set (1)	$C \leftarrow 1$
RC	Reset Carry	1	1	The carry flip-flop, C, is reset (0)	$C \leftarrow 0$
RAR	Rotate A Right	1	1	The accumulator and C flip-flop are circular shifted one bit to the right	$A(8:1) \rightarrow \boxed{C}$
RAL	Rotate A Left	1	1	The accumulator and C flip-flop are circular shifted one bit to the left	$A(8:1) \leftarrow \boxed{C}$
MDR	Move Digit Right	1	1	The accumulator is shifted right 4 bits and the least significant 4 bits of the current RAM operand are placed in the vacated accumulator positions	$A(8:5) \rightarrow A(4:1)$ $M(4:1) \rightarrow A(8:5)$
MDL	Move Digit Left	1	1	The accumulator is shifted left 4 bits and the most significant 4 bits of the current RAM operand are placed in the vacated accumulator positions	$A(8:5) \leftarrow A(4:1)$ $A(4:1) \leftarrow M(8:5)$
SB	Set Bit (n)	1,2	2	The specified bit of the current RAM operand is set (1)	$M \leftarrow M \vee 2^{(n-1)}$
RB	Reset Bit (n)	1,2	2	The specified bit of the current RAM operand is reset (0)	$M \leftarrow M \wedge \overline{2^{(n-1)}}$
B	Branch	1,2	1,2	The specified address is placed in the P-register	$P(7:1) \leftarrow I1(7:1)$ If $I1(8)=1$, $P(14:8) \leftarrow I2(7:1)$

Table 3-1. List of Instructions (Continued)

MNEMONIC	NAME	BYTES	CYCLES	DESCRIPTION	
				VERBAL	SYMBOLIC
BDI	Branch, Disable Interrupts	2	2	Same as B. Additionally, the interrupts are disabled	P(7:1) ← I1(7:1) P(14:8) ← I2(7:1) Disable Interrupts

BL	Branch and Link	1,2	3	The specified address is placed in the P-register. The previous contents of the P-register (incremented) are saved in the L register together with the state of the C flip-flop. The previous contents of the L register are pushed into the stack	L → (S+1,S)
					S ← S+2
					P → L(15:9,7:1)
					C → L(16)
					If I1(6)=1
					    P(14:8) ← SP$_u$(7:1)
					    P(7:1) ← SP$_1$(7:1)
					If I1(6)=0
					    P(12:8) ← I1(5:1)
					    P(7:1) ← I2(7:1)
					    P(13) ← I2(8)
					    P(14) ← 0

RT	Return	1	3	The P-register and C flip-flop are loaded from the L-register. The uppermost 2 bytes are popped from the stack and placed in the L-register	P ← L(15:9,7:1) C ← L(16) S ← S-2 L ← (S+1,S)
RSK	Return & Skip	1	3	Same as RT except that the next instruction (i.e., the instruction at the "return" location) is skipped	P ← L(15:9,7:1) C ← L(16) S ← S-2, L ← (S+1,S) Skip next instruction
RTI	Return, Enable Interrupts	1	3	Same as RT. Additionally, the interrupts are enabled	P ← L(15:9,7:1) C ← L(16) S ← S-2, L ← (S+1,S) Enable interrupts
NOP	No Operation	1	1	No function is performed. The branch condition tag is used	
SKC	Skip if Carry	1	1	The next instruction is skipped if the carry flip-flop, C, is set	Skip if C=1
SKNC	Skip if No Carry	1	1	The next instruction is skipped if the carry flip-flop, C, is reset	Skip if C=0
SKZ	Skip if Zero	1	1	The next instruction is skipped if the accumulator equals zero	Skip if A=0
SKNZ	Skip if Non-Zero	1	1	The next instruction is skipped if the accumulator does not equal zero	Skip if A≠0
SKP	Skip if Positive	1	1	The next instruction is skipped if the most significant bit of the accumulator is zero	Skip if A(8)=0

Table 3-1. List of Instructions (Continued)

MNEMONIC	NAME	BYTES	CYCLES	DESCRIPTION	
				VERBAL	SYMBOLIC
SKN	Skip if Negative	1	1	The next instruction is skipped if the most significant bit of the accumulator is one	Skip if A(8)=1
SKE	Skip if Equal	1	1	The next instruction is skipped if the accumulator and the current RAM operand are equal	Skip if A=M
BBT	Branch if Bit (n) True	2,3	2,3	A program branch is executed if the specified bit of the current RAM operand is true (1)	If $M \wedge 2^{(n-1)}=1$, then $P(7:1) \leftarrow I2(7:1)$ & if I2(8)=1, $P(14:8) \leftarrow I3(7:1)$
BBF	Branch if Bit (n) False	2,3	2,3	A program branch is executed if the specified bit of the current RAM operand is false (0)	If $M \wedge 2^{(n-1)}=0$, then $P(7:1) \leftarrow I2(7:1)$ & if I2(8)=1, $P(14:8) \leftarrow I3(7:1)$
BC	Branch if Carry	2,3	2,3	A program branch is executed if the carry flip-flop, C, is set (1)	If C=1, then $P(7:1) \leftarrow I2(7:1)$ & if I2(8)=1, $P(14:8) \leftarrow I3(7:1)$
BNC	Branch if No Carry	2,3	2,3	A program branch is executed if the carry flip-flop, C, is reset (0)	If C=0, then $P(7:1) \leftarrow I2(7:1)$ & if I2(8)=1, $P(14:8) \leftarrow I3(7:1)$
BZ	Branch if Zero	2,3	2,3	A program branch is executed if the accumulator equals zero	If A=0, then $P(7:1) \leftarrow I2(7:1)$ & if I2(8)=1, $P(14:8) \leftarrow I3(7:1)$
BNZ	Branch if Non-Zero	2,3	2,3	A program branch is executed if the accumulator does not equal zero	If $A \neq 0$, then $P(7:1) \leftarrow I2(7:1)$ & if I2(8)=1, $P(14:8) \leftarrow I3(7:1)$
BP	Branch if Positive	2,3	2,3	A program branch is executed if the most significant bit of the accumulator is zero	If A(8)=0, then $P(7:1) \leftarrow I2(7:1)$ & if I2(8)=1, $P(14:8) \leftarrow I3(7:1)$
BN	Branch if Negative	2,3	2,3	A program branch is executed if the most significant bit of the accumulator is one	If A(8)=1, then $P(7:1) \leftarrow I2(7:1)$ & if I2(8)=1, $P(14:8) \leftarrow I3(7:1)$
BNE	Branch if Not Equal	2,3	2,3	A program branch is executed if the accumulator is not equal to the current RAM operand	If $A \neq M$, then $P(7:1) \leftarrow I2(7:1)$ & if I2(8)=1, $P(14:8) \leftarrow I3(7:1)$

Table 3-1. List of Instructions (Continued)

MNEMONIC	NAME	BYTES	CYCLES	DESCRIPTION	
				VERBAL	SYMBOLIC
I04	Digit I/O (C, D)	2	2	Command C is transmitted to I/O device D. Bits 8-5 of the accumulator are transmitted to the device and bits 1-4 are received from the device	I2 → I/D(8:1) A(8:5) → I/D(8:5) A(4:1) ← I/D(4:1)
IN	Input (C, D)	2	2	Command C is transmitted to I/O device D. The accumulator is loaded with a data byte transmitted by the device. If D is omitted, a zero (all-call) device address is transmitted	I2 → I/D(8:1) A ← I/D(8:1)
OUT	Output (C, D)	2	2	Same as IN except the accumulator contents are transmitted to the device	I2 → I/D(8:1) A → I/D(8:1)
RIS	Read Interrupt Status	2	2	The accumulator is loaded with the interrupt status word from the highest priority I/O device currently requesting service.	I2 → I/D(8:1) A ← I/D(8:1)

361

Appendix

INSTRUCTION SET FOR THE NATIONAL PACE

(Courtesy National Semiconductor Corporation.)

TABLE VI. PACE Instruction Summary

Mnemonic	Meaning	Operation	Assembler Format		Instruction Format
1. Branch Instructions					
BOC	Branch On Condition	(PC) ← (PC) + disp if cc true	BOC	cc,disp	0 1 0 0 | cc | disp
JMP	Jump	(PC) ← EA	JMP	disp (xr)	0 0 0 1 1 0 | xr | disp
JMP@	Jump Indirect	(PC) ← (EA)	JMP	@disp (xr)	1 0 0 1 1 0
JSR	Jump To Subroutine	(STK) ← (PC), (PC) ← EA	JSR	disp (xr)	0 0 0 1 0 1
JSR@	Jump To Subroutine Indirect	(STK) ← (PC), (PC) ← (EA)	JSR	@disp (xr)	1 0 0 1 0 1
RTS	Return from Subroutine	(PC) ← (STK) + disp	RTS	disp	1 0 0 0 0 0 | 0 0 | disp
RTI	Return from Interrupt	(PC) ← (STK) + disp, IEN = 1	RTI	disp	0 1 1 1 1 1
2. Skip Instructions					
SKNE	Skip if Not Equal	If (ACr) ≠ (EA), (PC) ← (PC) + 1	SKNE	r,disp (xr)	1 1 1 1 | r | xr | disp
SKG	Skip if Greater	If (AC0) > (EA), (PC) ← (PC) + 1	SKG	0,disp (xr)	1 0 0 1 1 1
SKAZ	Skip if And is Zero	If [(AC0) ∧ (EA)] = 0, (PC) ← (PC) + 1	SKAZ	0,disp (xr)	1 0 1 1 1 0
ISZ	Increment and Skip if Zero	(EA) ← (EA) + 1, if (EA) = 0, (PC) ← (PC) + 1	ISZ	disp (xr)	1 0 0 0 1 1
DSZ	Decrement and Skip if Zero	(EA) ← (EA) − 1, if (EA) = 0, (PC) ← (PC) + 1	DSZ	disp (xr)	1 0 1 0 1 1
AISZ	Add Immediate, Skip if Zero	(ACr) ← (ACr) + disp, if (ACr) = 0, (PC) ← (PC) + 1	AISZ	r,disp	0 1 1 1 1 0 | r
3. Memory Data Transfer Instructions					
LD	Load	(ACr) ← (EA)	LD	r,disp (xr)	1 1 0 0 | r | xr | disp
LD@	Load Indirect	(AC0) ← ((EA))	LD	0,@disp (xr)	1 0 0 1 0 0 0
ST	Store	(EA) ← (ACr)	ST	r,disp (xr)	1 1 0 1 | r
ST@	Store Indirect	((EA)) ← (AC0)	ST	0,@disp (xr)	1 0 1 1 0 0
LSEX	Load With Sign Extended	(AC0) ← (EA) bit 7 extended	LSEX	0,disp (xr)	1 0 1 1 1 1
4. Memory Data Operate Instructions					
AND	And	(AC0) ← (AC0) ∧ (EA)	AND	0,disp (xr)	1 0 1 0 1 0 | xr | disp
OR	Or	(AC0) ← (AC0) ∨ (EA)	OR	0,disp (xr)	1 0 1 0 0 1
ADD	Add	(ACr) ← (ACr) + (EA), OV, CY	ADD	r,disp (xr)	1 1 1 0 | r
SUBB	Subtract with Borrow	(AC0) ← (AC0) + ~ (EA) + (CY), OV, CY	SUBB	0,disp (xr)	1 0 0 1 0 0
DECA	Decimal Add	(AC0) ← (AC0) +$_{10}$ (EA) +$_{10}$ (CY), OV, CY	DECA	0,disp (xr)	1 0 0 0 1 0
5. Register Data Transfer Instructions					
LI	Load Immediate	(ACr) ← disp	LI	r,disp	0 1 0 1 0 0 | r | disp
RCPY	Register Copy	(ACdr) ← (ACsr)	RCPY	sr,dr	0 1 0 1 1 1 | dr | sr | not used
RXCH	Register Exchange	(ACdr) ← (ACsr), (ACsr) ← (ACdr)	RXCH	sr,dr	0 1 1 0 1 1
XCHRS	Exchange Register and Stack	(STK) ← (ACr), (ACr) ← (STK)	XCHRS	r	0 0 0 1 1 1 | r | not used
CFR	Copy Flags Into Register	(ACr) ← (FR)	CFR	r	0 0 0 0 0 1
CRF	Copy Register Into Flags	(FR) ← (ACr)	CRF	r	0 0 0 0 1 0
PUSH	Push Register Onto Stack	(STK) ← (ACr)	PUSH	r	0 1 1 0 0 0
PULL	Pull Stack Into Register	(ACr) ← (STK)	PULL	r	0 1 1 0 0 1
PUSHF	Push Flags Onto Stack	(STK) ← (FR)	PUSHF		0 0 0 0 1 1 | not used
PULLF	Pull Stack Into Flags	(FR) ← (STK)	PULLF		0 0 0 1 0 0

TABLE VI. PACE Instruction Summary

Mnemonic	Meaning	Operation	Assembler Format		Instruction Format
6.	**Register Data Operate Instructions**				
RADD	Register Add	(ACdr) ← (ACdr) + (ACsr), OV, CY	RADD	sr,dr	`0 1 1 0 1 0` dr sr not used
RADC	Register Add With Carry	(ACdr) ← (ACdr) + (ACsr) + (CY), OV, CY	RADC	sr,dr	`0 1 1 1 0 1`
RAND	Register And	(ACdr) ← (ACdr) ∧ (ACsr)	RAND	sr,dr	`0 1 0 1 0 1`
RXOR	Register Exclusive OR	(ACdr) ← (ACdr) ⊽ (ACsr)	RXOR	sr,dr	`0 1 0 1 1 0`
CAI	Complement and Add Immediate	(ACr) ← ~ (ACr) + disp	CAI	r,disp	`0 1 1 1 0 0` r disp
7.	**Shift And Rotate Instructions**				
SHL	Shift Left	(ACr) ← (ACr) shifted left n places, w/wo link	SHL	r,n,ℓ	`0 0 1 0 1 0` r ℓ
SHR	Shift Right	(ACr) ← (ACr) shifted right n places, w/wo link	SHR	r,n,ℓ	`0 0 1 0 1 1`
ROL	Rotate Left	(ACr) ← (ACr) rotated left n places, w/wo link	ROL	r,n,ℓ	`0 0 1 0 0 0`
ROR	Rotate Right	(ACr) ← (ACr) rotated right n places, w/wo link	ROR	r,n,ℓ	`0 0 1 0 0 1`
8.	**Miscellaneous Instructions**				
HALT	Halt	Halt	HALT		`0 0 0 0 0 0` not used
SFLG	Set Flag	$(FR)_{fc}$ ← 1	SFLG	fc	`0 0 1 1` fc `1` not used
PFLG	Pulse Flag	$(FR)_{fc}$ ← 1, $(FR)_{fc}$ ← 0	PFLG	fc	`0 0 1 1` fc `0`

INDEX

Absorptive property, **15**
Accumulator, 78, 95
ACIA, 183, 255–58
A/D converter, 183–85
Addressing modes, 105–8
  direct, 105
  immediate, 108
  indexed, 107
  indirect, 106
  page relative, 107
  page-0 relative, 107
  register indirect, 107
  relative, 107
Algorithm, 118
Alphanumeric numbers, 56
ALU, 1, 75, 94
American Standard Code for Information Inter-
  change (ASCII), 70–71
Analog-to-digital (A/D) converter, 183–85
AND gate, 8–10, 21
AND-OR-NOT form, 18
Angelo, E.J., Jr., 23
ANSI, 189
Architecture, 74–112
  Harvard, 74, 104
  von Neumann (Princeton), 74, 104
Arithmetic:
  BCD, 68
  Binary, 49–53
  complementary BCD, 69–70
  hexadecimal, 58–59
  octal, 54–55
  1's complement, 60–62
  2's complement, 62–66

Arithmetic logic/unit (ALU), 1, 75, 94
ASCII, 70–71
Assembler, 116, 142
Assembly language (*see* Symbolic language)
Associative property, 15
Astable multivibrator, 178
Asynchronous counter, 49
Asynchronous transfer (*see* Programmed-data
  transfer)

Backler, J., **192**
Balanced line, 174
Base of number, 46
Bass, J.E., 273, 318
Baud rate, 188
BCD (*see* binary-coded decimal)
Benchmark, 291–96
Bennett, T., 252
Binary-coded decimal (BCD), 66–70
  addition, 68
  8421 BCD, 67
  excess-3, 69
  subtraction, 68
  2'421 BCD, 68
Binary numbers, 46–54, 57, 59
  addition, 49–52
  conversion to decimal, 46
  conversion to hexadecimal, 57–58
  conversion to octal, 54
  counting, 47–48
  signed, 59–60
  subtraction, 52–53
Binary tape, 187
Bistable latch, 37

Bit, 3
Bit-slice processor, 112
Block 188, 189
BNPF tape, 187
Boole, G., 8
Boolean algebra, 8, 14–16
Boolean variable, 8
Boonton 76A capacitance bridge, 310
Bootstrap loader, 144
Branching, 133
Breadboarding, 303
Buffer, 177
Bus, 75
    input/output, 98–99
    memory address, 98–99
    memory data, 98–99
Byte, 3

Calebotta, S., 85
Capacitance bridge, 310–16
Carr, W.N., 78, 85, 89, 94
Carry flag, 99
Cassells, D.A., 320
Cassette, 189–90
CCITT V 24, 176
Central processing unit (CPU), 1, 75, 94
Character, 187, 189
Checklist, 198
Checksum, 188
Chu, Y., 69
Clare, C.R., 118
Clock, 30–31
CMOS logic, 29–30
Codes:
    ASCII, 70–72
    BCD, 66–69
    excess-8, 69
    Gray, 69
    9's complement, 69
    1's complement, 60–62
    operations, 105
    10's complement, 69–70
    2's complement, 62–66
    unweighted, 69
    weighted, 67
Coincident selection, 82
Combinational logic, 14, 17–19
Command pool, 270
Common-emitter configuration, 23
Common-source configuration, 25
Commutative property, 15
Compiler, 116, 145
Complementary-MOS (CMOS) logic 29–30
Complementation, 11

Complete set, 18
Computer:
    Harvard, 74, 104
    von Neumann, 74, 104
Conjunction, 8
Control instructions, 100–101
    conditional, 100
    unconditional, 100
Control unit, 1, 75
COSMAC, 259–65
Counter, 49
CPU, 1, 75, 94
CROM, 215–19, 276
Cropper, L.C., 317
Cross-assembler, 144
Crossbar matrix, 80
CRT terminal, 317–20
Cushman, R.H., 252
Cycle:
    execute, 76
    fetch, 76
    instruction, 76
    machine, 76
Cycle-stealing transfer (DMA), 150, 168–70

D/A converter, 183–85
Daisy-chaining, 165
Data:
    parallel, 38
    serial, 38
Data, transfer of, 99–100, 150–70
Data acquisition, 304–7
Data concentrator, 307–13
Data pool, 270
Data word, 77–78
Davis, S., 79, 92, 190
Dc noise margin, 27
Decimal numbers, 45–46
    BCD, 66–69
    conversion to binary, 46–47
    conversion to hexadecimal, 57
    conversion to octal, 53–54
Decoder (1-of-8), 18–19
Deem, W., 27, 69
Delimiter, 124
De Morgan's theorem, 16, 19
Demultiplexer, 173
Design methodology, 287–304
Development system, 4
D flip–flop, 36
Dibble-dabble algorithm, 46
Dietmeyer, D.L., 14, 37, 105
Differential input, 174

Digital-to-analog (D/A) converter, 183–85
Diode-transistor logic (DTL), 25–26
Direct Addressing, 105
Direct memory access (see DMA transfer)
Disjunction, 10
Diskette, 192
Distributive property, 15
D latch, 37
DMA controller, 274
DMA transfer 112, 150, 168–70
Dot-OR connection, 41
DTL, 25–27
Duality, 15
Dynamic memory, 86

ECL, 28–29
ECMA standard, 189
Edge-triggered flip-flop, 32, 34
Editor, 116–17, 141–42
EIA RS-232B standard, 176
Electronic lock, 316–18
Emitter-coupled logic (ECL), 28–29
Emitter-follower, 24
Enke, C.G., 49
Even parity, 70–71
Excess-3 code, 67, 69–70
Exclusive-OR gate, 17–18
Execute cycle, 76, 78, 110

Faggin, F., 97, 243, 250
Falk, H., 144, 150, 168
Fan-fold paper tape, 186
Fan-in, 25–26
Fan-out, 25–26
Fetch cycle, 76, 111
File, 189
FILU, 215–19
Flag 99, 151
  carry (link), 99
  overflow, 99
  parity, 236, 245
  sign, 99
  zero, 99
Flip-flop, 30–37
  D, 36–37
  edge-triggered, 32, 34
  J-K, 33–36
  master-slave, 32–34
  R-S, 31–33
  T, 34–35
Floppy disk, 192
  sector, 192
  track, 192

Flores, I., 119, 186
Flow chart, 119–21
Fox, W.A., 275
Frequency-shift keying (FSK), 191
Frohman-Bentchkowsky, D., 79, 85
FSK modulation, 191
Full-adder, 51–53
Full-duplex, 180
Fundamental mode, 170

Gate:
  AND, 8–9
  logic, 7
  NAND, 12–13, 40–41
  NOR, 13–14
  NOT (inverter), 11–12
  open-collector, 40–41
  OR, 10–11
  tri-state, 40–42
General-purpose (scratch-pad) register, 97
Gladstone, B., 131, 132, 140, 150, 157, 161, 168,
  316
Gray code, 69

Half-adder, 50, 53
Half-duplex, 180
Halkias, C.C., 80, 86, 89, 92
Handshake I/O, 138
Harvard architecture, 74, 104
Heilwell, M.F., 77
Hexadecimal numbers, 56–59
  addition, 58
  binary conversions, 57–58
  decimal conversions, 57
  subtraction, 58–59
Hexadecimal paper tape, 187
High-level language 116, 145–47
High-speed TTL, 27
Hill, F.J., 14, 27, 37, 74, 138, 150, 157, 161
Hoff, M.E., Jr., 92
Holt, R.W., 75, 110
Huntington, E.V., 15
Hurley, R.B., 46
Huskey, H.D., 69

IBM Selectric typewriter, 288
IC (see Integrated-circuit)
IEC Publication 117-15, 9
IEEE Standard No. 91-1973, 9, 31
Immediate addressing, 108
IMP-4, 215–23
IMP-8, 223, 307
IMP-16, 223, 275

Indexed addressing, 107
Index register, 107
Indirect addressing, 106
Input/output (I/O), 104, 138–41
    devices, 1, 183–92
Instruction, 99–105
    cycle, 76
    encoding of, 104
    execution of, 108–12
    register, 99
    word, 77–78
Integrated-circuit (IC), 22–30
    CMOS, 29–30
    dc noise margin, 27
    DTL, 25–26
    ECL, 28–29
    noise generation, 26
    noise immunity, 26
    TTL, 26–27
Intel Corporation:
    integrated-circuits:
        1702A PROM, 208, 213, 241
        2102 RAM, 213, 241
        3002 Bit-slice processor, 112
        3216/26 Bus drivers, 213
        4001 ROM, 201–2
        4002 RAM, 202–3
        4003 Shift register, 204
        4004 CPU, 1, 197–209
        4008/4009 Interface, 208, 213
        4040 CPU, 209–15
        4201 Clock, 209, 213
        4207/09/11 I/O, 213, 293
        4289 Interface, 209, 213, 292
        4308 ROM, 213
        4316 ROM, 213
        8008 CPU, 2, 234–43
        8080 CPU, 2, 243, 252
    Intellec:
        4/MOD 4, 208
        4/MOD 40, 214
        8/MOD 8, 241
        8/MOD 80, 4, 252, 304
    MCS-4, 1, 197–209
    MCS-40, 209–15
    MCS-8, 1, 234–43
    MCS-80, 1–2, 243–52
    MDS, 252
Interface, 150
    IC elements, 173–83
    programmable 180–83, 255–58
Interrupt (see Programmed-data transfer)
Interrupt-service routine, 161

Inverter, 11–12, 42
I/O (see Input/output)

J-K flip-flop, 33–36

Karnaugh, M., 14
Kildall, G. A., 145
Koehler, H. F., 86
Kohonen, T., 68, 69, 110
Korn, G. A., 69, 70, 96, 138, 150, 161
Kroeger, J.H., 86

Language:
    assembly (symbolic), 116, 124–41
    high-level, 116, 145–47
    machine, 104, 116, 121–24
Large-scale integration (LSI), 22
Last-in, first-out (LIFO) array, 96
Latch, 32, 37
    D, 37
    R-S, 32
Lavell, J., 252
Least-significant bit (LSB), 47
Lee, R., 310
Lemos, M. R., 75
Level synchronizer, 172–73
Level translator, 117
Lewis, D. R., 3, 108, 240, 287, 290, 291
LIFO array, 96
Linear selection, 80
Line drivers and receivers, 174–76
    balanced, 174
    differential, 174
    single-ended, 174
    unbalanced, 174
Lippman, M. D., 259, 264
Literal, 126
Literal pool, 270
Loader, 117
Logic:
    gate, 7
    negative, 19–22
    networks, 17–18
    positive, 19–22
    state, 7
    variable, 7
Logical product, 8
Logical sum, 10
Loop, 129
LSB, 47
Luecke, G., 79, 85, 89, 94

McCluskey, E. J., Jr., 14, 37
McDermott, J., 110
McFarland, H. L., Jr., 75, 110
McPhillips, S., 196, 197, 215, 243, 296
Machine cycle, 76–78
Machine language, 104, 121–24
Macro, 127
Magnetic tape cassette, 189–90
  block (record), 189
  character (word), 189
  file, 189
  track, 189
Maley, G. A., 77
Malmstadt, H. V., 49
Mark parity, 72
Master-slave flip-flop, 33, 35
Medium-scale integration (MSI), 22
Memory 1, 78–94
  addressing, 80–83
  crossbar (rectangular) matrix, 80
  dynamic, 86, 90–94
  map, 299
  page, 107, 208
  plane, 84
  pROM, 79
  RAM, 86–94
  read cycle, 87–88, 91–92
  RMM, 79
  ROM, 78–85
  ROS, 79
  RWM, 78, 86–94
  segment, 84
  sense line, 84
  static, 86–89
  write cycle, 87–88, 91–92
Memory address register (MAR), 77, 94
Memory data register (MDR), 77, 94
Microcomputer 1, 74–75
Microcomputer system:
  benchmark, 292
  breadboarding, 303
  design of, 296
  evaluation of, 290–96
  selection factors, 296
  simplification of, 303
  testing of, 303
Microinstruction, 110
Microprocessor 1, 94–112, 196–284
  applications, 3
  checklist, 198
  evaluation, 290
  Intel 4004, 1, 197–209
    4040, 209–15

Microprocessor (*cont.*):
  Intel 4004 (*cont.*):
    8008, 2, 234–43
    8080, 2, 243–*52*
  monolithic, 110–11
  Motorola 6800, 252–59
  National IMP-4, 215–23
    IMP-8, 223, 307
    IMP-16, 223, 275
    PACE, 275–81
  RCA COSMAC, 259–65
  Rockwell PPS-4, 223–34
    PPS-8, 266–75, 317
  selection of, 196–98
  terminals of, 110
Microprogrammable controller, 108
Millman, J., 80, 86, 89, 92
MIL STD 188B, 176
Minterm, 17
Mize, J. P., 79, 85, 89, 94
Mnemonic, 116
Moden, 190–92
  FSK, 191
  PSK, 191
Monitor, 117
Monostable (one-shot), 178
Morrison, R., 174
MOSFET, 23–25, 29–30
  n-channel, 24
  p-channel, 24
Most-significant bit (MSB), 47
Motorola Semiconductor:
  ACIA, 255–58
  microcomputer systems, 258
  PIA, 255–57
  6800 microprocessor, 252–59
MSB, 47
MSI, 22
Muchow, K., 27, 69
Multiplexer, 111, 173
Multivibrator, 178–80
  astable, 178
  bistable, 30
  monostable (one-shot), 178

NAND gate 12–13, 21, 40–41
Nash, G., 191
National Semiconductor:
  CROM, 215–19, 276
  DH0006, 297
  FILU, 215–19
  IMP-4, 215–23
    -4P development system, 281

National Semiconductor (*cont.*):
  IMP-4 (*cont.*):
    -8, 223, 307
    -16, 223, 275
  PACE, 275–81
  PACE microcomputer system 275–84
  RALU, 215–19, 276
n-channel MOSFET, 24
Negative logic, 19–22
Nesting, 137
Noise generation, 26
Noise immunity, 26
NOR gate, 13–14, 21
NOT gate, 11–12, 21
NPN transistor, 23–25
Number systems, 45–70
  base of, 46
  BCD, 62–69
  binary, 46–53
  complement:
    1's, 60–62
    2's, 62–66
    9's, 69
    10's, 69
  decimal, 45–46
  hexadecimal, 56–59
  octal, 53–56
  positional notation, 45
  signed binary, 59

Octal numbers, 53–56
  addition, 54–55
  conversions, 53–54
  subtraction, 54–55
Odd parity, 71
Ogdin, J. L., 95, 97, 196, 197, 209, 215, 243, 296
Open-collector gate, 40–41
Operand, 105
Operations code, 105
OR gate, 10–11, 21
Output buffer, 40–42
Overflow, 64–65, 70

PACE microprocessor, 275–84
Page, 107, 208
Page-relative addressing, 107
Page-0 relative addressing, 107
Paper tape, 185–88
  binary, 187
  BNPF, 187
  character (frame), 187
  checksum, 188
  8-level, 187
  fan-fold, 186

Paper tape (*cont.*)
  hexadecimal, 187
  level (channel), 187
  parity, 187
  punch, 185
  reader, 185
  record (block), 188
Parallel-to-serial converter, 39
Parity, 70–72, 187
  even, 70–71
  flag, 236, 245
  mark, 72
  odd, 71
  space, 72
Party-line I/O, 152
p-channel MOSFET, 23–25
Peatman, J. B., 40, 150, 157, 161
Peripheral interface, 150
Peripherals, 183–92
Peterson, G. R., 14, 27, 37, 74, 138, 150, 157, 161
Phillips cassette, 189
PIA (*see* Programmable interface)
Plane, 84
PL/M, 145
PNP transistor, 23–25
Polled interrupt, 161
Pool, 270
POP operation, 96
Positional notation, 45
Positive logic, 19–22
PPS-4, 4, 223–34
PPS-8, 266–75, 317
Princeton architecture, 74, 104
Priority, 161
Program counter, 95
Program–interrupt transfer (*see* Programmed-data transfer)
Programmable interface, 180–83
  ACIA, 183, 257–58
  PIA, 182, 255, 257
  UART, 180–83
Programmed-data transfer, 150, 153–68
  asynchronous (handshake), 138, 150, 157–61
  program-interrupt, 97, 140, 161–68
    daisy-chain, 165
    polled, 161
    priority, 161
    software polling, 163
    vectored, 161
  synchronous, 138, 150, 153–56
pROM, 79, 85–86
  programming of, 85

Prototyping system, 4
Pseudo-instructions, 125
PSK modulation, 191
Pull-up resistor, 41
Pulse synchronizer, 171
Pushdown (push-pop) stack, 96
PUSH operation, 96

Quine, W. V., 14

Radix, 46
RALU, 215–19, 276
RAM, 86–94
Random-access memory (RAM), 86–94
RCA:
    COSMAC, 259–65
    COSMAC Microkit, 264
Read-only memory (ROM), 79
Read/write memory (RWM), 86–94
Record, 188, 189
Register:
    accumulator, 78, 95
    index, 107
    instruction, 99
    LIFO, 96
    map, 299
    memory address (MAR), 77, 94
    memory data (MDR), 77, 94
    program counter, 95
    scratch-pad (general-purpose), 97
    stack, 96
    status, 99
Register-indirect addressing, 107
Relative addressing, 107
Resident assembler, 144
Reyling, G. F., Jr., 275
Rhyne, V. T., 14, 17, 37, 53, 67, 69, 170
Richards, R. K., 69
Riley, W. B., 82
Ripple counter, 49
Rockwell International:
    DMA controller, 274
    parallel data controller (PDC), 274
    PPS-4, 4, 223–34
      –4MP Assemulator, 4, 233
      -8, 266–75, 317
      -8 microcomputer Systems, 274
    TDI, 274
ROM, 79–86
Rose, C. W., 304
Rostky, G., 79, 85
R-S flip-flop, 31–32
Russo, P. M., 259, 264

Schmid, H., 76, 183
Schoeffler, J. D., 304
Scratch-pad register, 97–98
Sector, 192
Segment, 84
Self-assembler, 144
Sense line, 84
Serial-to-parallel converter, 37
Sevin, L. J., Jr., 23
Shannon, C. E., 8
Sherman, P. M., 129
Shift register, 37–40
    left-shift, 38
    parallel-entry, 39
    right-shift, 38
    serial-entry, 38
    universal, 39
Shima, M., 97, 243, 250
Shultz, G. W., 75, 110
Siena, W. R., 3, 108, 240, 287, 290, 291
Sign-and-magnitude, 59–60
Signed binary, 59–60
Signed number, 59
Signetics Corporation:
    integrated-circuits:
        555 timer, 178–79
        74121 monostable, 179
        8T09 bus driver, 176
        8T10 bus flip–flop, 176
        8T18 interface buffer, 177
        8T90 interface buffer, 177
Sign flag, 99
Single-ended system, 174
Small-scale integration (SSI), 22
Snyder, F. G., 112
Software, 116–49
Solomon, L., 192
Souček, B., 99, 150, 157, 161
Space parity, 72
Stack:
    pointer, 97–98
    pushdown (LIFO), 96–97
Standards:
    ANSI, 189
    CCITT V 24, 176
    ECMA, 189
    EIA RS-232B, 176
    MIL STD 188B, 176
Stark, P. A., 119
State, 7
Static memory, 86–89
Status register, 99
Status word, 103

Subroutine, 101–2, 134–38
  linking, 101–2, 136–37
  entry pool, 270
Sum-of-products (SOP), 17
Swithenbank, T., 192
Symbolic language, 116, 124–41
  branch statements, 133–35
  input/output, 138–41
  literal, 126–27
  loop, 129–33
  macro, 127–28
  pseudo-instruction, 125–28
  subroutine, 134–38
Symbols, logic, 9–14, 21
Synchronizer, 170–73
  level, 172–73
  pulse, 171
Synchronous transfer (*see* Programmed-data
  transfer)

TDI, 274
Teletype Corporation, 188
Teletypewriter (TTY), 188–89
Texas Instruments:
  Silent 700 terminal, 189–90
  6011 UART, 181–83
Text buffer, 142
Thompson, R., 307
Track, 189, 192
Transistor, 23–25
  n-channel MOSFET, 24
  NPN, 23
  p-channel MOSFET, 24
  PNP, 23

Transistor-transistor logic (TTL), 26–27
  Schottky–clamped (STTL), 27
  Unit load, 27
Trap cell, 138
Tri-state gate, 41
Truth table, 8
TTL, 26–27
TTY, 188–89

UART, 180–83
Unbalanced line, 174–75
Universal asynchronous receiver-transmitter
  (UART), 180–83
Unweighted code, 69

Vectored interrupt, 161
Voltage curve, 22–23
von Neumann architecture, 74, 104

Walther, T. R., 94
Wayne, M. N., 119
Weighted code, 67
Weiss, C. D., 145, 197
Weissberger, A. J., 3, 196
Weitzman, C., 99, 161, 192
Whiting, J. W., 317
Wire-OR connection, 41
Word, 3

Young, L., 252

Zeppa, A., 27, 69
Zero flag, 99